AF469911

The Modern Flower Garden

BOOKS BY

C. E. LUCAS PHILLIPS

The Small Garden
Roses for Small Gardens
The Rothschild Rhododendrons (*with P. N. Barber*)
Climbing Plants for Walls and Gardens
The Modern Flower Garden

Cromwell's Captains
Cockleshell Heroes
Escape of the 'Amethyst'
The Greatest Raid of All
The Spanish Pimpernel
The Vision Splendid
Alamein
Springboard to Victory

The Modern Flower Garden

by

C. E. LUCAS PHILLIPS

HEINEMANN : LONDON

William Heinemann Ltd

LONDON MELBOURNE TORONTO

CAPE TOWN AUCKLAND

First published 1968

434 43653 4

Printed in Great Britain by
Cox & Wyman Ltd
London, Fakenham and Reading

CONTENTS

PHOTOGRAPHS

All photographs were taken in the author's gardens, the majority by Mr Arthur Hunt, Mr Harry Smith and Mr Bernard Alfieri.

(Short titles)

Photographs

DRAWINGS

Drawings

Drawings

Drawings

THANKS

I am grateful to many specialists for their very kind help in various chapters of this book, of which they have read my drafts and offered suggestions from their great knowledge. In particular, I am much indebted to the following gentlemen.

Mr O. E. P. Wyatt, MC, MA, VMH, for lilies.
Mr E. B. Anderson, M.Sc., VMH, for rock gardening.
Mr Rowland Jackman, for trees and shrubs.
Mr J. D. Taylor, for irises.
Mr Alan Bloom, for herbaceous plants.
Mr Howard Crane, for violas.
Dr C. J. H. Topping, for daffodils.
Mr James Rooke, for dahlias.
Mr T. H. Findlay, MVO, VMH, for primulas.
Mr Anthony C. Ayton, for pelargoniums.

I am further very much obliged to Mr C. D. Brickell, B.Sc., for having helped me to keep on a reasonably true botanic course throughout and for much other help besides, and to Mr D. Pycraft, who has advised me on the tricky subject of limy soils.

Mr E. C. Haes, B.Sc., kindly provided the drawings in Figures 105, 106 and 107. Of the remainder, the better ones were done by my wife and my daughter, Mrs Wendy Griffin. C.E.L.P.

GARDENER'S JARGON

On the sound principle of logic that one should define one's terms before stating one's propositions, this glossary of general gardening terms and phrases is placed at the beginning of the book rather than at the end. It will also thus more readily bring itself to the reader's notice. Where a definition needs to be rather a lengthy one, I have included it in the general text, so I fear that you will have to follow up the reference or else seek the exact page in the Index.

Fanciers of this or that particular flower, such as the chrysanthemum and the iris, have their own esoteric jargons, which will be introduced in the appropriate chapters. Terms specially applicable to pruning are in Chapter 7.

For terms used in the anatomy of a flower, see Fig. 6.

n = noun
v = verb

acid soil. Soil with a low lime content.

alkaline soil. Opposite to acid.

anther. The pollen-bearing part of the stamen (*q.v.*)

axil. The angle between the stem and a branch or leaf-stalk; hence axillary.

bed out, *v.* See Chapter 13.

bract. See Floral Anatomy, Chapter 3.

bud, *n.* There are flower- or fruit-buds and wood- or growth-buds; the term is used not only of a well developed bud, but also, in growth-buds, from the moment when there is a tiny mark or swelling on the stem.

bud, *v.* To propagate a desired variety by inserting a bud of that variety into a suitable root stock.

calcareous. Chalky, of soil.

calcicole. A plant that is happy in alkaline (limy) soil.

calcifuge. The opposite of calcicole.

calyx. See Floral Anatomy, Chapter 3, and Fig. 2.

chlorosis. Loss of green pigment (chlorophyll) in foliage.

clone. A named variety or cultivar propagated vegetatively (*q.v.*), not by seed. Thus in lilies the Mid-Century "strain" is an assemblage of seedlings from the same parentage and having the same general characteristics, but differing from one another in detail; from this brood of seedlings one was selected for its special qualities, named 'Enchantment' and propagated vegetatively. 'Enchantment' is thus a clone and all bulbs resulting from the original seedling through propagation by division, bulbils or from scales will normally be identical for ever and ever, but their own progeny grown from seed will be something different. Correctly, "clone" is thus a group name and does not apply to a single plant, but is sometimes so used casually.

FIG. 1. A shoot showing: (*a*) terminal or extension bud; (*b*) leaf axil; (*c*) axillary bud or "eye"

compost. Has two meanings – a special mixture of soil components made up for pots and seed-boxes; and decomposed organic matter from a "compost heap" used as manure.

corm. A bulb-like swelling of a stem underground, e.g. gladiolus and crocus.

corolla. The whole whorl of petals in a flower.

crock. A piece of broken flower-pot, or other stony material in lieu, laid in the bottoms of pots or seed-boxes for drainage.

cultivar. (abbreviated cv), See The Botanic System, Chapter 1.

cutting. See appropriate section of Chapter 6.

daisyform. My own word for flowers of the *Compositae* family, as exemplified by the common daisy, having two sets of florets – the outer ray florets and the inner mass of very small, crowded disc florets, usually yellow.

dead-head, *v.* To remove spent flowers from plants. See p.p. 76–7.

disbud, *v.* Usually, to remove a small quantity of small flower buds below or around the main one so that it may develop to its best.

drill, *n.* A tiny trench, maybe only a ¼in. deep, made in the soil for sowing seed.

eye. A rudimentary bud.

fastigiate. Slender, columnar, the branches erect and pressed close together, like a bundle of sticks.

fibrous. Of roots; thin, hairlike roots, more or less dense. "Fibrous loam" is old turf with plenty of dense grass roots.

genus. See The Botanic System, Chapter 1.

glabrous. Hairless.

glaucous. Sea-green or blue-green.

harden-off, *v.* See end of Chapter 6.

heavy soil. One preponderating in clay.

heel-in, *v.* To make a rough trench, lay in the plants, and cover their roots with soil as temporary protection until ready to plant; or, as with spent tulips and other bulbs that have to be got out of the way, to allow them to complete their cycle of life.

hose-in-hose. A very old term for a flower with a calyx (often enlarged) of the same colour as the flower, giving the appearance of one floret within another, as, e.g. in some primulas and azaleas. Not the same thing as a "double flower".

humus. See Chapter 4.

inflorescence. See Floral Anatomy, Chapter 3, and Fig. 7.

light soil. One predominating in sand.

loam. A blend of clay, sand and humus.

mulch, *v.* See Chapter 5.

new wood. A shoot (branch or twig) that has sprouted and grown in the current season.

node. The joint on a stem, often slightly swollen, from which a leaf-stalk will sprout or has sprouted.

nursery. A small reserved part of the garden, especially the kitchen garden, in which young plants are reared; it has a seed-bed and a pricking-out bed.

off-set. A young growth on the perimeter of the parent plant which can be detached to be established as a new plant, e.g. the small, rooted outgrowths of herbaceous plants and the bulblets of bulbs. "Offshoot" would be a better name.

old wood. A shoot that grew last year or earlier.

open weather. Weather in which the soil is neither frost-bound nor saturated with rain.

pan. A shallow pottery vessel in which seed is sown, often in preference to a seed-box; also a hard, compressed sub-stratum of soil.

FIG. 2. The unfolding sepals of a calyx.

perennial. A plant that lives on from year to year; usually applied particularly to the herbaceous border perennials.

perianth. See Floral Anatomy, Chapter 3.

pinch, *v.* To nip out, commonly with the finger nails, the growing point of a plant or one or more of its shoots.

pinnate. Used to describe a compound leaf having many small leaflets on both sides of a central rib, as in the wisteria (see Figs. 108 and 75).

pistil. The whole female organ of a flower including stigma, style and ovary.

pot-on, *v.* To move a plant from a small pot into a larger one as it grows.

prick-in, *v.* To work fertilizers, etc., into the top inch or two of soil with hoe or fork.

prick-out, *v.* See Multiplying by Seed, Chapter 6.

rhizome. Often mistaken for a root, this is a prostrate fleshy stem, often an underground one, emitting roots from the lower side and leafy shoots from the upper; most familiar in the flag irises and, alack, in couch grass, which travels underground. Pronounced "ryzome".

rub-out, *v.* To remove, usually by a simple rub of the thumb, an unwanted embryo growth bud, such as an inward-growing rose bud.

runner. A prostrate shoot thrown out by some plants, which roots at several points and forms new plants, e.g. strawberry.

scape. Naked, leafless flower stem rising direct from the ground, as in many bulbs.

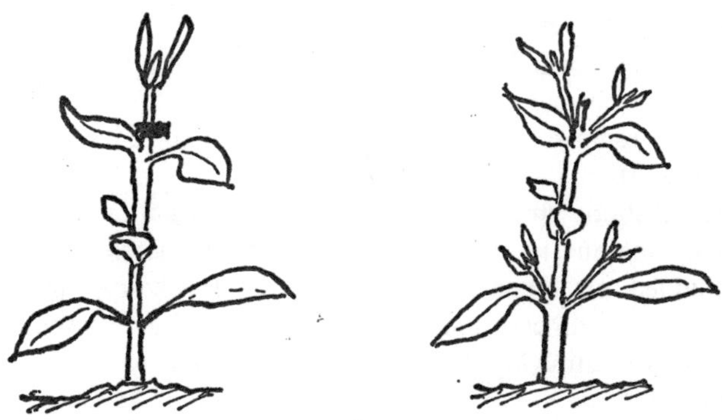

FIG. 3. "Pinching" or "stopping" the tips of some young plants to make them branch freely.

scion. A cutting or bud of a desired variety of tree, shrub, etc., that has been grafted on to a different root stock, often of a wild species, as in roses, fruit trees, lilac, etc.

seed-bed. Any strip or patch of soil specially prepared for sowing of seed.

sepal. See Floral Anatomy, Chapter 3. Pronounced "sepple".

single. A flower that has only one whorl or circlet of petals, as in the wild briar or dog rose and the common buttercup. Contrast with the "double" flowers of most modern hybrid roses, chrysanthemums, etc.

south wall. That side of a wall that faces south.

species. See Botanic System, Chapter 1.

spit. The depth of one spade in digging. (10in.)

spur. (*a*) On fruit trees and berrying shrubs, a very short branch bearing first one and later a close cluster of flower or fruit buds; or (*b*) an elongated tail of a petal or sepal, as in columbines and delphiniums.

stamen. The whole male organ of a flower, composed of the filament, or stalk, and the pollen-bearing anther.

standard. Of trees, an erect stem without branches below a certain height, usually 5 or 6ft; also erect petal or sepal of some flowers, e.g. iris and sweet-pea.

start, *v.* To stimulate a plant into early growth, e.g. dahlia and begonia, by planting it under glass in pots, boxes or in the greenhouse border.

stigma. The sticky or feathery part of the pistil or female organ of a flower; it receives the pollen.

stock, or root-stock. The rooted growth, often of a wild species, on which a cultivated scion is grafted or budded.

stop, *v.* To remove the growing tip of a plant to induce branching (see Fig. 3).

sucker. A shoot springing from the root formation of a plant, usually noxious, as in the rose and lilac, where a cultivated variety is budded on other stock; but in the raspberry, blackberry, pernettya, gaultheria and many other plants they are the normal means of multiplying. On standards, suckers may appear on the stem also.

tap-root. A thick tapering root growing straight downwards, as in the lupin and dandelion.

tilth. Cultivation. A "fine tilth", as of a seed-bed, is soil worked down to small, loose, fine crumbs or particles.

transpiration. The giving-out of moisture-vapour by a leaf.

truss. A popular, non-botanical term for any compact cluster of many florets, as in the rhododendron and the polyanthus.

tuber. See opening section of Chapter 15.

variety. See The Botanic System, Chapter 1.

vegetative propagation. The raising of plants by means of cuttings, grafts, buddings or division, not by seed. Plants so raised are clonal (*q.v.*) and will exactly resemble their parents.

whorl. ("Whirl") See Floral Anatomy, Chapter 3.

A Few Botanical Terms

Below are some of the dog-Latin (and a few Greek) terms most commonly encountered in the botanical names of plants. A knowledge of them will help to overcome the feelings of rage of those who have forgotten (or never learnt) their Classics. When used to describe a species they are adjectival and so must agree in gender with the genus, which is very frequently Greek. Thus *albus* (white) becomes *alba* for a feminine genus and *album* for a neuter one; and *officinalis* stands for both masculine and feminine, but changes to *officinale* for the neuter. I give below the masculine forms only.

Many other terms sufficiently explain themselves, as in *grandiflorus, roseus, alpinus, spinosissimus,* etc., and a great many are named after persons in the genitive, as in *forrestii, delavayi, fortunei, wilsonae,* etc.

See further in the appropriate section of Chapter 1.

acaulis. Stemless.
albus. White.
-anthus. Flower; as in *polyantha*, many-flowered, and *macrantha*, large-flowered.
arboreus. Tree-like.
argenteus. Silvery.
argutus. Sharply notched or toothed.
atro-. Deep in colour, as in *atropurpurea.*
aureus (and *aureo-* in compound words). Golden.
-cephalus. Headed, as in *macrocephalus*, large-headed.
chamae-. Close to the ground, as in *Chamaecyparis*, dwarf cypress (the "ch" pronounced "k").
chinensis. Chinese.
coccineus. (pronounced "koksineus"). Scarlet.
coeruleus or *caeruleus*. (pronounced "serrooleus") Blue.
cordi-. Heart-shaped, as in *cordifolius*, with heart-shaped leaves.
cyaneus. Dark blue.
-dendron. Tree.
dentatus. Toothed; *denticulatus*, with very small teeth.
elatus. Tall.
eximius. Beautiful.
flore pleno, abbreviated to *fl. pl.* or *f.p.* Doubled-flowered. See "single" in previous list.
-folius. Leaved, as in *longifolius*, long-leaved.
frutescens and *fruticosus*. Shrubby, often used to distinguish a shrubby species from an herbaceous one, as in potentillas.
hetero-. Diverse, as in *heterophyllus*, having leaves of different forms.
incanus. Hoary, white.

japonicus. Japanese.

lacti-. Milky-coloured.

lanceolatus. Lance-shaped, tapering at both extremities, usually applied to leaves.

lati-. Broad, as in *latifolius*, broad-leaved.

leuco-. White, as in *Leucojum*, the snowflake.

luteus. Yellow.

macro-. Large or long, as in *macrocarpus*, large-fruited, or *macroglossus*, long-tongued.

micro-. Small.

mollis (*molle-* in compound words). Soft.

mono-. One or once only, as in monocarpic, fruiting (or seeding) once only and then dying, as usually in the Himalayan poppy.

nanus. Dwarf.

officinalis. Of commercial or medicinal use; often applied to herbal plants, such as in *Salvia officinalis*, sage. Means the same as the old English "wort".

-oides. Similar to, as in *jasminoides*.

paniculatus. With flowers composed in panicles (see Fig. 7).

persicus. Persian.

-phyllus. Leaved, as in *microphyllus*, small-leaved.

platy-. Broad.

poly-. Many, as in polyanthus and *polyantha*.

praecox. Early, precocious.

procumbens. Procumbent, lying flat on the ground.

pubescens. Covered with short soft hairs.

radicans. Having rooting stems, usually of prostrate creepers.

repens and *reptans*. Creeping, prostrate.

ruber (*rubri-* or *rubro-* in compound words). Red.

rupestris and *rupicola*. Rock-loving or rock-dwelling.

sax-. Rock-loving, as in saxifrage and in the English adjective saxatile and the Latin *saxatilis* (*saxatile* in the neuter).

scaber. Rough to the touch.

scandens. Climbing.

schiz- (pronounced "skyz"). Split, as in *Schizanthus*.

serratus. Saw-toothed, usually of leaves.

serrulatus. Finely saw-toothed.

sessilis. Sessile, stalkless.

sinensis and *sino-*. Chinese.

speciosus and *spectabilis*. Showy, splendid.

steno-. Narrow.
strictus. Erect.
sub-. Semi, as in *subserratus*, partially toothed.
tomentosus. Thickly hairy.
umbellatus. Having flowers arranged in umbels (see Fig. 7).

CHAPTER 1

A NEW PRESENTATION

The Aim and the Method – Floral Curriculum – "Those Awful Names" – The Botanic System in Brief – The System of this Book

THIS book is intended as a follow-up, as it were, of *The Small Garden*, which was published in 1952. In part, it unavoidably travels the same terrain and even, for short stretches, unashamedly employs the same vehicles of words, yet it is a completely new book in outlook and content, journeying much farther afield in search of richer floral treasure.

Thus I have aimed to suit the aspirant to gardening who rightly expects a sure grounding in the elements but whose interest will not be satisfied to stop at the commonplace and the stereotyped. I therefore begin by trying, as far as I am qualified to do so, to demonstrate how you, Reader, may overleap the fences and ditches that bothered me when, enlisting among the "ancient gentlemen" of Hamlet, I took to the spade some forty years ago.

If you are no stranger to that honourable implement, you may perhaps pass fairly quickly through these passages on basic gardening and emerge speedily into the flowery meads beyond. Here you will find that Sixth Form plants, as well as those of the kindergarten, have their share of the allotments, together with many others of man's desiring that lie in the comfortable beds between. Even some "specialist's treasures" (pet name for plants that are just plain difficult) are cautiously admitted, especially among the pygmies that lurk in the crannies of the rock garden. Here also modern practices and modern plants, where they seem better than the old, are given prominence. There is much emphasis on those aspects of gardening that reduce effort and save time and there is special notice of the appreciable impact on modern gardening of the flower "arranger", as well as of those plants that I call the "vogue flowers" of today.

Do not, however, look within these pages for guidance on how to win prizes at the flower shows; there will be no splendid solitaire roses, no aldermanic dahlias, no mayoral chrysanthemums. These are the topics of the specialists. Our study here will be the garden, not the exhibitor's bench.

It is part of my gardening creed that, in the conditions of today, people who do not set their hearts on the show bench should adopt the maxim "profusion rather than perfection".[1] Perfection in this or that flower may be sought in specialist books (including two of my own), but in this one we are more concerned with getting the best possible garden display with the least possible fuss.

I have been obliged to omit also the arts of fruit and vegetable culture, partly because I no longer seriously pursue them myself and partly because my acreage of print is too small. Nor, unfortunately, will you find anything here about hot-houses, orchids, cacti, water gardens or "house plants"; for the simple reason that my own inclinations have not led me down those ways and my knowledge of them is limited to that of the admiring onlooker.

I shall keep outdoors nearly all the time, restricting myself to those plants that are hardy in the British Isles as a whole, or nearly so; but shall not forget, as is so often done, those gardeners who live in what I call the "Gulf Stream" counties – the moist and relatively warm west coast, from Cornwall far up into Scotland – where they grow so many beautiful things that we inlanders regard with envious eyes.

In the lists of plants that follow later I have been selective rather than comprehensive. In a good many instances, moreover, I am silent about particular *varieties* (or "cultivars") of popular flowers. The reason is that in these instances new varieties are brought out so thick and fast that in a year or two my choices would have little validity. The star of today is often down in the Third XI tomorrow. In other instances, the space factor alone bars me from giving more than the briefest mention of chosen varieties and there you must refer to the better catalogues for further details of this or that.

Nearly all gardening books should be read with those qualifications as to place and circumstance which are, no doubt, in the author's own mind, though not always expressed. Nature herself may disprove

[1] Propounded in my address reported in the *RHS Journal* of May, 1957.

usages that are commonly accepted. One man's experience may not be another's. A very distinguished horticulturalist once said to me: "Five men can advise five different ways of growing rhododendrons and they can all be right."

In all such matters one can only guide. Every gardener finds his own way of doing things, and where I have found a particular method good I advocate it. Let me not, however, deter you from venturing forward on your own nor from putting on the wings of imagination.

I hope, Reader, that you may be stimulated to a love and knowledge of flowers and to look upon your garden, of whatever size, as an integral part of your home, as full of delight as your house, for that is what a home should be.

Floral Curriculum

The modern gardener of limited means has simply got to make himself more or less independent of the jobbing gardener, except for mowing lawns and keeping the place tidy. The really knowledgeable jobbing gardener is nowadays a rare bird, though honest workers are not everywhere lacking. In particular, unless you are very sure of your man, do not trust the itinerant with any pruning jobs, for, if you put a pair of secateurs into his hand, ten-to-one he will become Milton's "blind Fury with th'abhorred shears".

Be careful also about that grade of so-called "landscape gardener" who, unlike the properly qualified professional, is merely Jobbing Gardener writ large, the extent of his skill reaching little farther than laying crazy paving. Undoubtedly there are good ones, but there are many shockers.

You can learn much, if you have an observant and calculating eye (even more if you have a sceptical one), by visiting the more famous gardens. Go to Kew, the Royal Botanical Garden and Saughton Park in Edinburgh, the Royal Horticultural Society's garden at Wisley (Surrey), the Northern Horticultural Society's garden at Harlow Car (near Harrogate), Roath Park in Cardiff and the beautiful garden in Regent's Park, London. Visit the better nurseries. Haunt all the flower shows you have time for, but fortify your mind against the bewitchments that you may see on the show bench, for the beauty in the vase may be a dying duck in your garden. Always inquire into its hardiness, its soil fads, its height and breadth and any proclivities that it may have. In particular always cock a sceptical eye at any new plant, especially new roses. Despite the fact that "all with one accord praise new-made gauds", experience has warned me to let other people be the guinea-pigs and to wait until the newcomer has been "tested in commerce".

Unless your wants are very simple, it usually pays to go to the larger or the specialist nurseries with national reputations, a list of which is given in the appendix; your small local nursery may be very good (if so, stick to it), but its range will be small. Whenever I quote a particular nursery in the text, the reason is that the plant in question is not generally available but that it is grown by that specified nursery to my knowledge, though occasionally it may be by others also.

Collect all the catalogues you can, but be on your guard against those that are too gaudily dressed in glorious technicolour, for they can be fearfully misleading and the all-colour catalogue usually gives the least information on the things you need to know. Most nurserymen have a high standard of integrity and will frankly tell you a plant's failings if you ask them, but only the most distinguished will volunteer the information in print. Also, do not let yourself be cozened by "bargain lots" advertised in the Press; you get what you pay for.

You will get great pleasure and profit from joining the Royal Horticultural Society; besides its other benefits, its staff of specialists is at the service of all subscribers. Join also the specialist society of any particular family of flowers that appeals to you, such as the Royal National Rose Society (which has splendid gardens near St Albans and promotes displays elsewhere), the Alpine Garden Society, the Scottish Rock Garden Club, and those dedicated to the delphinium, chrysanthemum, dahlia, carnation, sweet-pea, iris, etc. Their secretarial addresses are obtainable from the Royal Horticultural Society, in Vincent Square, London, S.W.1.

"*Those Awful Names*"

I have done all that seems reasonable to avoid technical jargon, but what I have not been able to do, or only in part, is to avoid "those awful Latin names" that do not come trippingly to the tongue.

Most of us, I am sure, would prefer to use vernacular English names, many of which have a native euphony and charm (and occasionally a pungency), and I shall use them freely whenever they seem to be appropriate. But to use them wholesale, without discrimination (in so far as there is any English name at all) is likely to lead us up quite the wrong sort of garden path. We really must be sure what we are talking about. The "bluebells" of Scotland are not those of the rest of Britain.[1] "Black-eyed Susan" may be either a thunbergia or a rudbeckia or anything else for aught I know. "Burning bush" may be the old dittany or the little cypress-like kochia. Sun-rose, rock-rose, autumn crocus, "japonica", winter cherry, and arum are a few other ambiguous nonsenses.

More troublesome are those instances where the authentic botanical name for one plant is applied by the multitude to another. "Nasturtium", which legally is the specific name for watercress, doesn't matter a great deal, but other instances definitely lead to confusion. A glaring one is "geranium". The real geranium is a hardy, leafy perennial, usually with deeply cut foliage and blossoms that are often blue or mauve, spreading widely and densely and used in the herbaceous border or rock garden or as a ground-cover. The more effulgent, tender creature used for summer "bedding out" or window-sill pots is no "geranium" at all, but a *Pelargonium*. If we so miscall it, what shall we call the true geranium? The answer may well be its old English name, cranesbill.

Another glaring instance is *Syringa*. This is the authentic name for the lilac, and not for that white-flowered bush of spicy fragrance which is properly called *Philadelphus*. By all means call *Syringa* "lilac", but don't call *Philadelphus* "syringa".

Likewise, we call the robinia an "acacia" and the true acacia we call "mimosa", and the true mimosas are tropical plants that few of us have ever seen.

One could go on and on with examples of such nonsenses. So inconsistent are we, indeed, that we have often abandoned a perfectly good English name in favour of a foreign one, as in cranesbill, mullein, meadow saffron, meadow rue and stone crop.

So far the weight of argument has been mainly in favour of Latinists. The purpose of the botanical name is, of course, to identify every plant precisely all over the world, so that there shall be no confusion, and that you, Reader, may be sure of getting exactly what you want

[1] The little Scottish bluebell is *Campanula rotundifolia* and the English one that adorns the woodland is *Endymion non-scriptus* (formerly *Scilla non-scripta*).

from the nursery. On the other side of the House, we argue that botanical names are so constantly changed by the erudite people who order these matters, nearly always to something even more jaw-cracking than the long-familiar name, that there is a great deal of confusion instead of clarity and a lot of aliases are bandied about. Very often a name that has held good for generations will be altered by the botanist in obedience to the wretched "species priority" law. Some of the changes make sense but a great many, to the gardener and the nurseryman, are just infernal nuisances, for they come upon us thick and fast. Not that the botanist is the only cause of confusion; very often a nurseryman or amateur will introduce a new plant of his own naming and fifty years may pass before it is checked and corrected.

Precious few nurserymen take any notice of the botanist, so that most catalogues, even of some of the top nurseries, are full of invalid names (Hillier's being, save for some trifles, a conspicuous exception). An immediate result is that the unfortunate author, in trying to help his reader, is impaled on the horns of a dilemma - whether to call a plant by what he believes to be its orthodox name or by a catalogue one (if all nurseries would but use the same); for it is the catalogue name that the average reader wants. As a result, I have to plague my text with a rash of synonyms, as maddening to me as it must be to you. Even the director of a world-famous horticultural institution has often to ask his botanist:

"What are we calling this today?"

The Botanic System in Brief

Since I began gardening forty years ago the apparently simple business of naming a plant has been turned into a complicated and forbidding affair amounting almost to a mystique. I shall not dream of wearying you with this tiresome formalism, but a nodding acquaintance with the basic method is really necessary for an understanding of flowers above the nasturtium and marigold level. I shall therefore set it out in the simplest terms, avoiding the frills.

Like people, all plants have at least two names, many have three and others may be encountered with a whole string of Tennysonian "jewels five words long" (often illegally).

First in the group names comes the genus, such as *Rosa*, the generic name for all roses, or *Anemone*, the like for all anemones. Thousands are Greek names (as in *Anemone*), not Latin.

Next comes the name of the species, as in *R. spinosissima*, the very spiny rose (which is our native Scotch or burnet rose), and as in *A. pavonina*, the euphonious name for the peacock anemone.

After the generic and the specific names there may follow a varietal name, as in *R. s. altaica*, the spiny rose from the Altai mountains of Siberia, and as in *A. p. ocellata*, the peacock anemone with a brilliant eye (an ancestor of the popular De Caen anemones of florists today).

The varietal name is very often a vernacular one in English, French or any other modern language, as in *Syringa vulgaris* 'Madame Lemoine', a famous white lilac, and *Erica carnea* 'Ruby Glow', a heather with red flowers instead of flesh-pink (*carnea*). Many have a rather bogus Latin varietal name, such as *Erica carnea* 'Atrorubra'. Note that in these instances and in all other varieties that have originated in cultivation, rather than in the wild, the varietal names are not in italic but are in single inverted commas.

In the modern jargon these may be called "cultivars", a much misunderstood term by many who use it, for the International Code that prescribes these matters lays down with emphasis that "cultivar" is the "exact equivalent" of "variety". It is therefore an unnecessary and somewhat affected term. Moreover, to a gardener, as distinct from a botanist, it doesn't matter a hoot whether a particular form of any plant originated in the wild or in someone's garden. Indeed, it is often extremely difficult to discover what its origin was.

The specific name of a plant is often given in honour of some person, in which case it terminates in *-ii*, or in certain cases in *-i*, as in the familiar mauve *Buddleia davidii* (usually pronounced "david-eye"). If the person is a woman the termination of the species name is *-ae*. See also what has been said in "Gardener's Jargon" about specific names that are adjectival.

In these days of the new pronunciation of Latin, many people are needlessly bothered about how to speak these botanical names and those who are younger than I think it right to pronounce them as they were taught Latin at school. This is not all so. As I have said, many names are Greek and what is "Latin" is usually only dog-Latin. Some, as in Berberis, Yucca, Sequoia, Ginkgo, are neither Greek nor Latin and a few are a mixture of the two, as in Taxodium. One is right to pronounce them, therefore, as though they were English words or as in the old pronunciation of Latin. Thus *Acer*, the maple, is "Aissa", not "Akka". *Iris* is not "Eerees" and *Spiraea* is not "Speereya". So also *alpinus* is as in the English "alpine" and not "alpeenoos" and in *wilsonae* the termination is "ee".

All these things are matters of quite minor importance and there are no Median laws about them, but they bothered me mightily when I began gardening and I still go wrong often enough after forty years of gardening. One picks them up slowly and by degrees. So I have given these few brief pointers, touching the fringe of the subject only, for the benefit of people similarly perplexed.

The System of this Book

Now for the method, or apology for it, that I shall normally employ in this book. I have to steer a middle course between orthodoxy on the one hand, not departing from it entirely, and simplicity on the other, not frightening the unaccustomed reader with indigestible mouthfuls when they can be avoided. On consideration I think it best to use the conventional italics when appropriate and the inverted commas for those particular plants which I apprehend to be "cultivars" (having in mind the monitory case of the lady who threatened to sue an editor for libel when he wrote "Mrs A has very loose habits").

I shall, however, omit the orthodox hybrid sign × and the abbreviations "var" and "cv" for variety and cultivar and shall often simplify in other ways. Thus *Camellia* × *williamsii* 'J. C. Williams' will be written without the ×, or better still will just be *Camellia* 'J. C. Williams', and, when writing about thrifts, 'Bee's Ruby' will be quite sufficient.

I have adopted these heretical methods in the interests of the general reader, who, as I know well, is irritated by botanical formalism, especially when it assumes the appearance of an algebraic proposition. Furthermore, in my lists of plants in each chapter I shall enter them under those names which are commonly accepted in current usage. Often they will be English vernacular names, such as snowdrop, hollyhock and lily-of-the-valley, but when in doubt and where a botanical name has largely superseded a popular one in current speech, as in antirrhinum for snapdragon, I shall use the botanical one. The Index will give both forms for readers who are uncertain what to look for. The guiding rule will be convenience and normal usage among laymen. The Index also gives a little guidance on pronunciation for those in doubt.

For similar reasons I have passed by certain changes or revisions of botanical names pointed out by my botanical counsellor, as they rarely, if ever, appear in catalogues; those I use remain valid synonyms even though, maybe, they are not "correct".

There are, of course, thousands of plants for which we have no English name and the poet Christopher Smart tells us wisely that "the right names of flowers are yet in heaven".

And now we must get on with the job.

CHAPTER 2

RECONNAISSANCE

Lay-out – Aspect – Design

BEFORE ever we put a spade in the ground, we ought to decide what sort of garden we are going to have and what shall be its form and features. This is not the usual approach in a gardening book, but I think it is the right one. Quite a lot of factors have to be assessed. Special considerations apply to seaside and town gardens and these are discussed in Chapter 25.

Lay-out

By lay-out I mean simply the apportionment of various parts of the garden to their separate uses according to its size and your desires. Design comes later, but, if you have the same concept of a garden as I have, bear in mind, right from the beginning, Gertrude Jekyll's advice that our aim should be "to paint a garden picture" or, in Andrew Marvell's, a pleasaunce in which "to weave the garlands of repose". You alone can decide whether, subject to space, you will also grow fruit and vegetables, make a tennis court, provide space for children's games and so on. In an inviolate acre all these things can be done, but in any area much smaller something usually has to be sacrificed. In very tiny plots you will be sorely taxed and may find a cottage-style mixture the only thing, where, as old Thomas Tusser, of Elizabethan days, wrote:

The Gooseberry, Respis, and Roses, all three
With strawberries under them trimly agree.

Vegetables occupy a great deal of time, labour and space, but if you decide to grow them you will be rewarded. In your lay-out you must put them in full sun but, if possible, out of sight of the house, except for a few herbs and lettuce, for which, if you wish to earn merit, you will make a little bed near the kitchen. Fruit, if confined to cordons (apples, pears, gooseberries, red currants) plus a row of raspberries, are less demanding in all factors.

Whether your garden is a new one, littered with builder's trash, or an old one that you have inherited, formulate a once-for-all plan after careful thought. Don't be in too much of a hurry. Wander about, take rough measurements, consider the environment, stick canes in here and there as experimental sites for trees or other features. In particular, study the view from the principle windows of the house.

Most gardens that are inherited from a previous owner have not been designed at all but have "just growed" haphazardly, with no conception of garden unity. Paths, trees, greenhouses and so on may all be in the wrong places. While it is sensible to preserve anything that is good, have no compunction in scrapping those things that stand in the way of your long-range conception. In all the gardens that I have made I have always initially considered the ground as a vacant plot, then made my plan and, maybe with some modifications, scrapped anything that did not fit the plan – dug up concrete paths, demolished greenhouses, felled trees, grubbed up hedges and so on.

It will surprise most people when I stipulate that the first things actually to be sited are what I call the workshops of the garden. These are the greenhouse and frames, the tool-shed, compost bins, bonfire and other features of great importance but of no decorative value. These, with the possible exception of the glassworks, have to be got out of sight, but are usually out of mind when garden-making begins, creating awkward problems later. The greenhouse must go in the sun usually, the compost heap in the shade and the bonfire must not give offence to oneself or neighbours; but, if you possibly can, group all these things together. They are complementary to each other, and if well placed will save an awful lot of trapesing to and fro.

Aspect

This is one factor that may have a decisive influence in all your deliberations.

Reconnaissance

Observe with some care the cardinal points of the compass and keep these ever in mind. In most parts of the country and for most gardening purposes the ideal situation is one on relatively high ground, with the land falling away to the south or south-west. Here the frost will drain away and here the aspect of maximum sun will give scope to plants on the danger list of hardiness. Westerly aspects have much in their favour, being kindly to those plants that like warmth but not too much direct sun. Open northerly or easterly aspects are exposed to strong and biting winds.

Aspect is of particular importance in considering how to use walls, fences and hedges. Solid brick or stone walls are the most valuable, for they hold warmth in any aspect, but at the seaside and in other places liable to violent gales they have their own perils (Chapter 25). Hedges hold no warmth but break the force of the wind.

A "south wall" is one that faces south, and the other side of it is consequently a north wall. A south wall is of precious value for sheltering anything of doubtful frost-hardiness. A south-west wall is virtually as good, and, indeed, often better. Unexpectedly, a north wall, so often a place of gloom, does, as I shall show, offer good opportunities for adornment and use, for here we can without difficulty grow winter jasmine, clematis, fine red currants and many other delights.

On easterly walls there is a special catch. A plant may be perfectly hardy, but, if it is an early flowering one, the early morning sun may beam down on the fattening buds and, by sudden thawing, rupture them. This is liable to happen up to May, or later in the north. Camellias, early rhododendrons and peaches are examples.

The aspect factor, however, goes even further than this. Every shrub, every plant of more than about three feet high creates its own problem or offers its own opportunity. Thus the shady north side of any large shrub offers a golden opportunity for a clematis to climb over it, but the same side will be of no service to plants that demand plenty of sun at their roots. Large trees obviously affect the issue to a certain extent, so whatever we think of planting, the aspect is one of the factors always to be considered.

It follows from all this that you must begin your outline design by reserving the sunniest corners and areas of the garden for whatever you most set your heart on, unless it is a shade-loving plant, such as the rhododendron. Roses, herbaceous borders, carnations, irises, all vegetables, most fruits and most rock plants should be in full sun.

Roses should be right out in the open if possible, not shut in by walls, fences or high hedges. If you have a wall facing any part of the southerly quadrant don't waste it by running a path close to it, but make there the widest border that you can. It is astonishing how often this quite obvious precept is ignored.

Design

Here we come to the pleasaunce, the garden picture, which is what this book is really about.

In a book of this size I can do no more than set out some basic considerations and accepted precepts, evolved from study of the best examples and my own practice, but these should be quite sufficient as guiding lights to the intelligent gardener, who will also, I hope, augment them by releasing the forces of his own imagination.

DESIGN IN THEORY

Keeping in mind the preliminary factors discussed in the two previous sections, start by mentally sketching out a very simple overall key plan, with strong outlines and silhouettes and with the dominant features firmly determined. When quite satisfied, no doubt after much cogitation, commit it to paper. Leave the detail to be filled in gradually, even perhaps over a period of years.

Design is usually best studied initially from the windows of the principle living-rooms. The view as a whole is the first, though certainly not the only thing. In gardens of the British manner, this usually means emerging from the house on to some sort of terrace, raised or otherwise, and of size conformable to the house. From the terrace one steps out on to a lawn – one of the dominant elements of the garden – unless the garden is a tiny plot among crowded town houses, in which case the lawn may well be replaced entirely by an expanse of paving.

After and beyond the lawn, anything may happen, but here we come to our first and usually inflexible precept: keep the centre of the garden open. Any cluttering up of the middle of the lawn foreshortens perspective, distracts the eye and upsets the values of other garden features.

The next concept in our mental planning is to make all the lines in the garden flow, smoothly and easily, without zigzags or jagged angles. This applies especially to the lines of beds and paths, which should all more or less conform to one pattern, though, in gardens not too small, there may be different patterns for different parts. This concept of flowing lines does not necessarily rule out straight ones.

At every stage of thinking endue the plan with a sense of **proportion** appropriate to the plot – no trees that will grow to forest size (a common fault, which will be discussed later), no lawns of excessive extent with a mean little border running all round, nor, conversely, any beds, terraces or paths too skimpy for the size of the place.

Closely linked with the quality of proportion is that of **balance.** By all means have a "strong-point" of some sort, but do not let it overwhelm the scene and reduce all other features to insignificance. Avoid also a lop-sided lay-out – a commandment which is not always easy if the whole garden itself is of an awkward shape.

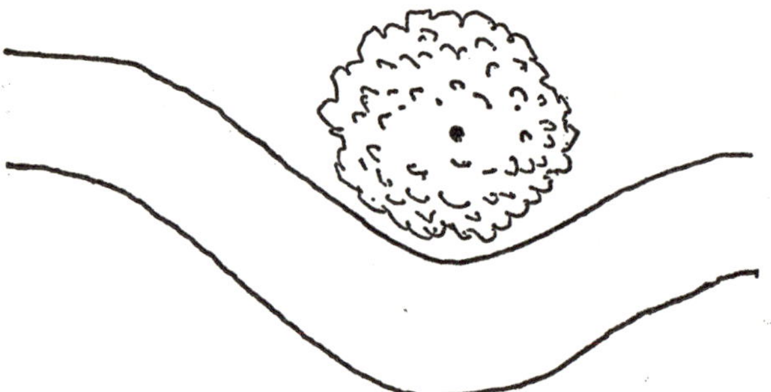

FIG. 4. Justifying a curve in a path.

Length of **perspective** is much to be desired, and there are several dodges for simulating length in a short garden. One is a central path, preferably of grass, which is broad near the house and gradually diminishes in breadth. If this path is made on a gentle curve, so that its termination is just hidden behind shrubs, it will be all the more effective, giving the impression that there are hidden treasures round the bend.

Where this impression cannot be contrived, the "focal point" practice can be employed, in which the eye is instinctively directed to a seat, a sun-dial, a prominent tree, or better still, a distant feature, when one is happily offered to you. In tiny town gardens, where the path unavoidably leads up merely to a blank wall or fence, the focal point might take the familiar form of the *trompe l'œil*, a deception trick fabricated from lattice work, which takes the eye up to a false door that seems to lead to a secret garden beyond. Another dodge is a very large mirror on the far wall, reflecting what is in the garden and seeming to give it length; but this is a tricky piece of conjuring, for it looks terrible if the sun shines on it.

Conversely, there may be an overriding call to screen oneself from overlooking neighbours or to hide some hideous feature outside one's own domain. In extreme cases this may be the governing factor in one's design and usually the answer is trees, probably fast-growing conifers such as Leyland's cypress, *Thuja plicata* or Jackman's 'Green Hedger'.

Unity is a quality that Aristotle would certainly have insisted upon and is the real test of what constitutes a successful garden picture. Its application to us is not easy to define shortly, except by saying rather vaguely that the whole thing should hang together, without any "sore thumb" sticking out. It is more easily done in small gardens and most difficult where, in a limited space, your ardours goad you into including displays of roses, irises, dahlias, chrysanthemums and other exhibitors' flowers into a general garden scheme. Unity means, in fact, discipline – a disciplining of one's tastes to avoid a hotchpotch and to assemble a harmonious combination of beautiful forms. I suggest that, where space is available and taste is concordant, a background or a framework of evergreen shrubs and trees, forming rich piles of foliage, is a first-class matrix for the moulding of a beautiful garden and for providing the basis of unity.

DESIGN IN PRACTICE

Having glanced at these few theoretical precepts, we shall consider some of the material factors that influence them.

The dominant features in garden design are trees, lawns and paths. These set the tone and create the atmosphere, so that their locations are the first things to be determined (after the workshop area).

Trees provide the architectural element of a garden's design and elevate it into a third dimension. Choose their stations with care. Two frequent mistakes are to forget that young trees may grow into big ones and to plant them too close to the house. The weeping willow, that looks so bewitching in its juvenile state, and the Atlantic cedar, with beguiling blue foliage, are two of the trees most commonly misused in small gardens, for they grow to very large dimensions.

Lawns provide the stage for the garden's coloured drama. One constantly hears the unwilling gardener say that he intends to have as much grass as possible, in order to save labour. This is a complete fallacy, for a lawn needs more frequent attention than any other part of the garden, except the vegetable plot.

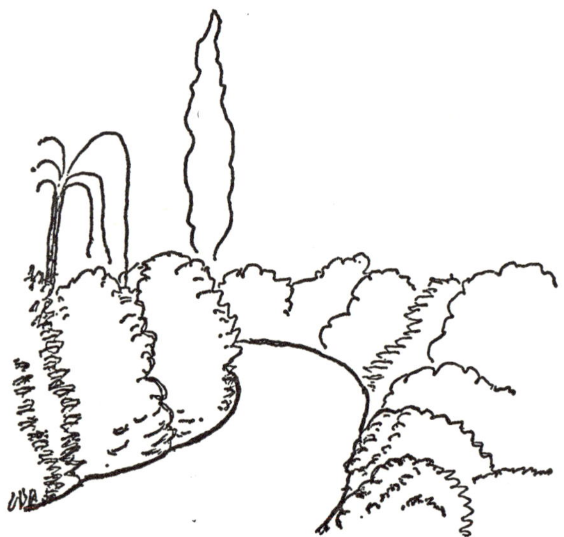

FIG. 5. The path of deception, seeming to lead to a hidden garden beyond.

One also hears a good deal of nonsense about "not cutting up the lawn too much". In fact, if you want to have a good floral display, in small gardens you *must* cut up the lawn, provided that the centre is kept open. Indeed, one of the dodges for making a small garden site appear larger than before is to have a succession of beds in depth as one looks from the house, the only objection being that of having extra edges to trim weekly.

Paths should be as few as possible, decorative in themselves and go direct from A to B. If a straight line imposes too severe a strain upon your sensitivity, create some justification for forming an easy curve, by placing a shrub or pool or piece of stonework that the path must refuse. Avoid self-conscious and meaningless wriggles and avoid a path that crosses a lawn diagonally or laterally when seen from the house, although a longitudinal one is, of course, right and proper if you want it. The kindest of all paths are grass ones, but these are not practical where there is a lot of wear and tear or where one wants to be able to walk dry-shod in all weathers. A paved ambulatory that goes right round the perimeter of the garden is a blessing on a wet day.

The construction of paths is outside my brief, but you will find helpful advice in Barry Bucknell's *Do It Yourself in the Garden*, published in paperback by Pan Books. I will add only that, when a stone path, whether crazy or sanely rectangular, is intended for no weight greater than the human frame plus a wheelbarrow, I have found it quite unnecessary to base it upon quantities of hardcore, as we are so often exhorted to do. An inch or two of builder's soft sand is quite enough.

Other factors. Odd though it may seem, there are several maxims of war that apply equally well to garden design. I have just exemplified one in the doctrine of "defence in depth". Another is "mass", of which more later. Equally potent is the doctrine of "surprise". Some sudden curve in a path, a hedge tactically sited, disclosing unexpectedly some embowered place, a retired rose-garden, a pool, give charm and variety to the otherwise commonplace. The division of the garden into separate compartments, connected by a central path, straight or curved, is in our best garden traditions and is an excellent device for many of the long, narrow suburban gardens, each compartment a garden within a garden, secluded and intimate:

Let not each beauty ev'ry where be spy'd,
Where half the skill is decently to hide;
He gains all points, who pleasingly confounds,
Surprises, varies and conceals the Bounds.

Garden and house being one, the house itself must be embraced in the design. If the style of the house permits, some sort of paved terrace, however small, will give unity to the whole and this unity will be further emphasized by shrubs and climbers providently planted on the walls. Climbers have particular value in small town gardens, in which the wall area often much exceeds the ground area.

The style of the house may also dictate whether the garden shall be formal – of geometrical outline, maybe embellished with a sunken enclosure – or naturalized, simulating a slice of nature, a style that is seldom practicable in small places. In the very wee plot of the town house, an all-paved garden is often a happy answer, enamelled with rock plants and adorned with trees in tubs. But whatever the *motif*, avoid fussiness. Simple and bold effects are the best. Shun all bearded gnomes, concrete frogs, reflective storks and all whimsies and oddities.

Design may also be strongly influenced by natural factors – the soil, the climate and the site. The merits of soils are dealt with in Chapter 4 and climate is often related to it. The west coast from Argyll to Cornwall – soft, balmy, wet, caressed by the Gulf Stream, but often violently windy – offers quite different prospects from the drier, colder east coast. In these Gulf Stream counties you may confidently plant the most sumptuous shrubs that would die from drought or cold in Kent or Norfolk. The south coast also is warm, though not wet, and in many places inland there are sheltered inglenooks where beautiful, half-hardy plants may be grown, and sometimes one finds them in the most unexpected places, as in parts of Northumberland.

Related to both these factors is site – whether hill-top or valley, meadow, heath, or woodland. The top of a hill will be windswept but will be more free of frost than a lush valley bottom, where 'frost pockets' will persist. In large towns the impregnation of the atmosphere by sooty chemicals will tax the functioning of the leaf-organs of many plants, yet will protect roses from the ravages of the black-spot fungus.

All these diversities mean that you must, like Pope, "consult the genius of the place in all", for you must consider all its moods and feelings if you would win its favour.

PLATE 1.

The south-west corner of the new garden photographed in its first spring. A few good perimeter trees have been retained, but everything else scrapped, and the "First Key Plan" has been given shape. This provided for banks of evergreen flowering shrubs, planted "in depth", to form a background for roses. The Key Plan allowed for later changes according to experience or caprice, and it allowed particularly for some extension of the plantings.

PLATE 2. *Top*: a corner of the winding "hydrangery". *Below*: Hydrangea 'Lilacina'.

CHAPTER 3

EMERGENCE

Root and Branch – Tender and Hardy – The Span of Life – Floral Anatomy

THE plants that adorn our gardens or feed our bodies have come to us from all over the world, and gay strangers from China and Peru, Persia and Africa, mingle cheerfully with our own natives. The tomato and potato go into the same plot as our coastwise cabbage and seakale. Our foxglove and heathers dwell at peace with the exotic rhododendron and the dahlia. Their origins are as mixed as their nationalities – stony mountain-top, lush meadow, chalky down, shadowy woodland, the dry and open moor and many other diverse conditions.

These mixed origins have through the ages caused many plants to evolve special characteristics to ensure their survival, conditioned by more or less heat, more or less water, more or less lime, and so on. The cactus and the water-lily, the buttercup basking in the sun, and the ivy creeping in the shade bear witness to a wonderful adaptability. Yet, if we except such freaks as the mushroom, all plants clamour in common for certain essentials. It is the gardener's business to know a little about them.

Root and Branch

The plant derives its nourishment principally through two organs – the leaf and the root. Through its root it obtains its food from the soil, which it absorbs in the form of soluble salts, i.e. through the agency of water.

Through the leaf, which is pitted with an immense number of tiny pores (stomata), the plant performs a much more involved and indeed mysterious process. It transpires or sweats, getting rid, in vapour form, of the water in its system; it breathes, taking in those gases it needs and rejecting others; and, through the agency of the vital green substance known as chlorophyll, it transmutes the elements of the air into carbohydrates, its energy food.

From this much-simplified outline of plant processes, we see that there are five elementals for healthy growing.

First, like human beings, plants need air; therefore they must not be overcrowded.

Second, light, in order that the leaves may absorb the radiant energy of the sun. Direct sunshine is not always essential, but a film of dirt on the leaf or the obscurity of overhanging trees restricts light radiation. Most plants require light all day, but many have conditioned themselves to living in the diffused light of partial shade, notably plants with large, thick, extra-green leaves such as rhododendrons, camellias and laurels. A very few are accustomed to even deeper shade. The shady spots often give gardeners a lot of trouble, so they have a section to themselves in Chapter 25.

Third and fourth needs, complementary to one another, are heat and water, in varying degrees. Though most of our garden plants like warmth, the process of transpiration may be critically affected by excessive heat, by wind and by a dry atmosphere. All these may cause the plant to transpire faster than it can take in water by the roots, and it then droops, just as a man droops in the tropics if he drinks less than he sweats.

Therefore watering is terribly important; but it is devilish hard to get the average gardener to believe just how much watering plants do need, in spring as in summer. Except for those accustomed to drought, our plants in general need a full inch of water, or 4½ gallons per square yard, every ten days, or about ½ a gallon per day. Calculating in more practical terms, this means that, using a mist-sprayer delivering not more than quarter of an inch an hour, our hoses should be on for three hours every week without rain. This represents an annual rainfall of about 36in., which is a great deal more than the heavens provide over that very large slab of our islands, barring local exceptions, which lies east of a line from the Tees to the Exe.

Tender and Hardy

Besides their varying likes and dislikes plants have diversities of even greater general importance to the practical gardener.

One such diversity is in their resistance to frost, and in this characteristic we classify them thus:

A TENDER plant is one that at all times requires warm and genial conditions; we shall have few dealings with them here.

A HALF-HARDY plant, such as the antirrhinum, may stand fairly low temperatures, or possibly a light ground frost. It must usually be raised in a greenhouse and not planted outdoors until the danger of frost is past.

A HARDY plant is one that can stay outdoors all its life, enduring hard frosts, some more than others. This is all that hardiness means in this country. It does *not* mean that you can treat the plant roughly, stick it anywhere without proper cultivation, and leave it to fend for itself. This misconception explains why thousands of pounds' worth of good seed is wasted every year, especially in hardy annuals, by those who imagine that the seed has merely to be broadcast light-heartedly anywhere. Of only a few plants is it true that they thrive in poor and rough conditions.

Other connotations of hardiness are sometimes met, as in drought-hardy, wind-hardy, sun-hardy and rain-hardy.

The Span of Life

Our next classification for garden purposes is according to span of life.

An ANNUAL is a plant which germinates from seed, flowers, dies, and produces its seed again all in one year or season. It may be hardy, half-hardy or tender. Most vegetables are annuals, and there are annual forms of several longer-lived flowers, such as the annual chrysanthemum, the annual lupin, and the annual delphinium (which includes larkspur). We gardeners also in practice treat as annuals some plants that by nature would live longer, e.g. antirrhinums.

A BIENNIAL is a plant that germinates from seed this year, and blooms and dies next year. Sweet-William, forget-me-not,

Iceland-poppy and Canterbury-bell are examples. Here again there are hardy ones and others.

A PERENNIAL has a continuous life over a period of years, and it may be hardy or otherwise. A very large group, varying from the oak to the violet. A herbaceous perennial is one which hibernates by shedding all its upper growth in winter, stem and leaf alike, right down to ground level, but retains life in its roots and crown. This class includes all the popular families that dwell in the herbaceous border, from the delphinium downwards, as well as the humble rhubarb.

In gardening practice, however, a few plants are included among herbaceous perennials although they do not, in fact, lose their foliage; of such are violas, pinks, thrifts, geum, hellebores, stokesia and others.

Another special category of perennials is the large and assorted congregation of bulbs and their kind, such as the daffodil and the dahlia.

Floral Anatomy

Flowers vary greatly in their construction, but in a normal one there will be one or more "whorls", or circlets, of different members, all springing from the same level on the stem, a very useful word for describing the characteristics of some plants.

The most obvious one, as a rule, is the whorl of petals, which are known collectively as the corolla. A whole ring of flowers may also girdle the stem in whorls, as in the candelabrum primulas (Fig. 31) and the monarda.

Enclosing the corolla protectively in the bud stage, there is normally a whorl of sepals, collectively called the calyx. Usually the sepals are small and green but sometimes they, rather than the corolla, form the plant's main decorative feature, as in the clematis, delphinium, anemone and hellebore. See Fig. 2.

Immediately below the corolla and the calyx there may be a whorl of rudimentary leaves called bracts, which are usually insignificant but which in some flowers, notably the poinsettia, are similarly the plant's most beautiful feature. Leaves also may be arranged on the stem in whorls, as in many rhododendrons and some lilies.

A good many plants have the calyx and corolla, or part of it, fused together or visually indistinguishable, with no apparent sepals, when they become jointly known as a perianth, a term that is specially familiar in the daffodil, the perianth being the array of rounded or pointed segments forming the background to the trumpet. Less obviously, the flowers of tulips, snowdrops and many other bulbs are formed of perianths.

Within the corolla appear the creative organs of the plant. The male organ is known as the stamen, its filament or stalk being crowned with

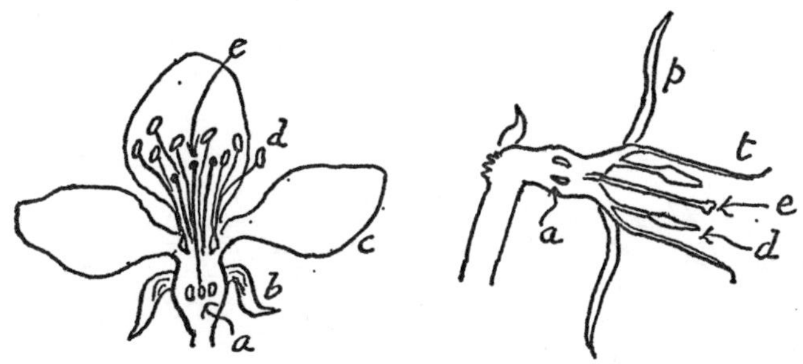

FIG. 6. Sectional sketches of apple blossom and daffodil, showing: (*a*) ovary; (*b*) sepal; (*c*) petal; (*d*) the male anther; (*e*) the female stigma; (*p*) perianth; (*t*) the trumpet-form corona.

an anther loaded with pollen that is usually brightly coloured. The more complicated female organ is known collectively as the pistil, of which the sticky terminal point is the stigma, and, when the male pollen falls upon the stigma through the agency of the bee, the moth, the wind or the hand of man, germination takes place and a seed is formed.

Many plants carry separate male and female blossom, when the plant is said to be monoecious, and others (particularly berrying shrubs) bear males on one plant and females on another, when they are called dioecious. In general, self-fertilization is abhorrent to nature. Even when both male and female organs are carried in the same flower there is often a device to forestall self-fertilization by the bee or other agency. If a holly fails to berry, it is not because of any occult prescience about the approaching winter, but merely because the female has not been successfully pollinated or else because it is a male. Similarly many fruit trees are self-sterile and need a close companion of another brand to form their fruits.

Plants display their glories in many floral forms that are termed

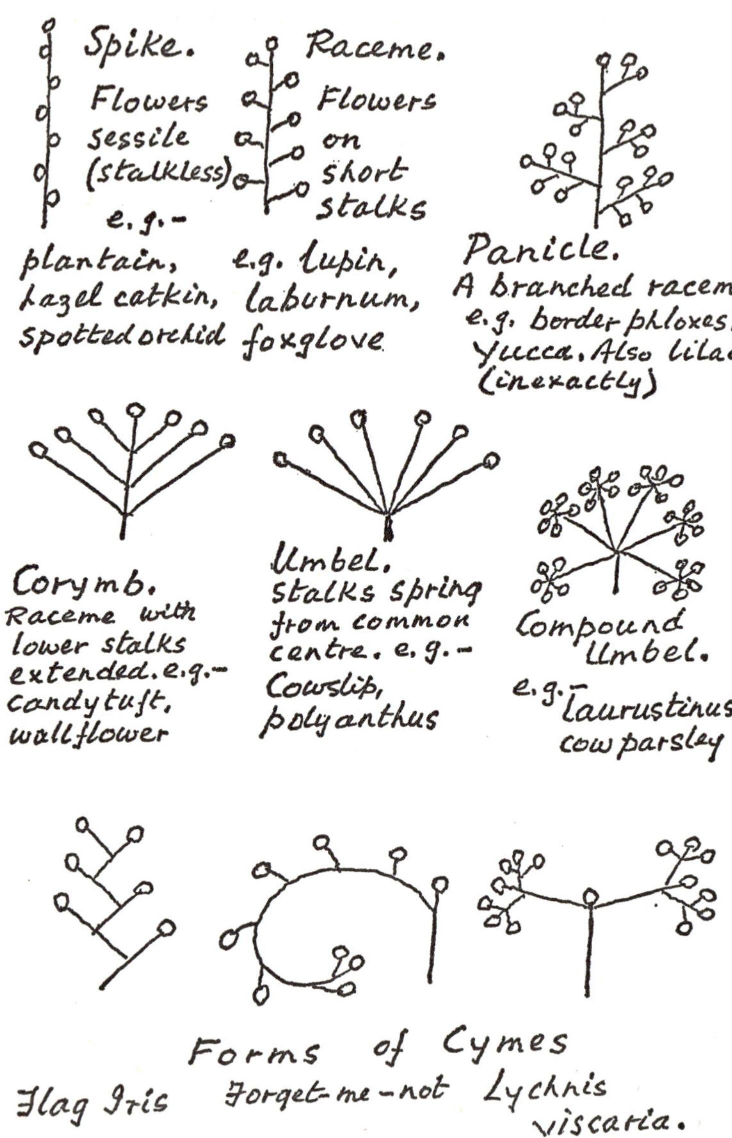

FIG. 7. Some forms of inflorescence.

inflorescences. These terms are often encountered in catalogues and garden literature and, although they are often technically wrong, they give one an idea of what sort of floral assemblage to expect. The inflorescence may consist of a solitary flower, as in the pansy and (usually) the tulip, or it may be a cluster of many florets arranged in a variety of ways; e.g. all the way up a tall stem, as in the delphinium, lupin and foxglove (which are inaccurately called "spikes" by gardeners) or in rounded or flat clusters, as in the lilac, rhododendron and border phlox, or a "composite" flower, such as the daisy and the thistle. Various styles of inflorescence are shown in Fig. 7, but it is more usual (as generally in this book) to use the informal words "cluster" or "truss" for any multi-flowered assemblage not in the shape of a spike or raceme.

CHAPTER 4

"DEAR EARTH"

The Living and the Dead - Sand, Clay and Humus - Peat - Chemical Elements - Organic Foods - "Fertilizers"

KING RICHARD II, grasping a handful of his native soil when he returned to England, exclaimed: "Dear earth, I do salute thee." For our part, less dramatically, we should do well to treat it with respect and understanding before we ask it to grow even a marigold.

Since plants imbibe their food through their roots, the gardener should always be asking himself: "What goes on underground?" To understand your soil and keep it in good heart and sweet temper is the beginning of wisdom. Project your thoughts underground, and ponder what is happening around the roots and whether the feeding and physical condition and the drainage are adequate and balanced.

Over most of the land formations of the earth the forces of nature have since times of prehistory gradually manufactured a thin film of soil compounded partly of pulverized rock surfaces and partly of decayed vegetable and animal wastes of countless centuries. This film we call top soil or fertile soil. It is alive, for it teems with tiny organisms, which we may refer to as bacteria.

Among them are bacteria whose purpose is to transmute the elements that are in the earth into soluble forms which plants can imbibe through their roots. Thus some of the ammonia contained in dung is converted by degrees into nitrates.

To retain fertility, top soil needs aeration by some means and it needs replenishment in some degree with animal or vegetable wastes such as dung, fallen leaves or decaying bodies. We say of a soil, therefore, that it contains, or does not contain, a high proportion of organic matter – that is to say, matter which has originated from some order of animal or vegetable creation having the organs of life and growth.

Below this thin film of top soil there is a subsoil. It may be only an inch or two below the surface, as on stony slopes or it may be some feet below. Relatively it is a solid and inert mass, lacking organic matter. For this reason subsoil should not be brought to the surface, except by the experienced hand who knows how to deal with it, but should be kept at its proper level. It can, however, be made fertile by creating those conditions that will encourage the bacteria to explore it, namely, by letting in air and digging in organic matter. When therefore we speak of a "good depth of soil" we mean one that has been deeply worked by man or nature, and unobstructed by rock, gravel, chalk, water and so on.

Sand, Clay and Humus

We need to look first of all at ingredients that make up the *physical* structure of the soil. These are: air, water, sand, clay, lime (including chalk), and humus.

Water we have touched on. Air is necessary to prevent the soil from becoming compacted and to assist chemical processes below ground. Air and water have to be in balance, for if the ground, through lack of drainage, becomes so saturated that it is waterlogged, air is expelled and you are likely to be in trouble.

SAND, being composed of relatively large, rough, and loose particles, holds air (and therefore warmth) but not water, which drains away through it quickly. It makes a soil "light" and easily workable, but it has no food value and its properties are purely physical or mechanical. Soils containing too much sand dry out quickly, and are said to be "hungry", needing frequent feeding with organic matter and copious watering in dry spells.

CLAY, by contrast, is a tightly bound mass of tiny particles. There are several types of it, including the boulder clay of the north and the yellow clay of London. It holds water too much and obstructs the passage of air. It is cold, stiff, sticky, and stubborn to the spade. When really dry it becomes brick-like and cracks. But it is chemically active and itself provides valuable plant food. Gardeners may curse it, but most plants love it. Clay and sand together thus balance and correct each other's faults. Soils preponderating in clay are called "heavy".

LIME. This is a many-sided matter and is of such importance to many gardeners, especially those who toil in chalk, that I have devoted a whole section to it in Chapter 25, where I deal with the whole matter in one piece.

We should, however, take careful note right at the beginning of two terms that will constantly recur in these pages – "acid" soil, meaning one with a low lime content, and "alkaline" soil, having a high one. To certain plants, known as "calcifuges", a limy soil is obnoxious, but to others, called "calcicoles", it is acceptable.

HUMUS is the precious element, so elusive of easy definition, that is the product of the decomposition of vegetable and animal (i.e. organic) matter. It is the heart and soul of the soil, which, without it, would be an aggregation of lifeless mineral particles. You can maintain the humus content of a soil only by frequent replenishment of organic matter, whether dung, compost or leaves, which is nature's method of replenishment.

None of these qualities by itself is of great value. What the gardener wants is a mixture, nicely balanced, of sand, clay and humus, which provides him with the joy of his heart – loam. A special form of loam that will be often referred to is "fibrous loam", which is a loam containing many fine fibrous roots in decay, as of old turf – a champion plant food.

One of the very nastiest soils is GAULT, a blue-grey blend of clay and marl, slimy when wet, rock-like when dry. A gault subsoil, I am told, is best undisturbed and cultivation confined to amassing quantities of organic material on top.

Peat

Peat does not come into the list of soil essentials that I have mentioned, but is found in various parts of these islands and millions of bales of it are now being incorporated into the clay, sandy and chalky soils in regions where it is foreign. When I began gardening peat was (like spent hops and coke) almost given away; today it has got into the hands of Big Business, with the inevitable result that its price has shot sky-high. Yet it is worth every sovereign you can spare for the majority of flowering plants (not all).

Peat is vegetable matter long decayed in waterlogged conditions. Most peats originate from mosses, sedges, or bracken. Not all are acid, but I imagine that all those sold for horticultural purposes are. By reason of its waterlogged origin, peat is *not* a plant food, though it may resolve itself into humus in time.

Its great value lies in its happy faculty of improving the physical structure of other soils. It holds moisture in the manner of a sponge, without clogging drainage, and is thus of particular value to plants that can't abide a dry soil, especially when young. It has a marvellous effect on the structure of stiff clay soil, liberating acids that precipitate the clay colloids, thus reducing the obstinate stickiness.

This in its turn enables the roots of plants to spread easily and quickly through the loosened soil; and if a young plant (or an old, transplanted one for that matter) is cradled in a nest of peat its roots are given a soft and unresisting medium in which to establish themselves quickly and push out in search of the rich foods beyond.

In sand, which is usually already loose, the main effect of peat is to serve to some extent as a water reservoir but it needs to be fairly often replenished. In chalk, where it should be used as liberally as the purse allows, it has a similar effect and loosens and aerifies the stubborn native material.

Peat is of particular value to all plants that need an acid soil, such as rhododendrons, camellias, most heathers and many lilies, although (contrary to popular belief) it is by no means essential to them. But it is a mistake to suppose that peat counteracts lime and that soils containing much lime can be made acid by incorporating peat in it. Lime is a pretty dominant element and will permeate the most acid peat in time, and, once there, will persist.

The uses of peat are many. It can be dug into the soil, used as a top dressing to conserve moisture, as pockets or nests for individual plants and as an essential element in potting composts. Impregnated with appropriate chemicals, it is also marketed as a medium for sowing seed and for potting – a very expensive medium, too.

For whatever purpose it is used it must be damp and, if used in or on top of the garden soil, it must be wet. Peat absorbs an enormous amount of water. My own method, in a small garden, is to keep a 60-gallon household water cistern in the "working area". Into this I put some 35 gallons of water and the tank will still hold two-thirds of one of the large, hundredweight bags of peat. I put in about five gallons of water to about every seven inches or so of peat at a time, stirring the while with a spade until the whole is almost, but not quite, like a porridge. It is darned expensive, but I keep the tank always replenished and every year I add peat to some part of the garden in turn.

Bearing in mind that peat has no food value, it should usually be fortified by a small quantity of fertilizer, preferably an organic and nitrogenous one. This could be of manure, of "Maxicrop", which is made from seaweed in both liquid and granular form, or of "Eclipse" fish manure, which is itself extremely acid, or of hoof-and-horn meal. This little gingering-up is particularly important when the peat is used as a top-dressing, but the ginger should be spread *below* the peat, unless it is mixed with it, which means more labour. Equally important, the soil itself should be at least moist when such a top-dressing is laid on. More about peat in Chapter 21.

Chemical Elements

As important as the physical properties of a soil are its chemical qualities. These, when converted into forms that plants can assimilate, are what they feed on. The primary and principal are: nitrogen, which improves foliage, phosphates, which promote root action, and potash, which ripens and hardens, and calcium.

There are several others, such as magnesium, manganese, boron, and so on, known as "trace" elements, but they are matters for the professional soil chemist and are much better not monkeyed with.

The important thing in a soil's chemical make-up, as in its physical structure, is correct balance, though not necessarily a balance in the same proportions for all plants. An excess of nitrogen or of calcium may be as harmful as a deficiency of potash. What the practising gardener must be ready to do, therefore, is to correct any imbalance that may be present or that may occur through heavy rain or through wastage by the appetites of plants, for to a certain extent the soil is eaten by what grows in it. As far as the flower garden is concerned, the elements that need frequent renewal are nitrogen, phosphates and potash; lime is only occasionally involved.

The chief method by which nature herself corrects this wastage is by leaf-fall and other forms of decay, returning to the soil what came out of it. Therefore all the law and the prophets, or nearly all, is that the gardener must frequently feed his plants (except for a few) with liberal platefuls of organic waste. We shall therefore consider these first before going on to the inorganic foods, but shall leave the versatile properties of lime till Chapter 25.

Organic Foods

Compared with the chemical fertilizers, the organic ones are slow in action but enduring in effect. The bulkier ones also make a potent contribution to the physique and structure of the soil and the ferment of chemical and micro-organic activity that they provide is absent in most substitutes. The outstanding ones for general use are animal manures, old turves, "compost" and leaf mould; and bonemeal is a commodity the gardener should never be without. I shall list first the bulky sorts that are so good for soil structure.

MANURE generally means animal dung and that is the sense in which I shall use the term. The best are those of the cow, horse and pig, but the droppings of poultry, sheep and goats have some value. All animal manures vary greatly in merit, according to their origins.

Horse manure is usually considered best for heavy (clay) soils, cow and pig manure for light (sandy) soils, but the odour of pig manure is too much for me.

For most purposes all animal manures should be fairly well rotted. You are fortunate if you can get it ready-made like that, but if fresh, you can rot it down before use. Fresh manures liberate excess acids harmful to some plant life. A raw, stiff clay seems to be the exception; fresh horse manure with plenty of long straw, I am told, is then an advantage.

Animal manure should not be left standing out in the open for any length of time, but should be firmly compacted in a ridge or pile and covered all over with broad sheets of black polythene, weighted down with stones. It will then rot down nicely.

For people who live in places where the right stuff is hard to get, particularly in towns, there are now several brands of ready-composted manure on the market, sold in polythene bales or sacks. Some may be of rather questionable value, but those that bear a branded name and are nationally distributed seem to be reliable. I have used "Stimgro" with satisfactory results. All that I have tried visibly contain lime, so I don't use them on lime-hating plants. Also, lacking bulk, they have little effect on the physical structure of soils.

Poultry manure is best used in the compost heap, where it is of great value. If used separately, apply it to the ground dry, partially or wholly decomposed, preferably in spring. Used raw, it tends to burn. Keep it under cover and dry. It is deficient in potash. The manure from deep litter chicken houses, in which the litter is peat, is reported to be good, but I have had no experience of it.

COMPOST. The compost heap or pile has attained special favour recently, though it is as old as the hills. Volumes have been written about it, fierce battles waged and a lot of hot air spouted by the advocates of one system or another. It should really, in fact, be called a decomposition heap, for it is made up of vegetable and animal wastes in the process of decay. It is a humus factory.

I shall not attempt to examine the numerous methods, especially as some of them contradict others. It is far better to advise the busy amateur to buy one of the inexpensive proprietary "activators" used for hastening decomposition and follow the manufacturer's directions. There are several good ones, such as Fertosan, Q.R. ("Quick Returns"), Garotta, Adco and Alginure. Liquid manures such as Maxicrop and Murphy's Murtonic can also be used. I have used them all, and found all good. The well-known Indore method and the Ministry of Agriculture system require no proprietaries. There is no better activator than manure if you can spare it.

The general idea is to heap up different types of refuse in an orderly manner. Heat must be generated. Thus the heap should hold a certain amount of air and not be too squashed, and it should be moist but not too wet. Exposure to sun, drying winds, and heavy rain are all alike to be avoided.

Prepare a pen in natural or artificial shade, such as the north side of a large tree. There should be free circulation of air round the sides, so don't build it against a wall, and the base should be plain earth or brick rubble, not anything impermeable. My own pens or bins are of two types – one of narrow, wooden boards, with air gaps between the boards, and the other of chain-link fencing nailed to wooden posts. About four feet square is a suitable size and one side of the pen should be removable, to enable the compost to be dug out when ready.

In small gardens and small families there is rarely enough material available to make the heaps as they should be made – quickly. Usually the main ingredient is lawn mowings, of which there is too much. What can be done is to accumulate the material as it becomes available in one pen and then, when there is enough of it, make a proper heap, using the activator, and finally cover the whole with a large sheet or sheets of black polythene (very important).

The stuff that can go on to the heap comprises any *soft* animal or vegetable matter from the house or the garden, except virulent or tough weeds, such as dandelion, dock, couch-grass, and ground-elder, and except the leaves of trees, which should be rotted down separately. Non-virulent weeds are entirely acceptable, but, unless one has enough material to make a quick, hot heap, it is safest to keep out any weeds that have flowered or gone to seed. Exclude all woody stuff, such as rose prunings.

Mix all the matter up well; especially mix the grass mowings up with other components, or they will make a thick, slimy blanket, obstructing air. It is usually best to turn the heap over at least once, bringing what was formerly on the outside into the centre.

Test when the material is ready by taking out a spadeful. When completely decomposed it will be black-brown, slightly moist, friable, and crumbly, faintly sweet-smelling, and bearing no marked resemblance to the original structure of leaf, grass, or stem. Such material is dug into the top spit only of the soil. Those people who are clever enough to make perfect compost, in which all weed seeds are destroyed, can use it as top-dressing, otherwise it is safest to dig it in, keeping it a good four inches below the surface of the soil.

LEAF-MOULD. This also is a form of compost, and a first-class food for all soils. Precious for lilies. Use only oak, beech, hornbeam, or hawthorn leaves. I haven't nearly enough of such leaves in my present garden, so I get them barrowed from neighbours who have a surplus. All one has to do is to stack them in an open-sided pen in autumn until about June, then turn the heap over and apply an organic lime-free activator.

The leaves of most other trees, particularly sycamore, chestnut, ash and so on, are unsuitable, as their tough foot-stalks and veins take years to decompose. They are better burnt, together with the leaves of roses and fruit trees, which may be infected with disease. Conifer foliage may well rest where it falls, and so may thick leaves, as of laurels and rhododendrons, provided the soil is given an occasional dressing of a nitrogenous fertilizer.

TURF. Old turf, full of fibrous roots, is one of the finest of plant foods. It is particularly good for light, sandy soils, giving it body and staying in the ground long after manures have been washed away. For chalky soils it is splendid, too. In default of your own turves, invest in two or three pounds' worth and stack them upside down in a shady place, with a thin spread of manure between each layer if you have any to spare. For rhododendrons and other plants that may be ill-affected by lime, use turves from lime-free soil if you can get them.

Fresh, green turf seems to be just as good as old turf, but must be chopped or broken up into small pieces and be accompanied by some sort of nitrogenous fertilizer. Old turves, if not thoroughly rotted down, should also be chopped up. Whichever is used, dig it in at least four inches below soil level. Turf, manure and peat are the three standard ingredients of all my digging and nothing enjoys this treatment more than roses.

Well rotted turf makes excellent loam for pots and seed-boxes when rubbed through a sieve.

HOPS. "Spent hops" is another commodity that used to be practically given away, but here again Big Business has stepped in and snaffled nearly the lot, using it as a base for "hop manure".

The spent hops are the residue from the breweries, containing precious little food value but excellent for improving the textures of all soils and for use as a top-dressing to retain moisture. If you can get a supply, make sure to spread a light dressing of fertilizer on the soil before applying the hops. Expect a pretty strong public-house atmosphere.

Hop manure – a misleading term – is merely spent hops impregnated with chemical fertilizer. It has a small organic content and is good stuff for general use by the amateur. Easy to handle and to store and is economical. Apply to the top spit in spring or beneath a top-dressing of leaves, spent hops or lawn mowings.

SEAWEED. One of the oldest manures known and rich in potash and salt. The best is the kind with long, broad ribbons or streamers and crenulated edges. Next best are the "bladder" seaweeds that children like to pop. The smaller, bushy kinds, often prettily coloured, are of least value. Weed thrown up early in the year is better than summer or autumn weed, and dried weed is more valuable than wet. Dry it under cover, not in the open. You can also compost it.

The proprietary "Maxicrop" is manufactured from seaweed and can be had in both liquid and granular form.

LIME. Soils with a low lime content may sometimes need a remedial dressing of it; but never at the same time as animal manure or any artificial fertilizer.

BONEMEAL. For general garden use this takes precedence. Mostly phosphatic and of special value for promoting root growth. Good for almost everything. Can be incorporated in the top spit when digging or, among plants already growing, spread on the surface and lightly pricked in with the tips of the fork or with a hoe. The usual rate is about 4 oz. per sq. yd.

Bonemeal is available in coarse, medium and fine grades, the last being known as bone flour. The coarser the grade the slower but longer lasting the action. Bone flour is thus applied in spring or summer, the others in autumn or winter.

Probably even better than bonemeal, particularly for roses, is meat-and-bone meal, which contains more nitrogen, but is not to be had everywhere.

FISH MANURE. These are made from desicated fish refuse and, if from a good source, are first-class plant foods. The best-known brand is Eclipse, which is a complete, balanced food, and it is extremely acid, making it acceptable to all plants uncomfortable in the presence of lime. It can be worked into the top spit when digging, but is perhaps more valuable as a top-dressing among growing plants, where it is lightly pricked in with the tips of the fork. Very good also as an under-spread for mulches of leaves or peat. Use at the rates recommended by the manufacturers.

DRIED BLOOD. Primarily a nitrogenous food, quick acting. Not cheap, but goes quite a long way and can be kept for the more precious plants. Excellent for mixing with the top-dressing of leaf-mould that most lilies need. Use at 2 oz. per sq. yd. in spring or early summer.

HOOF-AND-HORN MEAL. A very good plant food, having much the same effect as dried blood, but much slower in action and more permanent. Apply to the top spit in autumn or winter at 2 oz. per sq. yd.

MUNICIPAL COMPOSTS. Many local authorities now make a fertilizer from sewage and/or other waste materials. The few that I have tried make excellent, all-round feeds, but contain a good deal of lime and so are not suitable for calcifuges.

LIQUID MANURES. A valuable means of feeding plants quickly while in growth, either in the ground or in pots. Home-brewed liquid manure is made by filling a small sack or sandbag with rotted, not fresh, animal manure, adding a trifle of soot if available, and suspending it in a tub or tank of water. When the resultant solution is of deep tawny hue, draw off a small quantity, dilute it to the colour of straw and apply through a watering-can when the soil is moist.

Commercial brands of liquid manures (not all organic) can be bought in the shops.

"Fertilizers"

The majority of the inorganic foods are what are called artificial or chemical fertilizers. They are quick acting, easy to handle, and in experienced hands can be nicely adjusted to the needs of a particular crop. But their effect is not enduring, they feed the plant only and not the soil and they have as a rule little physical or mechanical influence on soil structure. Many are caustic to foliage, and should therefore not touch any portion of the plant and should be applied when there is little wind. Their best use is as a supplement to organic foods, and they are of particular value in the vegetable garden.

The artificials are pretty strong meat. The golden rule in their use therefore is "little and often". The rates of application are measured in terms of an ounce or two per square yard, which can be a tedious business if you are a precisionist. They are applied in spring or summer.

The chief artificials are:

Sulphate of ammonia, which provides nitrogen; superphosphate of lime, which provides phosphate; sulphate of potash, which provides potash.

There are many others. With two exceptions, however, I don't advise anyone who is not experienced, or who is not a chemist, to use any of these or other chemicals singly, nor to do his own mixing. They are tricky things. Nitrate of soda, for instance, makes sticky soils stickier, and sulphate of ammonia makes acid soils more acid. Moreover, there is always a danger of the soil's essential balance being upset.

Therefore, whatever the experts of the Press or the Air may say, it is far sounder for the amateur to buy only proprietary fertilizers, of which there are many excellent brands. For general use he should get a "complete" or balanced fertilizer made by a good firm or old friend Clay, while the "National Growmore", though devised for the vegetable garden, is good for flowers, too.

To this precept the two exceptions that I have mentioned above are the lawn, for which a spring dressing of sulphate of ammonia is excellent, and rose beds, for which an ounce of sulphate of potash per square yard in late winter can be valuable.

For special purposes there are excellent preparations to be had, such as various lawn fertilizers and Tonk's formula for roses and special preparations for chrysanthemums, etc. It is only for exhibition that you need to fiddle about with odd ounces of nitro-chalk or whatnot.

Soot from coal fires has a fertilizing value, dependent on how much sulphate of ammonia it contains. A good general stimulant with wide uses. Store it under cover for three months before using it among growing plants; or fresh on open ground. Almost useless if allowed to get wet. "Soot-water" is also useful, and is made in the same way as liquid manure.

Soot from oil-fired boilers should on no account be used.

CHAPTER 5

"COME, MY SPADE"

Modern Tillage – Drainage – Double-Digging – Modern Weeding – Watering – Mulching – Planting

IN modern practice good tillage or cultivation, as far as our pleasaunce is concerned, consists in sound preparation of the soil before planting and then leaving it alone, except for weeding, feeding and watering. After planting, any disturbance of the soil, beyond a mere scratching of the surface for weeding or feeding, is to be avoided, for it is damaging to roots, dangerous where there are bulbs and upsetting to the hegemony of the soil. The great thing is the beneficent practice of mulching, which keeps the top soil sweet, moist and less liable to weed infestation (unless the mulch be of manure). The exception to this curriculum is when bedding schemes are indulged in, requiring one lot of plants to be dug up and replaced by another lot.

We must, however, get the soil right in the first place. "Replenish the earth and subdue it" is a divine command. For our garden plants this is as vital as its foundations are to a house or its capital finance to a business. "Sickly plants", Gray tells us straight, "betray a niggard earth."

Drainage

Except for a bog garden, good drainage is the first commandment of good cultivation, an absolute *sine qua non*, to which constant reference will be made in these pages.

To all normal garden plants a waterlogged soil is fatal. The soil must, of course, be capable of holding such moisture as plants need – and some need a lot – and this we provide for by ensuring that plenty of decayed or decaying organic matter is incorporated, if not already present in the soil. But excess water must be able to drain away.

What is meant by "excess" water depends on the personality of the plant. Very often the drainage has to start at the ground level itself, when it is called "fast" or "brisk" drainage, and these also, or others like them, are terms that I shall frequently use. I am most anxious, Reader, that you should get a clear idea of this concept, which is so often passed over lightly. The fastest form of drainage,

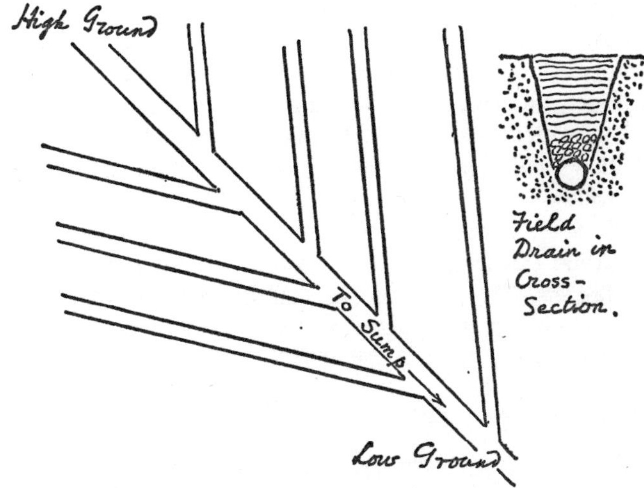

FIG. 8. Lay-out of a drainage system.

one may say, is a sieve. You create sieve-like conditions in a top soil by mixing in quantities of grit, stone chippings, gravel and so on. Through this the rain drains away fast, but sufficient for the plants' needs is retained in the soil that is mixed with the grit. Fast, gritty drainage is specially important for most rock plants, for the silver-leaved plants so important today and for many others and it is seen in its extreme form in the scree, in which there is often more grit than soil, and in which some of our most charming plants prosper (Chapter 21).

For other classes of plants the disposal of "excess" water means only lower spit drainage. In most existing gardens today there is little that need be done, but in new ground or in major operations, such as terracing, a drainage operation is likely to be necessary.

Pools of water lying on the surface for protracted periods show a need for drainage; but often the necessity is less obvious. Tests should be made in any new garden by digging holes about three spits deep in different parts and if the level of water – or "water table" – appears to remain permanently nearer to the surface than 18in., then there is a need for drainage, either in that part of the garden or throughout it.

The first problem is to decide where the waste water is to be directed. If there is no ditch or other outlet, the only thing to be done is to dig a sump-pit or a soakaway.

This is a terrible sweat. It means a large hole at the garden's lowest level, three-quarters filled with clinker, breeze, broken bricks, large stones, tin cans, etc., followed by a layer of smaller stuff and topped up with some 8in. of soil, which can be turfed over or used for shallow-rooting plants. For a small job a sump 6ft deep and square will do.

Excess water is led into this sump by a herringbone system of drains, using earthenware field drains or coarse rubble or even twiggy faggots. These are laid in shallow trenches which will be about 18in. deep at the highest point and will fall gradually deeper before reaching the sump. A fall of 1ft in 50ft is enough.

Double-digging

We still dig today in much the same manner as the "ancient gentlemen" to whom Hamlet's gravedigger, exclaiming "Come, my spade," paid his classic compliment; but we are not so thorough, nor even so thorough as in my own young days. The full "trenching" operation, digging three spits deep, was then the common practice of husbandry. Nowadays only a few enthusiasts, among whom sweet-pea fanciers are still numbered, go so deep. Most people are satisfied with mere double-digging, or bastard-trenching, and I must say that for general purposes this is adequate. Except in the more brutish soils, it is not particularly hard work for the average man. In both my post-war gardens virtually every inch has been double-dug and the full trenching only very rarely.

Nothing less than double-digging, 20in. deep, will provide a sure foundation. If our plants fail, we should probe our own hearts with the poet's blunt truth:

If vain our toil
We ought to blame the culture, not the soil.

The thing is done this way.

Divide the plot into rectangles. Rather narrow ones are best, but as long as you like. Twelve feet is a nice easy width. Across this width take out a trench a full spit deep and of, say, 30in. breadth. Wheel this soil away to the far end of the plot.

Step down into the trench and fork over the bottom spit, to the full depth of the fork.

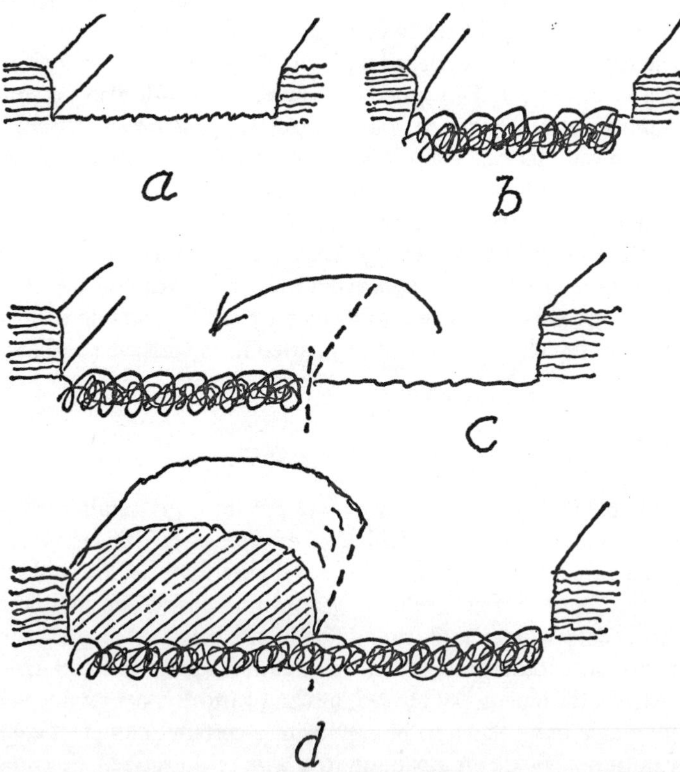

FIG. 9. Double-digging. (*a*) the initial trench opened up and the spoil barrowed away; (*b*) the second spit forked over and manured; (*c*) the second spit opened up and the spoil thrown into the first; (*d*) the second spit of the second trench forked over and manured.

Return to ground level, dig out another trench 30in. wide and throw the spoil from it into the vacant trench in front of you. Fork over the bottom spit of the second trench as before.

Repeat this sequence until the end of the job is reached, when the final trench is filled in with the spoil that was wheeled away from the first. This method ensures that the fertile top spit is kept always at its own level.

During the operation apply whatever manures or other additives may be wanted. In the normal way the bottom spit gets a liberal dressing of animal manure and you may also toss in unseeded weeds other than dandelions, ground-elder, bindweed and couch-grass. In sandy and chalky soils put in plenty of old turves, broken up smallish. In pig-headed clays, pea-haulm, straw and similar materials in limited quantities will help to open and aerate the soil.

The top spit can be enriched with all sorts of things. Priority is for peat and bonemeal. For general purposes there will also be some manure and, by my recipe, more broken-up old turves. Compost may take the place of manure and all these three commodities are best kept in the lower part of the top spit. Avoid making layers or sandwiches, however; mix the things up well.

Don't attempt at this stage to break the soil down into fine particles or rake it. Leave it rough. Above all, don't tread on the newly dug soil. Air must get deep into it. Don't plant anything in it for at least a month. Then is the time to smarten it up with rake and fork.

Modern Weeding

The nimble-witted chemist has of late put into our hands such an array of potions for the liquidation of weeds with the minimum physical effort that one would almost suppose that the hoe could be cast aside as an obsolete relic of ancient husbandry. We now have abstruse concoctions that can differentiate between one kind of herbage and another, others that seem to seal up the soil surface so as to arrest the emergence of seedlings and various other stratagems. These magic brews have to be used with a certain amount of care; they must not trickle off a path on to a lawn or flower bed, nor must a drop fall upon the leaf of any treasured plant.

Of old, the sovereign cure for weeds on paths and drives was sodium chlorate, which kills pretty nearly everything, including shrubs. It is still excellent for clearing large areas of matted weeds, as may be encountered when one inherits a house from a non-gardener. It acts quickly and goes down fairly deep, so that it is a danger to plants that spread their roots beneath a path, and it does not destroy all seeds, so that weeds will regenerate. When used for clearing land, nothing can be planted there for six months. Apply in spring, summer or autumn.

As regards modern weed-killers, my space allows me to give them only a brief mention; you must get the do's and don'ts of each from their leaflets. New concoctions are being brewed up even as I write. Watering cans used for any of these poisons must be very thoroughly washed out after use, but it is better to keep one or more specially reserved for them and distinctively coloured.

SIMAZIN. For paths. Supersedes sodium chlorate, inhibiting germination of weed seeds for nearly a year. Marketed under various trade names by Murphy, Fison ("Weedex") and Boots.

SPOT WEED-KILLERS. For use where a fluid might trickle on to lawns, beds or paving plants: Atlacide (a powder), P.B.I's Spot-weeder, Berk's Touchweeder or Killer-kane.

"HORMONE" weed-killers as used on lawns. For virulent un-diggable weeds growing in flower beds. Use at the same strength as for lawns, *not* stronger. Go round with some in a jam jar. Dip the leaves of bindweed into it and paint the leaves of dandelions. If the treated weed-leaves are in contact with a desired plant, keep them off with a piece of sacking.

BRUSHWOOD KILLER. For the tougher hooligans – brambles, nettles, ground-elder and possibly mare's-tail and horse-tail (the worst of all). Known by the magic symbol "2,4,5 – T". Two applications are likely to be needed.

PARAQUAT. Used to suppress weeds among shrubs, in rose beds and the kitchen garden. Best known so far under the trade name Weedol (not to be confused with Weedex). Preeglone Extra may be better.

DALAPON. Specifically for couch-grass, but kills other grasses also.

FLAME GUNS. Warlike-sounding weapons, but there is nothing really very intimidating about them, provided you have a sweet disposition, are patient enough to understand their captious temperaments and don't mind the rather messy job of keeping them clean. A really efficient pump is an absolute necessity. Ruthless destroyers of all top growth but do not prevent regeneration. Also useful for burning up accumulation of trash in odd corners and for starting awkward bonfires.

Despite all these wizardries, there is still plenty of work in the general garden for the ancient hoe. Get at the fibrous-rooted weeds early, before they have flowered. Tap-rooted weeds such as the dandelion, underground creeping horrors such as ground-elder, couch-grass and bindweed, and a few bulbous weeds laugh at the hoe, however. You may slice them off, but they will sprout again. In the absence of a poison, the only ways to get rid of dandelions, docks and thistles mechanically are either to delve down to the very extremities of their root tips, or else persistently to harass them with the hoe, when they will perish from lack of nourishment.

Watering

In Chapter 3 I have already asserted that a large part of England does not get nearly enough rain – a statement likely to arouse outraged protests from non-gardeners thirsting for eternal sunshine. Apart from quantity, *regularity* of rain or water is also very important. A sudden heavy fall of rain does not make up for three weeks lack of it and in some cases may do more harm than good. It is a great mistake to wait till plants are wilting and haggard before watering. In my own garden the hoses come on every ten days from April till September if there has been no rain. They are then on more or less continuously in some part of the garden until rain falls.

All watering must be *gentle* and *thorough*. Never use a hose or can without a rose, sprinkler or similar fitting (except the very small cans with thin spouts). On a hose, always use a fitting that will produce a fine rain or mist. Coarse sprays or sprinklers ruin blooms (especially roses), beat down the plant and deliver a volume of water too large for the earth to absorb. Give a gentle, steady and prolonged soaking and don't play about by holding the hose in your hand.

The gadget I use for producing a fine spray is a flat plastic tube with tiny pinholes all the way along, pierced at varying angles. They are quite inexpensive and I have them in three lengths – very short, rather long and medium. These I join up to short lengths of the usual round hosing, which in turn are screwed into one of several standpipes teed into my alkathene ring main.

These tubular sprinklers however, give a very uneven delivery and the ideal sprinkler has not yet been marketed. All vary tremendously in the size of droplet they deliver, the area they cover, the evenness and rate of their delivery, the soil disturbance they create and the amount of water they use. Many have gross faults. The most important thing, for which other faults may be forgiven, is that they should deliver a fine mist.

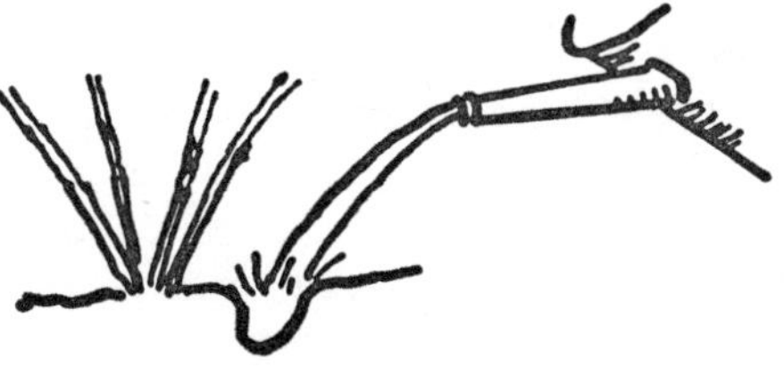

FIG. 10. How not to water.

Some plants, such as hydrangeas, rhododendrons and camellias, need repeated heavy waterings in dry weather. So also does anything newly put into the ground, especially conifers and other evergreens, which, in addition to rain or water every few days ought to have a fine mist from a syringe directed on their foliage at least once a day in their first spring and summer, according to the weather, and large-leaved shrubs, newly planted, ought to have it two or three times a day, if one were truly conscientious. Syringing is far better on such plants than the hose or the can, since the larger droplets from a hose quickly run off the leaves. Better still is a machine that automatically directs a squirt of mist every fifteen minutes or so, but not all of us can run to it.

One is often told that hose water from the tap should never be used on rhododendrons and other lime-sensitive plants and I followed this advice as best I could myself for many years. I now know it to be invalid. However, I catch as much rain-water from the roof as I can and this is of special value when planting or when watering single plants.

Another thing that one is often told is that plants should not be watered while the sun is shining. This also is largely invalid. Certainly evening is the best time to water at the height of summer, but one would never get round the garden in periods of drought if watering was so restricted. Only a very few plants, of which the pieris is one, suffer damage from watering in the sun.

Mulching

I have already extolled the virtues of mulching. The forests of the world proclaim how rich in food are fallen leaves and almost everything in our gardens benefits from a thick autumn mulch of them, especially shrubs and trees of all sorts, climbers, hedges and the herbaceous border. Manure, compost, peat and grass mowings also serve well, but all except peat may carry the seeds of weeds.

You must mulch only when the soil is moist and warm. Thus leaf, peat and compost mulches (contrary to what is often said) are best given in autumn. Grass mulches, which must be free of seed and occasionally stirred, for they get very hot, go on in the mowing season. On the other hand, mulches of animal manure should be given as the sap begins to rise in spring, or its elements will be washed away by winter rain. Keep animal manures well away from the stems of plants.

Do not mulch irises, carnations nor any prostrate or lowly plant. On the contrary, leaves falling on them should be picked off; but in low-growing shrubs, such as helianthemums, they may be tucked underneath.

Rock plants demand a special technique in mulching, for which limestone or sandstone chips are the usual thing. Indeed, a mulch of stones is good for almost any plant, serving to keep the collar of the plant dry as well as to prevent evaporation of water from the soil.

Planting

The operation of starting off a plant really well in its new home is of critical importance to its whole future.

In general terms the requirements are – a well-worked soil, friable, damp but not sodden; a hole slightly deeper and slightly wider than would appear necessary; an arrangement of the roots in the hole so that they are let well down or spread well out and not crowded, twisted or cockled up; a firming of the soil with hand or foot; a good watering-in, using rain-water if available.

A few plants have their special requirements, which we shall note as we go along. Depth of planting is often critical. Generally it suits

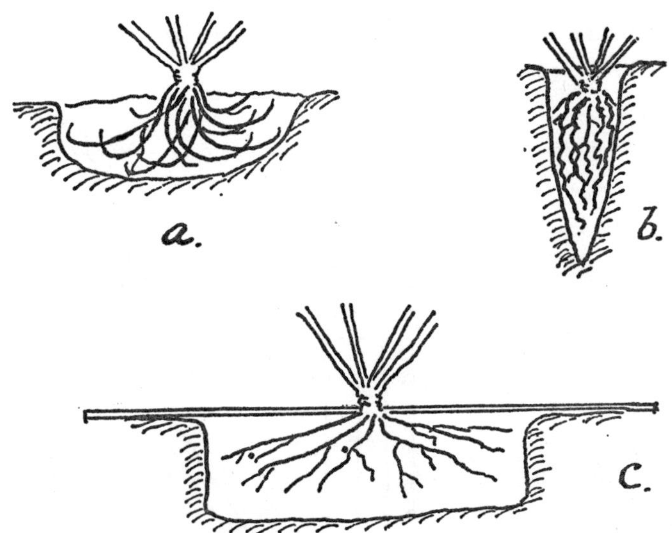

FIG. 11. Wrong and right planting: (*a*) roots crowded, cockled up and crossing, crown above ground level; (*b*) roots cramped, crown too low; (*c*) right, showing use of rigid stick to keep correct depth.

the need barely to cover the crown, but rhododendrons and carnations should be planted very shallow, phloxes and clematis rather deeply, and so on.

Trees, *particularly standard trees and conifers,* and *evergreen shrubs* need a little extra care. Having dug a hole of ample size, put in the plant, work some fine soil or peat in among the roots, leaving no air spaces, cover the roots with some of the excavated soil, tread down fairly firmly, *spread a layer of manure or good compost,* top up with more soil to ground level, water copiously and mulch heavily. Standard trees need strong stakes, which are best placed first. Be careful to plant all trees and shrubs *exactly to the level of the old soil mark* visible on the stem; this you may ensure by laying a cane across the hole before completing its excavation.

Syringe evergreens as ordered earlier and, in the absence of a mulch, water liberally in all dry spells for the first year.

Plant always in what is called "open" weather – that is, when the ground is neither frost-bound nor saturated. The soil should be damp, but not so wet that the boots clog. If, as often happens, planting has to be done in a dry spell, soak the ground thoroughly the night before if the job is a big one, or water the plants in extra thoroughly as you plant.

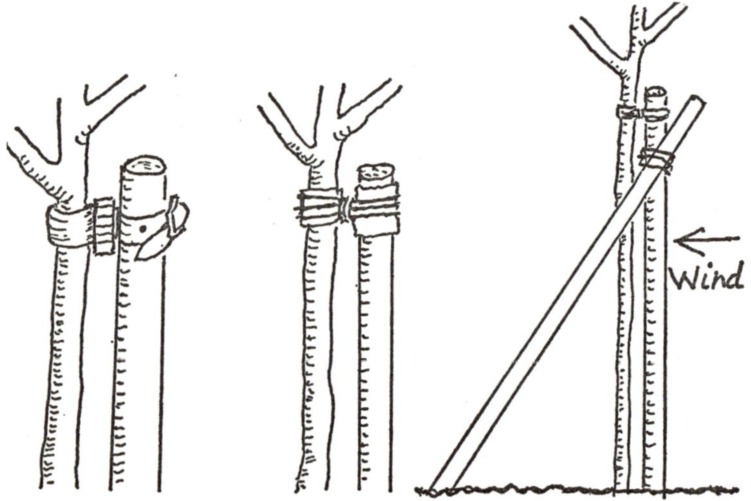

FIG. 12. Staking young trees. *Left*: with rubber or plastic tree-tie. *Centre:* with cord and sacking. *Right:* against a strong prevailing wind.

I have spoken of firm planting, but a word of caution is needed. The requirement is often stressed and is often overstressed, especially in relation to rhododendrons. Do not make your firming so drastic that the roots, particularly of fibrous-rooted evergreens, are damaged, the soil compacted and water unable to get through. This warning applies particularly to clay soils. Water itself is a highly efficient firmer of soil.

When plants come from a nursery get them into their homes as soon as possible. If delay is unavoidable, unpack and "heel" them in somewhere convenient (see "Gardener's Jargon"). They are then safe for a substantial time. Trees and shrubs, including roses, which may arrive in time of severe frost or continuous rain are reasonably safe in their packings in a shed for probably a couple of weeks. If they are evergreens, remove part of the top covering, spray the foliage and wet the roots through their covering every day or two.

Plants in pots, before transplanting, should be tapped out, the crocks removed, and, if somewhat pot-bound, a gentle squeeze given to the ball of soil so that the roots may be loosened and spread out. If the roots have got very packed and are coming out of the drainage hole, the pot may need to be broken.

Evergreens should arrive from the nursery with their roots in a ball of soil, wrapped in sacking or open-mesh netting. Do not disturb the ball of soil and, if the wrapping is a loose and open net, it need not be removed.

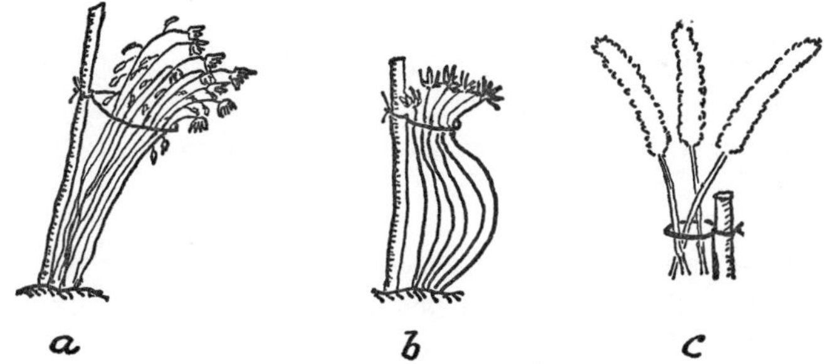

FIG. 13. Shocking examples of staking perennials: (*a*) the Weary Willie method; (*b*) the hangman's noose; (*c*) the lolling delphinium.

CHAPTER 6

"LIVE AND MULTIPLY"

Propagation Generally – Multiplying by Seed – By Cuttings – Root Cuttings – Layers – Air Layering – Division – Garden Glassworks

VIRTUALLY all plants can be grown from seed. In practice however, there are often objections to this method of propagation, whether because germination is difficult, or because growth is slow or because the offspring may not resemble their parents.

Nature herself employs other methods, as by stolons or suckers, by layers, by the formation of new bulbs, and so on. The tips of blackberries, drooping to the earth, will take root and form new plants. The strawberry sends out its "runners". The stems of jasmine, hydrangea, clematis, ivy and many other plants, laid on the ground, may take root anywhere along their lengths. The gardener takes advantage of these propensities of nature, and has invented some other methods himself to induce his plants to "live, and multiply, and go in to possess the land". By his choice of method he is able to perpetuate a particular strain or to develop new ones. For the gardener is the first to echo the sentiments of the immortal sonneteer when he engrossed the golden lines:

From fairest creatures we desire increase,
That thereby beauty's rose might never die.

The methods of propagation otherwise than by seed are called "vegetative". Their prime merit is that they are certain to be exactly like their parents, whereas seed, especially of the modern hybrids, may produce something quite different.

Broadly speaking, in modern practice annuals and biennials are raised from seed and other categories of plants are more usually

PLATE 3. *Top*: Heathers and dwarf golden conifers in the front garden. *Below left*: dwarf golden cypress *Chamaecyparis pisifera* 'Plumosa Rogersii' among heathers. *Below right*: the green-gold *C. lawsoniana* 'Minima Aurea' in another heather bed.

PLATE 4. *Top*: *Hypericum patulum* 'Hidcote' flowers profusely right up to the bole of a wide-spreading cherry, together with the carpeting cotoneaster 'Autumn Fire'. No weeds here!

Below: Close-up of the hypericum.

multiplied by one or other of the vegetative means. Thus the typical (but not only) method of increasing carnations and rhododendrons is by layers, shrubs by cuttings, fruits and roses by budding or grafting, many herbaceous perennials by division of roots, while some begonias will take root merely from a leaf laid flat on the soil.

Multiplying by Seed

Quite a wide range of plants, however, can be raised perfectly easily from seed besides annuals and biennials, if one is content to wait a bit. Many trees and shrubs, herbaceous and rock plants, bulbs and climbers will "be fruitful and multiply" by this means at the gardener's command.

His three main methods are by sowing:

(*a*) Outdoors, direct into the plant's quarters (*in situ*); many hardy annual flowers are so raised.

(*b*) Outdoors, but in a seed-bed in a special nursery, whence they are moved on to their permanent quarters, or often into an intermediate station, as soon as they are large enough to handle; this is the usual method for hardy biennials such as wallflowers and sweet-William, and for hardy perennials such as delphiniums and lupins.

(*c*) Indoors in a greenhouse or a frame, the seed being sown in boxes, or earthenware pans, or in pots; this is the characteristic method for starting half-hardy plants (e.g. antirrhinum and stock) and for tender subjects, but hardy plants may also be so started for special purposes.

Two golden rules of sowing, whether out or indoors, should be taken to heart early:

Sow sparsely.

Sow not too deep. Flower seed, as distinct from some vegetables, rarely needs to be covered by even a quarter-inch of soil and very fine seed, as in begonia and rhododendron, needs a mere film of sand. On heavy soils sow even less deeply than on light or thin ones.

Sowing Outdoors. Whatever method of sowing is adopted – whether in a nursery bed or *in situ*, and if *in situ* whether in long straight ranks or broadcast – make first a fine seed-bed. The soil must have been dug at least a few weeks beforehand and allowed to settle. Preparation of the seed-bed then consists in reducing the top two or three inches to a fine tilth; the smaller the seed, the finer the tilth.

First, lightly fork over the top few inches only, and give it an initial raking. Next, lightly tread down the soil with the feet to crush lumps, shuffling along the row sideways. Then rake thoroughly to-and-fro, removing stones. Repeat the process of treading and raking as often as may be necessary, according to whether the soil be light or heavy. The last process is always raking.

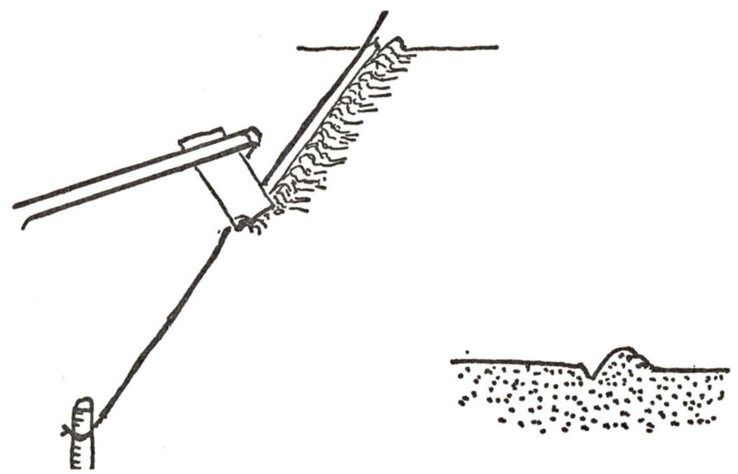

FIG. 14. "Drawing" a seed drill with a hoe. The drill shown in section.

This work should be done when there is plenty of moisture below ground but when the surface is sufficiently dry for the hoe to work easily without soil sticking to it. Conditions are generally just right after the east winds of early spring have dried off the surface moisture.

Having worked up a good tilth, make a "drill" for the reception of the seed (see "Gardener's Jargon"). Often it will be only a quarter-inch deep. Use a taut garden line to keep you straight and "draw" the drill with the corner of a hoe of some sort.

If the soil is dust-dry after a long spell without rain, make a rather deeper drill an hour or two beforehand, flood it with water and draw the soil back as soon as the water has soaked through.

In clay soils, whether dry or moist, lay half an inch or so of peat in the bottom of the seed-drill, which should be drawn that much deeper; this will give an easy start to the tiny roots of the seedlings.

Now sow the seed along the drill, either by pouring it gently out of the packet, or a pinch at a time with finger and thumb, or by means of a seed-sowing gadget. The finer seeds may be mixed with sand for easy handling and distribution.

After sowing, cover the seed from the little ridge of spoil from the drill by drawing the back of a rake or edge of a hoe gently over the surface. Very fine seed can be covered by sprinkling fine potting soil or sand from a fine-mesh sieve. Then lightly tamp down the soil of the filled-in drill with the hoe or the inverted head of a rake.

Seed may also be sown by broadcasting – sprinkling more or less at random and raking lightly to cover the seed. This is often done with annuals, but is not a method I care for. It is preferable to sow in irregular drills – serpentine, circular, as you will. Better still, however, for annual flowers, is the method of sowing "at stations" – dropping two or three seeds at selected spots, and subsequently thinning the seedlings to the most promising one when large enough. This enables seedling weeds to be more easily identified and the hoe plied with greater safety.

A good way of sowing annuals at stations is to scratch a rough criss-cross pattern, like squared paper, on the soil, and to sow at the intersections, the lines being at distances apart suitable to the plant – about 9in. for the general run of medium-sized annuals.

When the seedlings have fully developed their second pair of leaves – i.e. the first pair of *true* leaves after the cotyledons or seed-leaves – they must be thinned out to their appropriate final spacings if they have been sown in their permanent quarters, or "pricked out" if they have been sown in a preliminary nursery bed.

Thinning means reducing them so that those that remain stand at their final distances apart.

Pricking-out means lifting the seedlings from this nursery bed (or seed-box) – all of them – and replanting them more widely somewhere else, either into their permanent quarters or into some intermediate quarters. Lift them gently by means of an implement, with a little soil adhering to their roots. Handle them by the leaves, not by the stems.

Seedlings that cannot normally go into their final homes for some time, such as biennials (wallflowers, Canterbury bells, etc.) and perennials (delphiniums, columbines, etc.), are pricked out into a nursery bed first. This is a vital period for them. Give them a bed generously treated, in an open position, not under trees; some will appreciate a degree of shade. In this bed they are planted out at distances suitable to their nature – wallflowers at about 5in. apart, delphiniums at 8in. or more.

Sowing Indoors. For the general run of plants use wooden seed-boxes or shallow earthenware seed-pans, but pots are usually better for trees and shrubs. All must have holes or slits in the base for drainage and must be clean. Scrub old pots and boxes with hot water and soda, or a fungicide. Soak new clay pots for some hours.

"Crock" the receptacles, by layering their drainage holes or slits with pieces of broken flower-pot (which are "crocks"), or small stones, to control drainage. In pots, add a few half-decayed leaves on top of the crocks. Then fill the receptacle with either John Innes Seed Compost or one of the newer soil-less ones, which are of treated peat. There is little difference between these two types of rooting medium; the soil-less ones are the more expensive, but are stable and constant in quality. The J.I. composts are sometimes shockingly made; the best makers I know are Walter Unwins and L. S. Beckett. The best soil-less mediums are Fison's Levington Compost and Croxden Soil-less, which is the less expensive. In the Levington seedlings certainly root well.

Whatever compost is used, fill the receptacle to within quarter or half an inch of the rim the day before you intend sowing the seed. Make the surface quite level by pressing down rather firmly with a flat pressing-board. Then partially immerse the receptacle in water so that the water seeps up from below and nearly reaches the surface soil. Treat with Cheshunt Compound and leave to drain overnight.

After sowing, lightly sprinkle a little compost over the seed through a fine sieve, cover the receptacle with a sheet of glass and on top of it a sheet of brown paper. Usually the seed-box or pan is then put in a shady part of the greenhouse. Wipe the glass dry every day and reverse it.

As soon as the seedlings show their noses, remove the paper, tilt or shift the glass slightly to give more ventilation, and put the receptacle close up to the roof of the greenhouse or frame. After a few days remove the sheet of glass altogether.

From now on see that the soil is kept fairly moist, preferably by immersion as before. If watering is done from overhead, use a fine rose or a syringe.

When the seedlings have developed their first pair of true leaves, prick them off into other pots or boxes. If into a box, I like it to be 3–4in. deep, instead of the shallow trays into which most nurseries crowd their seedlings. Use the same compost as before, treated likewise with Cheshunt Compound. Space average-sized plants, such as antirrhinums, a good 3in. apart instead of the usual jungle. Keep them well watered and move them up as close to the light as possible. Seedlings of shrubs, other than the small ones, are pricked off singly into small pots and, if hardy, are "plunged" into a bed of sand or ashes outdoors or in an open frame.

This method of raising seedlings in a box or pan need not be confined to a greenhouse, if the plants are hardy. The boxes or pans can be put outdoors in the shade. This is the way I always raised delphinium and polyanthus, my favourite spot having been the north side of a red currant bush.

Seedlings of plants that are not fully hardy, however, must be hardened-off before being marched out to face the harsh world in the open. The method of doing this is given in the section "Garden Glassworks" at the end of this chapter.

By Cuttings

Here we depart from the ways of Genesis and enter an outer Eden, in which the hand of man has devised new ways of bringing fruitfulness to the earth, not by creation, which is still a divine prerogative, but by regeneration. As far as I know, Holy Writ does not record who was the first man to discover that, by sticking a twig into the ground, he could manufacture a new plant. I wager that it was the vine, whose bouquet so liberally flavours the Scriptures, that first showed the way to Adam and his sons.

Today we manufacture, very cheaply and often very easily, a very large quantity of new plants by this means, from the pygmies of the rock garden to big shrubs and trees. For the greater part we use stem cuttings ("slips" to our forefathers), but occasionally root and leaf cuttings. A stem cutting is simply a limb removed from a living plant at the right time of year and plunged into suitable soil. The base of the cut stem, after insertion, forms a callus or healing tissue over the wound and from this roots form. Only perennials are normally so multiplied, not annuals or biennials.

"Live and Multiply"

Some plants are so eager to regenerate that they will sprout if you merely push a twig in the ground in a shady place; of such are the willow, forsythia, artemisia, dogwood and pelargoniums ("geraniums"). Usually, however, you must:

Choose the right "wood" or branch.
Spot the right cutting point.
Use a soil in which it will "strike", or take root.
Provide a shady site and, in most instances, a moist, close atmosphere.

In no case are hollow-stemmed shoots any use for cuttings.

Choosing the Right Wood

Cuttings may be of "hard wood", "half-ripe" or of "soft wood".

A HARD-WOOD cutting is a mature or nearly mature shoot, usually 9–12in. long, of the *current* year's growth (what one might call a young adult shoot, not an aged one), taken from an established plant in autumn or early winter. Plants for which the use of this kind of cutting is typical are: bush-fruits, roses and the tougher shrubs and trees, such as buddleias, spiraeas, forsythia, laurels, privet, etc.

Side-shoots rather than "leaders" are generally best, especially young shoots springing from near the base.

Such cuttings are simply stuck in the ground in a shady place protected from cold winds. Make a narrow, V-shaped trench by waggling the spade to and fro, about 6in. deep, and line the bottom with an inch of sharp sand. Put in the cuttings, return the soil, making it fairly firm, and water well. Some cuttings will remain dormant all winter. When new growth does start, water thoroughly. Plant out in the following autumn or possibly in summer.

A SOFT-WOOD cutting may be either a young growth from a hard-wooded plant, frequently a growing tip, taken while the plant is actively developing in spring or summer (as for fuchsias and hydrangeas), or it may mean a cutting of a soft-wooded plant, such as viola, pelargonium and penstemon, which may be taken either in spring or in September, or of delphiniums and lupins, which are taken in early spring only.

HALF-RIPE cuttings, taken in early July as a rule, are side-shoots which have sprouted in the current season and are just starting to get firm and woody at the base but are still soft and still growing on at the

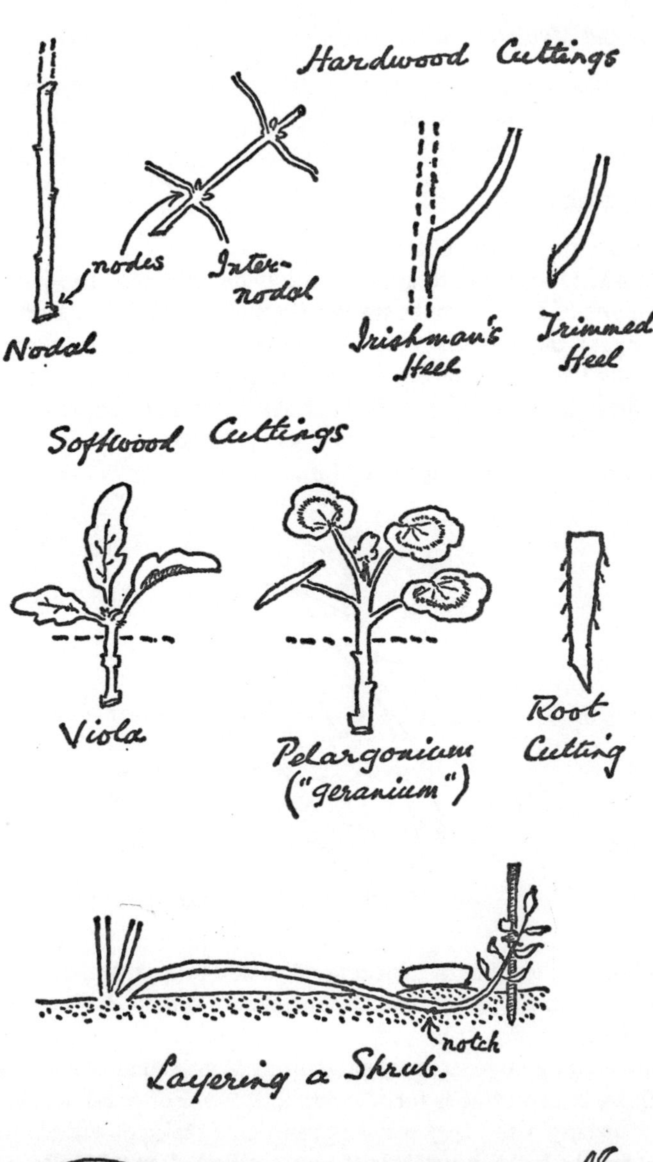

FIG. 15. Some cuttings and layers.

tip. Nearly all evergreens are propagated this way, as are a very wide range of deciduous shrubs.

The Cutting Point

There are three types of stem cutting:

NODAL: those cut precisely below a node or joint or leaf-junction (examples of a node are the swollen rings of a carnation or bamboo). In general, these are the best. The chosen shoots may be severed in any way that is convenient and it is then cut back below the node cleanly with a very sharp blade horizontally, without slope. A razor-blade is just the thing for softer plants or shoots.

INTERNODAL: used typically for clematis.

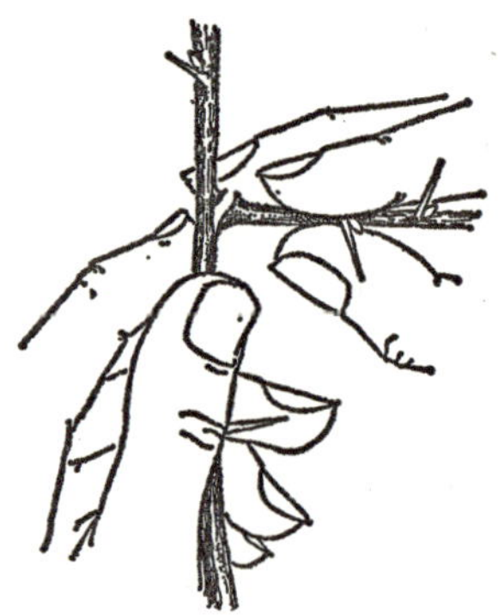

FIG. 16. Taking a heel cutting.

HEEL: those made by plucking off a side branch at the point of junction with its parent branch, and taking a wisp, or heel of the parent with it (Fig. 16).

Heel cuttings are extremely good for half-ripe and most hard-wood cuttings, but sometimes for soft cuttings, too. For rough-and-ready work on easy plants they may be pushed into their pot without more ado, but the better practice is to trim the heel clean with a razor.

Rearing the Cuttings

No more need be said about hard-wood cuttings, so we deal now with the soft-wood and half-ripe sorts.

As the cutting has to be inserted in soil, all leaves are removed from that portion which will be underground, leaving a small tuft by which normal leaf functioning can proceed. If the limb taken from the parent is too long, shorten from the tip, not the base.

After trimming, it is helpful to dip the basal ends of the cuttings lightly into one of the root-forming "hormones", such as Seradix (of which there are three grades) or Murphy's rooting hormone.

Now prepare the receptacle. For the amateur's small-scale work, pots are usual (I prefer clay pots for this purpose) or else clay pans or half-pots, much favoured by some growers of delphiniums and lupins. After crocking, fill the pots or pans a little short of the rim with a compost made up of one part medium loam, two parts peat, and one part sharp sand; or use the Levington seed compost.

Insert the cuttings round the edge, nearly touching it and nearly touching each other. The one time that plants like to be crowded together is when they are cuttings. Plant very firmly, pressing the soil about the stems hard down with the fingers. Intimate contact of the basal wound with the soil is essential; a dribble of sand in the bottom of each hole helps. Water thoroughly by immersion of the pots. Afterwards be sparing with drinks until the cuttings have rooted, but keep the soil just moist.

Nearly all soft-wood and half-ripe cuttings, taken with the sap still running freely, require a *moist, close atmosphere in the shade.* Otherwise they will transpire too freely and wither up. Accordingly they are best housed in a propagating box of some sort, which may be home-made, as mine are for all hardy plants; they are simply deep boxes with close-fitting glass lids and are kept (preferably in an outdoor frame) on the shady north side of a wall, being frequently syringed. Tender plants may need an orthodox propagating case with soil-warming cables, kept on the greenhouse bench.

When the need is to raise only one or two pots of cuttings, an easy and trouble-free method is by the use of polythene bags. Two fairly stiff wires, bent into the shape of a hoop, are thrust deep into the pot at right angles to one another, the polythene bag pulled over and secured round the pot by two elastic bands. The wire hoops must be fitted before the cuttings are planted (Fig. 17). This is the "Wisley pot".

The close and humid conditions I have described do not, however, suit those plants that have soft, grey or silver, felty or silky foliage. They include the senecios and so on that are the flower arranger's dream, together with pinks and lavenders.

All these should be housed in the shade, but *not* closely covered.

In some three weeks, or thereabouts, the emergence of new growth on the cuttings will provide evidence (but not certain proof) that they have taken root. Let them grow on for another few days and then test them by a cautious tug of the leaves. If they resist they have

FIG. 17. The "Wisley pot", showing the wire framework in position ready for the polythene envelope.

rooted. Tap out the pot by knocking its rim on the edge of a bench or other firm projection and transplant the rooted cuttings into other pots separately or into a nursery bed or into permanent quarters.

Root Cuttings

The roots of several herbaceous plants, if cut into small lengths, will grow into new specimens. Examples are phlox, gaillardia, mullein, anchusa, oriental poppy and romneya.

Lift the plant, or expose a portion only of its roots, between November and April. Cut the root into pieces 1–3in. long (some plants longer). Cut the lower end diagonally and the top square, for identification (in Fig 15). Plant vertically 2–3in. apart in a blend of sand and peat and a little loam, square-cut end uppermost, and cover with not more than an inch of sand or sandy soil. Thin cuttings, such as phlox, may be planted horizontally. Plant in deep seed-boxes, pits or a frame; if in boxes or pots, cover with glass as for seed. Water moderately until the shoots appear, then more liberally before transplanting into a nursery bed.

Layers

A layer is much the same thing as a cutting, except that the shoot is not detached from its parent until after it has rooted. Layering is the favourite means of increasing carnations, and the special method appropriate to them is dealt with in the chapter on that subject. Many shrubs are also increased either by the plant's natural habits or by man's inducement, such as rhododendrons, winter jasmine, hydrangeas, clematis and heathers.

Choose a well-grown young shoot that has not flowered, low down on the shady side of the plant and on its circumference. If it is not reasonably close to the ground, build up a mound of soil. Make a slanting cut or a notch in the bark on the underside of the shoot, press it down into a small cavity scratched in the soil, making sure that the soil gets well inside the lips of the wound and adding some sharp sand to the soil at that point. Cover that portion of the stem with an inch or two of soil, tread or press it in firmly and weight it down with a fairly heavy stone (better than pegging). Bend the tip of the shoot up as sharply as may be done without breaking and stake it with a small cane to induce upright growth as in Figs. 15 and 46. Water. Late summer is the usual time.

Air Layering

Man's latest stratagem (a refinement of an old Chinese one) is to trick a shrub into putting out roots high above the ground. It is a pretty dodge when a shrub is too tall or its branches too stiff to be bent down to ground level for ordinary layering; the magnolia is a favoured specimen and spring is the season. The method is still useful for amateurs not equipped with mist propagation gear.

Picking a young shoot of last season's growth, and a point about 8in. from its tip, you make a longitudinal cut about 1½in. long from below a leaf joint and passing through and above it, as in layering a carnation. Using a camelhair brush, dust the gaping wound with a hormone powder (special ones are marketed) and stuff in a pinch of sphagnum moss moistened in rain-water. Remove any leaf at this joint and any others 3in. above and below it.

Slip a polythene tube over the shoot and seal it very firmly about 3in. below the cut with electrician's insulating tape. Pack into the tube, tightly, a large handful of the moss which has been soaked in rain-water and then wrung out, completely enveloping the wound.

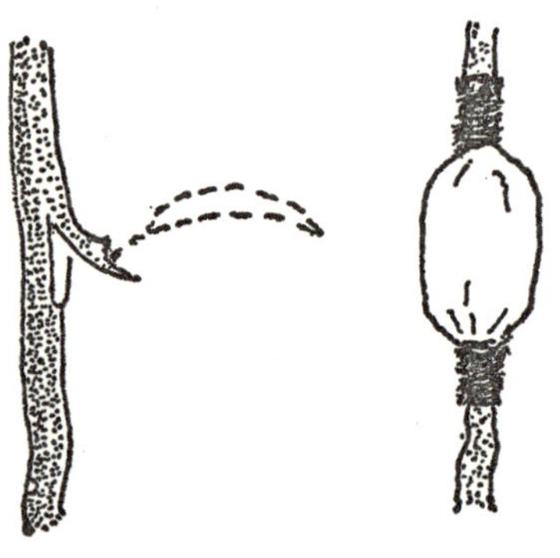

FIG. 18. Air layering—the initial cut (with leaf removed) and the finished job.

Crimp the polythene above the wound and seal it very securely with insulating tape, which must overlap the end of the polythene, so as to prevent entry of rain. The result is a plump polythene sausage about 5in. long. Sheet polythene can be used if it is cut into a strip and bound bandage-wise from the base upwards, so that the overlap bars the entry of rain.

In due course you will see the roots forming and the layer may be ready for potting in two to three months. Having severed the shoot from the parent and disengaged it, cut off the stub of stem below the rooting point and pot up in 3 or 4in. pots, using John Innes No. 1 Potting Compost mixed liberally with wet vermiculite. Keep in a closed frame or glass-covered box in full shade for a fortnight, syringing the foliage daily.

Division

This is the easiest of all methods, used largely on herbaceous plants and others whose habit is to extend themselves from the centre outwards, forming a dense clump, such as Michaelmas daises, golden-rod, helenium.

You simply lift the whole plant, with its roots, and divide it with the fingers or a knife or, if it is a matted clump, by driving two garden forks back to back through the centre, and levering them against each other. On tough and obstinate roots use a lawn edging iron. Use only the younger shoots on the outside of the plant and discard the centre of the old clump.

Autumn or winter are the usual seasons, but polyanthus and a few others are divided after they have finished flowering.

Garden Glassworks

Greenhouses and frames are outside my terms of reference except as auxiliaries to the outdoor garden, especially for propagation, for storing the stools of chrysanthemums and heliotropes and over-wintering pelargoniums.

A greenhouse, though obviously a great boon, is by no means essential to a garden, but a frame is, if one intends any kind of floral procreation.

A few plants covered by this book will need a little warmth in the greenhouse in winter and spring, but as a rule the needs will be met by the conditions of a "cool" house – one in which about 45° F. can be maintained. For the more tender plants a small propagating box, heated by electric cables and seated on the greenhouse bench, will suffice. What is more fundamental than heat is good greenhouse management: exemplary hygiene, the maintenance of a buoyant atmosphere, ample ventilation, the control of sunlight and the right degree of humidity. Except for cleanliness (the first principle) all these things can be done by a gang of submissive slaves if you treat yourself to an all-electric greenhouse. Blue-flamed oil-lamps are quite good, but you can't control their output to meet the sharp fluctuations of our outdoor temperatures.

Frames are of many sorts and have a wide range of uses. They give perfect control of watering, of ventilation, of shading from hot sun and can, in really tough winters, be quilted with mats or sacking.

For general purposes they should be in a good light, though direct sunshine has often to be avoided, especially for cuttings. For this reason a light, portable frame is most handy, though you can't heat it satisfactorily, whereas a sound fixed frame, with brick or wooden sides, can easily and inexpensively be warmed up by electric cables, both in the soil and in the air.

The frame may need to be totally closed, totally open or only partially open. For the partial position, the glass lid should never be *slid* open (avoid frames that open this way only); they should be *lifted*, at the leeward side, and propped open to the extent demanded

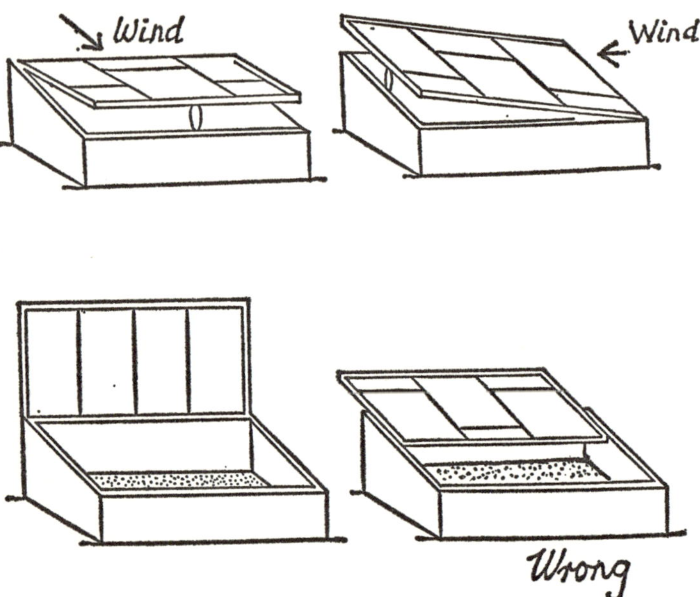

FIG. 19. Three correct methods of ventilating a frame and a wrong one.

by the circumstances. In heated frames, no matter what weather, always void some of the stale air by propping open the glass, even if only an inch for half an hour in times of frost.

Hardening-off. Besides its value for rearing cuttings and seedlings, the frame is of great value in hardening-off half-hardy plants. This means accustoming them by degrees to outdoor conditions. Heat is usually withheld about the end of March. Afterwards, when there is a risk of frost the frame is shut right up, but on warm days the lid is taken clean off and in many intermediate conditions it is propped partly open – more and more as the Zodiac advances. In early spring, better shut it up always at night, but in general always give ample ventilation rather than too little.

The last phase of hardening-off is to leave the plants fully exposed for the last ten days of May (barring frosts), after which they are marched off to their duty stations; but you may beat the pistol by planting out under cloches two or three weeks earlier.

Pots. All sorts of gadgets for rearing juvenile plants are offered these brisk days. Plastic, compressed peat, and fibre all compete with the old-fashioned clay pots.

I find clay pots (or pans) still the best for cuttings, but for other uses plastic pots have several advantages: they are lighter, less easily broken, more easily cleaned, more retentive of moisture. But they cost more and you can't so easily tell when watering is required. The gardener's traditional test for this is to give the pot a postman's rap with the knuckles (or an old reel of cotton on a stick); the clay pot gives a hollow response if water is needed, a dull, heavy thud if not.

Small peat pots are very good indeed for juveniles that have to be planted out in the open ground. You plant pot and all complete and the roots grow through the peat into the soil. No good, of course, for anything that has to be kept on the greenhouse shelf.

CHAPTER 7

"SUPERFLUOUS BRANCHES"

Why we Prune – When to Prune – How to Prune – Terms used in Pruning – Pruning Tools

To explain detailed pruning in writing is notoriously difficult and practical demonstration by an old hand is by far the best sort of tutorship. However, pruning is not a mystery, nor is it based on unreasoned rules of thumb, and the way begins to open up when it is realized that pruning is based chiefly on intelligent observation of the natural habits and behaviour of a plant.

Why we Prune

The celebrated gardener of Richard II summed up the matter well when, with Shakespearean aptness, he affirmed:

Superfluous branches
We lop away that bearing boughs may live.

That antique axiom sums up nearly all the law and the prophets on pruning. We may particularize by saying that the purposes of pruning are to maintain, increase or prolong the vitality of a plant, or to keep it in bounds, or to direct its energy to a special purpose. Thus, in a young tree, the first task is to build up a sound and well-shaped framework, but when it is well-grown we shall have a different purpose. In the apple we shall seek, as a rule, to induce new fruiting spurs; in a rose we may want a large shrub with many small flowers or we may want it to produce a few large exhibition blooms; in a hedge we shall want a dense barrier shrouded to the ground.

The most elementary pruning is "deadheading", by which we remove spent blooms in order to induce new ones or to interdict the formation of seed, and this is a form of pruning that should be constantly going on (though not on hydrangeas). If allowed to do so, a plant will put all its vitality into producing seed, which is not what the gardener normally wants. Accordingly no plant should be allowed to go to seed unless it is grown specially for its fruits or

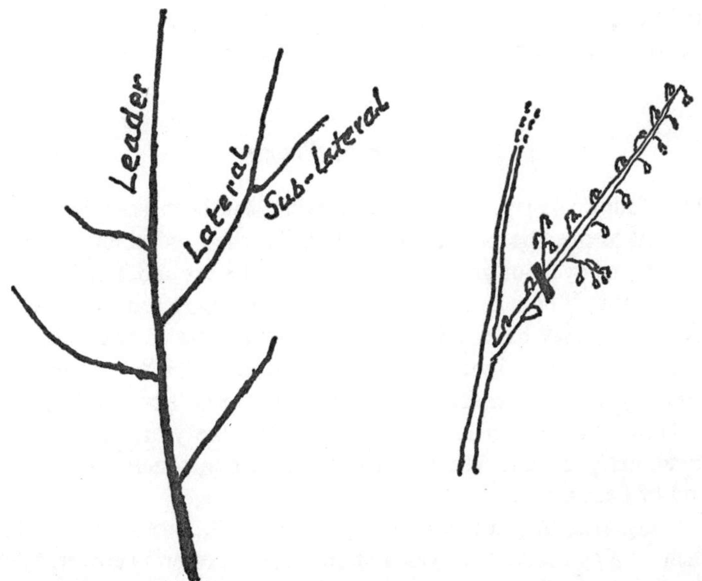

FIG. 20. Pruning terms. On right, drawing to show meaning of such jargon as: "Prune laterals to three buds of the base after flowering", etc.

berries or unless we specially want to gather seed; provided, of course, that the plant is not so big as to make the task unreasonable. We are also unconsciously pruning when we cut flowers for the house, and the canons of pruning should be observed when we do so. However, what we are really concerned with in this chapter is the annual overhaul of hard-wooded plants – trees, shrubs, roses, and climbers, while hedges of course are a subject to themselves.

This brings us to the really important topic of a plant's habits and behaviour. It is fundamental to note whether a plant blooms or fruits on:

(*a*) "new wood", i.e. whether it sends out a new branch or shoot and produces flowers on that shoot all in the same season; or (*b*) "old wood", i.e. a branch that grows this year but does not bear flower until next year, or even later.

This is the foundation of most pruning. For, broadly speaking, we may say that trees and shrubs that bloom in the spring or before midsummer do so on old wood developed the previous season, and those that bloom after midsummer do so on the new wood. More awkwardly, other plants, again, may flower on both old and new wood, such as some of the clematis and ceanothus.

When to Prune

This follows fairly logically upon what has been said before. In general terms, the period for pruning is when the plant has completed one cycle of growth and is about to start another. Thus the shrubs that bloom in the first half of the year are pruned (if at all) as soon as they have finished their floral display, so that they may direct maximum vigour into the new wood, which has begun to shoot up at the same time and on which next year's crop will appear.

Those that bloom in the second half of the year, on the other hand, are pruned (if at all) in winter dormancy, generally about the end of February.

Evergreens are not normally pruned at all, except to maintain them in a comely shape, which one does after flowering is over. Many deciduous shrubs also need no regular, annual pruning, though, as they age, they may need rejuvenation by cutting out old, whole branches, often down to the ground; these are usually the slower-growing shrubs, such as witch hazel and the winter viburnums.

The same applies to all plants of tree form, but take note that a few trees have special susceptibilities. Flowering cherries may become infected with bacterial canker if pruned before May and silver-birch, liquidambar and vines will "bleed" if cut after the sap has begun to rise.

On plants that bloom on both old and new wood, the gardener encourages whichever he prefers for early or late blooms, or he adopts a middle course, always remembering the principle of encouraging the newer wood.

How to Prune

The old axiom of "spare the knife and spoil the tree" is not always true except as demonstrated by the experienced hand. The beginner should therefore go easy with the knife until he has felt his way. There are a few basic ordinances that must be obeyed, but beyond these it is a mistake to be dogmatic. One man may want to produce a different result from his neighbour, as with roses. General principles are therefore best, and the intelligent man will soon find how to apply them. In the chapter on roses and flowering shrubs will be found specific injunctions where they are necessary, and many indeed, as for brooms and lavender, amount to emphatic commandments.

We may therefore conveniently ordain some general precepts to be observed in every sort of pruning and some particular ones that apply in various circumstances and that are not so emphatic or so precise.

General precepts

First, if in doubt about pruning at all, don't.

If in doubt whether to prune hard or lightly, prune lightly.

Always cut out dead, diseased and feeble, spindly growths.

Cut back into clean, healthy wood that shows no discolouration or scar.

Use only sharp tools and make clean, smooth cuts without ragged edges.

Cut always precisely above a new bud (or "eye") or flush with the junction of another limb; leave no "snag" or stub. Choose an eye pointing in the direction in which you want the new shoot to grow – usually an eye pointing outwards.

Always make either a sloping or a vertical cut, never a horizontal one on which moisture can lie.

Treat all large cuts – say anything more than three-quarters of an inch in diameter – with a proprietary wound-healer, such as Arbrex or Medo.

Never leave prunings lying about – burn them.

Particular precepts

That is as far as one may dogmatize unequivocally. The more

particular precepts deal with awkward problems of which wood should be pruned out? and how hard it should be pruned?

First, build up a shapely form and one suited to the purpose, whether it be a cordon apple, a pyracantha hugging the wall, or a rounded, bushy lilac clothed to the ground. Whatever its shape, the

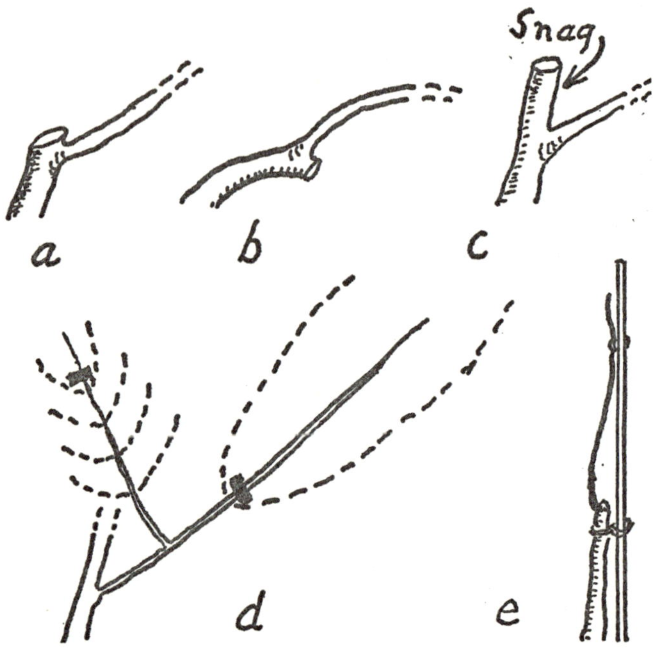

FIG. 21. Pruning methods. (*a*) and (*b*) cut immediately above the chosen shoot or bud; (*c*) leave no snag; (*d*) shows, on the left, the numerous, small, twiggy new shoots resulting from light pruning and, on right, the long, strong ones from hard pruning. (*e*) training in a new or "replacement" leader by tying it to a cane.

plant should be symmetrical and have the quality of grace – not lopsided, nor tufted, nor gaunt and scrawny. Balance is the thing.

Next, stimulate, year by year, the maximum display of flowers or berry, by the encouragement of new wood at the expense of the old. In some instances nearly all the old wood is eliminated yearly. Here again we differentiate somewhat between early- and late-flowering shrubs.

On EARLY-FLOWERING sorts shorten the spent flowering stems

as soon as the bloom is over hard back to a point where a strong young growth-shoot is sprouting near to the junction with the parent stem. Thus on the winter jasmine and on *Forsythia suspensa* you may cut to within 2in. or so of the base of the spent branch yearly. Occasionally cut older stems and boughs harder back still, so as to encourage new growth from low down.

On LATE-FLOWERING sorts remove altogether in late winter any old stem not carrying much new growth and lightly shorten others. Most of these need hard treatment, and some should be cut down nearly to the ground, such as David's buddleia (the big purple-plumed one), and the ceanothus 'Gloire de Versailles'.

These are good *general* guides for use when in doubt, but no more. We shall particularize in the appropriate chapters.

Old and neglected bushes must quite certainly have drastic treatment, applying the above principles in more severe degree, the main aim being to get rid of old unproductive spindle-shanks.

Terms used in Pruning

"Eye." A young bud. Before it waxes fat, is often identifiable as a pin-head with a little curved wrinkle above, rather like an upper eyelid.

"Leader." A growth by which a stem or branch extends itself along its own axis or line of advance.

"Lateral." A shoot springing sideways from any main branch.

"Snag." A superfluous stump resulting from a cut not having been made far enough back.

Pruning Tools

Secateurs. Do, for goodness sake, supply yourself (or be supplied) with one or more really good secateurs. The three best makes available are Wilkinson's, Rolcut and the Swiss Felco. The two former have several models. The Rolcut Ambassador is a beautiful, light, hollow-ground job, keen as a razor and with a long-lasting edge, and Wilkinson's Super Sword Pruner is a finely designed and engineered one, with a scimitar action. Both are of a price suitable to a Christmas present. Use all secateurs with a straight, squeezing action. Never wrench, twist or force them. If the job is too tough for them, use a bigger tool, such as the strong, two-handled secateurs or "tree loppers" – a huge blessing.

A pruning knife, of shape according to fancy.

A pruning saw. Various kinds available for jobs beyond the power of any secateurs. After using it pare the surface of the cut smooth with a keen knife. Shun double-edged saws.

For branches of large trees a carpenter's handsaw may be necessary. To prevent the under-surface of a limb splitting as the saw is about to come through, first make a short upward cut with the saw from the under-surface, then saw downwards in the same plane (Fig. 68).

Less essential, but very handy, is a "long-arm" pruner, enabling upper branches of trees to be lopped.

Keep a small carborundum for sharpening knives, but send your secateurs and saws to a professional from time to time unless you are a dab at that sort of thing yourself.

ENTR'ACTE

With a sigh of relief, we now leave behind the "mere mechanic exercises" and may begin to paint our garden picture. The design of our pleasaunce has been drawn, the ground cultivated and very soon, with Marvell at our side, we shall be able to

See how the flowers, as at parade,
Under their colours stand displayed.

I have picked these flowers with some care. It is not helpful to the reader to offer him a multitude of choices. He will wish, as one friend talking to another, to be guided to some extent and to be safeguarded from the brambles that lie in the path of those who tread with hasty feet. Much have my bonfires and my compost heaps benefited from plants that have been chosen merely from the pages of a catalogue or from among the beguiling darlings of the exhibition bench.

If I mislead you, you have every right to forsake me and you will apprehend, on occasions all too clearly, that I have my own likes and dislikes, which may differ from yours. If you have a passion for giant rhubarbs or monster thistles, read no further. I am no authority on such. Otherwise, however, I have tried to be faithful to my brief and to report conscientiously on all the genera of plants selected, even when I have no great enthusiasm for them.

Be wary about any plant that is described in catalogues or elsewhere as "choice". This usually, though not invariably, means that it is wayward, peevish and likely to be expensive. Be even more on your guard when a plant is described as a "specialist's treasure". This is merely a mesmeric hyperbole for saying that it is just plain difficult. The "choice" plant and the "treasure" are certainly what one will want to possess when one has qualified for the Sixth Form, but usually it is a mistake to attempt them when only in the Fourth.

The old saying has it that the apprentice starts gardening with annuals, journeys on to herbaceous plants, and, when he has reached the status of master-gardener, turns to flowering trees and shrubs; unless he is lured into those crevices where the pygmy sirens of the rock-garden dwell. Avoid that path. As you are exhorted in the section on design, begin with shrubs and little trees, which are easy and permanent and make a backcloth for whatever else you like to show on your stage. Plan an herbaceous or mixed border, rose beds, a carnation bed (separate, please), and use your annuals as short-term tenants for filling in, for the "odd spot" or for little bedding schemes.

Finally, *label your plants durably*, especially shrubs, roses, and clematis; it is vital for the purpose of pruning, which is one of the secrets of successful gardening. Also, it is maddening both for yourself and your friends if you have forgotten the name of "that red thing". For general use I commend the Hartley labels; they are cheap, reasonably enduring and adaptable. Pinches' solid metal labels are far more durable, but not cheap. Wooden labels remain readable for only a couple of months. Small plastic labels are handy in the greenhouse.

CHAPTER 8

"A SHORT LIFE BUT A GAY ONE"

All from Seed – Hardy Annuals – Sweet-peas – Half-hardy Annuals – Hardy Biennials

HERE we deal with the flowers that, in the words of the celebrated song, know they will "soon be dead" and accordingly make the utmost of their short tenure of the earth.

In Chapter 3 we have seen what are meant by the terms tender and hardy, annual and biennial. Eschewing all that is tender, I shall in this chapter deal with:

hardy annuals (with separate section for sweet-peas)
half-hardy annuals and
hardy biennials.

All from Seed

Included in them will be many gay favourites which are not truly within those categories, in the botanical sense, but are, as a rule, culturally treated as though they were, such as antirrhinums and wallflowers. We are able to grow some of these as annuals because, although strictly perennials, they have the happy knack of being able to flower from seed with the speed of annuals.

Everything in this chapter, therefore, is raised from seed, which is done in conformity with Chapter 6. The borderline between the hardies and the half-hardies, however, is often indeterminate, according to climate, so that what must be sown under some sort of glass in Durham may often need no protection in the south-west.

Though repetition is a literary sin, I shall for emphasis say again that if you really look for that "crowded holiday of scent and bloom" that the annual and biennial can give you, you must give them good cultivation just as much as you would to their longer-lived brethren. There are only a few exceptions, which we shall duly note. The popular notion that you have only to sprinkle a few seeds about the place to get a "riot of colour" is entirely mistaken. "Hardiness" means only what I have explained in the third section of Chapter 3. I implore you not to crowd them too closely together.

A few points need to be made at the outset:

> Pinch out all plants that are naturally bushy, such as wallflower and antirrhinums, when a few inches high to induce shrubbiness, but leave alone those of a different habit, such as larkspur and stock. When in doubt, refrain.
>
> Most plants in these classes, other than the lowly ones, need staking at a very early stage with twiggy sticks.
>
> Pick off all dead blossom persistently to encourage further blooming, though some sorts, such as stocks, make no second effort.

As a rule, annuals and biennials look best in their own beds, but many can also be used to fill up blanks in the border. The half-hardies are particularly well suited to bedding schemes, which I treat in Chapter 13. Foxgloves and evening primroses are entirely right among shrubs, and the Canterbury-bell takes her place with dignity and grace in the herbaceous border.

If cut flowers are a prime consideration, go for cleome, zinnia, clarkia, coreopsis, cornflower and stocks, plus of course sweet-peas. For places in partial shade, choose foxglove, evening primrose, nicotiana and forget-me-not. Several, if sown in late autumn, will give a fine early show in the cool greenhouse, particularly salpiglossis, nicotiana, antirrhinum, petunia and schizanthus.

The term "F1 Hybrid" will be frequently met in the better catalogues. These are hybrids raised afresh every year by controlled cross-pollination between selected parents, as they do not themselves produce true-to-type seed. They cost a bit more than other seed but are, or should be, of superior quality and very consistent.

Climbing annuals are dealt with in Chapter 22.

Hardy Annuals

The objective of all plants is to reproduce their own species and the hardy annuals are in a great hurry to do so. Many of them therefore can't stand the frustrating shock of being transplanted. They expect to be sown where they are to grow. Particular examples are larkspur, annual poppies and annual chrysanthemums.

For sowing in the open, dig the bed well in advance, allow the soil time to settle and then prepare a fine seed-bed by treading and raking. The usual time for sowing in the south is late March, if weather permits, but any time up to the end of April will suit; in northern counties about a fortnight later. For the reasons already given in Chapter 6, sowing "at stations" – either by the noughts-and-crosses method or in curvilinear patterns – is better than broadcasting. I implore you again not to make the learner-gardener's common mistake of burying the seed too deeply. A quarter-inch is more than enough for most seeds, and too much for poppies.

The minute the seedlings show their noses – or before – take anti-slug precautions. When the seedlings have grown two or three pairs of leaves, thin them out to their appropriate spacing.

The hardiest of the annuals can also be sown in late summer (about mid-August) to over-winter and to provide early bloom for next year. Those that will stand this treatment are often called "winter annuals" as a convenient term.

For those who would like a ready-made selection of hardy annuals, I should say that the pick of them is: sweet-pea (in a class by itself), larkspur, godetia, love-in-a-mist, mallow, flax and the convolvuluses that I name. But there are some delightful ones that are not so often grown; of such are the annual delphinium 'Blue Butterfly', the gentian blue *Phacelia campanularia* and bartonia. Some that do better in poor soils than in rich ones are eschscholzias, nasturtiums, cornflowers and pot-marigolds.

The following list contains a small trugful only of the more meritorious hardy annuals. The more difficult sorts, the very fleeting, and the less interesting are omitted. Named varieties are far too numerous to quote in this chapter, except occasionally, especially as nurseries have the annoying habit of calling a variety "So-and-so's Perfection", which may be much the same as someone else's "Wonderful". I have assumed that no one will expect me to describe such elementary delights as marigolds, "nasturtiums" and so on.

Alyssum. The familiar little carpeting plant, often called sweet alyssum, is so easy that it is overdone and much ill-used in hackneyed bedding schemes. The pink and the mauve varieties, such as 'Rosie O'Day' and 'Royal Carpet', are much nicer than the common white, a paltry thing. Delay sowing until late April or early May, or raise earlier in seed-boxes and plant out. Use alyssum as real carpeting at the feet of taller plants, not as a mingy "edging" or dot plants.

Sweet alyssum derives from *A. maritimum.* For the yellow one (*A. saxatile*) see Chapter 21.

Bartonia. The old name *B. aurea* is nicer and still more generally used than the new one, *Mentzelia lindleyi.* It is one of the gayest and easiest of summer annuals, with large, golden flowers like the rose-of-Sharon or like big buttercups, with a conspicuous brush of stamens. It grows to 15in. Sow *in situ* and thin to 10in.

CALENDULA. See Marigold.

Californian Poppy (*Eschscholzia,* pronounced Esholtzia). One of the easiest and most colourful, with festive trumpets in brilliant shades of orange, gold, red, pink above finely cut, sea-green foliage. Likes warm, dry conditions and flowers more riotously in poor stony soils than in rich ones. Height 9in. Sow *in situ* and thin to 7in. Keep spent blooms removed. Seeds itself profusely, even in gravel paths, but will not transplant.

Candytuft (*Iberis*). Easy cottagers, most familiar in the form of crowded heads, flat or slightly domed, of many wee flowers in mauve, pink or white. Some grow to 18in., but the dwarf varieties are usually preferred.

Less usual is the rocket candytuft, which forms a tall, hyacinthine column of pure white. This is *I. coronaria.* Inevitably seedsmen have their own fancy names, such as "hyacinth flowered" and "giant flowered".

Sow both *in situ* and thin to 8in., the thinnings being transplantable. Winter annuals.

For the perennial candytufts, which are better value, see Chapter 21.

Chrysanthemum. The annual forms of chrysanthemums are a great joy to both the gardener and his wife, when well grown. Their elegant, daisyform flowers have a smiling quality and often a rich blending of colour. There are both single and double varieties, of which the singles have much the more refined character. I like particularly those that have a bold band or ring of distinctive colouring on a white or cream ground and a dark eye – like "rings round the moon" or that phenomenon when a halo surrounds the sun. The white varieties with a primrose zone are also charming. Most varieties stand about 18in. high, but others go up to 4ft. There is an infuriating dissimilarity among seedsmen's fancy names and descriptions, many of which tell you nothing.

Give these chrysanthemums a favoured position in full sun, in good soil which is not too heavy and which is well drained. Sow the seed sparsely and cover it by no more than a quarter-inch. Thin them to 1ft apart at least, for they make bushy plants. They need staking. Winter annuals.

For the various perennial chrysanths, see Chapter 12.

Clarkia. One of our most beautiful and easiest annuals, which will thrive in partial shade as well as in sun, but does not seem to care for heavy clay soil.

In *C. elegans* the double, prettily fringed florets thickly encrust a spire-like plant in pink, red, mauve or white, to a height of about 2ft. In the very different *pulchella* the plant is a good deal shorter, much more branched and carries flowers of heliotrope, carmine or white.

Clarkias do not transplant, so must be sown *in situ,* not more than ½in. deep and thinned to 9in. By sowing in succession from March to May, they may be enjoyed from July to October. One of the best annuals for growing in pots in a cool greenhouse. Winter annuals.

Convolvulus. Some of this genus are weeds, but among the varieties or forms of *C. tricolor* (often mistakenly called *C. minor*) there is at least one little gem. This is 'Royal Ensign', which flourishes brave trumpets of an intense, glowing Oxford blue, with a golden throat and white rays. 'Royal Marine' is deep violet-blue with a milky throat and other pretty tricolor varieties are in rose-red or cherry. All these tricolors grow less than a foot high but bush out laterally. Any reasonable place in the sun suits them. Thin to 10in. Winter annuals.

Very different is the species often called *C. major*, which is a short climber to 5ft – one of the lesser "morning glories", in assorted colours. It thus needs a host on which to climb. Not fully hardy, it should not be sown outdoors until the middle of May and then only in full sun. In a pot it is a good greenhouse climber. Its right name is *Ipomaea purpurea.*

FIG. 22. *Convolvulus tricolor* 'Royal Marine'.

Coreopsis (or *Calliopsis,* or, in the old vernacular, tickseed). Characteristically, the annual tickseeds are yellow, daisyform flowers with broad petals, usually nicked or frilled on the margin, borne on slender but wiry stems, which makes them good for cutting. Some are crimson instead of yellow, or yellow with a crimson zone. Give them a sunny position in any reasonable soil.

For perennial tickseeds, see Chapter 10.

Cornflower (*Centaurea cyanus*). Our well-loved old wilding has donned many new dresses in modern times, but to my eye all cornflowers should be blue, not pink or white. There is much variation in height also, but one of the great favourites is the dwarf 'Jubilee Gem', only 1ft high. The tall varieties, which may reach 3ft are not very decorative in the garden and must be staked, but are useful for cut flowers, as indeed, are all cornflowers.

Sow in a soil which is not too rich and thin out to 10in. (18in. for the tall ones). A winter annual.

DELPHINIUM. For the charming little 'Blue Butterfly', see the delphinium section in the next chapter.

Dimorphotheca. Sometimes referred to as star-of-the-veldt, this is one of several South African, large-flowered daisies which have found a welcome in Britain and elsewhere and it has proved completely hardy. The long ray petals are in glistening white or pastel shades of orange, lemon or salmon, but the one that takes the cake is

FIG. 23. The easiest of the South African marguerites, hybrid dimorphothecas.

Sutton's 'Orange Giant' (or 'Goliath'). Like most daisies, the ray petals of dimorphothecas close up in the evening and in cloudy weather.

Delay sowing until mid-April, covering with the thinnest film of fine soil, and thin to about 8in. They grow very fast and will be in flower by June. The shorter varieties of about a foot, are to be preferred. In colder counties sow in boxes under glass in March and plant out in May.

D. barberiae, we may note here, is a mauve-pink perennial, of ragged habit and little garden value.

Flax (*Linum*). There are several species of flax, annual and perennial, notable for their graceful quality. Of the hardy annuals, one that is quite outstanding is *L. grandiflorum rubrum*, which bears very simple, five-petalled flowers of gleaming, satiny scarlet above slender, filigree foliage to a height of 15in. The individual flowers are fleeting but follow each other in rapid succession in July and August. Very easy and showy. Sow sparsely and thin out to 8in.

For the herbaceous border flaxes see Chapter 10 and for those of the rock garden, Chapter 21.

Godetia. One of the half-dozen best hardy annuals, forming bushy pyramids enlivened with sparkling porcelain cups in many colours. Succeeds in any good soil, in sun or part-shade. Is a winter annual and in fact the best results seem to come from an autumn sowing. Fine for cutting. Heights vary from 8in. to 3ft. Sow *in situ* and thin according to height. 'Kelvedon Glory' is a sunset variety that still keeps its place after many years. 'Sybil Sherwood' is a close rival.

Larkspur. Country-girl sister of the delphinium, yet a princess among annuals, rising in clustered steeples to 4 ft. in diverse colours. Repays good cultivation. Excels as a winter annual, sown *in situ* in September. Will not transplant.

Limnanthes douglasii. A 6in. plant with simple flower-cups in which the inner segments of the petals are yellow and the extremities white. Grows anywhere and can become an agreeable nuisance by spreading promiscuously, even in gravel paths.

Love-in-a-mist (*Nigella damascena*). One of the best-loved of simple cottage flowers, love-in-the-mist opens its curiously wrought blossoms of cornflower blue half-veiled in filmy foliage, a habit that explains its English name. Delightful for cutting. They are followed by large seed-pods that are almost equally fascinating. Inevitably the hybridist has broken away from the natural blue and you can now have pink, purple and other shades in what is called the Persian Jewels strain. But give me the blue, especially the variety 'Miss Jekyll', which grows to about 18in. Thin to 10in. A winter annual.

Love-lies-bleeding (*Amaranthus caudatus*). This is the old-fashioned amaranth, or flower-gentle, so loved by our ancestors for the wistful elegance of its long, drooping, catkin-like trails of blood-crimson. It looks at its best swooning down a bank or fainting over the edge of a terrace. Superior people lack the stomach for it. There is also a "greenery-yallery" form which goes quite well with the ensanguined one. Both go to 2½ft.

Give them a very sunny position in poor, stony soil and delay sowing until April. In colder regions treat them as half-hardy; there is also a half-hardy amaranthus grown for its many-coloured leaves, usually catalogued as "tricolor splendens".

Mallow or rose-mallow (*Lavatera trimestris*). One of the most splendid of annuals, developing shrub-like proportions with great speed and often growing 4ft high under good cultivation. The blooms are like those of a single hollyhock. The variety 'Loveliness' (or 'Sunset') has long held the field as champion of its species, but the new 'Aurora' may surpass it.

Sow two or three seeds here and there towards the back of your border or among shrubs (where they are quite at home) and thin each group to one. Surprisingly wind-resistant, independent of any staking and excellent at the seaside.

For the "tree mallow" (*L. olbia*) see Chapter 19.

Marigold (*Calendula officinalis*). In this section we deal with the familiar English, Scotch, or pot marigold, its dried petals being used to flavour stews and soups. A kindergarten plant. Grows best in soils that are not too rich. Sow the large, half-moon seeds 5in. apart and thin to 10in.; the thinnings will transplant. There are orange and lemon shades and various other quirks of the hybridist's inventiveness, of which we have by no means seen the end.

For the French and African marigolds, see under the half-hardies.

Mignonette. An old-fashioned flower much cherished for its sweet breath. Today there are varieties more enriched with colour than of yore, such as 'Crimson Fragrance'. Traditionally, it needs a limy soil and excels in chalk, but I am told that it is content with acid soils also. A firm seed-bed is needed. Thin out to 9in.

Nasturtium. I have already exposed the public scandal that this is a bogus name for what is really a tropaeolum. It is said to have been imported into this country as "Indian Cress" (their leaves being very good in a salad) and, as the true nasturtium is the watercress, that may account for the popular fallacy.

Anyhow, nasturtiums are gay, jolly, kindergarten plants that make their best floral effort in poor, stony soils, in sun or partial shade. Delay sowing till early May, as they are not bone-hardy. Sow the large seeds singly. There is a large choice of all sizes from dwarfs to quite vigorous climbers, singles and doubles, in various hues of yellow, orange and flame, the strain known as 'Gleam' being much favoured. Personally I avoid all these nasturtiums, as they are a magnet for all the black fly in the county.

Nemophila. An endearing dwarf annual of 6in., with buttercup-shaped flowers of sky-blue with a white eye amid leafy foliage. Excellent for shady and moist situations as for sunny ones. Is *N. menziesii* (or *insignis*). A winter annual. There is also a white one with purple veins and patches.

Phacelia campanularia is the poor man's gentian and one of the real stars among annuals. Growing about 8in. high, with broad leaves, it is adorned with trumpets of true autumn-gentian blue,

FIG. 24. The poor man's gentian, *Phacelia campanularia*

without a trace of mauve. It looks as delightful in the rock garden as in a mixed bedding or around the feet of roses. Choose a sunny position with good soil, sow the seed sparsely in mid-April, barely covering them, thin out the seedlings to 6in. It will be in full glory by July and will give a long season of flowers. Seedlings do not transplant,

Avoid the tall *tanacetifolia* unless you are a bee-keeper.

Poppy (Papaver). There are perennial, biennial and annual poppies. Of the annuals we have at our command:

Our native, scarlet poppies of the fields, *P. rhoeas*, from which has been derived the popular Shirley poppies in many brilliant and pastel colours, single or double, growing to 2ft.

The grey-leaved opium poppy, *somniferum*, which has similarly produced many colour forms, usually double, as seen in what seedmen's catalogues call the peony-flowered and carnation-flowered sorts. These may grow to 3ft. Make absolutely sure to decapitate the urn-shaped seed vessel.

Poppy seed is dust-like. Sow it *in situ* very sparsely and cover it with the merest sifting of fine soil or sand. Thin the Shirleys to 10in. and the opiums to 15in. The seedlings do not transplant. They are winter annuals.

The annual poppies are not a patch on the beautiful Iceland poppy, which is a biennial. For the flamboyant oriental poppies, see Chapter 10.

Salvia. The salvias are the sages and in this versatile genus we find one decorative annual in *S. horminum*, which throws up 18in. spikes remarkable not so much for their flowers as for their brightly coloured bracts, of purple, pink or white, which last for a long season. Very appropriate in an herbaceous border. Thin the seedlings to 1ft.

For the scarlet salvias, see in the half-hardies and for other salvias, see Chapters 10 and 18.

STOCK, night-scented. Included in the section on half-hardies.

Sunflower (*Helianthus annuus*). All the helianthus are "sun flowers", but the one traditionally so-called is the giant with rubicund face nodding cheerfully over the cottage wall. How any plant can grow to such a size in five months and become, as the Italian poet has it, so "impassioned with light", is always a matter of wonder.

Sow a seed or two here and there in good soil in a sunny position against a wall, where they always look their smartest. If the seeds that they themselves produce at the end of the summer are wanted for chickens or parrots, cut off the flower heads as soon as the seeds begin to loosen in September and dry them off indoors in a sunny window. Excellent also for human consumption if the cook of the family has the know-how. Where rust disease is prevalent, better not grow them.

In addition to the orange giant, there are several smaller hybrid brethren, even as dwarf as 2ft, and in various shades of orange, lemon, chestnut or maroon, each nurseryman having his own fancy names. Sutton's have a nice strain.

Sweet-Sultan (*Centaurea moschata*). Brother of the cornflower, sweet-sultan is an old-time favourite about 15in. high brandishing mops of fluffy flowers in many colours, like an idealized thistle. Good for cutting. Very easy if given ample sun and not too wet a soil. Sow when the surface of the soil is dry and crumbly and thin out to 10in.

Sweet-peas

"Here be sweet-peas, on tiptoe for a flight." Since Keats's day the sweet-pea has flown far and wide and established so many new colonies that Keats would scarcely have recognized them. When I began gardening there was virtually only one strain of the cultivated hybrids – the waved and frilled Spencer strain, which had by then just established its superiority over the small but richly scented grandifloras – but today there are several quite new groups and styles, apart from the innumerable named varieties. Which sort you elect to grow will depend largely upon whether or not you intend to test your skill against others in the challenge of the exhibition hall. If so, you will still opt for the classic and beautifully poised Spencers. Otherwise there is the following choice before you.

MODERN BREEDS

Galaxy. A fine strain that grows as strongly as the Spencers with five to seven waved blooms to each stem and lacking only their balanced placement and refinement. Grow them on tall "pea-sticks" or climbing on other plants.

Knee-Hi. Another fine introduction. Raised in California with the idea of producing a sweet-pea that could be grown as casually as a bedding plant, without any staking. But in Britain they grow much taller and are "Waist-Hi" rather than "Knee-Hi", so we have to stake them. The Knee-Hi's produce stems up to a foot long with four to six large, well-placed blooms.

Americana. Another intermediate type, 3–4ft high, with five to seven well-placed blooms. Vigorous and free.

Bijou. The best of several dwarf strains so far. Some 12 or 18in. high, the plants bush out laterally to a width of 2ft and carry plenty of large flowers on stems good enough for cutting. O.K. for window-boxes if the soil is good. The very dwarf strain 'Little Sweetheart' has little merit.

Royal Series. Huge and often double-standard blooms on very long, strong stems, five to seven on the stem, on tall plants. Possibly good enough for exhibition.

Early multiflora gigantea. A tall climber, flowering early, which has found favour in Australia and South Africa.

We may be sure that, before this book is much older, the scheming hybridist will have produced yet more "novelties", for the sweet-pea is a very marriageable maid. For lovers of old-world things there are also the wild species of *Lathyrus*, including *L. odoratus*, from which the modern sweet-pea is derived, and the cottage "everlasting pea", which is *L. latifolius*. And one may still get (e.g. from Unwins) some of the old "Grandiflora" sweet-peas, such as 'Daisy Eckford' and 'Prima Donna', that ruled the roost until the Spencers flew in.

For whichever breed of sweet-pea one elects, two basic qualities of theirs must be understood: that they are sun-worshippers and that they are greedy feeders, demanding quantities of rich, organic food. For the dwarf and half-dwarf breeds, if the ground has been generously treated in the last year or two, I dare say that little further need be done than to turn the soil over to the depth of one spit and work in a good fertilizer. Having done that, sow the seed an inch deep and about 5in. apart in casual groups – not in straight lines, for heaven's sake – and not too scattered, for they look best in bold clumps or swathes whatever their type.

The taller breeds, however – the Spencers, Galaxies, Royals and so on – make larger demands on the gardener. The methods he will employ will depend on whether he wants specimen blooms, for exhibition or superior flower arrangements, or simply for garden adornment and casual cut flowers.

FOR GARDEN DECORATION

For this one may grow them in clusters of 3 to 4ft in diameter or, if wanted only to cut for the house, in double or treble rows in straight lines in the kitchen garden.

Prepare the site in autumn or early winter; never later than February. Double-dig the ground according to the commandments of Chapter 5, giving the soil all the riches you possess. If it is not naturally limy, spread lime at the rate of 2 oz. per sq. yd. in January every other year, provided soot has not been used.

In early April work the soil to a good tilth and sow the seed an inch deep and about 5in. apart. If mice are feared, dip the seed in paraffin and roll them in red lead. The black seeds are apt to have hard seed-coats, so soak them in water for twenty-four hours and lightly nick the seed coat at a point opposite the eye.

FIG. 25. Sweet-pea. When growing for big blooms, remove leafy axillary shoots A and B, but not the young flowering stem C.

As soon as the seedlings send up their wiry little shoots, take anti-slug precautions and plant bushy pea-sticks, 5ft high, thickly and firmly. Pinch out the tip of each seedling after the second pair of leaves has expanded. When the plants are growing away well and showing their first buds give them a liquid feed of one of the sorts mentioned in Chapter 4.

Pick the blooms for the house as soon as you like, go on picking and always remove spent blooms at once. In the absence of rain water liberally and regularly. Irregularity (or other physiological imbalance) may cause the buds to drop before they can open, as in scarlet runners, camellias and other plants.

When flowering is over, cut the plants down to the ground, wet the haulms, chop them up and add them to the compost heap, leaving the nitrogenous roots in the soil.

For early results, the enthusiast will start his seed in pots in the autumn, two to a 3in. pot or the long peat pots of square section made for the job; these are planted out, pot and all, in late March, after hardening them off.

FOR SPECIMEN BLOOMS

The roots of sweet-peas go deep. In my early gardening days it was *de rigueur* to do the full trenching operations three spits deep, with gross feeding. Nowadays it seems that people haven't enough strength for such effort, yet they get very good results by a mere double-digging. If you opt for the treble-digging method, treat the third spit

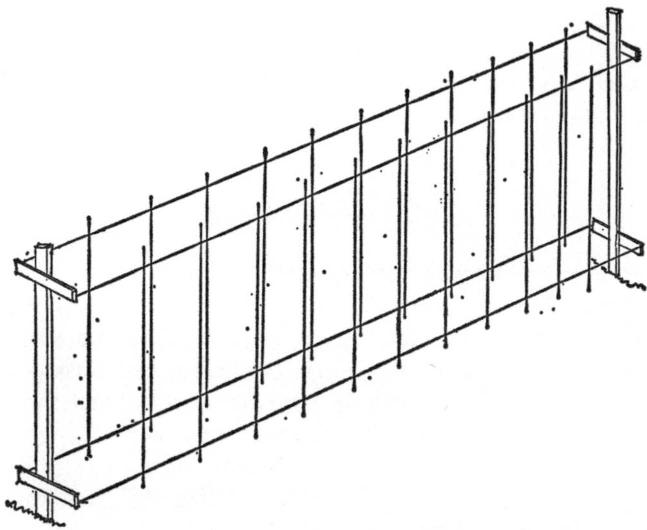

FIG. 26. Orthodox structure for cordon sweet-peas.

in the same way as the second, but the only breed of sweet-pea that justifies the effort is the Spencer.

Make your trench 4ft wide and as long as you need. Along the centre line of this bed erect a framework of 2 × 2in. timbers 6ft high (one per 10ft), with 16in. cross-bars near the top and bottom of each. Connect the extremities of the cross-bars with wire and plant 7ft canes all along the wires, 9in. apart in two rows 15in. apart (Fig. 26).

As the plants develop, fix them to the canes with the special split rings and pluck out all the leafy axillary side-shoots, but not, of course, the emerging flower stems. When the plants reach the tops of their canes, untie them carefully and make them start a second innings on a cane about 6ft away, those near the extremities of the rows having to be turned round the corner into the second row. A boring business.

COLOUR AND SCENT

One cannot start better than with a small collection of the standard varieties that all leading seedsmen offer. These give us a nice balance of colours. Beginners had better avoid the orange varieties.

The majority of the Spencers are nicely scented, many richly so. Scent often goes with particular colours, notably in the lavenders, lilacs, mauves, white and pallid shades and the picotees. Reds rarely excel and pinks are half-and-half.

Half-hardy Annuals

These must generally be raised in gentle heat in February or March in a temperature of about 55° F. in most cases, or they will mature too late; otherwise they must be got as seedlings from a nursery at the end of May, and this is what the beginner is best advised to do. Unfortunately, he is very unlikely to get the newer and better varieties from his small local nursery, which continues to grow only the same old strains of antirrhinum, petunia, ageratum and so on as forty years ago. And my experience of ordering seedlings by post from the larger nurseries has been unsatisfactory.

To raise your own, sow in boxes or pans and prick off into other boxes, using John Innes Compost or one of the new soil-less media at each stage. Take note that not all plants will be satisfied with the same temperature: salvias and verbenas, for example, need a high one and stocks and zinnias a low one. For the higher temperatures a propagating box within the greenhouse does the trick. On the other hand, in the absence of a heated glasshouse, those that need the minimum of heat (such as China asters, schizanthus and portulaca) can be germinated in the kitchen and pricked off into boxes in a frame against a warm, south wall.

Before being planted in their permanent quarters they must be "hardened off", as explained in the greenhouse section of Chapter 6.

In the half-hardies the F1 hybrids are particularly valuable, especially in antirrhinums, ageratum, petunias and the French and African marigolds.

In the following list are several elegant and richly dressed South African marguerites and their hybrids. I include them for the benefit of those readers who are fortunate enough to be able to provide the special environment that is their need: a fairly rich but light, rather gritty soil that warms up readily, with sharp drainage, such as would be provided by a slope, and a reasonably hot sun. No use attempting them in heavy, wet clay nor in the bleaker shires nor the rainier ones. In this brilliant company are the arctotis, gazania, ursinia, venidium and the radiant little Livingstone-daisy, whose demands are rather less exacting. Given these conditions they are not difficult, but they have the tantalizing habit of shutting up their ray petals towards evening and even whenever their friend the sun is obscured by a passing cloud.

Some of the half-hardies, such as nemesia, zinnia and the scarlet salvia, turn sulky if the gardener gives them a check in growth. This means becoming root-bound in boxes or pot. Accordingly, avoid sowing them too early and move them on quickly from stage to stage.

Ageratum. One of the comeliest edging or carpeting annuals (though technically a perennial), embellished with toy powder puffs in varying shades of blue or mauve. Get a F1 hybrid or a variety such as 'Blue Mink' and space out at 6in.

Antirrhinum. The snapdragon is really a perennial and jolly nearly a hardy one at that. Though a few get lost in a stiff winter, the older types are certainly hardy in my own garden, seeding themselves freely every year, especially in the very dry soils at the footings of walls. In the south of England, at any rate, they grow year after year in old walls and in my former Somerset home freely adorned the bleak upper elevations of the church tower next door to us. This habit should give a clue to its character, for I feel sure that the snapdragon is hardiest on a lean and stoney diet with good drainage; on a lush one it grows fat and soft. Its chances of survival are least in wet clays. We must also reckon that, as a perennial, it becomes pretty ragged before long, so that, except in the care-free garden, it is always best to grow some afresh from seed every year or two. If one cares to take the trouble, it is perfectly easy to grow them from heel cuttings taken in August and, indeed, the very first plants I ever grew as cuttings were antirrhinums.

Long strides have been made in recent years in raising better, bigger or smaller strains: double-flowered, base-branching, Tom Thumbs, Floral Carpets, ruffled tetraploids, penstemon-flowered (tubular), Super Giants or Rockets to 4ft, Majestic Nanum Grandiflorum (seemingly a triple contradiction in terms) and so forth. All very confusing until you sit down and think them out. One very positive improvement that has been made is the introduction of many varieties that are resistant to the rust disease, which used to be the scourge of the "snaps" in some seasons.

Unfortunately, these newer sorts are rarely to be got as seedlings in one's local nursery. In the absence of facilities to raise one's own, try at least to buy a box or two of rust-resistant varieties and of the normal "intermediate" type, growing to about 18in.; plant them out at 9in. intervals in the last week of May in a sunny bed. Stake them at once with twiggy hazel sticks and nip off the tips of the plants to induce branching, unless you want long central spikes for trying your luck at the flower show.

Those who have a warm greenhouse or a frame will have little difficulty in raising any strain they like. Apart from any special preference in another direction, get the sorts variously grouped as "intermediate", "semi-dwarf" or "nanum". The F1 hybrids are strongly recommended. Make an early start, sowing very thinly in February in the usual boxes in a temperature of 55° F. Guard against the damping-off diseases with Cheshunt Compound. Water only moderately. Thereafter, normal half-hardy treatment.

Aster. I suppose that the so-called annual or China aster owes its nurseryman's name to its superficial resemblance to the real aster (Michaelmas-daisies, etc.). In the courts of botany the China aster is the callistephus (*C. chinensis*), though it has wandered far from its simple origin and in the nursery catalogues now presents an appearance as diverse and confusing as the snapdragon, and become more and more like a chrysanthemum and less like an aster.

Among the various classes in catalogues there are the Californian Giants, like Japanese chrysanthemums, grown specially for cutting, the shaggy Ostrich Plumes, the more formal Comets, the Rayonnante, with slender petals rolled into quills like Rayonnante chrysanths, other quilled and semi-quilled sorts, Duchesses like incurved chrysanths, Princesses, ball-like Pompoms and heaven-knows what else.

Being a simple man, however, nothing pleases me more than the unaffected, open-faced candour of the old singles, which have the country-girl charm of the marguerite plus most of the colours of the rainbow.

Very little heat is needed for germination. Indeed, they can be started in an unheated, sunny frame in late March, or even in the open ground in early May in the warmer shires. Beware of damping-off diseases in seed-boxes. And if, after planting out, a plant suddenly wilts and collapses, burn it and treat the ground with Cheshunt Compound.

For the true asters, see Chapter 10.

Balsam (*Impatiens balsamina*). Sister of Busy Lizzie, the balsam can, I am told, be reared in the softer counties as a hardy annual by sowing in late spring. Elsewhere treat it as a half-hardy, choosing either the camellia-flowered or rose-flowered sorts. Very pretty, but the blossoms are a little apt to be hidden by the foliage. Water freely and beware of slugs. Excellent also in the greenhouse. 12 to 18in., with some nice dwarfs.

Cleome (*C. spinosa*). The cleome is a very distinctive plant indeed, sending up strong, rigid, thorny stems to 3ft, crowned with large, loose, more or less circular trusses of several gaping, four-petalled flowers in white or pink, from which the long, thread-like outspread stamens protrude for about 1½in. Very decorative indeed, but probably not to be attempted elsewhere than in warm, dry places with a light but rich soil. Normal half-hardy treatment. Excellent in the herbaceous border or as specimen plants on a terrace and very good as cut flowers.

Cosmos (or Cosmea). One of the most popular of all half-hardies, having slim, daisyform flowers borne with airy elegance up to 3ft high, without staking, on slender wiry stems above delicate foliage. In rich soils, or in partial shade, they may go higher still. Fine for cutting and dramatic when massed. The colour range embraces white, pink, red and orange. Blooms continuously from June to September if regularly deadheaded.

DIANTHUS. Included in Chapter 11.

Gazania. One of the gayest of the South African daises described in the introduction to this section. They are really perennials and growable as such in Cornwall and like places, but elsewhere are treated as half-hardy annuals, the seed being sown early in the year. Many spendid colours; 10in. Growing plants available from Hillier's. Having a greenhouse, you can propagate them quite easily from July or August cuttings. Good seaside plants.

GLORIOSA DAISY. See Rudbeckia.

Kochia (spoken Kockia). Graceful and shapely little bushes just like dwarf cypress in appearance, grown essentially for their foliage, which is a tender green in summer and fiery red in autumn. Equally good for the poor man's rock garden (instead of cypress) or for little avenues or other formal, rather prim effects, but not in a border. Can be raised without heat under glass early April. Is *K. scoparia.* Also sometimes known as summer cypress or belvedere.

FIG. 27. Hybrid gazanias in many colours.

LIVINGSTONE DAISY. See under Mesembryanthemum.

Lobelia. The ever-popular little plant with fine leaves massed with a multitude of tiny flowers, usually blue. Overdone in stereotyped bedding schemes, but charming at the feet of roses or massed as a carpet. The vivid, royal blue 'Crystal Palace' and the white-eyed 'Mrs Clibran' still hold their own. 'Rosamund' is watery claret and 'Sapphire' and 'Blue Cascade' are trailers for hanging baskets and window-boxes (where they need lots of water).

The seed is very fine; when sowing sprinkle it sparsely and give it only a dust-like covering.

Marigolds, African and French. These brazen splendours hail from neither Africa or France, but from Mexico. Both are species of *Tagetes.* The American breeders are mad on their brassy splendours and have inter-married the French and the African to such an extent (as in 'First Lady') that we might well call them American marigolds.

The African (*T. erecta*) brandishes bold knobkerries in lemon, brass or orange to a height of 3ft, though there are also some dwarfs. No one would call them restful, but they suit people who like savage and exciting colours and they look well at the seaside. New varieties succeed one another in America so rapidly that it is difficult to keep pace with them, but the F1 hybrids are usually a safe buy.

The Frenchman (*T. patula*) is usually not more than 9in. high, though there are a few that will top a foot. Despite several doubles, they are typically singles in blends of yellow and mahogany – jolly little creatures for many uses.

The brisk little lemon-coloured plants often sold in markets as plain "Tagetes" can, in mild districts, be raised as a hardy annual, sowing not too early.

Dead-head all these tagetes regularly and they will bloom for months.

For our native pot-marigold, see the section on hardies.

Mesembryanthemum. These are dwarf South African daises of a gem-like brilliance. Given the conditions prescribed at the opening of this section (though favouring a poor, stony soil instead of a rich one) they will sparkle in the most care-free way on a warm, dry bank, on a terrace or in the crevices of crazy paving, forming themselves into sheets of many colours on 4in. stems from late May onwards, provided the sun is shining. They seem fond of the seaside.

The sort most commonly available is the Livingstone daisy (*M. criniflorum*), but *tricolor,* deep rose and white on still shorter stems, is also very gay.

Nemesia. These showy little bedding plants of many colours are not easy to grow well, for they resent being checked in youth. Prick off at the earliest moment, keep consistently moist and rather cool, with plenty of peat in the soil, and move on into pots if threatening to flower too early. Young plants left too long in the pricking-out box become hard and woody – a common fault of plenty of plants bought in the market – and will never be a success. Their final beds must be of a fairly rich soil, with peat, leaf-mould, or manure to hold moisture, and in dry weather they must be copiously watered. Nemesias succeed in partial shade as well as in sun.

Nicotiana. Long famed for remaining shut up until evening, when they open to discharge its refreshing scent, the flowering tobacco will now, if you choose the right varieties, stay open all day. They are to be recognized by their long, narrowly tubular necks and widely expanded mouths and they come in many colours, of which 'Lime Green' is delightful. Apart from the inevitable dwarfs, they grow up to 3ft, prosper in partial shade as well as in sun.

No need to sow the seed until late March. When pricking out, use fairly deep boxes and put the seedlings in a good 3in. or more apart. Because of their scent, plant some beneath a sitting-room window. Excellent also in the greenhouse.

PANSY. Included under Viola, next chapter.

Petunia. Solomon in all his glory was surely not arrayed like one of these; for the petunia lends herself willingly to all the tricks and whimsies of the professional hybridist, so that almost every year she appears in a gorgeous new gown, particularly from America, where the petunia has an enormous vogue. There are, of course, dwarfs and there are large, floppy trumpets, nice compact bedding varieties, formless doubles, startling bicolours, ruffled and frilled ones and trailers for the window-box or hanging basket.

Apart from any fancy one may have, the safest course is to start with the bedding or "multiflora" strains, which are available in both civilized and savage colours. Or the dwarfs. They are effective when massed in beds by themselves, at 9in. spacing, or, using the softer colours, as foils for pelargoniums and scarlet salvia bedding complexes.

Delay sowing until March and, after pricking out (using deep boxes), make sure that they are grown on steadily without being checked, even to the point of moving them on into small pots if they outgrow the boxes. Good also for early adornment of the cool greenhouse if sown in autumn.

Phlox. Little sister to the big border phloxes, *P. drummondii* is a pearl among dwarf annuals, but appears to little advantage unless given a good soil, plenty of water and a place in the sun. At its best, it is richly laden with clusters of typical phlox flowers on slender stems, its charm being most apparent in the dwarfer varieties. The colours are many and have a richness of tone in even the more muted shades. Difficult to place satisfactorily in a garden, unless it be among rocks. For the perennial and the rock phloxes, see Chapters 10 and 21.

PINKS. Included in Chapter 11.

Portulaca. Another dwarf in Harlequin colours (from Brazil this time), to be reserved strictly for hot, dry situations, where they can be gorgeous. Six inches high, they may be clothed in orange, purple, rose, yellow, salmon or white. They are hardy enough to be sown *in situ* in early May, which is perhaps safer than the half-hardy method. Cover the seed with a mere dusting of soil.

Rudbeckia. The annual brethren of the herbaceous border genus include the gay Gloriosa daises, which are nothing to do with the hothouse gloriosa. They have large, showy, broad-petalled flowers in yellow or orange of the same floral style as sunflowers, from 1 to 3ft. Excellent for cutting.

For the perennial rudbeckias see Chapter 10.

Salvia. In the kingdom of the sages there are many clans but those that get the most popular cheers are the blazing scarlets, which are varieties of *S. splendens* (technically a perennial). If these are what suit your fancy, there are plenty whose names proclaim their character. They appear to better advantage when their excessive flamboyance is abated by gentler or contrasting colours, such as those of the ageratum or the bartonia.

Instead of the scarlet dazzler, however, one may opt for the salmon shades, including some dwarfs (not much catch) and some purples, which tend to go to the other extreme by their sombreness.

These salvias need to be started off in a temperature of a good 60°. After germination, prick them off, not into boxes, but into small pots first, and then, before they get pot-bound, into 4in. ones. Keep them in the greenhouse until early May and then move them into a frame for hardening. Plant out not before 1st June, a foot apart.

For other salvias, see in the hardies and in Chapters 10 and 18.

Schizanthus. The pretty and popular butterfly flower is recognized by its slim spikes of many, lightly poised florets, in rose, salmon, red or blush, amusingly marked with puckish little stripes and patches. Excellent and enduring as a cut flower. Best known as one of the easiest and most charming of flowers for the poor man's greenhouse, where it flourishes with a minimum of heat, but it can also be treated as a half-hardy annual. Choose a warm bed sheltered from the wind. For outdoors, the dwarf varieties of 1 foot are best. There is also a hardy annual strain (Dobie's).

Stocks. One of the garden's prime favourites, yet one which is too often confined to one strain – the Ten-week stocks. The classifications in some catalogues under fancy names can be confusing, especially as all but the night-scented stocks have a strong floral similarity. They vary, however, in their seasons and habits and not all can properly be classed as half-hardy annuals, but I put them all together here for convenience.

Night-scented stocks are insignificant little hardy annuals that hide their plain, lilac faces by day, but open in the evening to release their refreshing scent. Very fleeting. Sow in succession under a sitting-room window and mix the seed with that of the pretty little Virginian stocks to give a combination of scent and colour.

TEN-WEEK stocks. These are the general favourites in most parts of the country, flowering from June to mid-August. Sow late in March, keep the temperature well below 55°, ventilate freely, water with moderation after emergence and treat with Cheshunt Compound. Plant out at the end of May, 10in. apart, and do not pinch out the tips. Get the Hansen 100 per cent double strain and discard all seedlings that have leaves of a darker green than the majority.

EAST LOTHIAN stocks. Also called Intermediate. Popular in the north and flourish with hyacinthine splendour in Scotland. They carry on the stock innings when the Ten-weeks are run-out. Sow at the end of February. In the warmer counties they can be treated as biennials.

BROMPTON stocks. One of the joys of my early gardening days, surpassing wallflowers in their wealth of bloom and scent. These are biennials (see next section) and are raised in exactly the same way as wallflowers, the seed being sown in early July. They make lusty, branching plants up to 2ft high and need to be set 15in. apart, flowering in May and June, or earlier still in mild regions. The

Bromptons, however, dislike wet, cold clays. Grand in a greenhouse even unheated.

BEAUTY OF NICE stocks are usually regarded as greenhouse plants, to flower in winter. Sow in July and move them on by degrees from the pricking-out box to 3in. pots and then into 5in. ones. No heat is needed until the sun fails to provide 55°. They grow to perhaps 2ft.

Ask me not why all these pretty things are called "stocks". All but the little Virginian are, in fact, species or hybrids of *Matthiola.*

TAGETES. See under Marigold, African, etc.

TOBACCO-PLANT. See Nicotiana.

Ursinia. One of the South African daisies, with deeply cut foliage and flowers composed of vivid orange petals with a maroon base and jet-black disc. About 1ft.

Venidium. Another South African; the plant is rather coarse, growing 2–3ft, but produces the most elegant, very large flowers in which the long ray petals are in pastel shades of lemon, straw or ivory with basal maroon markings round a glistening black disc. See also Venidio-arctotis, next chapter.

Verbena (Vervain to our ancestors). One of the prettiest of annuals, but not the most tidy. It bears clustered heads of gay or tender hues, usually lit by a white or yellow eye. Vervains have a lax, sprawling habit, so plant them 9in. apart to create a floral carpet. At their best only in hot weather and light, warm soils. Excellent for window-boxes.

Sow the seed in January–February. The amateur's difficulty is that he must raise a temperature of not less than 60°, or germination will be slow and unreliable.

The celebrated scarlet 'Lawrence Johnson' can be propagated only from cuttings taken in late summer.

Zinnia. Either you rave about zinnias or else you consider them stiff and stuffy. Certainly they are not worth a lot of trouble if grown under poor conditions. Rich cultivation and a hot summer are their needs. Having grown them in volcanic soil in Africa chest-high, with blooms the size of many show chrysanthemums, I rarely find any satisfaction in them in this country. But, if you like zinnias and are not tied to a cold, wet clay, be not dismayed.

The best show is rarely obtained from market seedlings bought in boxes. In their race against the calendar they sulk if checked by becoming root-bound in box or pot. They must always be moved on quickly. Thus good results accrue, in the warm counties, by a direct open-ground sowing, in the manner of hardy annuals, in May. In not-so-warm regions cloches may be used. Elsewhere sow under glass, not before 1st April, with little or no heat, according to the weather, and move them on into small pots as soon as they are ready. Water generously.

The zinnia has had its full share of manipulation by ardent hybridizers. The simplest forms of other days are beginning to look more and more like dahlias or chrysanths of sorts and they range in stature from 6in. to 3ft. Stripes, bicolours and selfs abound in many colours. On the whole the new varieties in catalogues are the best, and, in this instance, the bigger the better.

Hardy Biennials

There are not many of these, but they provide some of our bravest and most popular plants and are pretty easy.

The normal drill is simply to sow outdoors in soil worked to a fine tilth, prick off into a reserve bed as soon as the seedlings are big enough to handle easily and then station them at their final posts in October. Sow in June in the north, in July in the south. When pricking-out into the nursery bed, plant at distances appropriate to the size of the mature plant – 5in. for wallflowers, 8in. for Canterbury-bells and so on. When planning the year's work, make allowance for the space that will be needed for these nursery beds. A few flowers are better sown in seed-boxes, and these we shall note.

Their posts of duty can be almost anywhere in reasonable sun, including the herbaceous border. Several, however, create an awkward problem through continuing their floral display right up till the end of June or longer. This means large blanks in the beds for the rest of the summer, unless something already growing strongly in pots is ready to replace them. The awkward ones are sweet-Williams, Siberian wallflowers, Canterbury-bells and, to a less extent, the Iceland poppy. Good replacements for them are bedding begonias and dwarf dahlias if they have been grown in large pots.

Canterbury-bell (*Campanula medium*). One of our grandest old favourites, very easy to raise and surely needing no description. Some have a bell only, others a circlet of coloured sepals as well, which gives them the name of "cup and saucer" varieties. Both sorts grow to 3ft in white, pink, blue or mauve and are very broad and bushy, flowering in June.

DIGITALIS. See Foxglove.
ERYSIMUM. Included in wallflowers.

Evening primrose. The traditional flower of this nickname is a very easy biennial, growing some 3ft high and broadly bushy, breaking out into a succession of gay, lemon flowers, set off by red calyces, but not opening until late afternoon. Rather a slatternly plant, it looks best among shrubs, tolerating their shade very well. Flourishes in the poorest soils. Simply sow the seed where the plants are to bloom. Space at 18in. It is *Oenothera biennis*.

A dwarfer one, with white flowers richly scented of honeysuckle and open most of the day, is *O. trichocalyx*, of 18in. Raise either in biennial fashion or as a half-hardy annual, sowing in February.

For the more desirable perennial oenotheras, see Chapter 10.

Forget-me-not (*Myosotis*). This very old favourite prefers moist places, but dwells as happily in shady places (even pretty dense shade) as in sunny ones. It is lovely among shrubs and in woodland and is a beautiful groundwork for Darwin and other tulips. One or two plants heeled-in in a moist and shady corner will present you with all the seedlings you are likely to want for next year, without any kind of preparation.

Foxgloves (*Digitalis*) are dwellers in the open woodlands, looking their most stylish in partial shade among shrubs and small trees. They seed themselves with the utmost freedom, even to the point of excess. The older sorts with the drooping tubes that suggest their popular name have now been largely superceded by the Excelsior strain, which lift their blossoms up to the horizontal, looking like a massed band of bugles. The American strain Foxy is more compact and branching, only 3ft instead of five.

We may as well deal here with the few perennial foxgloves also. *D. grandiflora* (alias *ambigua*) is pale sulphur, 2ft, June–August, and *mertonensis* is its short-lived offspring in prawn-pink.

Honesty. Almost a weed by the exuberance of its natural increase. Scatter the seed in some unimportant corner, shady for preference. The purple flowers are followed by the flat, transparent seed-pods so popular for winter decoration. The two outer valves of the pod should be lightly rubbed off. Is *Lunaria annua.*

Iceland poppy (*Papaver nudicaule*). To me this is the most delightful of all the true poppies, though admittedly there are people who exult more loudly in the savage splendour of the oriental one (which belongs to the Chapter 10). The Icelander grows a basal tuft of leaves from which arise an exuberance of leafless but hairy stems a foot or more tall, crowned with flowers that have a luminous radiance in orange, lemon, apricot, salmon or vermilion. A delightful adornment in any garden and a gay cut flower for the vase.

The seed being very fine, and needing to be covered by a mere dusting of sifted soil or sand, it is best to start off in a seed-box instead of the open ground. Alternatively, they can be raised in the manner of the half-hardies by sowing early in spring in a cool greenhouse temperature. The conditions needed for success on planting out are: a sunny position, well drained, a light loam mixed with ample supplies of leaf-mould or peat and plenty of water. Heavy clays, soils that dry out too quickly and those that may become waterlogged are all alike abhorrent. Space 1ft apart.

In a favourable environment the Iceland poppy will behave as a perennial and develop into large clumps.

PANSY. See under Viola, in the next chapter.

SWEET-WILLIAM and Sweet-Wivelsfield. See Chapter 11.

VIOLA. The hybrid viola of gardens is often raised as a biennial, but is truly perennial, so I have placed it in the next chapter, together with others of its kin.

Wallflower. The common wallflower of gardens seems to be a good deal less hardy today than in my youth. We planted them out in autumn and expected them to stand the stiffest winter without a shudder. Nowadays many of them give up the ghost. This is particularly noticeable in rich, fat soils, which cause lush growth that easily succumbs to frost. The proper place for wallflowers is in poor, stony, alkaline soil with sharp drainage – in fact, walls, or their like. On the other hand, they don't make a big splash in their first season unless given a good soil and accordingly are normally grown as biennials.

To raise them is child's play. Sow in an outdoor seed-bed, prick off 5in. apart and pinch out the growing tip before autumn, planting out 10in. apart. There are all sorts of colours to choose from, all charged with an ineffable scent. These are derived from *Cheiranthus cheiri.*

Much more vivid is the Siberian wallflower, which grows into a glowing ball of fire, immensely warm and stirring, but lacking a sweet breath. For sheer colour it will see-off everything else in the garden except the azaleas when it starts blooming in May. It creates the same kind of problem as the sweet-William, not ceasing to flower till the end of June. The Siberian wallflower is *C. allionii.*

We may as well deal here with the perennial wallflowers also. These begin in late spring and have a long innings. Most celebrated is the double, sweet-scented, bright gold "Harper Crewe", which flourishes in the stoniest or chalkiest soils in May–June if in the sun; increase it by July cuttings.

Another choice for us is the charming little Spanish wallflower, which is evergreen, dressed in lilac or mauve, densely flowered, grows only to about a foot and flowers from May and into July. Use it informally wherever there is stone or rock, as at the flanks of steps or in walling stone, or in any dry sunny place. This is *Erysimum linifolium.* Easy from seed.

An erysimum perhaps more beautiful is "Moonlight", which, from evergreen foliage, throws out 9in. racemes of pale primrose in late April and goes on for most of the summer. Give it full sun and a gritty, fast-draining soil in a raised bed. Short-lived. Increase by July cuttings.

For rock gardens, there is *C. rupestris* (or *pulchellum*), which makes 2in. mats of primrose hue. Now called an erysimum.

CHAPTER 9

THE FLOWERS OF THE BORDER: THE ELECT

The Border Proper – Delphiniums – Irises – Primulas – Violas and their Offspring

WE have constantly been told during the past twenty years or more that the herbaceous border, so long one of the great glories of British gardens, is passing away; yet it still clings to a place in our hearts and, in one form or another, will go on doing so. For not only are herbaceous plants lovely to behold, but also they are relatively cheap, give very quick results and are usually very easy to propagate.

Apart altogether from the formal border, herbaceous perennials have immense value in all sorts of other situations and often fulfil functions not easily entrusted to other plants; they may adorn odd corners, occupy small beds, embellish the banks of pool and stream, garnish the woodland scene, or mingle happily with shrubs. They have an enormous versatility, so that there is virtually no part of any garden and no circumstances of soil or situation in which one or other of them will not be entirely at home – whether sunny or shady, wet or dry, acid or alkaline, rich or stonily poor.

Many, indeed, are *not* at their best in the heterogeneous company of the open border and must be allotted some special mission or mingle with other company; violas, lily-of-the-valley, hellebores and the waterside primulas are some examples. Carnations and the tall bearded irises ought to be allotted territories reserved for themselves alone. Hostas, Himalayan poppies (*Meconopsis*), peonies and euphorbias have their own special uses. Others again, being essentially flowers for cutting and not very showy in the border, can with advantage be grown in the kitchen garden in straight lines, such as pyrethrums and scabious.

It will be seen, therefore, that, whether in the formal border or in casual beds, it is unprofitable to select plants just because you like the look of them; they must be chosen according to the condition of the soil, the locality and the setting. What will flourish in the peaty soil of a Scottish garden is likely to fail in the chalk of the Yorkshire wolds and in the sand of Bagshot.

The Border Proper

With these few general observations, we may proceed to consider a few precepts for the establishment of a more or less formal "border", whether large or small, but bearing in mind always that the "mixed" border, in which some shrubs are incorporated, has many attractions in smaller places and that bulbs of one sort or another gracefully diversify the form and features of the herbaceous plants. Dahlias also are entirely suitable and are valuable for filling or obscuring blanks left by plants that finish flowering before July.

THE SITE AND TREATMENT

Borders can be of many shapes and sizes – straight or curved, broad or narrow. They can face in any direction, but the south-facing border is the easiest, and the north-facing one requires a special technique in the choice of plants, giving priority to those that like shade. As a backing for the border, nothing is better than a bank of shrubs, but there is seldom room enough in a small place. Stone or brick walls are excellent, giving shelter for the less hardy things and allowing the employment of wall plants, but of course a border can quite well be put in the open, though shelter from stiff winds is to be desired.

In siting the border, try to have it running directly or obliquely away from the main windows of the house, so that one looks or walks down its length in perspective. A border should not be looked at full in the face, for there are always seasonal gaps. The "island" borders, about which so much has been written, I find most unsatisfactory. They can be fine in very large places, like Mr Bloom's celebrated garden in Norfolk, where they are composed with much expertise and on different levels, but elsewhere – especially in small gardens – I find them a flop. Better to fill island beds with roses, dahlias, heathers, what you will.

Borders should never be directly overhung by large trees, but some slanting shade for part of the day will be appreciated by some inhabitants, such as phlox and campanula.

In general, herbaceous plants can be put out any time from November to March if the ground is not frostbound or saturated by rain, but early autumn is usually the best time, as the soil still has some warmth. On cold, heavy clays spring is best and there are a few plants that should always be planted in spring only, including scabious, gaillardia, the amellus group of asters, and some others mentioned in the notes that follow. See also under pyrethrum.

In the after-care of the border, there are some important considerations. First, do *not* give it the usual kind of digging-over so often advised for the autumn; it tears up roots and disturbs or damages precious things such as bulbs and alstroemerias. A mere hoeing, or very shallow pricking-over, is quite enough. Much more important than digging is to mulch the ground with manure or compost in early spring, or with leaves in autumn.

Other after-care measures are the staking of any kinds of plants liable to flop as they attain full height, and the removal of spent blooms. A great many herbaceous plants will go on and on if dead-headed, particularly anything that has the form and shape of a daisy; it is surprising, too, how most lupins come on repeatedly after dead-heading.

Unless you have to get at the land for some operation, don't cut down foliage and stems too soon in the autumn – let them die right down till nearly black; then, if they are not hollow-stemmed plants, such as delphiniums, cut them down not too low, so that the stumps may trap wind-driven leaves to provide both a mulch and a frost protection.

About every third or fourth year the border, having become overgrown, will need sorting out. Leave alone the plants that resent disturbance – peonies, alstroemerias, fox-tail lilies, Japanese anemones, etc. – but lift most other herbaceous plants, divide them and replant. In big borders a portion can be done annually. If an annual top-dressing has been given, re-manuring will not be necessary.

The use of lime will depend on the condition of the soil and the nature of its inhabitants. The lupin does not care for lime, but gypsophila and iris do. In general, it is best not to apply any lime, except for specialized plants and except in old soils that have become very "sour".

DESIGN

The soil may have been well and truly made ready according to Cocker, but the border may still be a failure if it is not well laid-out. Composition, or design, is the touchstone. It requires, first, a little elementary knowledge of the characteristics of each plant – its height, spread, colour, season of flowering, and foliage – most of which can be got from any good catalogue, but it also requires something less easily taught – an eye. Variations in height, blends, or contrasts in colour, a bold handling of shapes and forms, a sympathetic grouping of different leaf textures, the counterpoint of light and shade – these are the things that make a border beautiful.

I have room for only one or two guiding precepts, but I must emphasize from the first that, just like any other artistic composition, it has got to be worked out with care, indeed, loving care, on paper beforehand. There is no other way, and the best paper to use is the large-squared paper of a child's arithmetic book (not graph paper).

Formality is to be avoided like the plague. The hand of man must be in no shape evident. No straight lines, no regimented gradations from the dwarf in front to the giant at the back, no plants dotted singly here and there, save one or two of the more high-pitched colours. Everything must seem as though "painted o'er with nature's hand, not art's" – and nature sheds her seeds in drifts and clusters. While obviously 7ft plants must not be right in front, nor miniatures right at the back, let a promontory of helenium or liatris thrust out towards the front, and a drift of penstemon sweep back towards the centre. Let the clusters be irregular in form – some roughly circular, some elongated, some sweeping away at an angle, and so on.

Another golden rule of border design (as in the military sphere) is Mass. It is a great mistake to crowd in a whole lot of different plants in "penny packets". Restrict the genera and have plenty of each. Have a dozen phloxes rather than a dozen different plants for the same flowering season; if you can afford only three phloxes, put them all together.

One of the major problems of border design is how to mask the ragged patches left by those plants that finish flowering early in the season. The worst offender is the oriental poppy, but anchusas, delphiniums and lupins can also look very tatty when they withdraw from the stage. Thus one of the touchstones of design is to station these behind plants that flower later and it is here that the purple salvias, achilleas, phloxes and Michaelmas daisies are so useful and here also we may recruit the dahlias.

If the border is a deep one, give yourself room to manœuvre. You will need to move about to tend the plants in all weathers, and this can be accomplished by laying down a few stepping stones, neatly arranged, or, as I do, by very narrow little stone paths, echeloned from front to back, which themselves form a feature of the design.

COMPOSITION

On colour composition one can say little in this small compass. Generally speaking, the mixed colours of nature make happy marriages (witness the fuchsia), and much that is written on this subject is rather arty and affected. No colour scheme, however, is entirely balanced without a few touches of white here and there, and nothing has a greater charm for this purpose than the white campanulas. A few plants of silver-grey foliage, which I cover in Chapter 20, also make melodious variations of the theme.

Grace and strength are given to the garden if the herbaceous border is made into a "mixed" one by inviting into it some of the smaller flowering shrubs. One that I would always have, which has the prettiest plumbago-blue flowers, goes by the forbidding name of *Ceratostigma willmottianum*. Other small shrubs particularly suitable for a mixed border are *Senecio laxifolius*, potentillas, *Hypericum patulum* 'Hidcote', the beautiful, silvery, lavender-flowered perovskia, some spiraeas, floribunda roses, the dwarfish varieties of philadelphus, hydrangeas if rightly placed, and the dwarf helianthemum, which is quite admirable near the front.

As for bulbs, lilies will be entirely happy among the shrubs and leafier plants, which will keep their roots cool. *Galtonia candicans*, the giant Cape hyacinth, is excellent for filling spaces that have become empty in August. Daffodils are almost essential, bringing life and light to the border while its other races are scarcely awake, but it is a fatal mistake to put them in the front; they should go right towards the back of the border, where their withering foliage will be concealed by the oncoming growth of the perennials.

Another class that keeps excellent company with border flowers are certain of the rock plants for the front edge. Some of the best for this purpose are *Gentiana septemfida*, aubrieta, dwarf phloxes, campanulas, flaxes, potentillas and geraniums. See Chapter 21.

Depth is a great boon in a border – more important than length. Those who can spare 12ft or more are fortunate, and anything less than 8ft creates problems in composition. For narrow borders or strips there are but two choices: be satisfied with a collection that will give you a full blaze for a short period, or have only a limited number of subjects and cluster them boldly. By way of example, the awkward 3ft strip is admirably furnished by using only lupins for early summer, followed by phloxes for mid-season, succeeded by medium or dwarf dahlias for final bloom.

A border about 5ft wide, if of reasonable length, could comfortably accommodate an arrangement of lupins, *Achillea* 'Moonshine', purple salvia, phlox or monarda, liatris, *Aster frikartii*, campanulas of several sorts and a few of the fine shorter delphiniums, together with pinks, flax, camomile, erigeron and cranesbill at or near the front.

In borders of more regal proportions the backbone must always be formed of lupins, delphiniums, phloxes and Michaelmas daises, in that order of flowering, filling in with whatever pleases your fancy. And if you are habitually on holiday in August, you can cut out all the flowers that bloom at that season.

PROPAGATION

Nearly all herbaceous perennials can be raised from seed, the majority with no great difficulty, but those of named varieties will not always be true to their parents. They are far too numerous for me to list here, but Thompson and Morgan's catalogue is a great help.

The great majority can also be increased by simple division of the roots, usually in autumn or winter, as explained in Chapter 6, and in the selections that follow this is to be assumed unless stated otherwise; several are raised easily by root cuttings.

Delphiniums

The delphinium is easily the sovereign choice of all the flowers of the border, not only for its own sumptuous floral display, unique among flowers, but also because it gives a serene and queenly air to the whole garden scene; so that, when it goes to rest in July, one's heart sinks at the terrible gaps left by its absence, until nature's curative balm awakens interest in other objects of affection.

New and exciting things are stirring in the heart of the delphinium as the promise of all the roseate colours of a tropical sunrise begins to gleam on the horizon. Hitherto the popular notion of the perennial delphinium has been of something more or less blue or occasionally white; these derive from the species *D. elatum.*

A few years ago, however, Dr R. A. H. Legros, a young Dutch scientist, evolved a method of marrying the elatums with the fine red, yellow and scented species of the wild. The progeny have been called University Hybrids, and have been greatly encouraged in this country by the Delphinium Society, so that a whole new range of colours in the elatum fashion is in prospect. Much has yet to be put to the proof, but the blood-red delphinium is already a fact.

Meanwhile, we still have plenty to delight us in the customary blues, mauves, whites and near-pinks. The elatum delphinium is remarkably free from natural enemies (except for the treacherous slug), is utterly hardy in Britain and in similar climates, has a long life and multiplies freely. Moreover, like other delphiniums, it is remarkably easy to raise from seed; provided the seed comes from a really reliable source, such as Blackmore and Langdon or Bakers, anyone can raise delphiniums that, from the garden point of view, are just as gorgeous as the named varieties, and far cheaper.

People who suppose that the majestic 7-footers mean an awful lot of trouble may take encouragement from the growing classes of "short" and "medium" varieties, as they are now officially grouped. The shorties, of which 'Blue Tit' was the first and still is the finest example, do not exceed 4ft and normally need no staking.

THE CULTURAL DRILL

Delphiniums can be grown successfully in almost any kind of soil, including chalk. Choose an open, sunny position, with good drainage. Double-dig the site and enrich it with bulky organic matter as in Chapter 5. Plant in September or October if you can. If you can't and if the soil is heavy and damp, wait until spring, though the first year's results will be only modest. Young rooted cuttings, whether your own or from one of the few nurseries that supply them, go into the ground in May or June, to flower the following year.

Plant so that the crown is level with the surface and the roots reasonably spread out. Cover the crowns and the immediately surrounding soil with a half-inch layer of sharp sand (I use Cornish sand) as a protection against slugs. Planting distances vary from anything up to 3ft for the talls down to 18in. for the shorts. In a mixed border it is usually best, space permitting, to have three or more of a kind in each cluster; if you mix them, keep the early, mid-season and late varieties separate.

When the new shoots have sprouted in spring they must be thinned out by cutting some of them down to the crown. This is the prime secret of getting the fine spikes that astound the beholder. Do this thinning when the shoots are a few inches high, though better late than never. Suffer only two shoots to a new plant, three or possibly four in the second year according to the vigour manifested by the plant, and anything up to six thereafter.

Next, staking, except for the shorties. Use 4ft canes, pushed 9in. into the ground when the stems are a foot high (or when thinning if you like). I use one cane per stem, tying in each with raffia, but plenty of people simply push in four canes (for an established plant) and tie raffia or soft string round the lot. Whichever you elect to do, make the first tie at about 10 or 12in. and a second one just below the bottom floret of the flowering spike when it develops. If using the single cane method, make the bottom tie with very little play, but the top one with plenty; thus the bottom tie arrests the stem from rocking at the crown and the second one allows it a certain amount of freedom to sway with the wind.

When the plants have finished flowering, cut down the stems to the level of the topmost leaves, *not* right down to the ground, which is damaging to the constitution of the plant. New basal shoots often develop after the first flowering and it is then in order to cut the old ones right out. Many varieties produce short flowering laterals below the main spike. These are very nice for a vase and should be retained when cutting off the main spike.

Sometimes a little mildew appears on the leaves. If so, spray immediately with Karathane and repeat after every heavy rain. The worst of all the delphinium's enemies is the occasional June gale accompanied by lashing rain. There is nothing you can then do to prevent the splendid spikes from being snapped clean off while in their full pride and your sole consolation is that your spouse will give them a welcome in the house.

Readers can get advice on the best modern varieties and on all cultural matters by membership of the Delphinium Society and overseas readers can get free seeds. Unfortunately only a few nurseries carry stocks of the best and newest varieties. Most of them are hopelessly out of date. The leading specialists are Blackmore and Langdon and Bakers. Jackman's have quite a good list, with some modern ones mixed with the old.

DELPHINIUMS FROM CUTTINGS

Common-or-garden varieties can be multiplied, like most herbaceous perennials, by ordinary division, but a far better method is to grow new plants from cuttings every few years.

Take the cuttings in spring, normally towards the end of March. Draw the soil away from the crown of the plant and select shoots about 3in. long (not too fat and not too thin and spindly), on which two or more leaves have opened up. Using a razor-sharp knife, slice off the shoot with a thin sliver of the crown attached; without this sliver of solid matter the cutting would never root. Treat the cutting with one of the root-forming "hormone" preparations.

Of the several methods of rooting the cuttings, I suggest that you use clay pans or pots filled with a very gritty compost made up of one-half Cornish sand and a quarter each of peat and loam. Put these in a home-made propagating box with a glass lid and no heat and put the whole thing in a closed frame in a shady place. Close, cool, moist and shady is the rule.

Rooting may take up to eight weeks. Give the plants then plenty of air for another week or ten days; then plant them out into a prepared nursery bed, protected against slugs by plenty of sharp sand. It will now be early June and the new recruits can be sent to their action stations in the autumn.

DELPHINIUMS FROM SEED

This is pretty easy, following the precepts of my Chapter 6 on propagation. Use clay pans, pots or the usual wooden boxes, rather than the open ground. Early March or August–September are the preferred times. Sow very sparsely and cover thinly. Prick off into deepish boxes, such as kipper boxes, or into small pots individually. Seed of the elatum hybrids should be bought from Blackmore and Langdon or from Bakers.

OTHER DELPHINIUMS

The Pacific Giants are a very fine American strain in the elatum manner. There are no named varieties but they are sold under colour groups or under King Arthur's Round Table names and are remarkably reliable. They are raised from seed sown in March and will bloom the first year. In this country many of them behave as perennials, though with not so long a life as the English sort. There is, in fact, some Giant Pacific sap in some of our newer elatum varieties. Seed is available from most of the leading (national) seedsmen and young plants from Carlile's.

Connecticut Yankees grow to about 3ft, branching freely and flowering over a long period, and are gay and jolly. Raise from seed.

Belladonna delphiniums throw up loose and airy spikes, from 3–5ft, in light and dark blue or white.

'Blue Butterfly', a variety of *D. grandiflorum*, is a charming 15in. dwarf in a brilliant deep blue. Theoretically a perennial, it is usually grown from seed as an annual for bedding and is also excellent in pots for the greenhouse. Sutton's 'Dwarf Porcelain Blue' is similar.

D. nudicaule is about the only true species delphinium commonly grown. A very pretty plant of brilliant orange-scarlet, only 10in. high, it is tuberous-rooted, expects to be given a hot spot and is a short-lived perennial usually grown in rock gardens. There is a paler hued form.

Other species, such as *cardinale, zalil, leroyi*, *brunonianum* and *wellbyi*, are for specialist gardeners.

Irises

This ancient and lordly race dwells in one of the more rarified strata of the horticultural atmosphere, with an aura and a jargon of its own and worshipped by the most devoted disciples, who often disagree with one another. Like other large races, it is segregated into clans, or sections and sub-sections, with forbidding names, according to their diverse qualities – all very confusing to those who have not been initiated into this freemasonry.

Many are very pernickety and difficult to grow in temperate climates, a fact that does not surprise us when we learn that some come from homes where they are accustomed to being sun-baked in harsh and stony soil and others from haunts where their feet are bathed in water.

If you are magnetized by their beauty you should join the British Iris Society, whose literature is very useful. In my crowded pages I can only skim along the ranks, like an impatient general anxious to get his inspection over, and pay most attention to those sorts that are the easiest and the most popular, particularly as I can myself claim no expertise.

We may begin by broadly grouping irises for our own simple purposes thus:

Those that grow from bulbs, in the manner of daffodils.

Those that grow from rhizomes (see "Gardener's Jargon").

The rhizomatous ones are sub-divided into:

Those that sprout little "beards" on their lower petals, these being dominated by the "tall bearded irises" or "flags" or "German" irises of martial carriage and popular image, though there is now also a whole tribe of most captivating dwarfs.

Those that are clean-shaven, so to speak.

I shall horrify the iris fancier when I say that I consider the tall bearded flags as doubtful aspirants to a place in small mixed gardens, and certainly unsuitable in very small ones. Their beauty is not long-lived and when their day is done their place looks pretty desolate and there is very little you can do about filling the ragged gap. Culturally, they ought to be allowed a little territory all to themselves, for integration with other races does them no good; their rhizomes must not be shaded by any leafage. So I suggest that the all-purposes gardener may find it profitable to consider the enchanting dwarfer sorts, the new "intermediates" and the bulbous ones, many of which are of rare delight and have the charm of surprise to the beholder.

TALL BEARDED FLAGS

These, the hybrid successors of the old, purple "London Flag", are the lords of June, growing from a thick rhizome with sword-like leaves, clothed now in many-coloured splendour, standing with exemplary rectitude at about 3ft, and cultivating neat little beards of

PLATE 5.

Left: A fastigiate hawthorn at the drive entrance.

Below: The annual *Eccremocarpus scaber* climbing up it.

PLATE 6. One of a matched pair of *Hydrangea paniculata* 'Grandiflora' at the foot of the old terrace.

stubbly growth at the top of each of the three falls. Until you have penetrated farther into the mysteries of the iris cult, be on your guard against other bearded species (such as the oncocyclus and regelia groups), as they are meats for the epicure only.

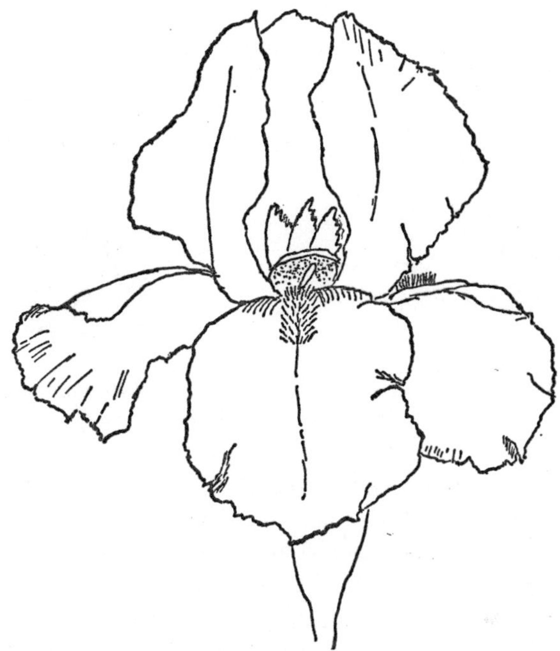

FIG. 28. Anatomy of a bearded flag iris, showing the three erect standards, the three drooping falls, the beard on each fall (one hidden), the small stamen in the shadow of the stigma, with the crests of the style behind.

The prime needs of what are still sometimes called the German irises (since they derive in part from the so-called *I. germanica*) are:

Full sun. They will grow in shade but not prosper. The rhizomes must be baked. So no mulching.

Fast drainage. They hate wet feet. Light soils are not always best, but in heavy clay the beds should be raised.

Soil treatment is a fairly simple matter. Avoid absolutely all animal manure, but dig in plenty of leaf-mould or good compost, mixed with bonemeal or hoof-and-horn. In acid soils add some form of lime. Iris pundits do not all agree on this point, but it is certain that this race of flags is happy in lime, particularly magnesium limestone (dolomite chalk).

Planting. The best time to plant flags is immediately after they have finished flowering, as the new roots are then just beginning to grow, but most people find it more convenient to do so in August or September.

The method of planting is governed by the fact that the rhizome is not a root, but a stem, from which the roots grow. Accordingly,

FIG. 29. Planting a bearded flag iris. On right, an end-on view to show roots astride a saddle.

lay it so that its upper side (it's "back") is fully exposed to the sun. This you do by first digging a hole of sufficient size for the roots and then building up a saddle of soil in the middle of the hole, so that the rhizome will ride on top of the saddle with its roots astride it. Plant the roots firmly, with the "fan" of leaves to the north, and cut the leaves down to a height of about 9in. Space the rhizomes about 10in. apart in triangles of three to a clump, but leave at least 18in. between clumps. Take precautions against slugs, the iris's worst enemy.

Servicing. In March, and again after flowering, dress the soil with a general fertilizer (best thing for non-specialists). Watering is seldom necessary, as these flags are pretty drought-hardy. The pundits disagree about whether the withered foliage should be removed in autumn.

Every three or four years, when the rhizomes will have multiplied considerably, crawling ever outwards, dig up the whole clump as soon as flowering is over in July, cut off each rhizome separately, replant the new ones in prepared soil and discard the old.

For the same reasons as before, I avoid suggesting named varieties. Price will rule out the newest ones except to the dedicated. You will find almost every imaginable colour and blend, including many of devastating beauty but also others that look like lumps of mud or handfuls of manure.

Among the newcomers are some "intermediates" or (in America) "medians", which are hybrids between the talls and the dwarfs, with flower seasons varying from April till June. These may be the answer to the small gardener's prayer, for they are hardy and very free-flowering. Planting time is the end of May.

DWARF BEARDED FLAGS

Except for size, these are just like their big brothers, but bloom in April–May and don't need rich feeding. They are most endearing creatures and breed rapidly when provided with sun and a free-draining soil. Very suitable for rock gardens. Two of the easier sorts are:

pumila. A real sweetie, like a plump-looking cherub, squatting almost right down on the ground. Quite hardy. There are blue, yellow and white forms, notably 'Blue Pygmy' and 'Amber Queen'.

chamaeiris is another charmer, a little larger in all its parts, on 6in. stems. There are blues and yellows and a white one, 'The Bride', which rises to a foot.

WITH RHIZOMES BUT NO BEARDS

Here we enter a very mixed company, many of them austere and aloof, but here and there we come upon a few that are easy enough to make friends with. Most of them want damp soils, and some very damp ones.

First of all, the **Algerian iris** our fine old friend *I. stylosa,* not yet accustomed to its ugly new name *unguicularis.* A moody fellow, sulking for no known reason in one man's garden, but blooming hilariously in another's and glorifying the chill winter months with its beautiful, marvellously scented blossoms in blue, lavender or white on 10in. stems. Nothing will scent a room more sweetly, nor last so long, if cut when the buds show colour.

One hears all sorts of stories of how *stylosa* flourishes in the most unlikely places, but the only sound advice is to give it a place against a dry, unshaded, south-facing wall, with a spartan diet of gravel mixed with some good loam and leaf-mould, plus lime, in the forms of magnesium limestone or limestone chips for preference. It succeeds in chalk. Good, fast drainage is absolutely necessary and a footing of broken bricks is sometimes recommended.

Plant in September or April and water well for the first month, but not afterwards. Do all you can to fight off the slugs, the deadliest enemy of *stylosa.* Cut the leaves down to 9in. from the ground each April.

The **Siberian iris,** *sibirica.* Easy, provided the soil is not too arid. Builds up into big, tough clumps, 3ft high. Numerous varieties, usually blue or violet. Too small flowers for too much foliage. Plant firmly in September to bloom in June. No artificial fertilizers.

chrysographes, closely related, but shorter, is much more beautiful. In its best forms it is a rich, velvety purple with delicate gold pencillings on the falls. Needs a damp soil.

The **gladdon,** or stinking gladwin, is our native *I. foetidissima*, with dingy mauve flowers, though there is now a good yellow one. Stinks only when you bruise the foliage. Its special value is in its capsules, or seed-pods, which, when allowed to ripen, split open to reveal its rows of large seeds, in brilliant sealing-wax red. Madly desired by flower arrangers. Moist soil in shade. Stake the weak stems.

laevigata is a beautiful water iris, of which there are many charming colour forms, growing with its rhizome just submerged, but quite content with any very moist soil.

kaempferi is to me the most beautiful of all irises and one of the world's most sumptuous floral creations, having enormous, broad-petalled flowers of stunning colours. But *kaempferi* is a difficult goddess to serve, demanding to have her toes in water all summer but dry all the winter, besides a very rich and acid soil; though the expensive German 'Care' strain is lime-tolerant.

The Pacific Coast or Californian hybrids, not yet easy to come by, have orchidaceous colourings, grow from 8 to 18in, flower in May, dislike lime and are said to be quite hardy and easy in shade or sun, provided the drainage is free. A valuable introduction. They make few roots. Plant only in April or September.

BULBOUS IRISES

Here again we have some difficult customers, which we shall leave alone, and some easy ones.

The best known are those which are popularly called Dutch,

Spanish and English irises. Inexpensive, easy and good for cutting, they have slender stems, short standards and falls that are strap-like and angular. They bat from early June to mid-July, in the order I have quoted. Plant in September, 3in. deep, in any reasonable soil. The English are the largest and most decorative, with broad falls like those of the flags, but they must have a damp soil. The others need a good sun-baking, and the Spaniards are sweetly scented.

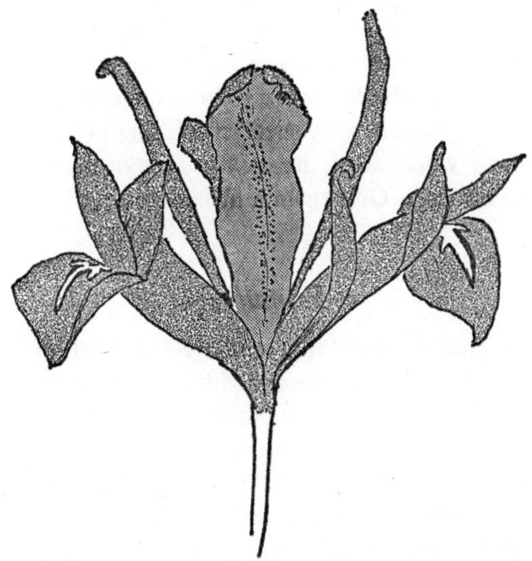

FIG. 30. *Iris histrioides* 'Major'.

Less familiar but far more endearing than these are the tiny winter irises that "warm the cold bosom of the hoary year" with their brave Cinderella charm. In the front of them all is:

histrioides 'Major'. A lovely minature jewel, like a three-pointed star in blue, hall-marked with gold, enamelling the harsh earth throughout January and February and gleaming seraphically through the snow when it is not deeper than 3in. As hardy in the Scottish highlands as in the south. Plant the bulbs in September 3in. deep in fairly rich soil in sun, being sure that the drainage is sound. They like lime. Delightful in bowls, in which they will probably bloom for Christmas; give no heat.

Another pretty toy is the violet-scented ***reticulata***, which is V. Sackville-West's

Blue-netted iris, like a small cry
Startling the sloth of February

Of vase-like silhouette, it is 5in. high and expects the same conditions as its cousin. There are several named varieties in shades of blue. The very long, thin, grass-like foliage that follows is rather a nuisance. Excellent in pots and bowls. Marriage with *histrioides* has produced some pretty children.

danfordiae, a pretty yellow pygmy, much written-up. Avoid it; the bulbs break up after flowering. Much more beautiful, much easier, but much more expensive is the lemon ***winogradowii,*** which flowers in February–March. Seems to be quite content with a heavy soil, provided it gets sun; very successful in the north.

All these little winter irises are easy in pots of porous compost in unheated greenhouses. Give them a little liquid feed after flowering.

Primulas

A great and glorious race that embraces a host of species and varieties that will gladden the hearts alike of the simple cottager and of the most erudite and skilful connoisseur. It includes the primrose, cowslip, auricula, polyanthus, the candelabrum primulas that haunt the waterside and tiny treasures that nestle in the crannies of the rock garden. Most of them expect a cool, moist and shady soil. A great many are for the expert only and these we shall politely pass by.

None, easy or difficult, is really a fit tenant for the artifices of the formal border; they expect to be given a more carefree way of life, each according to its disposition, whether among shrubs, or close to water or in some peaty bank, but always in a soil where its roots keep moist and cool, even though the sun may warm their leaves and blossoms.

Primroses. Primulas are classified in a number of "sections", which are often a helpful guide to the gardener. The easiest is the Vernales section, of which the undisputed queen is our "rathe" native primrose (*P. vulgaris*), one of the world's most beautiful flowers. Next comes a modern discovery in the bright purple cherub *P. juliae*, little parent of many hybrids, including the ubiquitous, claret-faced miniature 'Wanda'. Supporting them there swarms a charming, dancing chorus of "coloured primroses" in many hues, some fixed by name, others simply seed strains, which are as easy as pie to raise and for which the leading seedsmen have their own pet names, such as 'Mothers' Day' and 'Jewel Box'. There are also a few double primroses that may catch the eye, but they are not easy to maintain unless given ideal conditions and frequently divided. The violet 'Our Pat' is one of the easier sorts.

Polyanthus. From all these endearing little primroses, with their short-stemmed flowers usually nestling close upon their crinkly leaves, it is only a short step to the robust, jostling and pushful polyanthus, which thrusts up from its nest of leaves a thick, strong stem crowned with a large truss of many flowers well above the foliage. The Polly-Anns are the modern version of the oxlip, which arose, we surmise, from an idyllic marriage in some blissful Arcadian grove between the primrose and the cowslip (*P. veris*). Polly-Anns are dressed in raiments of the gayest of colours and are child's play to raise from seed in cool, moist, shady conditions in March or April, using a stiffish compost with more loam and less peat than in the J.I. compost. Alternatively young growing plants can be bought at no large expense.

Standing somewhat apart from others is a fetching polyanthus primrose called 'Garryarde Guinevere', with richly bronzed leaves and large pink flowers; easily lost unless frequently divided.

Polly-Anns need careful planting. Put them in a bit deepish, but without covering the crown. The best time is early September. To my eye they always look best in partial shade in informal settings, but they flower better out in the open, provided they never get dry. I loathe seeing them in the solid phalanxes of "bedding" schemes, but one can often compromise. In spring tuck some moist peat under the leaves to cover the surface roots. The worst enemies of the polyanthus are the birds, which mischievously pick off the flowers. There is no better way of defeating them than a line or two of black cotton strained between twigs two inches above the flowers; once the birds' feet have touched what seems to them a treacherous snare they keep away.

All these primrose-style primulas can be propagated by dividing the plant in late May. The robust polyanthus needs frequent division, or else it degenerates into matted clumps. In fact, the finest Polly-Anns come from seeds sown fresh every year or two, which is less trouble than lifting, dividing and replanting.[1]

[1] Anyone who wants to pursue the polyanthus to perfection should get Blackmore and Langdon's little pamphlet on it.

Auriculas. Almost as easy as these Vernales primulas, given the right conditions, is Keats's vestal flower, the chaste and fragrant auricula, the "bear's ear" of yore, which is characterized by its rather thick and fleshy leaves and often by its concentric rings of contrasting colours composed with beautiful symmetry. They are very hardy and are good in towns. Birds, so pestilent to polyanthus, usually leave auriculas alone.

In the poet's day the auricula was ardently venerated by dedicated societies, but today their sort of perfectionism is to be found (although they are quite hardy), only in the greenhouses of a few specialists, in which one may see the most heart-melting creations, often in ethereal greys and greens and dusted over as if with talc powder.

The outdoors gardener is denied these flour-sprinkled creations, but can enjoy instead what are called the "alpine" auriculas (although all auriculas are alpine in origin). Give them a free-draining soil, as on a raised bed, with leaf-soil and plenty of grit, a place in shade or part-shade and plenty of water in summer.

The easiest method of propagation is by the young offsets growing from the base of the plant. In July or August loosen the soil, detach the offsets with a portion of root and pot them up in 3in. pots, two or three round the edge of the pot. Be careful not to give more water than is necessary to keep the soil just moist. Use a normal compost of fibrous loam, leaf-soil and sharp sand.

Auricula seed is slow and erratic in germination. Sow in spring and be careful to cover the seed with only a fine dusting of sand. Keep them cool and shady.

Other primulas in the auricula section are the tiny varieties of *P. pubescens* and *marginata*, such as the lovely 'Linda Pope', which are Sixth Form plants and need alpine conditions, preferably in a greenhouse.

Candelabrum primulas. The candelabrum primulas have an unique beauty of their own as they stand with all the grace of water nymphs near the banks of some stream or in some moist spot in dappled shade. From a basal tuft of crinkly leaves, they send up slender stems encircled by whorls of small flowers rising tier upon tier to the summit, in the manner of a candelabrum. These tiers unfold in succession, so that the nymph has a long reign of beauty. Perhaps the easiest and best known are the tall Bartley strain of *P. pulverulenta*, in tender pink or buff, their stems and leaves dusted with white powder, or the varieties of *japonica*, such as 'Postford's White' and 'Miller's

Crimson', with rather coarse foliage. Another easy one is the rosy *bulleyana*.

Others are not usually so easy. Gold is provided in the 3ft splendours of *helodoxa* and in the new and even better *prolifera* and orange in the glowing, richly coloured *aurantiaca*. Yet others will be found in catalogues. All these you must plant in soils that are at least very damp, where they will freely sprinkle their offspring around them.

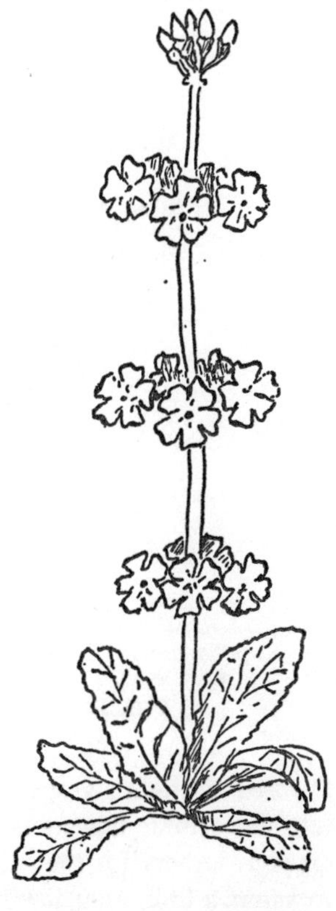

FIG. 31. *Primula japonica*, one of the easier candelabrum primulas, with flowers in whorls.

Sikkim primulas. The handsome Sikkim section, often scented, call for the same damp conditions. These follow the cowslip tradition, with many-flowered bunches clustered at the tops of their scapes or stems. The noblest is *P. florindae*, growing in midsummer sometimes to 3ft or more and topped with huge bunches in soft yellow, dusted with white meal; there are forms in other colours also. It is often seen in shallow water, but is quite easy in any moist soil and is quite happy in sun. The prettiest in my eye is *sikkimensis*, a 2ft beauty with deeper tinted crowns; and the easiest, perhaps, is *alpicola*, in various colours and 15in. high. All these are scented.

Given a soil really moist and cool, the pygmy darlings of the **Farinosae** section are also not difficult. They are ideal for the moist, peaty beds described in the rock garden chapter. Choose first

FIG. 32. A Sikkim primula, *Primula florindae.*

P. rosea 'Delight', a sparkling little charmer of 4in., bursting out into its carmine flowers in April before the leaves, a real little fire-cracker. Others for the same conditions are the wee, sugar-frosted *frondosa*, a Lilliputian jewel with lilac, yellow-eyed primroses dancing on 5in. stems, and the enchanting *involucrata*, with white, sweetly scented florets on 8in. stems in May–June; *frondosa* does not insist on things really wet, but *involucrata* does.

These little Farinosae primulas have no objection to lime but, except for *rosea*, they should be lifted and divided every year.

Outside any of these classes is the very easy drumstick primula, *denticulata*, which brandishes its knobkerries of blue, white or red (as in 'Prichard's Ruby') a foot high in early spring; it will gladly grow anywhere that the polyanthus does.

Departure from these various "primrose paths" may land us into difficult country, some of which is outside my experience. Gardeners who have slightly warmed greenhouses can easily enjoy the delights

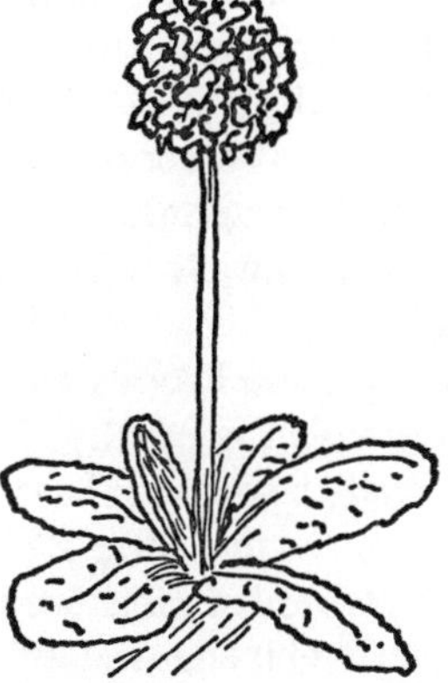

FIG. 33. The popular drumstick primula, *P. denticulata.*

of the pretty winter primulas – *sinensis, kewensis, malacoides* and *obconica.*

Forbes and Hillier have good lists of primulas of all sorts.

Violas and their Offspring

Pansies, violets and the little violettas are botanically all violas, as well as those popularly and confusingly known simply as "viola". While the identity of violets is pretty distinctive, there is often only a vague borderline between some of the modern pansies and the hybrid violas "of gardens". Not that it matters much to anyone but the fancier, who will, indeed, defy the botanist by calling the viola a "tufted pansy". There is no genus Pansy, so those of us who are not fanciers can in turn defy the fancier and call them what we like.

In broad terms we say that the viola of gardens and of catalogues has a tufted, compact habit, with many but not very large flowers, and lives on from year to year if cut hard back after flowering; while the pansy may have very large flowers indeed, as in the fine Swiss

Roggli strain (from Roberts), but has a looser habit and usually a shorter life.

The large, nearly black splodge seen in many pansies is the characteristic of the "Fancy Pansy", fostered so ardently by the pansy societies of Victorian and Edwardian days, but their earlier "Show Pansies" had only small markings or none at all.[1]

Except among a few dedicated practitioners in the north, the old standard of perfection has gone, but today we still have the big, dark, piratical patch (so regrettably disparaged as a "blotch") of the Fancy, but many other strains of pansy, following the Show tradition, are as free of markings and as prodigal of flowers as many garden violas, as in Unwin's well-known 'Clear Crystals' and Dobie's 'Gay Jesters'.

Many of these hybrids are perennials, but the Fancy pansy, with its looser habit, is usually classed as a biennial or even an annual and so really belongs to the last chapter. Its most significant ancestor was the enchanting little *Viola tricolor*, a native of our shores and my own favourite in this beautiful genus.

So much did it endear itself to our forebears that it acquired a very large collection of nicknames, starting, it would seem etymologically, with Spenser's "pretty pawnce" or with the very word "pansy" itself, derived, of course, from *pensées*. We all know that Shakespeare's Ophelia said that it stood for "thoughts", but Chapman's Cornelia said more decisively: "That's for lovers' thoughts." Not far removed from this were other tender or homely nicknames, such as Heartsease, Love-in-idleness, Kiss-me-at-the-garden-gate, Jump-up-and-kiss-me, Cuddle-me-to-you, and so on. Its lovely little elfin face is scarcely to be recognized in its hybrid descendants.

Today the non-specialist may enjoy both pansies and garden violas with carefree ease, raising both in the manner of biennials as I have previously described. There are a few named varieties that come remarkably true from seed, such as 'Arkwright Ruby' and 'Chantreyland', and every seedsman has his own strain with its own characteristics, including some with amusing kitten faces, such as 'Felix' and 'Bambini'.

My first love among the named varieties of the garden viola was 'Maggie Mott', which looks so charming at the feet of standard roses, followed closely by 'Pickering Blue' and 'W. H. Woodgate', all in blue tones, and the yellow 'Moseley Perfection'. Today very few

[1] Not as in the *RHS Dictionary*.

nurseries grow other named varieties, but John Forbes, of Hawick, still maintains a list of twenty or so.

Violas of all breeds expect to have a moist and pretty good soil. They are thoroughly accustomed to living in partial shade, though the pansy and the hybrid viola of gardens will behave splendidly in sun if watered well.

The normal times for sowing these hybrids in the open are June in the north and July in the south, but any time from March to early September will do, resulting merely in a different season of flowering. I prefer to sow in seed-boxes rather than in the open ground. By whichever method, keep the young plants at all stages cool, moist and shady. Beware of slugs when pricking out. Sowings can also be made under glass in January–February.

When the plants come into flower, keep them continuously dead-headed, removing both stalk and spent blossom. When flowering is finished, or nearly so, cut the plants down to 2in. from the ground, top-dress with a little fine soil, sand and peat, and they will probably bloom again.

Besides these jolly hybrids, there are a few garden-worthy species. One is *V. cornuta*, the "horned violet" of old. It is of violet colour in the true wild form, but most people prefer the white one, *alba*, which gives a non-stop production of its perky stars from May till October and agreeably covers the ground with its expanding mats; most charming when gleaming in some shady place.

Most violas of all kinds provide quantities of their own seedlings if wanted, though not all the children will be like their parents. The fancier therefore perpetuates his favourites by cuttings. These are taken from September onwards, 2 to 3in. long, from short-jointed, basal shoots.

Violets are assumed to be *Viola odorata*, though there are other, similar species, not all scented. They are very much perennials, spreading freely in all directions by runners and, indeed, making a good ground cover, quite content beneath trees but if superior flowers are wanted the runners should be removed.

Only a handful of named varieties is readily available nowadays. Three favourites are 'Princess of Wales' and 'The Czar', both sweetly scented and long-stemmed, and 'Sulphurea', also scented but coloured cream (from Forbes). Can be raised from seed in early autumn in boxes in a cold frame, but germination is sometimes erratic.

There are white and pink violets also, and double ones, such as the pale Parma violet and the richly scented 'Marie Louise', a great favourite among old gardeners for growing in frames.

All these can be multiplied from cuttings or, for general garden purposes, by simple division.

The American violet, *V. cucullata,* is scarcely less desirable, but lacks scent and is deciduous, growing from a rhizome. It has large white flowers, delicately pencilled with purple hair-lines, and seeds itself freely.

Violettas are pretty little hybrids said to have originated from a marriage between *cornuta* and a blue pansy. They have a neat carriage, rather small, rounded faces, with an air at once demure and perky, and a very sweet scent.

A little violet of particular note is the Labrador violet (*V. labradorica*). It has beautiful, purple-stained foliage and tiny flowers of true violet hue and is a most engaging little plant. It breeds deliriously, however, forming a dense mat and so can become a nuisance where you don't want that kind of behaviour. I find it a valuable and decorative ground cover among shrubs of various sorts. Flourishes in full shade as in sun.

Rock gardeners have a few small-flowered violas at their disposal. A very pretty one is *V. gracilis.* The flowers are delicately poised over a compact, creeping plant, but unfortunately it is of uncertain perenniality. Longer-lived if kept cut back, are some pretty hybrids in the lavender 'Norah Leigh' (a charmer), the lilac-pink 'Haslemere', the blue-and-gold 'Ardross Gem' (like a big brother of the elfin-faced *tricolor*) and 'Hunterscombe Purple'. Joe Elliott lists some of these; all grow happily in any part of the garden.

CHAPTER 10

BORDER FLOWERS: OTHER CHOSEN RACES

General Selection – And Another Trugful – For Special Conditions

THESE chapters on the herbaceous plants have been arranged separately simply in order to avoid having them all in one large chunk. Some of the flowers that follow would also well qualify for admission to the Elect, according to one's taste.

All but a few are indifferent to lime and all are easy to grow in their appropriate soils, except the fox-tail lily, the Himalayan poppy, the *Lobelia fulgens* hybrids, *Incarvillea delavayi* and *Salvia patens.*

Achillea. The yarrow or milfoil family provides some tiresome weeds, but also some excellent garden flowers with deeply cut foliage. The finest is *A. filipendulina* 'Gold Plate', a commanding border plant, vigorous and easy, carrying on its erect and rigid 5ft stems bold, golden platters, 7in. across, which gleam above the foliage throughout July and August. No staking, except maybe in windy places.

'Gold Plate' has some very well brought-up little brothers. 'Coronation Gold' is a 3ft replica of it with grey leaves and 'Moonshine' is a brilliant, shining, silver-leaved hybrid of 2ft with flowers of soft sulphur; a very distinctive and ornamental plant.

The pale primrose *taygetea,* also 2ft, and the shorter *clypeolata,* with silvery, frond-like foliage, are 'Moonshine's' parents and both splendid plants in their own right, the latter being preferred.

'King Edward' is an 8in. dwarf, of pale sulphur, exceptionally good and usually employed in rock gardens; so also are the pretty little *clavenae,* with ferny, silvered leaves and white flowers, and the yellow *tomentosa.* All pretty miniatures.

Quite different are two red-heads of the common yarrow, *A. millefolium*, named 'Fire King' and 'Cerise Queen', names that disclose their identities. They grow to about 30in. and spread like their vulgar brothers that infest lawns, but not so boorishly.

Even farther removed is *A. ptarmica* 'The Pearl', which produces tufts of white buttons on 2ft stems. Not much catch as a plant, but valued as a cut flower. Known in Elizabethan days as sneeze-wort, the powdered leaves having been used to cause sneezing.

ACONITUM. See Monkshood.

Agapanthus. Curiously nicknamed African-lily, the South African agapanthus is a handsome plant that develops copious sheaves of arching, green straps from which rise thick rods surrounded by large orbs composed of numerous bluebells. You might imagine them to be floral sceptres grasped by some monarch of the garden.

For long the agapanthus was a favourite plant for wooden tubs on baronial terraces and considered tender, but the modern Headbourne Hybrids, bred by the Hon. Lewis Palmer, have proved fully hardy in the open more or less throughout the British Isles. Their heights vary from 18in. to 4ft and their colours from white, through palest blue to violet, displayed in July and August. Most are deciduous; the few evergreen ones collapse in a horrid mess in a hard winter, but sprout afresh in the spring.

The prime needs of the agapanthus are full sun, brisk drainage in a sandy or chalky or gravelly soil and buckets of water in the summer for their thick, fleshy, rhizomatous roots. Heavy, rich soils are unfavourable and manure sickens them, but a feed of bonemeal is good.

Propagate by division in May. Easy enough from seed, but slow and variable.

Alstroemeria. One of the front rank of the border chorus. The brilliant and rampant orange species long familiar in many places (*A. aurantiaca*) has been displaced by the scintillating Ligtu hybrids, which, at a little distance, resemble azaleas in their sparkling array of pinks, flames and apricot, 3ft high. But they expect full sun, a deeply dug soil enriched with organic matter and a situation on the dry side. The brittle, fleshy roots can't stand disturbance, so, instead of buying them from a nursery, it is far better, and perfectly easy, to grow them from seed. Put three seeds in a 5in. pot, sown ¼in. deep. When the seedlings are about 2in. high, plant out the whole ball of soil from the pot with the least possible disturbance, each potful a foot apart. Guard against underground soil pests. Weed carefully by hand only. No staking.

Occasionally the alstroemeria is referred to as the "Peruvian lily" – a pointless name that deserves no currency.

Anchusa. Bushy plants for the back of the border, with tough, bristly stems and enamelled with brilliant blue flowers like large forget-me-nots, 4–5ft. Valuable for infusing the blue influence in May and June before the delphiniums and good for dry soils, being fairly drought-hardy, but very short-lived. 'Loddon Royalist', 'Morning Glory' and 'Opal' are fine varieties. They take up a lot of room, however, leaving an awkward, bare gap after midsummer unless provision is made to mask them.

Propagate by short root cuttings set upright in a sandy compost.

A. angustissima (alias *caespitosa*) is a beautiful 12in. dwarf, massed with brilliant, deep blue from May to July and again later if cut back, but likewise short-lived. Not suitable for heavy clays.

For *A. myosotidiflora*, see Brunnera, in "Second Choices".

Anemone. In this large, versatile and most beautiful family there are many very diverse children. Some are dainty woodlanders or rock plants. Others are the brash gauds of the florist that enliven a winter vase. For the herbaceous border and situations akin to it, only a few concern us.

One is the familiar, hybrid "Japanese" anemone (now *A. hybrida* but often wrongly catalogued as *japonica*). This has slender 3ft stems crowned with salvers of white, pink or rose-mauve in late summer and autumn, particularly striking when planted, fairly closely, in large, bold clusters. Whether in the border or elsewhere, it is of special merit for succeeding in the shade, even fairly dense shade, where the white and pale pink forms gracefully lighten-up the gloom. There they associate delightfully with the taller sorts of campanulas, which are happy in the same conditions and will give light and colour during the long wait for the anemones.

There are many good varieties and there is the beautiful Chinese species *A. hupehensis*, which is a parent of *hybrida* and of which the old, original "Japanese anemone" was in fact a cultivated form. All this breed are slow starters; they hate being disturbed and sulk for the first year. Plant in *spring*, not autumn (unless grown in pots) and label their stations, for they disappear below ground. The tough roots grip firmly, go very deep and are wellnigh ineradicable except by a hormone weed-killer.

Quite different from these immigrants is our lovely native Pasque-flower, *Anemone pulsatilla* ("shaking in the wind"). Also called *Pulsatilla vulgaris*; the botanists don't agree! In April it lifts up purple chalices enriched with golden stamens, on 10in. stems draped with a soft, silken down and arising from a shapely mound of deeply cut foliage. The Pasque-flower is a dweller of chalky downlands and so is accustomed to sun and a fairly dry situation, sustaining short periods of drought with equanimity.

Various colours other than the normal purple are available from some nurseries, should you want them. To my eye the Pasque-flower does not look right in a conventional herbaceous border, nor in the rock garden, but is more suited to small occasional beds or around the feet of shrub roses. Easily raised from seed.

Not nearly as well known as either of these anemones are the beautiful and easy *A. narcissiflora* and *magellanica* 'Major'. In the first the flowers are white, pink-backed and golden-eyed in many-flowered trusses growing to about 15in. in April–May. Full sun and moist soil. In the second the large flowers are of cream, 1ft. Sun or part-shade.

See Chapters 15 and 21 for other anemones.

Anthemis. The little "common camomile" (or chamomile), used of old as an aromatic herb and sometimes today for lawns, is *A. nobilis.* Its larger brethren are very flowerful and cheerful daisy-form plants particularly useful for light, soils, not overfed, flowering from midsummer till September. The best of the lot is 'Beauty of Grallagh'. Do not fail to cut the stems right down to the ground or it will perish.

Less common is St. Ivan's camomile, *sancti-johannis*, an awkward name for a gay and simple plant of 18in. that is massed with bright, gleaming, brazen-yellow daisies from grey-green, deeply-cut foliage. Thoroughly reliable; easy from seed.

Quite different from these is the pewter-leaved camomile, *cupaniana*, which quickly forms expansive mats of deeply incised foliage, massed with white marguerites on 15in. stems in May–June. Like most other silvers, it must have a stony, starved, limy, fast-draining soil and all the sun there is. Plant in spring. Cut the flowered stems hard back and divide in autumn. Not for the colder shires. Often grown in rock gardens.

FIG. 34. *Anthemis tinctoria*, of which 'Beauty of Grallagh' is the best variety.

AQUILEGIA. See Columbine.
ARTEMESIA. See Chapter "Silver and Grey".
ARUNCUS. Included under Spiraea.

Aster. We have noticed the popular "China aster" in the chapter on annuals. A far larger selection confronts us among the perennial, true asters, the most important of which are the Michaelmas daisies, mainstay of the border in autumn. They stand any amount of punishment from neglectful gardeners, but degenerate if suffered to spread into large clumps. Break up these clumps every three years or so, in autumn or spring, replant the strongest of the young, rooted shoots on the perimeter and discard all those in the middle. Otherwise, the only essential attentions are staking and a few squirts of Karathane against mildew (from which the "novae-angliae" section is free) at the end of June and early in August. It is profitable, however, to restrict each plant to three or four stems, rubbing out the remainder in spring.

Besides their formal employment in the herbaceous border, the Micks consort very well with shrubs, having themselves rather a shrubby appearance. Thus they are useful fill-ups while shrubs are still young and to give colour among the established shrubs that have done their dash for the year.

As for named varieties, there is a choice of at least one hundred and fifty on the market. I dislike the very double ones, which look more like footling little chrysanthemums than asters. An aster is not an aster unless you can see the golden eye of its disc. People who are just starting gardening had better avoid also the newer, large-flowered sorts, which are often the most prone to mildew and which need the most staking, getting bowed down by rain. Many of thc old guard, such as 'Harrington's Pink', still confidently hold their own.

The dwarf Micks, hybrids of *A. dumosa*, up to 15in. high, are pretty when at last they come into flower, but rather dowdy all summer and their uses are limited.

Another group of Micks offers us elegant sprays of very small, dainty, starry flowers, delightful for cutting and usually listed under *A. ericoides*. The chosen varieties here are 'Chastity', 'Ringdove' and 'Blue Star'.

Some of the smaller and earlier flowering asters equal or excel those of Michaelmas in grace and beauty. They can stay put for several years without dividing, make beautiful cut flowers, are not prone to mildew and are admirable plants in every way, whether in formal beds or elsewhere. Here are some to note.

The hybrid *A. frikartii*, beyond doubt the most beautiful of all asters. Some 3ft high, it breaks out in July into a profusion of large, lavender ray florets of peacock brilliance surrounding a large, orange disc and goes on till autumn, branching freely. One of the finest perennials we have. The variety called 'Wunder von Staffa' is inferior to the true *frikartii*.

The *amellus* varieties, gay and easy if not in heavy soils. These have big, deep-golden discs and softly brilliant rays, flowering generously from August till October and growing to almost 30in. Plant in spring, not autumn.

yunnanensis 'Napsbury'. A glowing heliotrope with golden disc, nearly 2ft high. Very flowerful and rewarding.

acris (now *sedifolius*). An old-timer of 3ft, with greyish foliage and massed with small, starry florets of soft blue on stiff stems, still esteemed by gardeners who are not bemused by grandeur; there is a nice dwarf form.

Most asters are pretty easy to raise from seed, but will produce a mixed bag.

Astilbe. An elegant and graceful race with feathery plumes in diverse colours, from 6in. to (rarely) 5ft high, often mistaken for spiraeas. The plumes rise from a low mound of beautiful foliage, so that the plants are becoming all summer. Give them a moist and partially shaded station, or else water them abundantly. Give them also plenty of peat or leaf-mould. Increase by division in April.

Astilbes need no staking and lend themselves to forcing in the greenhouse for a spring show, but must afterwards be replanted outdoors. Fine varieties with erect plumes are 'Rhineland', 'Koblenz', 'Etna' and 'Fanal'. Others arch over like ostrich plumes, as in the 4ft 'Betsy Cupreus' and the splendid white 'Professor van der Wielen' (Sunningdale). And do not miss the miniatures, such as the 6in. *simplicifolia* and the 12in., shocking-mauve *chinensis pumila.*

AURICULA. See section on Primulas in previous chapter.
BERGAMOT. See Monarda.

Campanula. No garden is perfectly harmonious without the music of the bellflowers, whether in the formal border, among shrubs, under trees – almost anywhere. They rise in airy steeples hung with bells of cool, clear blue or white, giving lightness and grace to their surroundings. They thrive not only in the sun, but also in dense shade, where the white and pale blue varieties are particularly welcome. They multiply themselves rapidly and most can easily be raised from seed. There are a great many species, as well as cultivated varieties, and from among them we may choose first the following.

The peach-leaved bellflower, *C. persicifolia.* From a basal tuft of leaves, slender rods, like drawn wire, rise steeple-like for some 3ft, hung with carillons of bells in a long succession from early June onwards. The most desirable varieties are the tender blue 'Telham

Beauty' and the white 'Fleur de Neige' or 'Snowdrift'. In my garden they spread themselves freely, coming up everywhere, but I am told that they are less at home in sandy soils. All need a little light staking with 1ft canes, for, though the stems are rigid, they rock at the crown of the plant.

FIG. 35. *Campanula persicifolia,* the peach-leaved campanula.

latifolia is our beautiful native, the broad-leaved giant bellflower, but it is an inveterate spreader and suitable only for the larger scene, where it looks lovely under trees, especially its white form. The soft-purple 'Brantwood' is more restrained and a great joy in the sun with its elegant, elongated bells, standing erectly at 3ft and needing no props.

lactiflora, pale blue and of bushier appearance, departs from the steeple habit and is topped with big, impressive, dense, branching trusses of rather small flowers that recurve in a form more star-like than bell-like, possibly reaching 6ft and needing support in windy places. Nothing is more beautiful than the true species itself, but the shining white 'Alba' is lovely in shade and the heliotrope 'Prichard's Variety' equally so in sun. 'Loddon Anna' is a washy pink, much over-publicized. 'Pouffe' is a miniature of 8in., spangled with lavender bells on leafy mounds, but its stems sometimes splay out flat on the ground, leaving a naked centre. All are excellent in shade or sun.

lattiloba (often called *grandis*) is a species with broadly lobed bells, of which 'Percy Piper' and 'Highcliffe' are splendid exemplars, with densely packed, wind-hardy spikes of deep blue, 2½ft high, growing from an evergreen basal rosette of leaves.

vanhouttei (violet) and *burghaltii* (lilac) have large, elongated bells in the fashion of *latifolia*, but are of floppy habit; 18in.

glomerata 'Dahurica' is a cottager, known of yore as bunch-of-nuts, with overcrowded clusters of violet bells at the top of densely leafy stems of 18in. Hard as nails but not top-class except in a few new varieties, such as the very fine 'Superba'.

Besides these taller campanulas, there are numerous dwarfs which are usually grown in the rock garden, but several of which are entirely suitable for the front row of the border chorus and for various other uses on the garden stage. See Chapter 21.

Closely resembling the campanula is a Chinese bellflower whose buds puff themselves out like balloons before bursting open dramatically in the form of very large, wide-mouthed bells. Very handsome. Normally about 18in. high, flowering in September. There are varieties in blue, white and pink, a more compact one called *mariesii* and a pretty, violet dwarf of 8in. named *apoyama*. These are aptly known as balloon flowers or, to the nimble-tongued, *Platycodon grandiflorus*.

CAMPION. See Lychnis.
CARNATION. See Chapter 11.

Catmint. This favourite old edging plant should be planted in spring rather than autumn at a spacing of a good 15in. A good place for it is in a hot, sunny, dry, starved, sandy or stony soil, as at the top of a retaining wall or a bank or spilling over a stone path. Do not cut down dead growth until spring. Correctly it is *Nepeta faassenii*, but is often wrongly catalogued as *mussinii* (one of its parents, very invasive). The hybrid 'Souvenir d'André Chaudron' has larger, tubular flowers, more richly tinted, but not until July. 'Six Hills' grows to 3ft in a deeper hue.

CHELONE. See under Penstemon.
CHRISTMAS ROSE. See Hellebore.

Chrysanthemums. Several of these in their great variety are entirely suitable to borders and mixed beds, including the Shasta-daisy, the *rubellum* chrysanths and others, but I have included them all in Chapter 12.

Columbine (*Aquilegia*). Few flowers are more charming than these dainty, wing-footed ballerinas dancing on slender stems. They have poise and grace and a carefree air. The most popular are those fitted with very long "spurs", such as McKana's Giants, the Blackmore & Langdon and the Scott-Elliot strains, besides one or two named varieties. Those with short spurs have been aptly known of old as Granny's-bonnets, which I find no less attractive when they are good, as in the beautiful blue 'Hensol Harebell' (a form of the alpine aquilegia) and the blue-and-white dwarf species *glandulosa.*

The gardener who is not in a hurry can perfectly easily raise the most charming columbines from seed sown in June, to flower the next year. They like the sun but prosper also in semi-shade. For the specialist there are also some pretty miniatures for the rock garden and scree.

Coreopsis (or Calliopsis). Besides the annuals of the last chapter there are some perennial tickseeds very suitable for the border or casual beds. They are yellow, daisyform flowers, usually with broad petals nicked on the margins. Though not distinguished, they are jolly and flower without a halt from June to September and in any reasonable soil. The best is:

C. verticillata, which differs from the typical coreopsis in having crowds of slender, pointed, lemon petals, like many-pointed stars, with fine, filmy foliage that nicely matches them. Light, airy and well behaved, needing no prop or stay. To 18in.

Other tickseeds are more robust and inclined to be coarse. In particular, 'Badengold' is to be avoided by all who have rich soil.

CRANESBILL. See Geranium, below.

Dahlia. See Chapter 15. Although not included here, dahlias of all sizes are excellent companions for the border, particularly for masking or filling gaps left by such early birds as the anchusa, doronicum and Canterbury-bell.

Day-lily (*Hemerocallis*). Another vogue-flower, especially in America, where it is ardently fostered. Today we have a very wide choice of colours, but my feeling is that, at any one time, there are too few flowers for too much foliage, which is dense, rush-like, 3ft high and spreading. All the same, day-lilies are easy, hardy, self-supporting and very long-flowering, for new trumpets constantly move forward to replace those that have finished their brief day's fanfare.

To show what they can really do, day-lilies expect rich soil, retentive of moisture, with copious waterings in dry spells, but a place right out in the sun; the notion that they are shade lovers is fallacious. One does see them, however, doing quite well in dry soils, and in the United States *H. fulva* covers vast areas of dry, poor soils. They must be divided about every four years. Plant about 18in. apart. They look well in bold clusters among shrubs, as well as in the border.

New (and expensive) varieties are constantly replacing the old and you have merely to choose the colours that most appeal to you.

DIANTHUS. See Chapter 11.

Dicentra (Bleeding-heart). Also known by such fond names as Lucy Locket, lady-in-the-bath and Dutchman's-breeches, *D. spectabilis* is a creation of wistful elegance extending arching wands from which are suspended strings of nodding pink-and-white jewels for which all its fond nicknames, diverse though they are, are marvellously apt. It is bleeding-heart because it looks like a broken one, forlorn and drooping; Lucy Locket from its resemblance to the little, heart-shaped lockets that nice girls wore on gold chains in the days of my youth; Dutchman's breeches because the baggy trousers on the old canal banks of Holland had the same silhouettes; and lady-in-the-bath because, when the flower is turned upside down you will see the little white lady peeping from her pink tub.

By whichever name you choose to call it, the showy dicentra is a charming and refined adornment of the garden in April, growing 18in. or so from beautiful, delicately cut, blue-green foliage. It must have a moist soil and it shows off its beauty best in some nook of dappled shade rather than in the rough and tumble of the average herbaceous border. No use attempting it in hot, dry soil.

The enemies of the bleeding-heart are the slug and the frosty breath of March, when its pink shoots peer out from the bare earth; so cover the tender crown and the top of the fleshy root with an inch of coarse sand and a blanket of leaves in winter. Mark the position of each plant with a cane or label.

Little sisters of the larger bleeding-heart are *D. eximia* and *formosa*, both 12in. high. Not so appealing as *spectabilis*, but tougher and longer-flowering; *formosa alba* and 'Bountiful' make pretty ground-cover.

All bleeding-hearts make excellent pot plants for the greenhouse. Increase by dividing in February.

Doronicum. Sometimes alluded to for an obscure reason[1] as leopard's-bane, this sturdy cottager is usually the earliest riser in the border beds, opening its large, brassy daisies with the daffodils in late March. Hard as nails, of the easiest culture and spreads freely. The best is *D. plantagineum* 'Excelsum', otherwise celebrated as 'Harpur Crewe', 3ft. 'Spring Beauty' is a good German variety of another species, double-flowered and half that height. Plant these doronicums at or near the back of a border, *not* the front. They prosper almost anywhere.

Echinacea. *E. purpurea* is a moisture-loving plant that gives us large daisies with empurpled crimson ray florets, slightly drooping, springing from a large, dusky disc. The standard variety is 'The King', standing at 4ft on rigidly erect stems, with blooms that may be 5in. wide, like crimson sunflowers. 'Robert Bloom', however, is perhaps a more acceptable plant of 3ft, with flowers of a glowing red-purple. Rich soil in sun.

Eremurus. The "fox-tail lily", sometimes so-called, is a very tall and dignified beauty crowned with enormous plumes of multitudinous little flowers, shooting up on naked stems from a base of long, narrow leaves for a short season in May and June. Expensive and one of the tests of a gardener's skill and fortune, but one that dazzles all beholders when he succeeds. It needs a rich soil in a position protected from wind and, judging by Lady Stern's Sussex garden, revels in chalk.

The eremurus has large, fleshy, starfish-like roots which are extremely brittle and must be handled very carefully. It has a strong

[1] The name of one of its species is Greek for "leopard strangler".

objection to being moved and is likely to sulk below ground in the first year.

Plant the queer-looking object tenderly in autumn on a slight mound, making sure that there is no gap beneath the hollow crown, and with the dormant buds of the crown barely covered with soil. Encase the crown in sharp sand as a protection against slugs. Mark the situation clearly and permanently, so that the roots are never worried by careless hoemanship. After flowering, cut the stems down and gather up the leaves as they wither in July – when you are left with an awkward blank.

The species and varieties of the fox-tail lily are surprisingly numerous. That usually known as *elwesii* and the similar *robustus* may shoot up to 10ft. 'Dawn' is a beautiful, rose-pink hybrid and 'Flair' a bright gold at the end of June, both about 8ft. Perhaps the most generally useful are the Highdown and the Shelford hybrids of 5–6ft, but the deep-gold *bungei* is also beautiful and seldom more than 4ft.

I suggest Hilliers as one of the few sources of a wide range.

Erigeron. Another daisyform genus of the easiest culture and nice for a prominent front position in any border or occasional bed. Usually about 2ft high, with ray florets in shades of blue or pink with a yellow disc, like large-flowered Michaelmas daisies. Chosen varieties are 'Wupperthal', 'Foerster's Liebling' and 'Darkest of All'. They need staking.

Quite different is the engaging little dwarf *E. mucronatus*, a little, pink-tinted daisy with finely chiselled foliage. Sow a few seeds in the crannies of informal pavements and steps. Not suitable for borders or beds.

ERYNGIUM. See Sea-holly, below.

Euphorbia (spurge). The spurges are one of the vogue-plants of today, largely due to the enthusiasm of the flower arrangers, but, as plants, the larger ones lack refinement and can't stand harsh wind. Some spread aggressively by suckers. However, they flourish in the poorest soils, don't mind chalk, fill untidy corners and many grow under trees. Their floral display is made by conspicuous bracts that remain in colour for a long time.

There is a choice of the following, the first three being the nicest.

polychroma. Best of the lot for garden use. Forms a compact, rounded hummock 1ft high, sometimes more, densely shrouded with brilliant gold from spring onwards, before gradually turning green. It is usually held to be synonymous with *epithymoides*, but the RHS botanist (in the *Journal* of May 1967) states that they are not identical, the real *epithymoides* being a less desirable plant of 6in.

pilosa 'Major'. Similar to *polychroma*, but a shade coarser and grows to about 30in.

myrsinites. Of softer colouring. Is a trailer, usually expected to hang down the face of a rock wall. Very nice.

griffithii. Large, regal crowns thickly studded with lustrous garnets, but suckers avidly and is a menace in small places. 'Fireglow' is a cultivar favoured by some. About 30in.

veneta (or *wulfenii*). The one most "written up". Stands 4ft with big, aggressive truncheons of "greenery-yallery". As a plant it is coarse and gross, woeful in winter and not 100 per cent hardy. Cut the stems right down to the base after flowering (if it does).

characias is similar but has a maroon eye; hideous.

sikkimensis. Usually 4ft, sometimes 6ft. Greeny-yellow bracts for much of the summer. Suckers freely and is a flopper.

robbiae. A rampant suckerer to be suffered only in waste, shady places, not too exposed. Shun *cyparissias* even more.

Evening-primrose (*Oenothera*). Besides the biennials noticed in the previous chapter, there are some more beautiful perennials, that stay open all day. Most people will be well satisfied with *O. missouriensis*, which, while growing no more than 9in. high, spreads out along the ground in mats of leafy, trailing stems with long narrow leaves and splashed with huge flowers of a soft luminous yellow unceasingly from June till late August.

Several other excellent evening-primroses offer us more compact little plants, with flowers that are all pretty much alike; the most readily available are 'Fireworks' (*O. fyrvekeri*), 'Cinaeus', 'Yellow River' and 'Highlight' (from Bressingham Gardens).

Something different is a bushy, leafy plant standing at 15in. with large, lemon flowers that open flat. This may be called *O. pilgrimii* or, perhaps more correctly *O. perennis rectipilis*. Very good indeed if you can get it.

Give all these oenotheras a sunny position, not too damp.

FILIPENDULA. Included under Spiraea.

Flax (*Linum*). Besides the annuals, there are some fine border flaxes, blue or yellow, that flower over a long period. They thrive in any reasonable soil but yearn for the sun.

L. narbonense provides multitudes of large flowers in brilliant blue of a shimmering, satiny texture throughout June and July on slender stems some 20in. high. Each blossom is ephemeral but is quickly replaced. The plant deteriorates quickly if the flowered stems are not cut down promptly.

Our native *L. perenne* is a lovely sky-blue on frail 18in. stems. Plant it where the stems can weave through and between other plants.

In contrast, *L. flavum*, 1ft, is a rather woody little bush bearing dense heads of bright yellow flowers freely and continuously nearly the whole summer, but I am told that it is not quite hardy in the north. Smaller still is a lovely pygmy, smothered with large, butter-yellow flowers on 6in. stalks, but in May only. This is 'Gemmell's Hybrid'. Usually regarded as a rock garden plant, there is no reason why it should not be enjoyed elsewhere, if the drainage is good. It tends to flower itself to death, so take some cuttings.

FOX-TAIL LILY. See Eremurus.

Gaillardia. One of the great favourites of the border and the vase, painting the scene with daisyform flowers in blazing yellow, orange, tawny or crimson hues. Give them a soil generously enriched, stake them at an early stage with bushy pea-sticks, and cut spent blooms down to the base of the stalk. Plant in spring, not autumn. Many fine varieties.

Increase by division or autumn root cuttings.

Geranium. Here we speak, of course, not of the summer-bedding pelargoniums, but of the true geranium – the hardy, leafy, herbaceous genus, usually with deeply incised foliage, like outspread fingers, and cup-shaped flowers, often blue or mauve. This is the cranesbill of old, aptly so-called from the very distinctive shape of its seed-pod; a very good name that we could well stick to.

The cranesbills are one of the most valuable plants in almost any garden, whether for the formal herbaceous border, for ground cover under trees (though not all are suitable) or for clothing some awkward corner. Nearly all are as hard as nails, will flower for long periods, need no propping up, will grow in any kind of soil, good or bad, in sun or shade, wet or dry and give no trouble at all. There are some pretty dwarfs for the rock garden or elsewhere.

For a real shocker, grow *G. armenum* (or *psilostemon*), a gorgeous, barbaric magenta-crimson with a wicked black heart, halting the beholder in his tracks. Superlative. Choose its neighbours with care and, for preference, put it next to a grey-leaved plant. To 30in. or more, June–August.

FIG. 36. *Geranium renardii;* pale lilac, pencilled violet, with velvet leaves.

Three other fierce beauties are:

'Russell Prichard'. Bold magenta-pink with grey leaves. Very fine. 1ft. June–August.

ibericum. Violet petals veined with red, on a broad, leafy plant of 2ft.

platypetalum. Similar in purplish-blue, with foliage covered in a grey down; plants sent out by nurseries as *ibericum* are usually in fact *platypetalum.*

From these we turn to quieter colours.

Where a leafy, low but fairly wide-spreading cranesbill of quiet colour is the order, far the best is *grandiflorum alpinum*, with large flowers of brilliant blue. Awfully good as a ground-cover around and beneath shrub roses and other deciduous shrubs.

sanguineum lancastriense. Found on the Island of Walney, this pink variant of our bloody-cranesbill is one of the best and most reliable of dwarf plants. Ground hugging, of almost no height, but spreading moderately with dense, many-pointed, dark-green leaves,

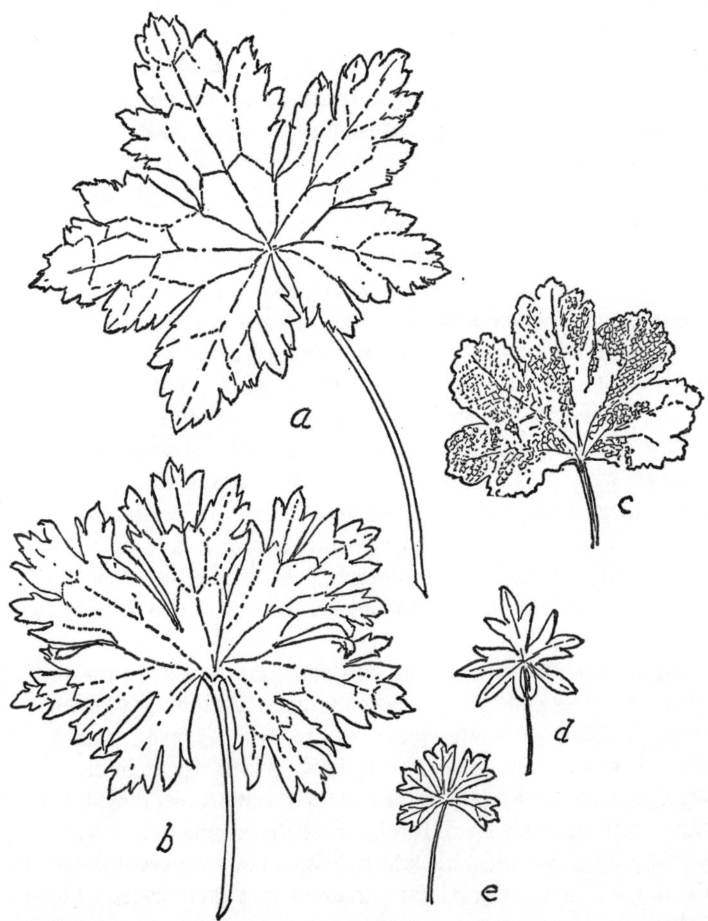

FIG. 37. Leaves of some true geraniums: (*a*) *endressii*; (*b*) *grandiflorum alpinum;* (*c*) *renardii*; (*d*) the Lancaster cranesbill (*sanguineum lancastriense*); (*e*) the Dalmatian cranesbill (*dalmaticum*).

it begins to throw up its salmon cups early in June and goes on for a couple of months. Keep it dead-headed. I have a very nice small-leaved form. The white form of *sanguineum*, known as *alba*, is also a delightful and much neglected plant.

renardii. A plant with a strong individuality, having beautiful, grey-green, felted leaves, not deeply cut but having rounded lobes, and adorned, though in May only, with delightful flowers of palest mauve densely veined with violet hair-lines. Sun.

endressii. Another of the leafy sort, growing 15in., spreading widely and loosely and good as ground-cover, but the flowers of its several varieties are too small and nearly all of washy tints.

dalmaticum. Makes a dense, spreading, most satisfying mat, only a few inches high with flowers of slightly shocking pink.

macrorhizum. Foliage sticky and aromatic when crushed; pink flowers in June only. 15in. Makes a mass of very tough rhizomatous stems and increases very fast; not suitable for small places.

Of all these the most suitable for ground-cover are:

Shade or sun: *grandiflorum alpinum, endressii, macrorhizum.*

For sun: *armenum, platypetalum, ibericum* and 'Russell Prichard'.

Besides these broad, leafy spreaders, the geranium gives us some vivid miniatures, usually classed among rock plants but perfectly suited to any place with good drainage in full sun. Akin in spirit to the stunning *armenum* is a beautiful 6in. savage in brilliant crimson with a black eye, usually seen lurking among boulders like a fierce little guerrilla; this is *cinereum subcaulescens.* It has a pretty sister named 'Ballerina' with a gentle face of lilac-pink, gypsy-eyed and charming, blooming for three months. Smaller still, with a pale-pink face and black anthers is one usually called *farreri.*

Gypsophila. Beautiful for its border effects as well as for cutting. Plant it where its misty shrouds will mingle, like a flung veil, with the flowers and foliage of other plants and you will achieve an enchanting effect. Dig deep, for the gyp's tap-roots go far. Plant in clusters of three, with the crown just below soil level, but protect it against slugs with a quilt of sharp sand. It relishes chalk or lime in any form. The best is still the beautiful old white 'Bristol Fairy', growing 3–4ft, but 'Flamingo', 30in., is good for gardeners and their wives who want pink.

Several dwarf or trailing gyps, normally recruited for rock gardens, can also be put to use with charming effect in the border or

PLATE 7. *Top*: *Campanula persicifolia* forms, self-seeded in one of the rhododendron beds.

Below: *Senecio laxifolius* at the back of one of the heather beds.

PLATE 8.

Left: *Euonymus fortunei* 'Silver Queen' begins to climb the front wall.

Below: The Irish juniper *J. communis* 'Hibernica', with a young plant of the dwarf thuja 'Rheingold'.

in occasional beds as bridal veils for other plants or overflowing little walls of stone or brick. These include:

'Rosy Veil', 9in.; *dubia*, prostrate, pink flowers, bronze foliage; *repens* 'Fratensis', prostrate, pink; *cerastioides*, white with purple veins, prostrate, having some named varieties.

Geum. Known also as avens. Easy old favourite in red or yellow shades rising from a rosette of evergreen leaves irregularly lobed, needing good soil and sun, but no staking and usually growing from 18in. to 24in. The flowering seasons are variable. Reliable varieties are in all catalogues, but two dwarfs are specially good: the fiery orange *G. borisii*, with kidney-shaped leaves, and the hybrid yellow 'Georgenberg'.

The genus include our native wood avens and water avens. The latter, *G. rivale*, is useful for very wet places in 'Leonard's Variety', with nodding, coppery pink flowers from hairy leaves. 1ft.

Some of the named varieties as well as the species are easily raised from seed.

Helenium. Bold, brassy or bronzy daisyform flowers are borne with great profusion to a height maybe of 5ft on plants that develop circumferentially into big clumps, in the manner of Michaelmas daisies. Somewhat coarse and proletarian and needing care in the choice of companions, they are none the less one of the mainstays of many borders throughout August and September. Easy as pie and as hard as nails and usually strong enough to stand erect without props. Plant 18in. apart. Many good varieties in catalogues.

HELIANTHUS. See Sunflower.

Hellebore (*Helleborus*). These are the Christmas and the Lenten roses, so-called, and their relatives. Elegant and expensive nymphs carrying white, pink, green or claret cups in damp, shady woodlands as a rule, though some are quite able to face the sun. They revel in chalk. The hellebores are not, of course, roses and are really winter buttercups. They have no true petals, the "cups" being sepals. There is some fuss and bother about correct names, but I am using those found in the best catalogues.

Earliest of the hellebores to open its buds is the evergreen Christmas-rose (*H. niger*), one of the best-loved of our winter flowers, but not the easiest and must, it seems, have a limy soil. The large, white cups are often stained a watery claret and open very wide, standing some 10in. high above a leathery leafage. The variety or strain 'Potter's Wheel' has huge white flowers, but perhaps the best is the one known in nurseries (wrongly, I am told) as 'Altifolius', with white flowers, sometimes tinted pink, often opening as early as November.

In January, or sometimes at Christmas, comes *atrorubens*, with large, drooping bowls that are deep claret without and green within, standing at 18in. Very soon afterwards comes a sharp contrast in *foetidus*, with small, lolling cups, stained with wine and borne in clusters, a native of damp woods in our chalky downs.

FIG. 38. The lenten hellebore, *H. orientalis.*

Then in February there is our variable native green-hellebore (*viridis*), with very coarsely toothed leaves and nodding, bright green cups for a few weeks. About the same time the much more handsome Lenten-rose (*orientalis*) arrives, dressed in claret, *vin rosé*, cream, white, or green, with coarsely toothed leaves, 18in., flowering for up to three months; the best all-round hellebore of all.

Overlapping all these, and sometimes starting in November, is the robust and scarcely less handsome *argutifolius*, shrub-like and large in all its parts, growing sometimes to 3ft, with spiny leaves and nodding, pallid green flowers in large and opulent clusters. Hardy even in the north of Scotland. More familiar to most of us as *corsicus*, but, if you want to be slap up to the minute, you will call it *H. lividus corsicus* – until it is changed again.

Hellebores are very slow to raise from seed, but they often drop their young about them freely. Propagation by division is not always easy.

HEMEROCALLIS. See Day-lily.

Heuchera. Light, graceful and airy plumes of very small flowers are tossed up from a basal rosette of leaves on slender stems, in the manner of London-pride, though much taller and more impressive. Today there are many fine varieties in pink and red, mostly 2ft or more, flowering from May through to July, such as 'Scintillation', 'Red Spangles', 'Bressingham Blaze' and others from Bressingham Gardens. Of easy culture in any decent soil in a sunny position. Plant rather deeply.

Heucherella. This new genus is the result of marriages between heucheras and two species of *Tiarella*. One of these resulted in the charming 'Bridget Bloom', which throws up filmy clouds of tiny flowers in tender pink to 18in. Very nice.

Hollyhock (*Althaea rosea*). These fine old cottagers are best raised from seed. Sow in the open ground in May or June, prick out to grow on in a nursery bed and station them in their permanent posts in autumn, to flower next summer. They are not long-lived, but seed freely and never look so well as in the odd corners and crannies that they choose for themselves. Traditionally, one plants them close to a wall. There are double and single varieties in diverse colours.

In country districts, but not in the neighbourhood of towns, hollyhocks are prone to attacks from a rust disease, which explains itself. Better burn the plants and grow something else.

HIMALAYAN POPPY. See Meconopsis.

Hosta. Another great vogue-plant, distinguished by bold, neatly tailored clusters of leaves, which are deeply ribbed longitudinally, or variegated in colour or undulating on the margins, and sometimes all three, forming a low, compact mound. Beloved of flower arrangers, some of whom, however, seem to neglect the fact that the hosta has also hyacinthine spires of the most elegant, lilyform flowers.

The herbaceous border is hardly the place for hostas and they look most picturesque in informal locations, especially in light, open woodland, even nestling at the foot of trees, including nooks at the base of the trunk. The soil must be rich and, for preference, damp, though some species seem content with a fairly dry one. They are tidy plants, needing no supports, but may spread fairly widely, when they quickly subjugate most weeds. The usual flowering season is July–August and the average height 2ft. Their cruellest enemies are slugs, which eat holes in their beautiful leaves.

There have been the usual frequent and maddening changes of name, including the name of the genus itself, which was formerly *Funkia*. The following, however, are the most generally accepted names of those most widely available.

H. albomarginata. Leaves are long and narrow, light green except for a narrow white piping along the margins. Mauve lily-flowers borne high. Content with a fairly dry soil, but (it seems) prefers shade and the leaves cannot stand a lot of wind. 1ft. Not quite as good as:

crispula. A hosta of rare elegance and distinction. Leaves dark green, broadly margined with white, handsomely and sinuously waved. Lavender flowers carried high. In full sun the white margin gets scorched. 18in.

fortunei. Bold, broad, heart-shaped, more or less flat leaves of apple-green, above which rise purple scapes (stems) hung with heliotrope funnels. In 'Hyacinthina' the leaves are blue-green, soft and cool, and in 'Albopicta' the young leaves are primrose in the centre, but slowly turn all-green. Good in sun. 2ft.

lancifolia. Leaves glossy, pure green, pointed, spear-like, overlying each other densely, with fine spires of profuse pale-lilac flowers. July–September. 1ft.

plantaginea. A beautiful hosta; large, apple-green, glossy leaves and very large, white, scented, lilyform trumpets of firm, waxy texture. Late-flowering and sometimes shy. 18 to 24in. Best in sun.

sieboldiana (or *glauca*). The most frequently seen of hostas and the most persistently vexed by those who constantly change "the beauteous names of things". It is a very fine creation with very large, broad, thick, heart-shaped leaves, crinkled and ribbed, of a delicate blue-green with a subtle patina. The pale-lilac flowers, which come in June, are dense, but do not always rise far above the foliage. 2ft. The variety 'Elegans' has extra-large leaves.

tardiflora does not flower until September–October and is of dwarf proportions; flowers pale purple, 1ft.

tokudama 'Variegata'. A newcomer. Broad, rounded, striped leaves flushed with a blue sheen.

'Thomas Hogg'. Very like *crispula*, but having blunter leaves and a less regular white margin. 18in.

undulata. A very handsome plant with spectacular leaves which are boldly and crisply waved and finely pointed and in which the whole heart of the blade is heavily splashed with ivory and broadly banded with dark green round the margin – the opposite arrangement

Fig. 39. The Kaffir-lily, *Schizostylis coccinea.*

to *crispula.* The flowers, borne high, are lilac. Its fine variety *erromena* is all green in the leaf.

ventricosa. A very tall plant, Large, dark green, slightly incurved leaves and delightful violet bells, lined white inside. One of the best for flower. Sun. 3ft.

Propagate by division with a sharp lawn-edging iron in winter.

Kaffir-lily (*Schizostylis coccinea*). Specially welcome for cheering up the late autumn, these 18in. flowers grow in the habit of a gladiolus, with many small flowers on a slender stem from grassy foliage. As South Africans, they expect a warm spot in the shelter of a sunny wall, but with a soil that does not dry out. Examples are reported of it growing in shade, but this is not to be advised. They shut up shop in the evening. Plant the fleshy roots in April and see that they have plenty of water in summer. They spread by underground stems. Divide when they get overcrowded. In the colder shires protect them in winter with a quilt of leaves.

The standard varieties are the rose 'Mrs Hegarty' and the pink 'Viscountess Byng', but the latter comes out so late that it needs cloches or a frame to protect the blooms, which can be cut for the vase up to Christmas.

Kingcup or Marsh-marigold (*Caltha palustris*). This old favourite of our native valleys is not a marigold, of course, but a marsh buttercup. Its bright, golden lamps light up the scene in April and May, standing at 10in., and are as easy as you please to grow in any moist soil where you might have primulas and astilbes. Most people want the double form, *C. p.* 'Plena'.

Liatris. Fine border plants that shoot up erect stems developing into long truncheons, densely wreathed with small tassels in bright colours all July and August. No staking. Any deeply dug and well-drained soil suits them, but they like plenty of water. You can choose between the rosy-purple, monstrously named *L. pycnostachya* ("densely clustered") of 4ft or *L. spicata* 'Kobold', a little shorter.

Propagate by division in March–April.

Lily-of-the-valley (*Convallaria majalis*). No need for any description. Not suitable for the herbaceous border and should be planted in shady places (or sunny ones) among shrubs and under small trees, where they will spread densely, forming a close ground-cover, if the soil has been richly cultivated, with ample leaf mould. Disentangle the roots as well as you can and plant the small, white, fleshy tips an inch deep, covered with leaf-mould, and about 6in. apart. They will sulk the first year. 'Fortin's Giant' is a large variety, if you want one; avoid the dirty pink 'Rosea'.

Give them an annual sprinkling of old cow-manure, if you can, or of leaf-soil mixed with a complete fertilizer. When they get overcrowded, lift, divide and replant them immediately after flowering in manured soil.

Limonium is the modern name for what has long been familiar to us all as *Statice*, or sometimes as sea-lavender. The usual one is *L. latifolium* 'Blue Cloud', which throws out large, airy sprays massed with tiny lavender florets on stiff, 2ft stems in August and September with rather coarse leaves. Prettier still, however, and smaller is *L. vulgare* 'George Butler' with dense sprays of gleaming amethyst at 15in. Full sun. Plant in spring. No staking. Good by the sea. For winter decoration indoors, cut the stems before full bloom and hang upside-down under cover for a week or two.

Propagate by autumn root cuttings.

LINUM. See Flax.

Lobelia. The tall, effulgent lobelias of the border are totally different from the pygmy blue bedding annual – and very much more difficult. Growing 2ft tall, they are robed in handsome foliage, sometimes beetroot-coloured, and push up spires of curiously wrought, prick-eared florets of blood-red, purple or pink in August–September. These are the plants catalogued as *L. cardinalis*, but in fact they are usually hybrids of *fulgens*.

Much has been written on the causes for the failure of these lobelias, especially their failure to over-winter. My own recipe is: a rich, well manured, very moist, frequently flooded soil, in full sun, with lots of sharp sand on the crowns against slugs and a dressing of BHC against soil pests. I am told that in the colder counties you should lift and house them in a cold frame in November with as much root as possible.

Plant in spring. Good varieties are 'Bees' Flame', scarlet (from Bressingham Gardens), 'Queen Victoria', blood-red, and 'Purple Emperor' (from Forbes). They need staking.

Propagate by cuttings in close conditions in June or by division in March.

Less sought after is the bright blue *L. syphilitica*, which is overburdened with foliage. In *L. milleri* Mr H. C. Pugsley has raised a promising and apparently hardy strain which bursts forth into all sorts of colours from screaming magenta to muted salmons.

LOOSESTRIFE. For the purple, see Lythrum. The yellow is *Lysimachia vulgaris;* not for choice gardens.

Lupin (*Lupinus*). These are the glory of the border before the delphiniums bloom in mid-June. The modern strain of Russell hybrids has displaced virtually all others and is of easy culture, provided that the soil is acid or neutral and that they are not planted in recently manured beds. Their thick, fleshy tap-roots drive deep, however, so they expect the soil to have been dug a good two spits, with some peat and any humus-making material other than manure. About the only fault of the Russell lupin is that it is short-lived, because the sap of an annual species is in its veins.

Plant to the full depths of the roots; it usually suffices to drive the spade in and work it to-and-fro, so that a V-shaped opening is made. Space them about 18in.

The moment that flowering is over, cut the spikes down to a point a little below the bottom floret, in a fashion not to rob the plant of its foliage. Lateral flower spikes will then develop. Limit the number of spikes in the manner described for delphiniums, allowing only six or seven to a fully-grown plant.

There are quantities of named varieties and new ones come out every year from Bakers, so I shall not attempt to quote any.

First-class plants can also be raised very easily from seed from Bakers. The seeds being hard-coated, nick them lightly as you do sweet-peas. Spacing them out well, sow in boxes 6in. deep from March to May or in a well-prepared nursery bed outdoors in partial shade. When large enough, prick them out into reserved beds or direct into their ordained positions. Those that you may not care for when they first flower can be scrapped.

Lupins can also be propagated by cuttings in exactly the same way as I have described for delphiniums.

For convenience, the tree-lupin (*Lupinus arboreus*) may be mentioned here. This is an excellent, bushy, evergreen shrub, growing very quickly some 5ft high, densely covered with scented yellow blossoms from June onwards and particularly successful at the seaside. There are varieties in mauve and white as well as yellow. Short-lived but easily raised from seed. Sow in pots and plant out when 9in. high; they transplant ill from the open ground.

Lychnis. A pretty and versatile family that serves us well for many purposes, all coming easily from seed.

L. chalcedonica is a bold, erect grenadier, 3ft tall, terminating its stems with orbs of scarlet throughout June and July. One of the things best dotted about singly or in small clusters, when they look like guardsmen among the nurses in the park. No other plant is quite so good for the purpose. Try it among the purple salvias.

Then comes a group of old-time shorties, formerly called *Agrostemma*, which may not perhaps be eligible for the classiest borders, but are very acceptable for informal, cottage-style plantings.

A fine fellow with a long name is *L. viscaria* 'Spendens Plena', the double-flowered catchfly, with sticky stems, native of rocky places in North Wales and Scotland. Rather like a stock, with double, rosy-purple flowers in cymes on 15in. stems in May and June, rising from cushions of grassy foliage. Catalogue names vary, but make sure of the 'Splendens Plena' whatever else precedes it.

L. flos-jovis is the old flower-of-Jove, flower-of-love or pink campion, with charming rose-pink flowers arranged in little clusters like those of a phlox, rising a foot high from soft, grey, velvety leaves. A delightful plant. Space at 10in.

FIG. 40. *Lysimachia clethroides.*

L. coronaria is the rose-campion, a dear old cottager, with stems and leaves sheathed in a pearly grey wool and simple flowers of a deep, velvety crimson, white or rose from June to August. 18in.

We might as well complete the picture by adding that our native cuckoo-flower or ragged-robin, of watery places, with deeply cleft petals that explain the latter name, is *L. flos-cuculi.*

Lysimachia. A family of varied habits that contains one good border plant, which would be widely used by flower arrangers if it were better known. This is *L. clethroides*, a plant with erect stems, 30in. high, with slender leaves and topped by the most amusing and ingenious trusses that bend themselves in the shape of a duck's head, densely packed with innumerable, white, five-pointed stars. July to September. Good, I am told, on chalk.

punctata is a proletarian with a lot of foliage that partially conceals the crowded whorls of undistinguished yellow flowers.

L. nummularia is the jolly little yellow creeping-jenny of cottages, nice for window-boxes and hanging baskets.

Lythrum. The purple loosestrife, quite unlike the yellow, is *L. salicaria*, a gay and easy plant with 4ft steeples thronged with many small pink or red florets throughout July and August. For moist soils in shady places and very fine indeed at the waterside. Has done well for me in full sun also, but with ample watering. Standard varieties are the carmine 'The Beacon', the rose 'Prichard's Variety' and the clear pink 'Robert' of 30in. only.

Meconopsis. The blue Himalayan "poppy" is a divinity that inspires a devoted ardour in all her followers. That graceful carriage, that slightly inclined head, that soft, celestial blue and orange in the poppy-like flower have the beholder immediately in thrall. But *Meconopsis betonicifolia* (still sometimes called *baileyi*) is exacting in any garden that does not provide the right environment, as so many gardens in Scotland do. A shady, cool, woodland situation and a moist, acid soil, deep in the accumulated leaf-mould of generations, or artificially enriched, are the prime demands.

Furthermore the blue meconopsis is not a true herbaceous perennial (and so has really no right in this chapter). For it is usually monocarpic, meaning that it dies as soon as it has set seed, though strains are reported that are truly perennial. However, we may possibly defeat nature by removing the flower spike the first year after planting (for which the right time is March) and the plant should then develop quite strong crowns and sometime behave more or less as a perennial. Even if this is not done, it will annually drop a litter of its offspring from its own seed, whenever it is truly happy. Protect it from slugs as I have so often described. It will grow anything from 3 to 5ft tall, flowering in May and June.

The Himalayan poppy can be raised yearly from seed sown in autumn or spring in a compost of equal parts fibrous loam, sharp sand and powdered leaf-soil or peat. Merely sow the seed on the surface. Place in a warm, moist greenhouse or frame. After pricking off, however, keep them moist, cool and shaded. The resultant plants may vary a good deal in colour.

A safer bet in average gardens, but yielding a less celestial dividend, is *M. grandis*, a true perennial. The poppy-flowers vary from purple to a good deep blue. In the expensive clone 'Branklyn' they have the vivid hue of the star-gentian (Hillier) and there is a charming cream, flushed pink in the bud, named 'Miss Dickson' (Jack Drake).

Another good bet (given the right conditions) is a hybrid between the above two species named *sheldonii*, a vivid blue, pretty reliable as a perennial, growing to 3ft. (Jack Drake or Reginald Kaye). There are also some hybrids between other species.

MICHAELMAS DAISY. See Aster.

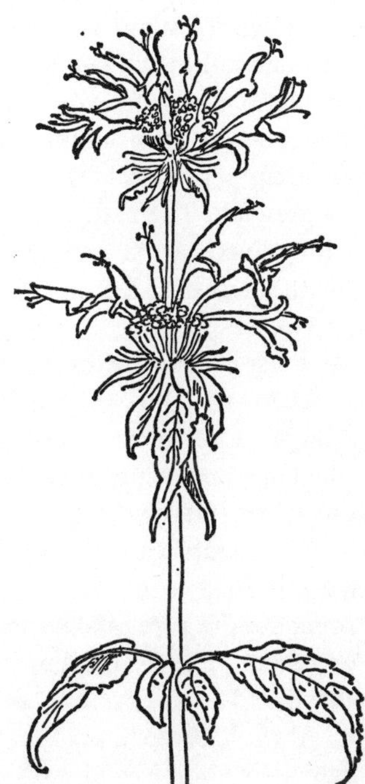

FIG. 41. *Monarda didyma.*

Monarda. An old-world plant with aromatic leaves and curiously wrought flowers of audacious colours, which girdle the stems in whorls and crown the tips. Blooms prodigiously from July to September to a height of 4ft. The dazzling 'Cambridge Scarlet' is the best known, but 'Croftway Pink' is a softer colour, and there is a whole range in other shades. A splendid substitute where phloxes fail, but not long-living. Needs a moist soil or generous watering and mulching and is a success in town gardens. Top-dress in spring with an inch of fine soil and bonemeal after the shoots emerge. Easy from seed. Is *M. didyma*, the bee-balm. Another species is the bergamot, a name sometimes used for any monarda.

Mullein (*Verbascum*). Also known of old as Aaron's-rod. We are back here to honest-to-goodness border plants. Though often short-lived, the mulleins are very good value indeed, flowering throughout June and July, with the general deportment of the hollyhock, but branching with upraised arms and, for the greater part, not much above 4ft. The florets follow each other in succession continuously up and down the stems and they consort very well with delphiniums. Any decent soil in full sun will do, including chalk.

The catalogues offer you several choices, but note especially the splendid *vernale*, in gleaming yellow, growing to 6ft, and *olympicum*, towering up pyramidally to 7ft from a rosette of large leaves covered with a grey felt. The many-coloured *phoeniceum* hybrids, though not very long-lived, are a gay surprise and seed themselves about. I wait with interest to see how the pretty new 'Frosted Gold' is going to behave.

The most surprising of all mulleins, however, is *bombyciferum* (alias *broussa*). This remarkable plant forms a basal rosette of very large, silver-grey leaves, from which a flower spike densely sheathed in a pure white fleece and studded with small, yellow flowers, rockets up to 10ft. or more, if the soil is sandy and warm, without the help of any crutches. This is a biennial, quite easy from seed and, once established scatters its own young freely about.

Propagate the perennial sorts from root cuttings in autumn.

Penstemon. These are plants that display longish, tubular bells, usually flared at the mouth, elegantly poised on erect and slender spires. A whole bed or a bold grouping of penstemons is a fine picture, for they are very flowerful, with a long season (but a rather short life) and are much more refined than the antirrhinums, which some of them resemble in stance and habit; but they are of slightly suspect hardiness. They need full sun and a light soil that warms up quickly. Plant in spring.

Apart from John Forbes of Hawick, few nurserymen have a very long list of named border varieties. The most reliably hardy and most readily obtainable are 'Garnet' and 'Firebird' (or 'Schonholzeri'); but 'Rajah' and 'Ruby' are prettier (Carlile's).

For the rock garden, however, and other places in hot, dry soils there are some charming small species, especially the violet *barrettae*, the lilac *scouleri* and the rosy 'Six Hills Hybrid' (Broadwell Gardens).

None, however, makes nearly as fine a show as penstemons grown from seed. There are annual strains, but the perennial ones are best for the exuberance of their flowering. Get a packet of mixed colours, sow in May, prick off into deep boxes and winter them in a cold frame, to plant out next April and to flower all summer. I used to pot them all up separately for the winter instead of leaving them in a box and they made a magnificent show. In the succeeding winter, if it is not a severe one, most of them will hold their own out of doors, but those that most take your fancy can be safely perpetuated by heel or nodal cuttings of young, basal, unflowered shoots taken in August and put into a cold frame.

Quite different from these are the winsome 'True Blue' and 'Blue Gem', on whose 15in. stems enchanting little sky-blue tubes dance with an airy grace; they are not hardy, but Thompson and Morgan have seed for annual raising. Grow them on in pots and do not plant outdoors until late April.

More rarely seen are a few penstemons that have a good record for perenniality, though I cannot swear for their hardiness. They include *deustus*, which, in June–July, has pallid blue flowers on erect, 18in. stems from a base of leathery leaves (Bressingham Gardens) and *diffusus*, with pale purple trumpets from a hummock of foliage.

The species named *barbatus* (sometimes called *Chelone barbata*) catches the eye at shows but is a poor thing in the garden.

Peony (*Paeonia*). A lovely (and expensive) genus whose beauty is all too fleeting. They pay us a short visit in May and June and are gone, though their decorative foliage remains. They flourish in sun or shade, but expect a deeply dug soil, rich in manure or other organic food. They hate being moved and may keep you waiting for a few years before they show how well they can do.

Plant in September if you can, taking care that the crowns are not more than an inch below ground. Plant firmly. Give them a mulch of manure every November, or alternatively of leaf-mould and bone-meal, but keep the manure away from the crowns. The herbaceous border is not really the place for them and they look better in some less formal place.

There is a long list to choose from. My own fancy is for certain of the species, though, being single, their display is short. Two of the most enchanting (but, alas, most fleeting), whose appeal must not be disallowed by their forbidding name, are:

mlokosewitschii (usually called "Mlok") which has huge bowls of lemon, and *cambessedesii*, with delightful, small flowers of rose, but very early-blooming and not frost-hardy. Both about 18in.

Popular choice, however, leans usually in favour of the extravagantly beautiful Chinese varieties, which may be very double and have a marvellous range of colours. Choose from the catalogues such as appeal to your fancy, but start with the luscious, soft pink, sweetly scented 'Sarah Bernhardt', which is nearly everyone's favourite. Some people still have an affection for the old cottage peonies, which are varieties of *officinalis*, in red, rose, or white, but they cost just as much.

The tree peony, being a shrub, does not really belong to this chapter, but we may as well polish it off here for convenience. The most celebrated and most difficult are the gorgeous hybrids that derive (in all probability) from the national flower of China, *P. suffruticosa*, known as the moutan, its Chinese name. These plants produce (in time) enormous, satin-textured flowers in a rich diversity of colours and of quite superlative beauty in May, but not many of them, on a small shrub that will reach 4ft after several years, sparsely clad with blue-green leaves of stag's-horn design. Nothing is more desirable, but nothing (except the large magnolias) is less suitable to the impatient gardener.

Those who yearn for the short-lived splendour of the moutans should plant them in October and provide them with a good loam, preferably a limy one, in a well-drained spot with a westerly or northerly aspect. Plant so that the swelling made by grafting them on to the stock of herbaceous peonies is buried by about an inch. On no account give them any manure, but mulch them every autumn with rotted leaves.

The moutan is a perfectly hardy plant, but unfortunately the young growths, on which the flowers appear, are not so in our variable climate. A mild spell in late winter starts these shoots into premature growth and a late frost, or even a cold east wind, shrivels them up. This in turn may bring on an attack by a wilt disease, for which the only remedy is to remove the wilted shoots and spray the plant with a copper fungicide.

Other tree peonies that are desirable and are much easier to grow are:

lutea ludlowii, a beautiful yellow, with finely cut foliage, slightly tinted purple, flowering in May and developing unto a luxuriant, finely leaved shrub that will reach 7ft or more. It seems to do better in chalk than elsewhere.

delavayi gives flowers of a very dark burgundy, sometimes almost black. A new variety resulting from the marriage of these twain, with large, lemon flowers, is 'Anne Rosse'.

Thirdly, a series of hybrids between the moutan and *lutea*, giving us many gorgeous creations, of which perhaps the best known are the magnificent yellows 'L'Espérance' and 'Alice Harding'. In some varieties the flowers are so huge and heavy that they fall over.

Sunningdale Nurseries have one of the best lists of both herbaceous and tree peonies.

Phlox. These are the pride and joy of the border in July and August, bearing big trusses of bloom in a handsome range of colours. They are hybrids but usually catalogued as *P. paniculata* (or *decussata*). To do well, they really must have a rich soil and they cry out all the summer for water. They have not much of a chance in sandy soils that dry out quickly. Apart from what is underneath, I mulch them in late spring with both manure *and* peat – the one to feed them, the other to keep them moist and cool. They very much appreciate a little shade. As far as your purse allows, plant them in mass, never in penny packets. Plant them rather deeply, covering the crowns by an inch or so.

There are nearly a hundred named varieties and all you have to do is to pick your choice of colours. Of a different parentage (one of the Arendsii hybrids) is a beautiful lilac phlox named 'Elizabeth', of 2ft, flowering from June onwards (Christopher Lloyd).

In a class by itself is the variety 'Norah Leigh', which is distinguished by foliage that is almost entirely of cream. The very pale-lilac flowers are a perfect complement to the foliage, but the trusses are often small. An attractive but rather capricious plant which, surprisingly, does best in light, sandy soils if well fed.

Border phloxes are liable to be attacked by a stem eel-worm, evidenced by a twisting, distortion and withering of the leaves and stems and a stunting of the plant. There is nothing you can do about it except take some root cuttings, burn the remainder of the plant and start again somewhere else – not on the same piece of ground. Alternatively you can grow monarda instead.

For the dwarf rock-garden phloxes, some of which can quite well be used in the front of the border, see Chapter 21, and for the half-hardy annual *drummondii*, Chapter 8.

PINKS. See Chapter 10. In contrast to carnations, pinks are useful and valuable in the border and in occasional beds.

PLATYCODON. Included under Campanula, above.

POLYANTHUS. Included in Primula, previous chapter.

Polygonum. The impatient polygonums, or knot-weeds, which are always in a great hurry, do not really qualify for our Chosen Races and too many of them are galloping weeds, with leaves like those of docks and sorrel, but the bell-flowered *P. campanulatum* is very useful for filling a shady place of rather poor soil. From a rounded and densely leafy mound it throws up trusses of little, pink bells, branching from wiry stems, 4ft high, all summer. Spreads too rapidly for small gardens but beautiful among trees.

Of other knot-weeds, the rose-red 'Donald Lowndes' is easily the best, spreading rapidly into a low, dense mat, tufted with 9in. spikelets and turning russet in autumn. Very decorative and excellent "ground-cover" in sun. Among rocks, in stony places and on banks, the still dwarfer *vacciniifolium* also colonizes prettily in the same style.

Propagate by division in March. For the climbing polygonum, see Chapter 22.

Potentilla. In this versatile genus there are shrubs, herbaceous plants and rock plants. The herbaceous sorts have strawberry-like leaves with cupped flowers in shades of red or yellow, produced the whole summer long, though never in a large quantity at any time. They are of the easiest culture in light soils that have not been richly fed. They have a floral resemblance to the border geums.

'Etna', 'Monsieur Rouillard' and 'Gibson's Scarlet' are all very attractive and thoroughly reliable; about 18in. See also the rock garden sorts, some of which may well be used in borders and occasional beds. The shrub species are in Chapter 19.

Propagate by division in March–April.

PULSATILLA. See Anemone, above.

Pyrethrum. These florist's favourites, like coloured marguerites, are one of the most desirable of cut flowers, but they are a bit too thin for anything like an herbaceous border and are best grown simply in straight lines in the kitchen garden. They need a richly manured soil. Nurseries usually deliver in spring, so they flower sparsely in the first year. Give them a little staking. For a succession of bloom, keep the flowered stems cut down to the ground. The salmon 'Eileen May Robinson' has for many years been a leading variety, but other good ones will be found in catalogues. Pyrethrums are in fact a species of chrysanthemum (*C. coccineum*).

Multiply by division in *early July*, just after flowering, and water well.

Red-hot-poker (*Kniphofia,* pronounced as in index). These flaming red or yellow torches are very liable to be extinguished unless given sun and a rich, moisture-holding but really well-drained soil, in which there is no danger of water collecting in the crown of the plant. Plant them in spring, feed them generously in the growing season and water them copiously in dry weather. No good planting them in any old soil. Place them with care so that the more strident colours do not quarrel with their neighbours. They look well among shrubs and the autumn species and varieties make a splendid marriage of form and colour with Michaelmas daisies. They are quite first-class close to the sea, being very resistant to wind and salt. The following are worth first consideration.

'Royal Standard'. Scarlet-and-gold, the most reliable and best for general garden use. 3½ft. July–August.

'Bees' Sunset' and 'Bees' Lemon'. The most spectacular. Enormous truncheons. 4ft or more. June–August.

'Buttercup'. Very reliable. 3½ft. June–August.

galpinii. A very fine, elegant, late dwarf. Orange. 2ft. September–October.

'Maid of Orleans'. A beautiful "white-hot-poker", but not bone hardy. Really a soft cream. 3½ft. July–September.

nelsonii. A good dwarf. 18in. Scarlet-and-orange. August–September.

Propagate by division in spring, just as growth begins to appear.

RODGERSIA. See Chapter 23.

Romneya. The "Californian tree poppy" is a splendid, queenly plant, half-shrub, half-herbaceous. It makes a branching bush of 6ft, bearing very large, immaculate, silky white "poppies" adorned with a boss of golden anthers, from July to September, and well set-off by lobed, blue-green foliage. Hardy enough in all but the colder counties. Plant in spring. Multiplies itself by underground runners, and thrives

FIG. 42. *Romneya coulteri.*

even on poor soils, given ample sun and a fairly dry situation. Sometimes reported difficult to get going; order pot-grown plants.

Two species are offered – *coulteri* and *trichocalyx* – but, to the gardener, they are virtually the same. You should cut the plant right down almost to the ground in April. Increase by root cuttings 2½in. long in early spring in a heated propagating box.

Rudbeckia. Daisyform flowers characterized usually by a protruding, cone-shaped central disc and reflexed or drooping ray petals, nearly always yellow. They expect a damp soil or a great deal of water. The tall ones are coarse and rank, and do not qualify for our Chosen Races and they expect the gardener to bolster up their rangy limbs. The shorter ones are more tolerable and 'Goldsturm' is a good, sturdy plant of 2ft in orange-and-black, with star-like petals; *deamii* is similar. The double-flowered 'Goldquelle', 3ft, is also decorative. They have a long season in late summer and autumn. I have ignored the confusing name complications.

FIG. 43. *Rudbeckia fulgida* var *speciosa*, parent plant of some of the best varieties.

Salvia. The sages provide us with some of our most splendid border plants. First choice is *Salvia superba*, a grand 3ft bush that throws up sheaves of erect stems, normally needing no staking and crowded with small bright-blue flowers set off by copper-crimson bracts, which give colour for months and blend happily with the grey-green foliage. It has three very well-behaved small brothers in 'Lubeca', 'East Friesland' and 'May Night', which are excellent in smaller borders. All these make good companions for the golden platters of the achilleas and for the blue-green foliage of romneya. Propagate by cuttings in spring.

For a brief ten days in June a salvia of elegant habit is *haematodes*, luxuriant with lavender branches, 3–4ft, from a base of ground-hugging leaves disfigured by slugs. You grow it from seed and it lives but a few years. For wet places there is *uliginosa*, with fine azure spikes up to 5ft high, but not reliably hardy.

A beautiful, pure, clean Cambridge blue that will certainly entice you at late summer shows, is *patens*, from Mexico. Its wide-mouthed florets look like pieces of a jigsaw puzzle cut out of the sky. But it is not hardy and its tuberous roots must be lifted in autumn with a ball of soil and parked in a box as one does non-hardy chrysanths.

For the superb foliage forms of the common sage, see Chapter 18. For the scarlet bedding salvia, which there is no law to stop you from using, see Chapter 8.

Scabious (*Scabiosa*). Like the pyrethrum, the scabious is essentially a flower for cutting rather than for the border and is most conveniently stationed in the kitchen garden. A creature of chalky areas, it is an ardent lime-lover, but strongly dislikes heavy soils. Plant in spring, not autumn. There is still nothing to beat the fine old blue 'Clive Greaves', but the white 'Miss Willmott' is also beautiful. Do not cut down the dead growth until spring. Renew by basal cuttings in a sandy compost in spring every few years.

SCHIZOSTYLIS. See Kaffir-lily, above.

Sea-holly (*Eryngium*). These are valuable plants for providing diversity of foliage and flower, having handsome, spiny leaves and flowers arranged in dense, conical, bristly clusters, very like teasels, encircled by spiky bracts of bright, metallic hues that often suffuse the stems also. Very variable in height. Good for winter decorations when cut, suspended upside-down and dried. Their need seems to be for a rather light and easily drained soil; avoid rich feeding.

The sea-hollies are available in species rather than in varieties, their names often declaring their colours. A dramatic one, with large, feathery bracts of pale violet is *alpinum*, of 30in.; while *variifolium*, at half that height, is sheathed all over in steely blue (Bressingham). A few, such as the handsome *bourgatii*, need staking.

Propagate by autumn root cuttings, by seed in March or by division. "Miss Willmott's Ghost" (which is *E. giganteum*) has a large, spiny ruff of pale silver, grows 3ft and can be raised only by its very slow seed. It dies after flowering, so is not for the impatient gardener. All prosper at the seaside.

Sedum. An easy-going and drought-resistant race characterized by fleshy leaves and a willingness to grow in poor, stony soils, provided they have sun. It includes our little native stonecrop (*S. acre*), whose bright yellow stars will happily overflow into a gravel path or anywhere else.

Many sedums are prostrate plants for rock gardens or trailing over little stone walls (see Chapter 21), but the following are excellent for the border or for any open, dry place. All flower in densely packed corymbs or cymes.

maximum 'Atropurpureum'. Pride and joy of flower arrangers and of gardeners with a discerning eye. Thick, leathery leaves and stems of a wonderful mahogany crowned with dusky-pink florets which are so-so. A most handsome plant, 18in.

alboroseum 'Foliis Medio-variegatis'. A frightening name for a beautiful plant with remarkable leaves, almost wholly primrose, and pallid flowers. God's gift to arrangers and lovely in a border. An old plant brought back into fashion, 15in. (Bressingham).

aizoon (or *euphorbioides*) 'Aurantiacum'. For sheer, glittering brilliance difficult to surpass. Leaves and stems suffused bronze, dense clusters of copper buds opening bright gold, 1ft (Bressingham).

spectabilis. The commonest. Pale-green leaves, pink flowers. 15in.

'Brilliant'. Of a deeper pink.

'Autumn Joy'. Magnificent floral domes of dark crimson, going on into October. Not decorous in hot weather. 2ft. Needs staking.

'Ruby Glow'. Wonderful colour, but the stems sprawl when in flower.

SHASTA DAISY (*Chrysanthemum maximum*). See Chapter 12.

Sidalcea. Sometimes called "Greek mallow", this is another very good border genus. Slender, erect stems thickly bedizened with pink or red blossoms like miniature mallows or hollyhocks. If neatly staked with canes, they make tidy and decorative plants from July to September. There are excellent varieties ranging from 2ft to 5ft. Any decent soil.

Spiraea (including *Filipendula* and *Aruncus*). The herbaceous spiraeas of my earlier days have all been expelled from the tents of that tribe by the botanist and ordered to set up on their own. In time we shall have to accustom ourselves to such diktats, but in the meantime most people and many catalogues still call them spiraeas. The shrubs of the same name have been allowed to retain it and are in Chapter 19.

Two new herbaceous genera have now been created. The first

affects the old goat's-beard, which tosses up 4ft plumes frothing with tiny cream flowers in June only; usually considered a plant for a deep, rich, moist, leaf-mouldy soil in partial shade, it succeeds in fairly dry ones also. This was long familiar to us as *Spiraea aruncus,* but is now *Aruncus sylvester.* Amputate the plume when it fades and you are left with a plant that resembles a big fern. There is also a 2ft dwarf, called 'Kneiffii'.

The other genus created embraces all the other border plants long familiar as spiraeas, but now labelled *Filipendula.* All but one like the same moist soils as the goat's-beard.

The nomenclature of filipendulas has become hopelessly chaotic and the unfortunate author is sorely perplexed how best to advise his readers on account of the maddening disparities in catalogues. The best thing is to be on the sure ground of the older names, which the leading nurseries will know; in this I am backed up by a professional botanist of high standing who advises me not to get entangled with *Filipendula,* "except in a general way". So here you are:

Spiraea venusta 'Magnifica'. A regal 6-footer with waving plumes of deep pink. June–September.

S. palmata. A crimson 3ft or more of foaming trusses over palmate leaves. Very fine, especially at the waterside. July-August.

S. filipendula 'Flore-pleno'. This is the old dropwort, like a gracefully drooping feather in cream, nicely matched to the delicate, ferny foliage. The only one of this team that enjoys a dry wicket, including a chalky one.

S. ulmaria 'Multiplex' or 'Flore-pleno'. Our old native meadowsweet in a double form, foaming in cream over ornamental leaves in June–July to 3ft.

S. camtschatica 'Rosea' is a very fine and robust plant, with handsome, fluffy, chocolate-soldier plumes of fawn pink, loftily borne above strong, upthrusting five-lobed leaves. 5ft.

STATICE. See under its modern name, *Limonium.*

Stokesia laevis. A much neglected plant with flowers of rare sculptural beauty. From a dense basal rosette of rather commonplace, but evergreen, strap-like leaves, there rise 12in. stems bearing curiously and delicately wrought blossoms of sky-blue, in which you may see something of the cornflower and something of the thistle, but in which you can also imagine the hand that had the skill to chisel the Passion-flower. A flower to look into closely, not for mass effect. Get the variety 'Blue Star'. July–September.

Thrift (*Armeria*). Most people are familiar with the neat, grassy domes, like green hedgehogs, of these hardy maritime or mountainous cliff-dwellers, surmounted in spring or summer by little drumsticks in pink, red or white. Of the easiest culture, they range from the tight 3in. tuffets of *A. caespitosa*, usually seen in rock gardens, to the 18in. of 'Bee's Ruby', which is appropriate to the border.

In between are the pretty and well-behaved native of our own seashore, *A. maritima*, called also the sea-pink, and various hybrids, also growing to about 6in. The little tufted ones and the maritimes look particularly charming at the edges of pavements and in low rock walls.

Among others that will be found in catalogues, 'Vindictive' and 'Bloodstone', flowering from May–July, will please most people.

Trollius (Globe-flower). These are sublimated buttercups of about 2ft which expect a moist soil, where they will shine like golden lamps in May and June and sometimes later in the summer also. They respond handsomely to a rich soil and succeed alike in sun or in partial shade if given plenty to drink. Charming with forget-me-nots and bluebells. Several excellent varieties are in the catalogues. Increase by division in spring.

VERBASCUM. See Mullein, above.

And Another Trugful

This is a small selection of other herbaceous perennials that may appeal to diverse tastes or suit special purposes. There are plenty more, but one has to draw a line somewhere.

Acanthus. Much favoured as models by old Greek sculptors. Strapping, erect spikes of hooded flowers with a sinister leer (as befitted the morals of Greek gods). The most reliable in this country is *A. spinosus* 3½ft. Suitable for larger gardens. Full sun; rich, deep soil. Protect in the first winter. Good in chalk and at the seaside. If you value your nylons, keep it clear of paths. Propagate by autumn root cuttings, seed in spring or division.

Baptisia australis. Bushy, 4ft plants with spikes of small indigo pea-flowers. Good substitutes for lupins in limy soils that are not too damp.

Bergenia. A vogue-plant. Large, cabbagy, leathery leaves which some people rave over but which usually look morose or tatty in winter. Quite nice sprays of flowers, usually pink, in March. Tough, spreading, rhizomatous roots, a good weed barrier. O.K. in shade and in chalk. The 'Ballawley Hybrid' ('Delbees'), *cordifolia* and *purpurascens* lead the field, but new German ones, such as 'Silberlicht', are creeping up.

Brunnera. Like a dwarf anchusa, with long sprays of vivid blue forget-me-nots in great profusion to 18in. in April–June, after which the leaves grow very large. Full name: *B. macrophylla*; there is a good variegated form, very like a hosta in leaf. Moist soil best. Raise from seed or autumn root cuttings.

Catananche. Nice old plant known to our ancestors as Cupid's-dart, supposedly because Greek women used it as a love philtre. Papery flowers borne abundantly in sheaves all summer (if kept cut down) from a low nest of grassy leaves. Good to dry-off for winter. Best in dry soils. The best is *caerulea* 'Major'. 30in. Propagate by autumn root cuttings.

FOXGLOVE. See in Biennials, Chapter 8.

Globe-thistle (*Echinops*). Bold plants crowned by orbs more like drumsticks than thistles. Useful for dry soils and the seaside. Choose 'Taplow Blue'. 4–ft, late summer. Dry off upside-down for winter decoration. Propagate by root cuttings or division.

Golden-rod (*Solidago*). Most are vulgar and weed-like, but some nice modern ones of modest stature are the pale gold 'Goldenmosa', like wan winter sunlight, 'Lemore' and 'Golden Gates', all about 30in. The very dwarf 'Golden Thumb' is remarkable for dense, green-gold foliage, with 3in. golden tuffets above it; a very pretty plant, but the leaves turn green in autumn.

Helianthus (Perennial sunflower). Coarse, floppy, ragged and thoroughly plebeian. If you must have one, choose 'Capenoch Star' and take anti-slug precautions, 5ft. July–August.

Heliopsis. Another sunflower, usually orange, a slight improvement on the above with neater foliage, but miserable in dry weather, Choose the rich orange 'Patula', 4ft, or semi-double 'Incomparabilis', 3ft. July–August.

Incarvillea. Beautiful but quite a Sixth Form plant. Large, open-throated trumpets, like gloxinias, in May–June, 18in. Must have full sun and a rich, humusy, briskly drained soil. Plant the fleshy roots immediately on receipt, the nose just covered. The foliage dies completely away quite early, so label each spot carefully. The usual one is *I. delavayi* in mauve-pink, but *mairei grandiflora* is more colourful with its orange suffusion.

FIG. 44. Mimulus hybrid.

Ligularia. Formerly included in the senecios, these are large, coarse creatures with big, shaggy, brassy daisies, fit only for damp wildernesses. But there is one elegant 6-footer with black, slender stems like iron rods thickly spangled with slim gold stars over large, broad, coarsely toothed leaves. You take a deep breath and ask for *L. przewalskii* 'The Rocket', a name of suspect validity (Bressingham Gardens).

Meadow-rue (*Thalictrum*). Thin, airy clouds of tiny, mauve florets on slender, tall stems, with delicate foliage, in July–August. The one usually preferred is the 6ft *T. dipterocarpum* 'Hewitt's Double'. Not easy and too dainty for the rough-and-tumble of the border; best in light woodland. Moist, rich soil, with heaps of peat, essential. Plant deeply.

Mimulus (musk or monkey-flower). For damp places, where they will spread like wildfire and may have to be restrained. 'Red Emperor' and 'Whitecroft Scarlet' are dwarfs. 'A. T. Johnson', yellow with red spots, is 18in. and will grow in shallow running water, but does not need it. Plant in spring.

Monkshood (*Aconitum*). Bushy plants with hooded flowers shaped like a monk's cowl, or sometimes like a Grecian helmet, and having a similar habit to the delphiniums, which they follow. Rather a dowdy plant florally, but useful for shady places and for windy ones, having wiry stems. Flowers dull violet to nice light blues and bi-colours and one yellow (*A. vulparia*). Good catalogues will tell you all you need to know.

Poppy (*Papaver*). People with strong nerves are much disposed to rave over the oriental poppy (*P. orientale*). Its huge blossoms, most of them in the fiercest of colours, have a barbaric splendour, but leave behind a sprawling, grizzly mess of decadent foliage, jagged and bristly, that will be an eyesore for months, unless cut to the ground, in which event you have a large gap. Few can stand erect on their own legs. The little Iceland poppies (Chapter 8) beat them hollow.

Pulmonaria. Familiar old dwarf, spreading, cottage plants called "Soldiers-and-sailors", "Spotted-dog" and so on because, in some species, the little flowers open pink and turn blue and because the broad leaves are speckled with white spots. The usual sort, commonly listed as *P. saccharata*, but properly *picta*, has evergreen leaves spotted heavily.

P. angustifolia, a much better plant, has no spotting and fine flowers of intense blue. Good, easy plants in sun or shade. March–May.

Solomon's seal (*Polygonatum*). Arching wands with white, hanging bells in May. For woodland and shady shrublands, not formal borders. The usual one is *P. multiflorum*, 30in.

Tradescantia. Small, three-petalled flowers nestle in over-dense, iris-like foliage. Of its several nicknames Moses-in-the-bulrushes is the most apt. Flowers are fleeting, but successive. Blue, pink, red or white. Very tough roots. Very invasive from seed. Any soil, anywhere.

Valerian (*Centranthus ruber*). Our common native is an excellent garden plant, especially in dry soils, stony places and at the feet of walls. There are deep red and white varieties, 3ft. June–July. Scatter a few seeds here and there and they will look after themselves.

Veronica. Slim, pointed spikes in various hues. Not as a rule sufficiently profuse to justify their ground space, but 'Pavane', 'Barcarolle', 'Minuet' and 'Crater Lake' are all very pretty, not exceeding 2ft. July–August. Of the taller ones, *virginica alba* tapers elegantly to 4ft in August–September with spires of white. The grey-leaved sorts such as 'Wendy' and *incana*, 18in., have their followers.

The nicest veronicas are the dwarfs of Chapter 21. The shrubby ones are now called *Hebe* (Chapter 18).

FIG. 45. Solomon's-seal, for woodland.

Zantedeschia. One of those plants called "arum lilies" by the multitude. Until recently the zantedeschias were called *Richardia* and before that *Calla,* with all sorts of nicknames. They are South African marsh plants and not hardy outdoors in Britain, except for the new 'Crowborough', which is hardy in the south and the cold Cotswolds at any rate. The spathe (the funnel-shaped outer envelope) is snow-white, elegantly furled and recurved at the margin, enclosing the deep yellow, truncheon-like spadix (a densely crowded spike), and grows to 30in., flowering in June–July. Plant the top of the crown 4in. deep in April in an open, sunny place in rich, wet soil. It would be as well to put on a protective blanket of litter in the first winter in the colder areas.

The sumptuous yellow *elliotiana* and *pentlandii* are warm greenhouse plants. The plants take their name from the Italian botanist Zantedeschi.

Venidio-arctotis. This very special hybrid, raised by Suttons by marrying two South African genera, has given us one of the most beautiful and most tantalizing of coloured marguerites. They grow 18–24in., in many brilliant or tender hues, flowering from May till frost. You must get them from Suttons in spring and give them a hot, sunny position in soil that is not too sticky. Plant 18in. apart.

Like so many South African daisyform flowers, they shut up in the evening and even at the passing of a cloud. They can be multiplied only by cuttings of young unflowered shoots in August.

For Special Conditions

As a general guide to gardeners who have to compete with some special conditions of soil or situation, I have picked the following short lists of herbaceous candidates. Of course, due regard must be paid to any qualifications that there may be in the preceding text. For chalk and other limy soils. See Chapter 25.

Damp soils

- Astilbes
- Candelabra and some other primulas (including waterside)
- The border phloxes
- *Monarda didyma*
- Kingcups (waterside)
- Some irises, as shown in the relevant section
- Purple-loosestrife (*Lythrum salicaria*) including waterside
- Goat's-beard and filipendulas, including waterside (both listed here under *Spiraea*)
- Echinacea
- Trollius (globe-flower)
- *Lobelia fulgens*
- Geum 'Leonard's Variety' (waterside)
- Day-lilies (*Hemerocallis*)
- Mimulus (waterside, some in running water)
- Zantedeschia (but in sun)

Dry soils

Camomile
Anchusa
Catananche
Baptisia australis as a substitute for lupins
Valerian (poor and stony)
Sedums (poor and stony)
Euphorbias
Globe-thistle (*Echinops*)
Thrift (*Armeria*)

For Shady places (See also Chapter 25)

Campanulas of several sorts, including dense shade
Nearly all primulas
Lily-of-the-valley, including dense shade
Columbines (or in the sun)
Foxgloves (perennial sorts as well as biennial)
Solomon's-seal (dense shade)
Goat's-beard (now *Aruncus sylvester*)
Japanese anemones
Purple-loosestrife
Astilbes
The leafy geraniums (or in sun of course)
Hellebores (or in sun)
Himalayan poppies (*Meconopsis*)
Bergenia
Hostas (part-shade or sun)
Dicentra (Bleeding-heart), dappled shade
Doronicum (or sun)
Euphorbias (or sun)
Peonies
Phloxes of various sorts
Violas
Tiarellas

CHAPTER 11

PINKS AND CARNATIONS

THE great and lovely *Dianthus* family includes carnations, pinks, sweet-Williams and many other plants of our desiring that have no fancy name but are simply Dianthus so-and-so. Their botanic name, given some 2,300 years ago by Theophrastus, is Greek for "divine flowers", and so may we think them today. They adorn many of the stony places of the earth, loving the sun, not expecting rich food or very much water and, with rare exceptions, having a taste for lime.

In English they have a long and romantic tradition as "coronations", "sops-in-wine", "gillyvors", "cloves" and so on. Why we call certain of them "pinks" no one knows, though various fanciful suggestions have been made. "Carnation" is, with reasonable certainty, from the old name "coronation". To the great benefit of gardeners, the morals of pinks and carnations are as promiscuous as those of the wicked old Greek gods, for they cross-breed freely, so that today the simple species that Theophrastus knew rub shoulders with a multitude of newcomers of divers forms and habits, though fortunately the majority have kept their heady mountain scent and nearly all still wear the steel-blue, grass-like livery of their foliage, so agreeable to the eye in winter as in summer.

We should begin by having a clear idea of the main types into which the vast family has become diversified. They are:

greenhouse carnations, not in my brief;
border carnations;
garden or border pinks of various sorts;
alpine or rock pinks;
sweet-Williams and related hybrids;
other annual and biennial sorts;
wild species, some being Sixth Form plants.

High, Dry and Sunny. In general terms, dianthus, if not intended for winning prizes, will prosper in any reasonable soil (which does not include stiff, yellow clay), on the strict understanding that the drainage is good and that they have ample sun. Nearly all like lime, but are quite happy in mildly acid soils. I grow some of my pinks in the rich soil at the margins of rose beds and others in the sterner stuff beneath crazy paving and they seem indifferent. In moderate clay I mix in lots of Cornish sand and build up the soil about 4–5in. to ensure good drainage. Indeed, "high, dry and sunny" is a rule of life that applies to dianthus as much as to nearly all other plants with silvery or grey foliage (see Chapter 20), though height is not necessary where the soil is light and naturally well-drained.

Better use no peat and certainly no leaf-mould. If the soil is poor or very thin and sandy, dig in plenty of old turfy loam with some bonemeal. If you have any fresh wood-ash, charcoal and burnt earth from the bonfire, work that in also. Better add lime in some form if the soil is acid; I jealously hoard a small store of genuine old lime-mortar rubble. Grit is extremely important, especially in clay soil; you can use limestone chips, Cornish sand, crushed brick or gravel.

A cardinal ordinance is that all dianthus must be planted *firmly* and *not deeply*; the ball of soil should be fractionally above ground level and the earth around the ball should be firmly rammed with the butt of the trowel. Better sprinkle a little BHC dust in the hole against soil pests.

The only other ordinance is to cut the stems of spent flowers low down, either to a point where a new flowering shoot is sprouting or, in the alpine style of pink, to a strong cluster of new foliage.

Propagation is also generally a simple matter. All the popular sorts come readily from seed, though, except for the true species, the result will be a mixed bag. Indeed, the little pinks that most engage my own affection are just selected seedlings of what are called "Allwoodii alpinus". Annual and biennial dianthus, including sweet-William, are, of course, necessarily raised from seed.

To multiply one's stock of the perennial varieties is also an easy matter, but the method for pinks is different from that for carnations; don't ask me why. Pinks are done from cuttings and, in most cases, this is child's play. Do it in late July or early August. Select compact, short-jointed, vigorous shoots that have not flowered, not long lanky ones. Make a razor cut just below one of the plump nodes, strip off the lower leaves with a downwards pull, leaving three or four pairs of fully developed leaves. Plant the cuttings firmly in a very gritty compost, with the lowest leaves just clear of the surface. Proceed as for any other cuttings, keeping the pots out of the sun but avoiding the close, moist atmosphere needed for most evergreens.

Border carnations, on the other hand, are normally increased by layers. This you do in the same season, using young, non-flowering shoots. With a razor-blade or a very sharp knife, make a slit longitudinally up the middle of the stem from the underside, starting just below a node and passing through and beyond the node – a cut of an inch or so in all.

Having reduced the soil to a fine tilth, remove all leaves from the portion of the stem which will be underground, and lay the stem

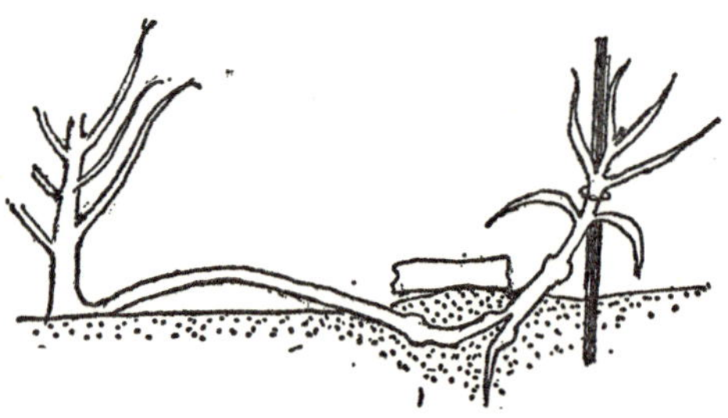

FIG. 46. Layering a carnation.

down in the soil, with the wound gaping and the tongue of the cut projecting downwards. Press in very gently, cover with half an inch of soil, and keep in position with a hooked peg, a special layering pin or a flat stone. See sketch. Some sand at the point of layering helps. Water.

Layers should root in seven to ten days if kept moist, and will be ready for severance from the parent plant in six weeks, but if the weather has been hot and dry, leave them longer; there is no hurry.

After severance from the parent, the layering may be lifted and transplanted; October is best, but spring will do.

Border carnations. By this term is meant hardy carnations of dense petallage that can be grown outdoors instead of in a greenhouse. Be careful about this when ordering, for I have known mistakes to be made. The term does not, however, mean that the right place to grow them is in the herbaceous border, for they are not generally good garden plants, demanding pretty rigid staking. I regard them as plants for cutting, to be grown in the kitchen garden with scabious and pyrethrums, which like similar conditions.

Plant 12–15in. apart, firm and high. Autumn is best. When the plants put on growth stake them with 2ft split canes. Do not "stop" or pinch out the main flowering stems, but some thinning out of the buds is necessary as they develop, even if you don't aspire to exhibiting, and you do this simply by pinching out the small buds that cluster just below the main terminal bud on each stem. Apply a systemic insecticide to keep off the aphis.

Varieties of the "borders" are numberless, new ones constantly replacing the old, so there is no point in my offering suggestions. Consult a good specialist, but don't fall for the latest "new-made gaud". Get established varieties and demand those with a stiff, erect stem, a strong calyx that will not be burst by heavy blossom and those that have a long flowering period. Most people will also demand scent, though this is not to be expected in the yellow varieties.

Cottage carnations are small border carnations. Hardy, easy, gay and flowerful; no disbudding.

Garden pinks. These are innumerable and scarcely definable. They may be like small carnations, densely petalled, or single, having five petals only, or partially double in rosette formation. Usually they grow 9–12in. high; for anything 15in. high or more graduates, we may say, as a carnation. Being often of lax growth, nearly all need staking, of a discreet sort that will not spoil their charm.

There are a few famous strains, such as the hybrid *allwoodii* and the similar Imperials and the laced London pinks of old-world aspect. For profusion of flower the *allwoodii* take the cake, blooming three times or more. The most famous is 'Doris', a beautiful salmon-pink that never stops until November. The finest double white is the *allwoodii* 'Lillian', closely followed by 'Whiteladies' (the right spelling), both of which are far superior to the untidy old 'Mrs Simkins', who bursts her bodice so shabbily. "Show" pinks are a sort of sublimation of the Allwoods, with flowers of charming exhibition form but not so freely borne.

Besides these strains there are all sorts of other garden pinks old and new, but unfortunately many of them have a short season. Some of the best are: the dark-red 'Casser's Pink', growing more than a foot high (from Hilliers), the ice-cool, green-eyed 'Charles Musgrave' (or other variations on the name of Musgrave), marvellously scented, the pink 'Inchmery', the old laced white-and-chocolate 'Dad's Favourite' (not good in clay) and the tall, red 'Highland Queen'.

These garden pinks you can use anywhere – in the border, as marginal plants, in little beds of their own or how you will. Do not dot them about, but concentrate them in bold squads or platoons.

Rock pinks. I use this term as one of convenience only, for the majority can be happily used anywhere about the garden where the conditions are as prescribed. They are miniature editions of the garden pinks, but with a rather stronger emphasis on the single, starry-eyed varieties that so much engage my own heart. All but a few stand erect on their own legs, needing no crutches, at anything from 4 to 9in. high.

Besides the seed strain known as "Allwoodii alpinus", there is also the original *Dianthus alpinus* itself, in rose or cherry, 3in., from seed or from nurseries. A few good and easy named varieties of rock pinks are the gay 'Little Jock', 'La Bourbrille' (variously spelt) and 'Nellie Clarke'. Seed of Little Jock hybrids is sold by Thompson and Morgan.

My own chosen ones, however, would be that dashing and vivacious squad of warlike Lilliputians 'Bombardier', 'Fusilier', 'Grenadier' and 'Mars', handsomely uniformed in scarlet or crimson and alive with *panache*; but you must give them extra good, gritty, almost scree-like drainage and must take cuttings fairly often, for they gallantly flower themselves to death in your service. Not inappropriately. you may match them with the beautiful pink-and-crimson 'Fair Lady' (through Jackman's).

Species. These include kindergarten plants and Sixth Formers. Among the former are:

The Cheddar pink, found wild in the Cheddar Gorge, with quite nice pink flowers, richly scented, 6in. This is *D. caesius*, though an attempt has been made to foist upon it a new jaw-cracking name which is mouthed only by pedants.[1] Best in its double form. Use it freely anywhere in the garden.

The maiden pink (*D. deltoides*). Easy as pie and quite delightful. Prospers in any soil. It has a trailing habit with slim, dark-green leaves and myriads of small, starry flowers in various shades of red. Not long lived, but seeds freely. A magnificent wall plant. Among the several very good varieties are 'Steriker' (from Broadwell Alpines), 'Huntsman', 'Wisley' and 'Bowles Variety'.

arvernensis. Another easy one, being a miniature edition of the Cheddar pink. Good anywhere, especially in paving stones, where it

[1] *D. gratianopolitanus.*

stands a certain amount of buffeting by boots. In a lean, stony soil it forms a compact, dense cushion. 4in.

neglectus. A variable species but noted for the buff reverse to its pretty, rose-red flower. For gritty rock gardens. Mistakenly said to dislike lime, though pure chalk may be another matter.

FIG. 47. Some simple pinks: (*a*) the cheddar pink; (*b*) the alpine pink; (*c*) the maiden pink.

petraeaus 'Plenus'. White, double flowers of the sweetest breath on grey mats. For the rock garden. 9in.

Besides these easier little pinks, there are Sixth Formers, whose place is the scree bed or a trough and which are difficult to get hold of, such as the pale pink *freynii*, the rose-red, densely flowered *simulans*, the pink, pincushioned *microlepis* and the prostrate *musalae*.

Sweet-William (*D. barbatus*). No need to describe our dear old friend nor to sing his praises. We can have red, pink or white varieties, the charming auricula-eyed ones and the dwarf 'Indian Carpet'. Sweet-Williams are hardy biennials and are easily raised from seed by the usual biennial process. Like some other biennials, they leave an awkward gap in the beds when they stop flowering in late July, so have something ready in pots to replace them. Another jolly dwarf, called 'Wee Willie', is a hardy annual, which precociously starts blooming when 2in. high and goes on majestically to 6in.

A pretty child of sweet-William is sweet-Wivelsfield, with larger, looser, slightly shaggy flowers, but the same heavenly breath. This also is an annual, usually treated as half-hardy. Shaggier still is 'Loveliness'.

Annuals and **Biennials**. Besides the sweet-William family, there are several other pinks and carnations in these classes. The leading seedsmen have their own strains of both. I specially recommend:

The Chabaud carnations. Very fine if you get the true seed from a specialist (e.g. Roberts of Faversham). Theoretically perennial, but best treated as half-hardy annuals in most counties, sowing the seed in a little heat in January–February. They have served me splendidly in Surrey in fairly light, warm soil.

The Japanese pinks, so-called (*D. chinensis* 'Heddewigii'), about 9in. high in many gay colourings. A hardy annual, but, for time's sake, best started under glass in March–April. Good for bedding.

Among other sorts, 'Baby Doll' and 'Bravo' are chosen as the prettiest and most charming.

CHAPTER 12

FREE-AND-EASY CHRYSANTHEMUMS

The Country Girls – The Mandarins

"CHRYSANTHEMUM" is botanist's Greek for "the golden flower". Those who know it only as the massive, aldermanic creation of today, whether golden or otherwise, would never recognize in it the simple daisyform wildings of the fields that were its ancestors and are surprised that the ox-eye daisy of our meadowlands and the greeny-yellow feverfew of old cottages are true chrysanthemums. Few flowers have been so transformed, for good or ill, by the hand of man, in this instance Oriental man. Fortunately, the pure daisyforms, with the golden eyes prominently displayed, are still actively cultivated and can be grown in any reasonable soil without any of the fuss demanded by the lordly mandarins.

The most exalted of these mandarins are the October and Late varieties, but, since they expect the luxury of a greenhouse for their maturation, they are outside my terms of reference and to a large extent outside my knowledge. Highly stylized, very sumptuous of their kind, they include varieties with tightly infolded petals, others with outspread, reflexing ones. These and all other specialist sorts are exceptionally well discussed in a very good little book *Chrysanthemums for Small Gardens*, by James F. Smith.[1] We shall, however, have a little to say about those specialist varieties that are known as Early-flowering, since they can perfectly well be grown outdoors in most regions, whether for exhibition or for ornamenting a vase.

[1] Published by Pan Books.

The Country Girls

Before coming to these mandarins, we will look at what I have called the "country girl" chrysanths, which have much interest and charm, are of the easiest culture and take their places best in the herbaceous or other borders. Except for the first, all are totally different from the popular conception of a chrysanth.

C. indicum. This is a seedsman's name for strains that, in form, resemble the shaggier of the mandarins. Doubles and semi-doubles, about 30in. Quite nice.

Annual chrysanthemums. Charming hardy annuals included in Chapter 8.

C. maximum. This is the justly popular Shasta-daisy or King Edward daisy, an extremely hardy perennial with white ray petals radiating from a yellow eye (when not obscured). Almost an essential in herbaceous borders. July onwards. 'Esther Read', 2ft, is the best known, but 'Everest', 3ft, is bolder and purer and 'Ben Lomond', 3ft, has fringed blossoms. The Wirral strain is also good value.

A delightful newcomer is 'Little Silver Princess', which averages about 2ft, with masses of silvery white, golden-eyed flowers, fine for cutting. Easy from seed.

C. rubellum. Elegant, scented, single, rather small, daisyform blooms in great profusion, about 2ft, from September onwards. Hardy and charming. 'Clara Curtis' is a radiant soft pink and 'Jessie Cooper' brick red (Waterer or Hillier).

Korean hybrids. Stocky, free-and-easy, averaging about 2ft. Single and double varieties in many colours, rather mat. September–October. No staking. Jolly and flowerful though not refined. Named varieties from nurseries or seed from Butcher's or Thompson and Morgan.

Pyrethrums. These are actually chrysanths (*C. coccineum*). Somewhat illogically I have included them in "Flowers of the Border".

Marguerites. Here I mean in particular what is also sometimes called the Paris-daisy (*C. frutescens*), a shrubby plant only half-hardy, much favoured for City window-boxes. Outstanding among them is the very beautiful lemon-yellow 'Jamaica Primrose', familiar to visitors at Wisley from July onwards (from Butcher's or Forbes).

Also of marguerite form and also not hardy is *C. foeniculaceum* having big, shining-white daisies and almost thread-like foliage. August onwards.

Feverfew. Our country wench already mentioned. A proletarian with a plain little face, but with foliage that delights people who are not too superior. For the little by-ways of the garden. 'White Bonnet'

FIG. 48. *Chrysanthemum rubellum.*

is a really handsome new cultivar, long in flower, a 2ft plant (Hilliers). 'Golden Feather' is a dwarf much used for the front rank of formal bedding schemes (raise from seed in heat in March and behead the flower buds).

C. haradjanii, the silver-leaved chrysanth. Now rechristened *Tanacetum*. See "Silver and Grey".

The Mandarins

Leaving these country-girl chrysanths, we now come to the first of those highly stylized and sophisticated groups that the specialist gardener tends with such ritualistic devotion. These are the group officially classified as "Early-flowering", meaning August and

September. We enter here a new world, with a jargon all its own, but, following the general spirit of this book, I shall avoid most of the jargon and shall not write for the aspiring exhibitor, which is better done by Mr Smith and others, but for the gardener who likes to grow some good blooms for his house.

The mandarin chrysanthemums (my term, not an official one) are numbered for show purposes in no fewer than thirty divisions, with many sub-sections, but all we need know here are the names used for the various floral styles, most of which are obvious enough. For our earlies the main ones are:

incurved decoratives, with the petals infolded;
reflexed decoratives, the opposite of the incurved;
intermediate decoratives, between the two;
pompons and semi-pompons;
sprays, with clusters of many small blooms.

There are also singles and anemone-centres, for which there is no large following. In the southern counties one may also borrow from the October chrysanths, particularly the elegant, highly sophisticated Rayonnantes, with long, quilled petals, longitudinally rolled, looking like an aristocratic and refined drawing-room spider. Deliriously popular with the arrangers.

Culturally, there is not a great deal to say, the main point being that these chrysanths are gross feeders and need heavy dressings of old (not new) manure or manure substitutes. Plant preferably in the first week of May, at least 18in. apart. Plant firmly, water moderately at first and tie each plant to a 4ft cane. Protect against the ravages of birds with black cotton.

After that the small chores consist of watering when dry, tieing in to the stakes as the plants grow and spraying occasionally with BHC. The main chore, however, is the rather boring one of "stopping" and disbudding; but for our simple purposes this need not be nearly so complicated as that which the exhibitor has to apply to the greenhouse mandarins.

If left to itself, the chrysanthemum will produce a flower bud on its single main stem quite early. This is called a "break bud", because the first branches break out immediately below it. The break bud is valueless and is plucked off at once. Some varieties, however, are slow in developing a break bud, so we accelerate the branching process artificially by pinching out the main stem at the topmost developed leaflet.

To the gentlemen of the fancy the date for this "stopping" is frightfully important, because they have to focus their calculating eyes on the date of the shows that they design to take by storm. To us, however, a good rule of thumb is to "stop" towards the end of May if a break bud does not sprout naturally.

New "breaks" (the fancier's name for growth buds) will now develop into lateral branches in the leaf axils and, in time, there will

FIG. 49. "Mandarin" Chrysanthemums. *Left:* A prepared cutting. *Right:* The "breaks" or lateral branches resulting from stopping, or truncating, the main stem.

be further breaks in the branches themselves. For good quality cut blooms, we confine the number of branches to six or eight by gradually pinching out all excess ones (except as noted in the next paragraph but one).

By late July each branch will have developed a terminal flower bud, which will be escorted by a number of smaller buds clustering beneath it, together with several leafy shoots. Pinch off these excess buds and shoots, a few at a time, with finger and thumb, as soon as they are large enough to handle. This process is what the fancier calls "securing the buds".

Apart from various niceties that affect the specialist, this is all that is necessary. If "sprays" of many small flowers are one's aim, all one needs to do is the first stopping, or one can adopt half-way measures, as I used to do in my chrysanthemum days. The "medium reflexed" varieties are well suited to this informal treatment. Alternatively, one can buy varieties specially cultivated for sprays – now very popular. The pompons need in any case only the initial stopping. The Rayonnantes also are often allowed to make multiple branches, so as to get many blooms of moderate size.

As always, keep your plants well watered in any dry spells. If rain does not descend, give them a good soaking once a week.

For the usual reasons, I refrain from suggesting named varieties. Go to a specialist nursery and tell him the sort of thing you want. The first three classes I have mentioned earlier give the largest blooms, but the poms and semi-poms are valuable for very formal "arrangements" and 'Denise' and 'Jante Wells' are much favoured for window-boxes.

Propagation. In the mildest regions one may leave the plants out all winter and may even allow them to grow on next spring without more ado; but old plants deteriorate and it is better to start with new ones. This you can do in spring by lifting new shoots with their small roots, choosing those farthest away from the main stem, potting them up and bringing them on in a greenhouse or frame.

In districts not mild enough for this carefree treatment the drill is to amputate the main stem at about 12in., cut all the strong, new basal shoots down to the ground and lift what is left of the plant, with its roots. This object is called a stool. Time, November. Pack the stools in deep boxes filled with peat and sand or with loose, gritty earth (not lumpy), water thoroughly and park them in the greenhouse or frame for the winter.

In February, or earlier if necessary, water them again, adding a mild stimulant. About 1st March pot up the new, rooted, outer growths as in the last paragraph.

The more ardent grower will take nodal cuttings from these new basal growths and treat them like any other cuttings.

CHAPTER 13

A BIT OLD-FASHIONED

ONE might well say that "bedding" was hardly a topic suited to a book with the title that this one bears. Though much Victoriana is being revived, nowadays we associate bedding schemes chiefly with public parks or occasionally with the larger private gardens; for they entail an awful lot of labour and, in their prim artificiality, seem out of keeping with modern gardening trends.

Yet there are plenty of people who still enjoy this primness, or at least enjoy the flowers so used, and it is certain that bedding schemes do particularly suit the little front gardens of the towns and suburbs and certain styles of house in the country. Where the plot is small the labour is no burden. Informal adaptations of the bedding ideas can also be applied to odd corners and spare patches of ground. Stone vases, tubs and window-boxes are particularly well furnished by the plants of this class.

Bedding, or bedding-out, is the practice of filling a whole bed with plants, yanking them out when they have finished flowering and replacing them by something else. This treatment is apt to be a bit taxing on the soil, which needs to be restored to vitality, preferably by farmyard manure, between plantings.

There are spring and summer bedding schemes. The spring bed is planted out in autumn. Bulbs usually take first place and there is still, indeed, nothing more lovely than the old, traditional marriage of the pink tulip 'Clara Butt' with the azure of forget-me-nots. You must, of course, lift the tulips and heel them in at the end of the display. Hyacinths put on a production of operatic splendour and may for this purpose be brought more cheaply than the fat bulbs used for bowls. "Polyanthus of unnumbered dyes" and the golden and variegated auriculas also delight the eye with their pageants of colour. So do wallflowers and Brompton stocks. The Siberian wallflower (*Cheiranthus allionii*) will stun beholders with its orange flames.

A Bit Old-fashioned

For summer there is a much larger band of volunteers to pick from. Most famous of the bedders, I suppose, is the pelargonium (or "geranium"), often in dual marriage with the calceolaria and lobelia, but this is a fearfully hackneyed and stereotyped affair. Other outstanding plants for bedding fresh to these pages are the heliotrope of tender associations, the dwarf begonias and plants with white or silver leaves, such as *Senecio cineraria* and *Centaurea gymnocarpa* (Chapter 20). Apart from these and a few others, the leading candidates are found among the half-hardy annuals that we have already reviewed and that need not be further examined. These are:

antirrhinums	French marigolds
scarlet salvias	nemesias
zinnias	ageratums
Drummond's phlox	stocks
petunias	alyssum
verbenas	schizanthus

All can be bedded out from the boxes into which they have been pricked-off as seedlings (in which state they can be bought from garden shops), but if you can get them sufficiently advanced to be grown-on into pots they will unfurl their bright banners all the sooner. You can parade them in rigid regimental ranks in Victorian fashion if you wish or put spurs to your imagination and display them in irregular formations.

A Few Bedding Plants

Begonia. The dwarf, ever-blooming, fibrous rooted varieties of *B. semperflorens* are great favourites in mixed schemes, but of course the tuberous ones are grander, though best kept to themselves. Chapter 15.

Canna. Having seen much of these tall South Americans in tropic climes, I have never thought that they fitted our native scene. In any case, they must have a warm, sheltered climate, a very rich soil and full sun. They ought to grow 5ft high or more and are of use for adding a vertical dimension to usually flat beds. The big flowers, rather like gladioli, may be yellow, pink or red and the big leaves, which are handsome of their kind but out of balance with the flowers, may be green or bronze. Plant the fleshy roots at the very end of May 10in. apart, or grow from seed sown singly in 3in. pots in a high temperature in February, after having soaked the seed in tepid water for twenty-four hours. Plants from Sunningdale or Dobie, seed from Dobie or Thompson and Morgan.

Give them a heavy, protective mulch of straw, branches, etc., for the winter, or else lift them at the end of September and store them in a greenhouse, like chrysanthemum stools, in nearly dry soil. Pot up again in March in 55–60°, water and feed ready for planting out again.

Echeveria. A popular bedder, with elegant sprays of red florets rising 9in. from a rosette of fleshy leaves. Raise from seed as a half-hardy in a fairly high temperature in March and proceed in the normal way.

Feverfew. The greenery-yallery foliage of our old cottage friend, neat and dense, is a good foil to strident colours. See Chrysanthemum chapter.

Heliotrope. "Cherry-pie" is another Victorian favourite back in fashion, valued for its honeyed breath as well as for its imperial colours. An excellent relief for the eye-strain of salvias and the fiercer pelargoniums.

A few nurseries, such as Forbes of Hawick, still supply plants of named varieties; alternatively, although a perennial, the heliotrope can be treated as a half-hardy annual, raised in a fairly high temperature, pricked-off, potted-on, hardened and planted not before the first week of June in the sunniest possible spot. Since they have a bushy habit, you can dot them about if you like, especially among pelargoniums. Water freely. A good seed strain is the deep violet 'Marine' (Suttons, Unwin or Dobie), but there are also strains in mixed colours. Those we grow are hybrids.

If you care to do so, you can lift the plants at the end of September, prune them fairly hard and pop them into the smallest pots that will take their roots and grow them in the cool greenhouse, keeping them on the dry side until February.

Increase by firm, green cuttings, 2in. long, in pots or boxes of very sandy soil in close conditions and winter them in a minimum of 45°.

Pelargoniums enjoy sufficient popularity to justify their own excellent specialist society, curiously called the British Pelargonium and Geranium Society as a sop to the multitude. They are among the most easily cultivated of plants, blooming continuously for months on end, needing absolutely no expertise when grown as garden plants and putting up with almost any condition, except sharp frost. They are perennial, but you need a cool greenhouse to keep them going from year to year. In the soft, western counties, however, they are sometimes left outdoors all winter and may grow very large indeed.

For our general garden purposes pelargoniums drop into the following broad pigeon-holes (which are not the official ones).

ZONAL pelargoniums. So called because most of them inherit the dark ring or zone on their leaves of their chief ancestor, *P. zonale.* These have hitherto been by far the most widely used, but they are being challenged by the —

IRENE pelargoniums, a recent introduction, large, branching and bushy, often with multiple flower-trusses. In spacing you reckon that two Irenes equal three of the normal zonals.

IVY-LEAVED. Very pretty, informal trailers for hanging baskets, window-boxes and tubs or amenable to being tied up to canes to simulate a climber if you care to take the trouble. Derived from *P. peltatum.*

REGALS. Florally the choicest of their race bearing magnificent blooms, usually marked with a very dark patch, often on bushy plants of considerable size; except in warm corners, these must be grown in cool or warm greenhouses.

MINIATURES. Charming little creations, many with beautiful leaves. Delightful in a sitting-room window or in a window-box.

SCENTED pelargoniums, having insignificant flowers and grown for their dense, curled or incised foliage, which, when pinched, puts a chemist's perfumes into the shade.

FANCY-LEAVED. Grown for the many-coloured beauty of their foliage.

The best soil for pelargoniums outdoors is a rather poor one, gritty and stony. Rich soils will boost the foliage at the expense of the flowers. The main reason why they are always grown in small pots in the greenhouse is precisely to starve the roots. Indeed, when the ultra-vigorous Irenes are grown outdoors you plant the pot and all, though with 2in. of soil above the pot. Otherwise, the first need, as always, is good drainage. Full sun is also in the usual recipe but I have seen plenty of zonals and ivy-leaves doing well in partial shade and for the fancy-leaved it is an advantage.

Planting time is again about 1st June. Afterwards there is nothing to do but remove the spent flowers. At the end of September you can lift the plants, pack them in boxes about 4in. deep in slightly moist soil and park them in the cool greenhouse at round about 42°, keeping them nearly dry all winter, then pot up again in spring.

A better practice, however, is to produce new plants every year from ordinary nodal cuttings taken in mid-August. This is a kindergarten job, for the zonals and ivy-leaves will often root well even if just stuck into sandy soil in a shady spot in the open garden. However, it is neater and surer to plant the cuttings in boxes, close together, in a gritty compost, move them on singly into 3½in. pots when they have rooted and harden them off in the normal way in April.

You will soon have more plants than you need and can of course, adorn your greenhouse or sitting-room with them, together with the many other charming styles of pelargonium, where you will keep them in 5in. pots, water them rather sparingly during the summer and give them an occasional feed of tomato fertilizer. You can flower the zonals in the winter also by pinching out all the flower buds that appear in summer, keeping the pots in a sunny frame from June to September and then taking them into the greenhouse.

As for varieties, there is an enormous multitude of the zonals, but the initiate cannot do better than start with established successes such as 'Gustave Emich', 'Orangesonne' and the purple-magenta 'Festiva Maxima'.

Of the Irenes, he might begin with 'Irene', 'Treasure Chest' and 'Toyon'.

For varieties with coloured foliage he can have 'A Happy Thought' (now 100 years old), 'Caroline Schmidt', 'Mr Henry Cox' and the merry 'Mrs Quilter'.

For the ivy-leaved: 'La France', 'Mme Crousse', 'Galilee' and 'L'Elégante', which has prettily variegated leaves.

Though strictly outside our brief, we must spare a brief word for the Regals, for the benefit of people able and anxious to grow them. Provided the greenhouse can be kept to a minimum winter temperature of 42° there is no difficulty at all. They can have a slightly richer compost than the zonals. The main thing is to pinch out the growing shoot at every five or six leaves, and repeat the operation on each of the four new shoots that result. This builds up a shapely plant. Also trim back the spent flower heads to a point of new growth, which will give you a further flowering. Water fairly well every other day. Feed the plants occasionally when in growth with an all-purpose fertilizer and move them on into larger pots each year. After flowering, stand them outside in the sun, but rehouse them before September.

Propagate as for zonals. Late spring cuttings will be in flower by Christmas in 5in. pots.

Well established varieties that will reward the beginner are the celebrated 'Carisbrooke', 'Grand Slam', 'Braque' and the fine new 'Renoir'.

In Riviera climates and in warm nooks elsewhere the Regals will do outdoors well enough in summer and they look elegant in tubs and hanging baskets.

CHAPTER 14

ROSES

As I have written on roses at considerable length elsewhere,[1] I must deal with them here in somewhat short order, rather for the benefit of those who have very little experience, and I shall plunge at once into the heart of the matter without preamble.

Like Cleopatra, the rose is a creature of "infinite variety". She displays her beauty in many forms, adopts many different habits and applies herself to many diverse purposes. We must begin by being clear about these things.

The Shapes and Forms of Roses

Everyone will know what is meant by a bush and a standard rose, but there is less clarity about the larger forms, particularly those that have far-reaching arms.

Ramblers usually produce long, flexible canes and are best used to clothe arches, pergolas and trellis screens, but *not* walls. Their pliant limbs can usually be bent to one's will fairly readily. They have one short and vivid season of bloom, with large trusses of small flowers, and then they are over.

Climbers are too often confused with ramblers and unfortunately many nursery catalogues group them together, but there are sharp differences, though mixed parentage sometimes makes the borderline rather faint. The typical climber has a strong, thick stem, and is not, as a rule, amenable to being bent over an arch but is seen at its best on a house wall or a large screen, well fanned out. It may easily reach the eaves of an average house. After it is established, it does not regularly throw up new canes from the ground, as a rambler does, and the methods of pruning the two sorts are totally different.

[1] *Roses for Small Gardens* (Pan Books).

A special group of climbers are the "climbing sports". These originate from extra long canes that have sprouted by chance on the dwarf bushes and their flowers are identical with those of their parents. They do not bloom until their second season and then on side-shoots. Very few give any bloom after their magnificent display in June.

Pillar roses are simply short climbers, or occasionally short ramblers that do not normally grow more than about 9ft. Their name implies their intended use, but they can quite well be grown on a wall, fence or as large, free-growing shrubs.

Shrub roses are of great value. Again their name implies their chief use and they may be liberally employed anywhere about the garden. They vary greatly in habit and carriage.

Miniature roses are toy models, seductive but sometimes deceptive. They are usually in bush form but you may easily fall a prey to the tiny standards also.

The Breeds of Roses

Our rough method of classification, very far removed from any botanical arrangement, will be directed towards grouping roses according to their *uses*.

Hybrid Teas (HT). These are the roses that most people acknowledge as the queens-regnant of the rose today, with spirally coiled petals that reflex as they open. The HT's have a distinguished drawing-room elegance but the plants have a rigid carriage. Their employment is essentially in formal settings.

Hybrid Perpetuals (HP). Very similar in appearance to the HT's, but only a few are grown nowadays.

Floribundas. This classification was intended to cover a wide range of free-flowering cluster-type roses. In practice today it is usually confined to that race of roses which has resulted from the marriage of the HT's and the older, cottage-style pompon roses called Polyantha (many-flowered). The result is a plant which has exactly the same carriage and bearing as the HT's but which bursts out into large clusters of flowers of moderate size. These great clusters succeed each other in such rapid succession that in some varieties, as in 'Allgold' and 'Red Favourite', the plant is in continuous bloom from June till November and later.

Today, the HT element has begun to take charge over the old pompon to such an extent that in many new varieties we have, in effect, HT roses in floribunda profusion. This process will intensify, for the 'HT-floribundas', as we may call them, are a highly satisfying form of garden adornment.

Polyantha roses, already referred to, are small bushes, or possibly standards, bearing large clusters of small pompon roses more or less continuously.

Species Roses. Strictly, these are roses in their natural state in the wild, or else crosses between them that are regarded in a similar kind of light. They vary immensely in style, habit and size and have personalities all their own. Most of them interest only the specialist, but others, such as *R. primula, moyesii* and *willmottiae*, are adornments to any garden. The majority of the species roses flower only once in the season, but some of them or their descendants play a phenomenally long part in the floral stage, such as the densely bushy rugosas, the exuberant and heavy-scented musks (somewhat removed from true species), and the enchanting Bourbon roses.

"Old" roses is an unofficial term often used to describe the roses cultivated in our gardens by our forefathers. They are totally different from the modern HTs and floribundas, being far less formal in their deportment and having flowers that are spherical or cupped rather than conical, and often densely petalled. As contrasted with the classic HTs, they are the roses of romance and of the great poets, who knew no other. Most play their parts for only a few weeks and need to have their feet adorned by other plants for the rest of the summer.

Rose stocks. This is a convenient place to say that all hybrids are normally propagated by budding the cultivated "scion" on to a root "stock" of a wild species. The quality of this root stock is of the greatest importance to the buyer. His safeguard is to go only to a rose *grower* with a good reputation.

Cultivation

The rose is one of our most willing and gallant triers, and will do well in many soils, but (contrary to popular belief) what it likes best is a medium loam a trifle on the acid side – one that is well drained, well aerated, and easily worked, but which will retain moisture and not dry out quickly in hot spells, as sandy soils do. What it will not stand is waterlogging or very acid peats.

Situation is almost as important as soil. Except for the sorts grown on walls, roses hate being shut in. They are fresh-air fiends, and demand an open situation where the air and the breezes can circulate freely. Apart from the woodland tree-climbers, they also demand sun, and must on no account whatever be directly under trees, but they do not dislike slanting or oblique shade at midday, especially those of orange and yellow shades.

If possible, do not plant roses where other roses have long grown. Soils become "rose-sick". If unavoidable, import some fresh top-soil from elsewhere in the garden or from outside.

Prepare the soil well before planting – a month ahead if possible. Double-dig it according to the canons of Chapter 5. Invigorate both spits with organic matter, but keep animal manure well down, as the roots of a newly planted rose should on no account have direct contact with it. Use broken-up turves freely. In the top spit use plenty of peat with a double handful of bonemeal per square yard.

Planting

The best period is October–November, in the north the earlier the better – but any time up to March will do provided the soil is neither frost-bound nor saturated.

When about to plant, bring out only one or two plants at a time if there should be a cold, drying wind. Look over the roots, cut out any coarse growth in the nature of a tap-root and trim back damaged roots with secateurs. Shorten any unduly long ones; a foot is quite long enough.

Before making the planting hole, observe how the roots lie. Nowadays most nurseries "lay in" their stocks (except for standards) with the roots all pointing to one side. Therefore make your hole in the shape of an open fan but, as you dig, avoid throwing any of the spoil on to the back edge of the fan, especially at the point where you would imagine the handle of the fan to be; for you must be able to see where the level of the soil-bed is and must not deeply bury the point of union of the scion and the root-stock.

Accordingly make the hole about 4–5in. deep at the handle of the fan, where the union will be, and about 6–8in. deep at the outer perimeter, where the tips of the roots will lie. "Offer up" the plant to be sure it will go in comfortably.

Line the bottom of the hole with peat an inch thick, with a sprinkling of bonemeal and mix it lightly with the natural soil. Put in the plant, with the point of union at the handle of the fan and only fractionally below soil level. Spread out the roots well (not always easy).

Now throw in some soil mixed with more peat and bonemeal,

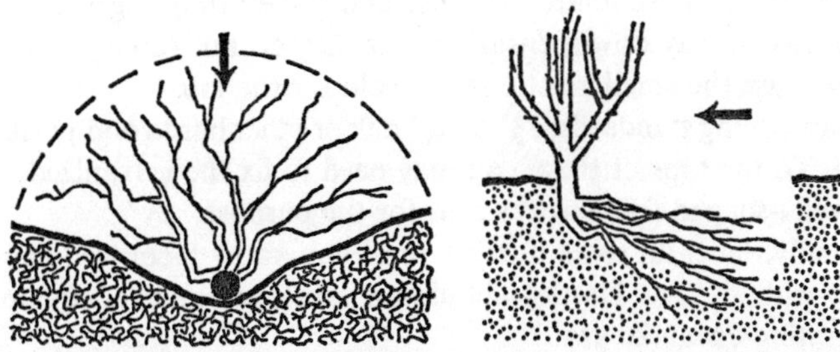

FIG. 50. The "fan" method of planting roses. *Left:* Seen in plan from above. The black ring is the crown of the plant, branches omitted. *Right:* Seen in section, with hole not yet filled in. Arrows show direction of prevailing wind.

making sure that it dribbles in between all the root spaces. If necessary, give the plant a little up-and-down shake.

Partially fill the hole with the natural soil and give the roots a *light* treading in, the extremities first. Then fill up the hole to soil level, *without* any second treading except such as to make sure that the point of union (which should be covered by not more than one inch) is firmly seated.

Standards need a slightly different planting technique. The roots are usually found to be growing circumferentially and often in two or more layers. The hole must therefore usually be a round one and of the right depth for each plant. This you ensure by laying a stick across the hole at natural ground level and offering up the plant.

Standards on *rugosa* stock will usually have two or more layers of roots. Retain the basal one, cut off the upper layers close to the stem and plant with the remaining roots not more than 4in. deep.

Brier stock on standards is recognizable by the fairly smooth stem, with few but larger prickles, usually rubbed off. Plant them to approximately the same depth as the bushes, ignoring the soil mark.

Equally important in planting standards is to have a really strong stake and plant it firmly in the hole before planting the rose. I normally use African hardwood stakes, 1in. square and paint them with the horticultural grade of cuprinol or solignum two months before I plant.

Put the stake in at least a foot deep and firm it decisively when you fill in the hole. The top should be about level with the point of union at the top of the standard. Tie rose and stake firmly together at the top and half-way down, ensuring that they do not rub against each other. I use the small plastic straps sold for the job.

For weeping standards, $1\frac{1}{2}'' \times 1\frac{1}{2}''$ oak or other hardwood posts will serve. To the tops of these you may need to fix the galvanized wire, umbrella-shaped frameworks sold for the purpose.

Finally, label all roses durably until you know them well enough to do without. The Hartley aluminium labels are quite adequate.

Planting distances are:

Bushes of all breedings: in general, 2ft suits for the modern vigorous ones, but those of modest growth, such as 'Allgold', 'Picture' and 'Lili Marlene' will do well at 18in. or even less, while very vigorous ones, such as 'Super Star' and 'Sutter's Gold' need 30in., 'Peace' 4ft, 'Iceberg' 4ft and 'Queen Elizabeth' up to 5ft (for it will grow 9ft high and a good 6ft wide by the third year).

Standards: at least 3ft.

Ramblers: an absolute minimum of 6ft.

Strong climbers: 10ft.

Species and shrubs: according to ultimate spread.

After-care

Pruning and spraying are the most important measures in the after-care of the rose, and these will be dealt with separately.

MULCHING

The thing that is really beneficial is mulching, particularly with manure, peat or the leaves of oak or beech. Use a mulch of manure every two or three years.

FEEDING

If the above practice is followed, the only additional feeding necessary is in early July, when the roses have finished their first flush and need building up for their next. Use any good complete fertilizer, organic or otherwise and lightly prick it in. Occasional watering with a solution of Murphy's Foliar Feed or Maxicrop is also good.

DISBUDDING

The HT's and, possibly, the old roses will need disbudding as they develop. This means simply removing any small flower buds growing

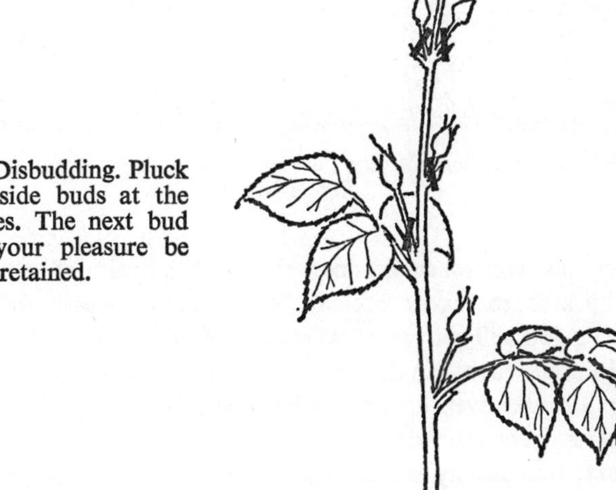

FIG. 51. Disbudding. Pluck out the side buds at the thick lines. The next bud may at your pleasure be retained.

out below the main terminal bud in each branch and threatening to compete with it. Buds appearing a foot or so down the stem may be left. Do no disbudding on other types of rose: floribunda, polyantha, species, climbers and ramblers.

SUCKERS

These insiduous fifth columnists are shoots growing from the wild stock from below the point of union. In a bush or shrub they appear from below ground, but on a standard they may sprout from the stem also. Suckers are recognizable from the fact that the leaves, and probably the thorns also, are quite different from those of the cultivated scion. Characteristically, they have seven or more leaflets to each leaf, instead of three to five (of HT's and floribundas), and are a paler colour, but this is not an invariable guide.

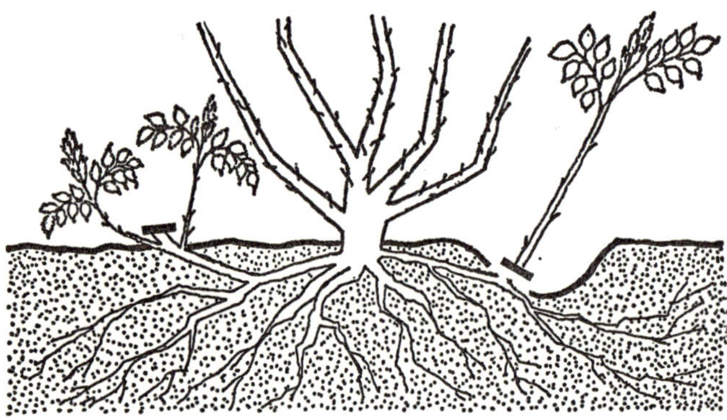

FIG. 52. Suckers. *Left:* Wrong; cut at ground, the suckers break again. *Right:* Right.

You must remove suckers completely at the point of origin on the root by a sharp tug or wrench. Never cut them with secateurs or knife, or you will get two suckers instead of one; so will you also if you do not excavate to the point of origin. This can sometimes be a tough job and even an impossible one when the suckering shoot originates from the side of the plant opposite to that on which it appears; but usually suckers come out easily if tackled when still small.

Pruning

Chapter 7 dealt with pruning generally, and the application of those principles to roses is not difficult, the main question being the degree of severity to apply to different sorts.

The problem is immensely simplified by an understanding of the natural habits of the rose. In a state of nature the rose is constantly throwing up new growth. Into these new shoots it gradually directs its sap, and the older growths become starved out. What the pruner does, therefore, is to hasten the natural rejection of the old wood before it becomes useless and to encourage the plant's instinct for producing ever fresh young shoots; especially does he encourage those from the base of the plant, though in some types new growth does not come readily from the base but sprouts from some point high or low on the existing stem. No rose effects this periodic replacement more continuously than the HT and the floribunda.

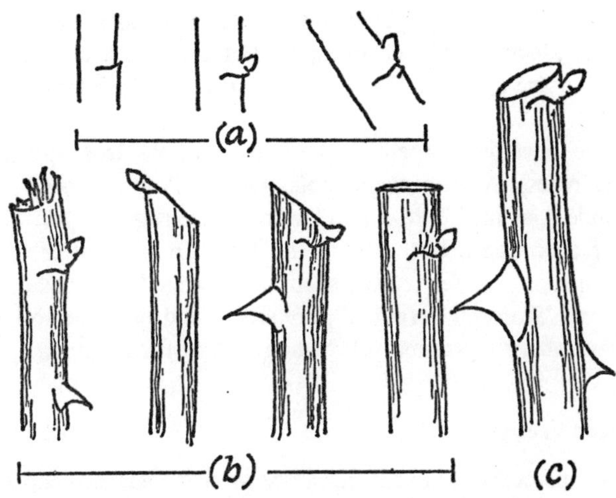

FIG. 53. (*a*) Typical rose "eyes". (*b*) Wrong pruning – jagged, cut below the eye, wrong way, too flat. (*c*) Just right.

That is the sum and substance of pruning in principle, and intelligent observation of the behaviour of each breed of rose will point the way. One will observe, for example, that the true, old ramblers flower on canes which grew last year and which, in their turn, will be superseded next year by other new canes growing now.

There is a lot of difference between pruning for exhibition and pruning for general garden adornment. Be guided by general principles rather than by rules of thumb, but there are certain basic ordinances deriving from these principles. Here again, as in Chapter 7, I divide them into two groups – General Precepts, applicable to all roses and all circumstances, and Particular Precepts, applicable to various types of rose and dependent on the sort of effect you want to achieve. The General Precepts are *in addition* to the General ones of Chapter 7.

General Precepts

Prune harder in the first year than in subsequent ones, spring-planted trees harder than autumn-planted, standards slightly harder than bushes, weak varieties and thin shoots harder than vigorous ones, not so hard on sandy soils as on rich ones.

Invariably cut right out, either down to the ground or, in a lateral, to its point of junction with a sound stem: all *dead* wood, all *diseased* wood and all *feeble*, spindly wood. These are what I call "the three primaries". Whatever other pruning is not done, these are obligatory. Even when the advice is "no pruning", the three primaries must be observed.

Always decapitate spent flowers (the whole truss on cluster-forming roses) as soon as possible. Don't allow any seed-pods to form, unless, as in *R. moyesii* and some of the rugosas, you want the hips for decoration, but, even then, don't do so until the plant is three years old. A few roses, such as 'Mermaid', 'Nevada', 'Frensham', and 'Stanwell Perpetual', are sterile and produce no hips.

Always observe pruning rules when cutting for the house.

Particular Precepts

These are precepts for particular cases or circumstances and are less precise and less peremptory than the foregoing. There is room for manœuvre in personal judgement, opinion and experience. They concern mainly the *degree*, and *times* of pruning for the different types of rose and the building-up of a shapely and decorative plant.

BUSHES, STANDARDS, and SOME SHRUBS, of whatever breeding (including the old roses). Seek to build up a cup-shaped structure, fairly open in the centre. This will give balance to the carriage of the rose and allow the free circulation of air. You do this by always pruning to an outward-pointing eye (except on very lax or prostrate growths) and rubbing out those that point inwards, especially those low down on the stems. Certain shrubs, however, such as the hybrid musks, the Bourbons and the rugosas, are by their nature not amenable to the open cup or goblet shape.

WHEN TWO BRANCHES CROSS, especially on bushes and standards, cut one back below the point of crossing. In some larger shrubs, as again in the hybrid musks, crossed branches are not easily avoided, but it is always important, in all roses, to prevent branches from rubbing against each other or against their supports.

SINGLING OF GROWTH-BUDS. If two or more growth-buds appear in a cluster at one point on a stem, as often occurs after pruning, reduce them to one by the thumbnail.

HTs. In the first season, prune each stem to an outward-pointing

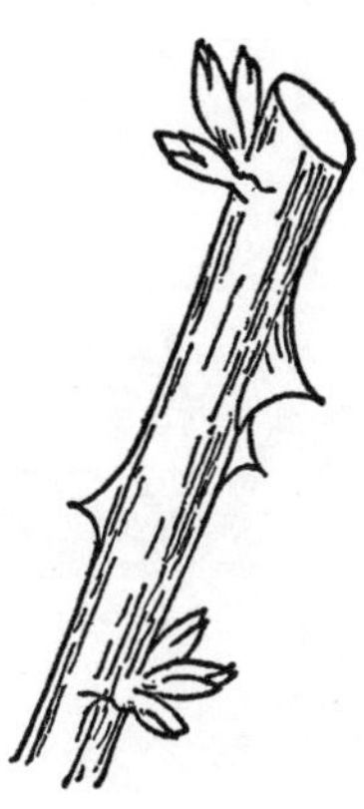

FIG. 54. Singling multiple growth buds after pruning; reduce each cluster to one.

eye about 4in. from the ground. In subsequent years, a good guiding light, after observance of the three primaries, is to reduce annually about one-third of the growth overall; on sandy and lean soils, remove rather less. Any laterals allowed to remain on the basal stems should be cut back to one, two or three buds according to vigour.

FLORIBUNDAS. As for HTs, but rather more lightly. In the first year, cut down to about 6in. from the ground.

OLD ROSES. The same general procedure, but prune more lightly.

SPECIES. No pruning except the occasional removal of old wood according to the extent to which new wood is produced. Some pruning for shape may also be needed.

RAMBLERS and CLIMBERS. Here classifications are not clear-cut and the boundaries of breeding indistinct. Habit of growth must be our guide. In one small group we amputate the stems at 15in. from the ground in the first season (*expecting no bloom that year*) and subsequently we simply cut right down to the ground, in early autumn, all the canes that have flowered and tie-in, as their replacements, the new canes that have been growing in the summer and on which next

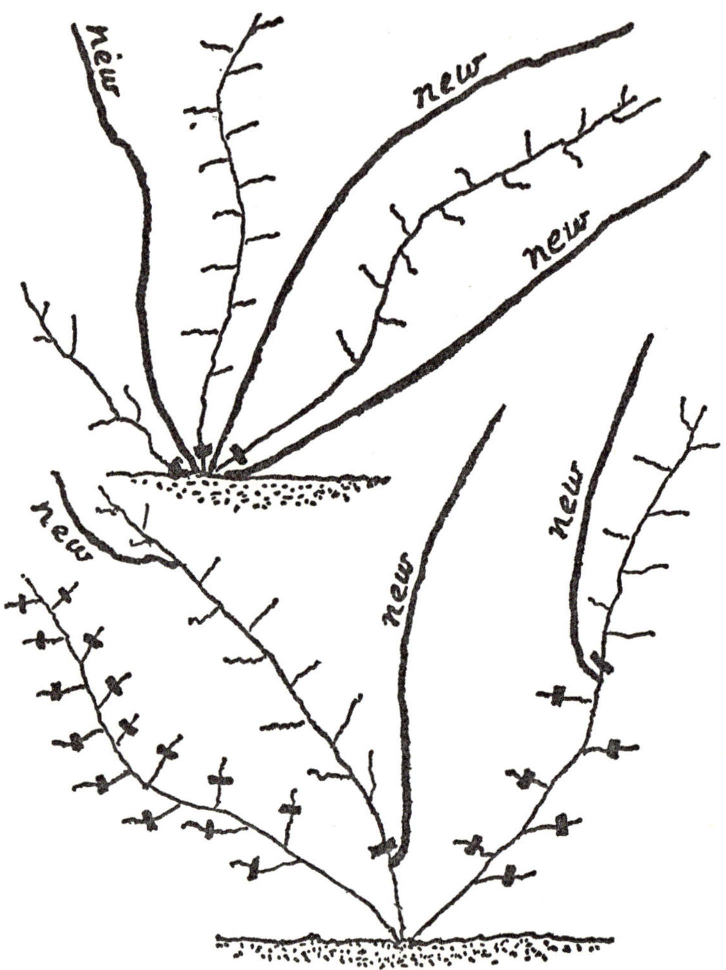

FIG. 55. Pruning rambler and climbing roses. The "new wood" grown in the current season is shown by the long, thick lines, and the old, flowered wood by thin ones. The very short, thick marks are the pruning points. *Top:* A rambler of the 'Dorothy Perkins' habit, with all old, flowered canes cut to the ground (unless no new canes). *Below:* On other ramblers and on climbers in general, prune according to the amount of new wood available to replace the old; on old wood that is retained, shorten the laterals.

year's display will come – in exactly the same fashion as raspberries. This group, now not so popular as of old, includes:

> Dorothy Perkins, Crimson Showers, May Queen, Excelsa, Dr Van Fleet, Sander's White, and (usually) American Pillar and Crimson Conquest.

For the remainder – all climbers and some rambler hybrids – the following formula is intended to simplify the problem on the basis of intelligent observation:

Prune not at all in the season of planting. In subsequent years cut out old, flowered wood in proportion to the extent that new wood is produced. Thus:

(*a*) for every cane springing right from the ground or near it, cut out the whole of an old cane, provided that the plant as a whole is not left too poorly furnished; if, for example, there is only one old cane and one new one, treat the old one as in (*c*).

(*b*) When new canes shoot, not from the base, but from somewhere higher up on an old one, cut the old back as far as the strongest of the new and shorten the *laterals* of the remaining old wood by about two-thirds.

(*c*) When there are no new canes at all, cut back the *laterals* as in (*b*) and shorten the tip.

There are, as always, a few special cases. Thus 'Mermaid', 'Emily Gray' and 'Easlea's Golden Rambler' need extremely little pruning, especially in the first year.

PILLAR ROSES. As for climbers (not as the first group of ramblers).

WEEPING STANDARDS. As for ramblers.

The Time to Prune

It is now the generally accepted practice, in most counties at least, that the right time to prune roses is the same as for any other deciduous shrub that flowers after midsummer – in winter dormancy. I start soon after Christmas.

In parts of Scotland and some other northern counties many growers think it best to wait until the hardest of the winter is over – usually late in March. If in doubt, let the roses themselves be your guide and bring out your secateurs as soon as there are signs of new growth.

The lax ramblers, however, as I have said, are cut back in early autumn, or even before.

The Rose's Enemies

The rose is preyed upon by many insects that relish its sweetness and "feed on its damask cheek". Greenfly suck the sap from young shoots. The spittle-bug in his frothy lair sucks more insidiously because protected. The slugworm delicately chisels out the skeleton of a leaf. The sawfly grub rolls up the leaf like a paper spill. The nimble capsid bug distorts the leaf and eats the bud. The caterpillars of the tortrix moth burrow into the heart of a young bud, the tiny thrip destroys its tissues and the rose chafer consumes the blossom itself.

Fortunately, several of these, particularly the greenfly, formerly the worst of all rose pests, are easily disposed of by the new systemic insecticides. These are sprayed on, or even watered on with a fine-rosed can, and are taken up in the sap of the plant, rendering it poisonous to all suckers and to some at least of the biters also. Very often one application in early May suffices for the whole season, but sometimes a second one is needed in July. I have not seen a greenfly in my garden for years. It acts for many other plants also.

In default of a systemic, there are a dozen or more insecticides on the market, based usually on BHC or pyrethrum. DDT is useless for greenfly.

Far more difficult to deal with are fungus diseases. They are carried by air-borne spores that settle in the tissues of the leaf and can be terribly debilitating, sometimes lethal. They cannot be cured, but can be prevented or arrested. The method of doing so is to spread a film over the leaf, of a substance that will prevent the entry of the spores, but this application has to be repeated about once a fortnight and more often still if there is much rain.

The commonest of the fungus diseases is mildew, which coats the leaves, stems and buds as though with white powder, manifesting itself first in a slight twisting and reddening of the leaf. Ramblers planted against walls catch it terribly. The most widely used correctives are Karathane or Dinocap. Start spraying in May.

Black spot is a terrible scourge in country districts, but seldom gets a hold in or near industrial ones, as the sulphur in the atmosphere protects the foliage. It is manifested by very pronounced black spots, roughly circular and faintly fringed on the perimeter. The danger time comes at the end of June and persists all summer. You have a choice of concoctions known variously as Maneb 80 (Bugge's Insecticides), Dithane (PBI and Shell), Tri-Spot (Rentokil, through Boots) and Orthocide (Murphy). Murphy and PBI both market a concoction for dealing with both black spot and mildew: but we have not yet really got the answer.

Purple spots, usually irregular in outline and the edges clearly defined, is often mistaken for black spot. This is merely a minor malady due to faulty feeding.

Rust is fortunately not a common disease, but when it comes, is a killer. The moist western counties are most susceptible. It comes in July, when the undersides of the leaves become freckled with orange spots, which turn black in August. May, with luck, be prevented with Dithane or Shell's Zineb Dust after pruning, in mid-April and again in late autumn.

Fungicides and insecticides can be mixed into one brew and sprayed on together.

Varieties to Choose and to Avoid

People who are not old hands are confronted with several difficulties, of which they are not aware, when ordering HT and floribunda roses today.

The catalogues of too many nurseries have become so plastered with glorious technicolour (in itself often far from reality) that no space is left to tell you the things you really want to know. At the same time scores of new varieties are thrown upon the market every year and receive adulation far beyond their deserts. Flower shows similarly tell you far too little – little more, indeed, than the colour and form of the bloom.

What the average gardener needs to know as well are the answers to the following questions:

Is the rose resistant to disease?

How big does it grow?

What is its habit? Will it grow upright, like 'Super Star', or sprawl sideways and tear your nylons like 'Grace of Monaco'?

Will its blossom become a soggy mass in rain, like 'Karl Herbst'?

Does it hang its head?

In a floribunda, is its performance really continuous or merely recurrent?

Very few catalogues give you answers to any of these questions. The only safe way to assess a rose is to see it growing, and even then you may get only some of the answers. Few nurseries can show you what a plant looks like when full-grown (the thing you want to know). Apart from private gardens, the best displays are those of the Royal National Rose Society at St Albans (the most comprehensive) and in some of the gardens mentioned in "Floral Curriculum", Chapter 1. For an extremely modest fee, much pleasure and advantage will be yours in membership of the Royal National Rose Society, Bone Hill, Chiswell Green, St Albans, Hertfordshire.

My overriding advice in this matter of selections is to avoid all new roses. Only rarely is there a real winner which holds its place for long, such as 'Peace', 'Super Star' and 'Wendy Cussons'. Others soon find their way into the catalogue's small print, after they have been "tested in commerce". Let others be the guinea-pigs.

Other types of roses – shrubs, climbers, ramblers and the old ones – present less difficulty; they are seldom the sport of the advertising agent and one is on surer ground.

All this time I have said nothing about scent. I must leave that to your own nose, merely observing (for the purpose of contradicting popular fallacy) that many new roses have better scent than many old ones.

The following curt lists of selections are intended only to open the doors. Apart from personal tastes, all are thoroughly sound. Details from the better catalogues.

HTs. I have space here to do no more than name a dozen of the leading varieties of today which seem likely to hold their own for a few years to come. Whatever new ones may come along, these are all of high excellence.

Wendy Cussons
Super Star (tall and slim)
Stella
Piccadilly
Silver Lining
Prima Ballerina (great vigour)
Pink Favourite
Rose Gaujard
Ena Harkness
Mischief
My Choice
Peace (great vigour)

Floribundas. The same introductory remarks apply.

Allgold
Paprika
Pink Parfait
Orange Sensation
Lili Marlene
Dickson's Flame
Anna Wheatcroft
Elizabeth of Glamis

Evelyn Fison — Nathalie Nypels (never stops)
Dearest — Red Favourite.

I exclude 'Queen Elizabeth' and 'Iceberg', both of which should really be classed as shrub roses.

Shrub roses have much diversity of habit. A few of the best are:

Rugosas. Clothed to the ground with dense, dark-green foliage. Long-blooming. Clove scented.

Hybrid musks. Usually have long, arching arms, prodigal of blossom and drenched with scent.

Bourbons. Usually slim and erect to about 6ft, voluptuously scented. Need a little staking.

Unclassified, all very fine indeed:

Nevada (the tops) — Queen Elizabeth
Golden Wings — Iceberg
Bonn — Sarah Van Fleet

Old roses. An enormous field, from which I can pick only a small bouquet. For a detailed treatise see Mr Graham Thomas's *The Old Shrub Roses.*

Rosa alba. Robust and upright. The best is 'Celeste'.

The Provence Rose (*R. centifolia*). Great floral swags on langorous, drooping branches. Needs good cultivation. Choices: 'Fantin Latour' and 'Tour de Malakoff' (dramatic colourings). Two little sweeties of better habit are 'Rose de Meaux' and 'Petite de Holland'

Moss roses (*R. centifolia muscosa*). The "moss" is caused by the enlarged, scented, glandular projections on the sepals. None better than *muscosa* itself (the Common Moss). More gorgeous are 'Nuits de Young' in maroon-purple and 'William Lobb', a stunning Parma violet on a gaunt, 8ft shrub.

The French roses (*R. gallica*). Great variety here. Most stand at about 4ft. Thrive on poor soils. Most famous is 'Rosa Mundi' (*R. gallica* 'Versicolor'), having petals painted in red and white stripes. A few others, all in gorgeous colours: 'Charles de Mills', 'Tuscany Superb', 'Belle de Crécy', 'Cardinal de Richelieu'.

Pillar or Short Climbers. Among these 'Golden Showers' stands out as one that never stops blooming. The pink 'Aloha' is nearly as good. More vigorous and spreading, but not so continuous are 'Nymphenberg' and 'Danse du Feu'.

Strong Climbers. For house walls, large pergolas and tall screens:

'Mermaid'. The tops. Hates moving. Must be pot-grown. Slow starter. Extremely vigorous but fails in Scotland.

'Allen Chandler'. Great vigour.

'Guinée'. Darkest of dark red.

'Mme Grégoire Staechelin'.

'Elégance'.

'Paul's Lemon Pillar'.

Any of the climbing sports, especially 'Climbing Mrs Sam McGredy'.

Ramblers. A few only:

'Albertine'. Treat for pruning as a climber.

'Emily Gray'. Treat as a climber. No pruning first three years. Almost evergreen.

'Easlea's Golden Rambler'. Same pruning as for Emily.

'Crimson Conquest'. A true lax rambler.

'Crimson Shower'. Valuable for late blooming. A true lax rambler.

Tree climbers. The following species will scramble high up into trees, laden with large trusses of richly scented, white flowers, once only: *R. gentiliana, noisettiana, longicuspis* and *filipes* 'Kiftsgate'.

Ground-hugging roses. The following are absolutely first-class for densely clothing wide areas of ground, suppressing weeds besides making a fine, once-only display of charming flowers:

'Max Graf', A variety of *R. rugosa*; *R. paulii* 'Rosea'. Larger than 'Max'; *R. macrantha* 'Raubritter' and *R. wichuraiana,* quite prostrate.

Roses for hedges. Several roses make very decorative hedges and are boy-proof and dog-proof to boot. 'Iceberg' and 'Dainty Maid' excel in this role, so does the old 'Frensham' but it mildews badly. 'Masquerade' and 'Shepherd's Delight' do well. 'Queen Elizabeth', much advocated, builds up into a tall hedge with all the flowers on the crown and the feet are rather naked. Some of the hybrid musks, such as 'Cornelia' and 'Penelope', are lovely, 6ft wide, but rather loose in structure.

Plant all of them a trifle closer that you would otherwise and prune lightly. Not suitable adjacent to a public pavement.

CHAPTER 15

BULBS AND THEIR LIKE

In general – After-care – Bulbs Indoors – Daffodils – Dahlias – Lilies – Tulips – Other Prime Choices – Second String

BULBS, corms, tubers and rhizomes are all forms of swelling that various plants have evolved as devices for storing the requirements of life during their periods of dormancy, as electricity is stored in a battery. They originate as a means of survival under some harsh conditions of life, particularly in arid conditions of semi-desert and rocky, sun-baked mountain slopes, or, less harshly, from shady woodlands and lush water meadows.

To the gardener their attractions are that they are easy to handle, usually easy enough to grow and that the flowers that they produce usually have their own special qualities of freshness and grace. Many will flower beautifully in the shade but most, I think, want a certain amount of sun to recharge their storage batteries. Most of them flower on leafless stems known as scapes.

Your true bulb is a compressed body made up of swollen leaf bases, which form a sheath round the flower within, complete in all its parts. Daffodils, hyacinths, onions, snowdrops and scillas are of this type. All these live in the ground for a number of years and propagate themselves not only by seed but also by sprouting a number of small bulbs, or off-sets, which will develop in close proximity to the mother and form a large clump unless broken up by man and separated to form new colonies. Tulips, on the other hand, have the peculiarity of forming one or more new bulbs every year, completely replacing the old.

Corms differ from true bulbs in that they are the swellings of stem bases, with the embryonic leaves and flowers compressed into a small bud, usually at the crown. The gladiolus and the crocus are familiar examples.

A tuber is a fleshy, underground swelling, which may be a root swelling, as in the dahlia, or a stem swelling, as (to one's initial surprise) in the potato. Together with them one may group what botanists call "false bulbs", of which familiar examples are the begonia, cyclamen, most anemones and the little winter aconite.

A rhizome has been explained in "Gardener's Jargon" and we have seen it in action in the iris. As rhizomes are more in the nature of herbaceous plants than of bulbs, they have been included in Chapters 9 and 10.

DEMANDS AND DESIRES

In the open garden the demands of bulbous plants vary a good deal, many expecting to be sun-baked in a gritty, fast-draining soil, others liking things cool and moist, as we have briefly seen from their lands of origin. However, some genera have been so much hybridized that, to a large extent, we may ignore their native origins, as particularly in the modern tulip, which has been in the hands of Dutch marriage-makers for centuries and is virtually a man-made article, ready to do service anywhere within reason.

In general, clay soils are not the best for bulbs, except for woodland and meadowland natives, such as bluebells, snowdrops, snake's head fritillaries and the hybrid daffodils. The first of all requirements is good drainage, which is best provided by light, rather sandy, porous soils. Observe carefully, Reader, how very often in the following notes you will meet the phrase "gritty, fast-draining soil". The lack of such a soil is the cause of many a failure. The average gardener who has not been provided by nature with a very porous soil can hardly produce one at will, except on a small scale, and the alternative is simply to avoid those bulbs that need it. In my young gardening days I learnt this lesson the hard way through relying too much on the allurements of catalogues. Heavy clays can, of course, be lightened somewhat and built up above the natural level, with coarse drainage material two spits down, but this means a mort of hard labour.

Most bulbs take quite kindly and sometimes even eagerly to lime. The few exceptions will be noted as we go along.

I shall assume that the ground has already been prepared in accordance with the canons of earlier chapters and impregnated with plenty of organic matter in the forms of compost, leaf-soil, old turf or peat. Bonemeal, we think in this country, is at all times particularly good. But *on no account whatever* plant any bulbs in ground that has recently been manured, with such few exceptions as we shall note later. Unless one is absolutely mad about bulbs, the sound thing to do is to plant none at all until the second year of beginning a garden, after the initial manuring has been done and after the main framework of other permanent plants has comfortably bedded down. To plant shrubs or herbaceous things after the ground has been plugged full of bulbs can be a jolly tricky operation.

Unimaginative arrangement can quite spoil the natural charm of the bulbous plants. Hyacinths, tulips and begonias do indeed look their bravest when dressed in ranks like regiments of light-opera soldiers. But the care-free beauty of all others abhors rigidity. Daffodils in straight lines are abominable, like ballet dancers in battle-dress. Informal drifts and clusters are their best formations. There is no better dodge for getting the right effect than the old one of taking a handful of stones, of size according to the bulb, tossing them down casually and planting where they fall.

A special problem of planting is that, once the beauty of their blossom has passed away, a great many bulbs become dowdy and unkempt in their foliage. Therefore, make a special point of planting these sorts – daffodils, tulips, muscari, hyacinths, gladioli, crocuses, etc. – where their sere and drooping foliage is not an eyesore, e.g. in the middle or back (*not* the front) of a border, where the early ones will enliven the naked earth before its other occupants are fully awake, but where they will be covered by the oncoming foliage of those others when they sink to rest; or among shrubs, where nearly all bulbs except the hybrid tulips look particularly well; or naturalized in grass; or in beds by themselves, where, if need be, they can be lifted and removed after flowering.

These, of course, are generalizations. You wouldn't plant tulips among shrubs, and rarely in grass. Nor is all bulb foliage disagreeable – anemones, for example, go excellently in the front edge of a sunny border. Taste and discretion must be the guides. But there is one place where virtually all bulbous plants are absolutely barred – the formal rose bed. Not only will the bulb be completely out of its element, but also it will do the roses no good, and the dying foliage on the bare beds will be an eyesore. I would allow only the miniature bulbous irises of winter.

In the pages that follow the reader who is acquainted with only the most familiar bulbs will, I hope, profit from some suggestions that may be quite new to him. He will find distinction and poise in the orbicular flowers of the alliums and slender elegance in the fritillaries, a more sumptuous beauty in the belladonna lily, the crinum and the starry nerine that decorate the declining zodiac in carefully chosen corners, an elfin charm in the little wild anemones and cyclamens and the miniature lily-form erythronium, besides many little cherubs that frolic in the rock garden and other stony places.

NATURALIZING

Those best for naturalizing are daffodils, snowdrops, crocus, fritillary, and chionodoxa, but the smaller flowers should, of course, not be in tall and rampant grasses. The mower should on no account go over places where these bulbs lie till their foliage has died right down, so plant them in clusters or drifts convenient for manœuvring the machine, preferably near the corners or edges of the lawn in small gardens.

Planting can be done with a special tool for naturalizing; alternatively, lift a few slices of turf with a turfing iron or spade, fold them back, dig and loosen the soil beneath, plant in the ordinary way with some bonemeal, and replace the turf.

PLANTING

Take care always to plant bulbs at their correct depths. In the cultural notes that follow, "plant 3in. deep" means that there must be 3in. of soil above the top of the bulb. In very light soil plant a bit deeper, in heavy soils not quite so deep. For most lilies a spade must be used, but generally a trowel is the best tool. In heavy soils seat the bulb on ½in. of sharp sand.

The time for planting most spring-flowering bulbs is September–October and for summer flowering ones March–April, but there are a few exceptions (particularly snowdrops and lilies), which will be given in the notes that follow.

After-care

When the flowers wither, nip off all seed-pods. Never, if avoidable, cut or damage the foliage. Leave it to die or wither completely. Water the spring bulbs well as they go to rest if there is a prolonged spell of dry weather, for it is then that they are making themselves ready for next year's effort.

LIFTING

With a few important exceptions, bulbs and their kind are best left in the ground once planted, until they multiply sufficiently to need dividing and replanting. The chief exceptions are begonia, gladiolus, tulip, ranunculus and dahlia, but others can be lifted if necessary to make room for other plants, though lilies, amaryllis, crinum and cyclamen should be moved for compulsive reasons only. If avoidable, do not lift till the foliage has died right down or is touched by frost, except gladioli. Then dry the bulbs, etc., clean off the earth, separate, grade, and store in a place that is cool, dry and airy, but frost-proof. You may store small quantities in cardboard boxes or paper bags, which you must pierce to give circulation of air.

Although lifting is best done after complete withering of the foliage, it may nevertheless be done earlier to make room. In such an event, lift carefully and complete with roots with a ball of soil, "heel in" the plant in a reserve quarter in a trench deep enough to cover the bulb, water, and leave till the foliage has died. This often has to be done to tulips, whose formal nature generally requires them to be put in a bed of their own, to be followed by a summer bedding-out of begonias, antirrhinums, etc.

PROPAGATION

Many bulbous plants can be raised from seed without great difficulty but usually it is a long business. For the general run of the more popular bulbs and corms proper, one's stock is more easily multiplied by detaching the young bodies that form at the base or side of the parent and planting them out separately, the smaller ones in a seed-bed. Tulips, as we have seen, thoughtfully produce new bulbs each year; so do gladioli, together with myriads of baby cormlets. Hyacinths unfortunately are a subject for the expert only. Tubers are treated differently.

Many of the most endearing little ones, however, happily multiply themselves in the most natural manner if left to run to seed, forming ever-widening colonies.

Bulbs Indoors

A limited range of bulbous flowers can be grown indoors to enliven the grim days of January and February, by growing them either in pots in a porous compost or else in prepared fibre in undrained bowls. Only a few can be successfully reared in fibre, and when ordering it is as well to specify if bulbs are wanted for this special purpose. Hyacinths excel in this mode of life, and so do some daffodils. Several tulips, crocuses, scillas and muscari also are good. Less usual and of rare charm are the dwarf irises, *histrioides* 'Major', and *reticulata*, which do particularly well in bowls. Many more grow bravely in ordinary flower-pots, reared in unheated greenhouses or frames.

September is the right time to do all such planting. The methods of cultivation are much the same whether by pot or bowl. Use pots large enough to take at least three hyacinths or five tulips. Bowls must be non-porous, and circular ones are better than fancy shapes. Pack the bulbs as closely together in the receptacles as you like, provided they do not actually touch one another. There is no need at all to bury the bulb, all it needs being a firm seating, and it is therefore quite enough to insert it to only half its depth. Leave sufficient space between the level of the soil and the rim of the pot to permit watering.

For bowls, the fibre should be thoroughly moist but not sodden, so that when squeezed in the hand moisture is not pressed out. If the fibre does not arrive in this condition from the shop or nursery, tie it up in sacking or similar porous material and suspend it with a weight in a cistern of water for at least a day.

The bulbs having been planted, they must now go into darkness for several weeks. The method of putting them in a dark cupboard or cellar should be adopted only by those who have no garden. They are much better outdoors. My own experience is that the best method is to bury them in peat, sand or ashes (that have been thoroughly weathered for a couple of months) to a depth of a good 6in. in a shady position, preferably under a north wall, and forget about them altogether for eight weeks at least. Then unearth and inspect, taking care not to damage any young shoots. Those that are well through by 1in. or more can be taken out, and the others must be put to bed again.

Whether the outdoors or the cupboard method is adopted, the pots and bowls must next go into a place of semi-shade, but still quite cold for a week, and then gradually move up into full light. From then on give them utmost light and careful watering, seeing that the soil or fibre is nicely moist but never sodden.

Continue to keep them coldish until the flower bud shows in the neck of the bud, when they can be brought into a warm room, though the warmer the room the sooner will the flower be over. Never hurry them; light is more important than heat. Quick forcing turns the bulbs "blind", especially crocuses. Keep them well away from any gas-fire, and out of any room with violently fluctuating day and night temperatures.

Bulbs in pots can go into a greenhouse, conservatory, frame or glass porch as long as one likes. In the little conservatories and glazed porches attached to many small houses there is no better method of providing early spring cheer. The taller sorts will need staking as the flower-heads develop, and for heavy-headed hyacinths in bowls of fibre thinly split canes with sharp points, or rigid wires, should be thrust firmly into each bulb itself.

Bulbs grown in this artificial manner get pretty exhausted and are quite unfit for similar use again, but if, after flowering they are planted among shrubs or in odd corners, they will provide a little quite cheerful bloom in subsequent years. Plant out the whole bowlful complete and add a handful of bonemeal. Hyacinths and other bulbs that have been specially "prepared" for early flowering are not worth saving.

BULBS IN WATER

Specially "prepared" hyacinths and a few daffodils can be grown indoors in glass vases made for that purpose. Fill with water up to about half an inch from the base of the bulb and drop in a few pieces of charcoal. Keep in a cool cupboard until the bulbs have become strongly rooted.

The daffodils 'Cragford' and 'Paperwhite' can also be grown in bowls or soup plates filled with small pebbles. Push the bulbs into the pebbles until they are comfortably seated and pour in the water carefully until it is not quite touching the bulb.

Daffodils

(Narcissus)

"Daffodil" is simply the vernacular name for any kind of narcissus, whether having a long trumpet or not. There is, however, an official regimentation of daffodils into various "divisions", devised largely for the benefit of exhibitors, and we who are not exhibitors had better get this tedious business out of the way in short order, ignoring the minor details and most of the sub-divisions.

FIG. 56*a*. Daffodil styles: "large cup" (Division ii).

Div. i. Large trumpet daffodils. There are four sub-divisions according to the relative colours of the corona (the trumpet in this case) and the perianth (the pseudo-petals that form the background of the corona).

Div. ii. Large cup (or short trumpet). Here we find brilliant orange-scarlets in the coronas and here also are most of the charming pink daffs that have won many hearts (including mine).

Div. iii. Small cups. Again much red in the cups.

Div. iv. Double daffodils. Abortions best passed by with averted eyes; why anyone should seek to distort the chaste features of the daffodil I can't imagine. But if your taste does go for scrambled eggs on sticks, have a dish of 'Golden Ducat' or 'Gay Times' until something better is cooked up.

Div. v. Derived from *N. triandrus* (aptly known as "Angel's Tears"), characterized by clusters of small, pensively nodding flowers with small cups and reflexed perianths. For porous, gritty soils.

Div. vi. Derived from the bewitching little *N. cyclamineus.* Quite a large division, with many delightful, dwarf, semi-dwarf or quite big daffs, which, though they look downwards with swept-back wings, appear extremely alert and intent. For damp soils.

FIG. 56*b*. Daffodil styles: "small cup" (Division iii).

Div. vii. Jonquils. Usually two or more flowers on a scape, often very sweetly scented.

Div. viii. Derived from *N. tazetta,* with multiflowered stems, some not quite hardy outdoors, about 15–20in. high.

Div. ix. Derived from *N. poeticus,* the cup reduced to a small, brightly coloured disc and the whole flower usually rather flat, as in the popular old 'Actaea' and the newer 'Cantabile'.

Div. x. Wild species and miniatures.

One may infer from this list that not all daffodils prosper in the same conditions and this is certainly true of the wild species and the tinies, but the larger modern hybrids have a wide tolerance and will flourish in any soil that, without having been manured for at least a year, is in good heart, retentive of moisture without being waterlogged.

Of course, daffs of all sorts never look so well as in naturalistic environments, such as meadows, open woodlands and orchards, but not all of us can give them these conditions. In smaller gardens their most appropriate places are among deciduous shrubs or at the back of herbaceous borders. Never plant them in straight lines or as "edgings" and for heaven's sake avoid the frightful habit of tying up their leaves in knots or plaits when flowering is over; what is important then is watering in dry spells and a sprinkle of bonemeal.

FIG. 56*c*. Daffodil styles: poeticus (Division ix).

Order early and plant early. August is ideal. September is O.K. Plant the bulbs to a depth according to their size and the nature of the soil, covering the larger bulbs by a good 3in. in average soils (which means a 6–7in. hole). For the tinies a hole 3in. deep is enough. Station the big ones some 8in. apart if you want them to stay and grow into big clumps; the little ones about 4in. When they get overcrowded, with a lot of flowerless foliage, dig them out, break them up and replant.

Choices. New varieties of daffodils, especially of the larger ones, come out every year, costing, per bulb, the price of a West End suit. Select from the catalogues according to your purse, but watch the falling prices of such superlatives as the white 'Cantatrice' and the pink 'Salmon Trout', which will soon be joining 'Kingscourt', 'Trousseau', 'Preamble' and 'Broughshane', now moving up into the front line as the favourites of the future.

One frailty of nearly all these big, modern hybrids is that they are liable to get flattened by heavy rain. This melancholy fate is usually escaped by the shorter species and their varieties in Divs. v to x, which have a delightful air and are well suited to gardens of all sizes, as well as to pots. Remember to give a sunny position and a warm, sandy, well-drained soil to the wistful *triandrus* varieties; the little ones, such as 'April Tears' and 'Hawera', are seen better in pots or in an upper stratum of the rock garden.

By contrast, the still more desirable *cyclamineus* hybrids should be chosen for the damper, shadier parts of the garden and there is nothing more enchanting than the little *N. cyclamineus* itself, a 5in.

FIG. 57*a*. Some dwarf daffodils: *Narcissus cyclamineus*.

cherub, with a tubular toy trumpet and perianth segments acutely swept back like the floral ears of the cyclamen. Its hybrid progeny are numbered among the most beautiful of all daffodils, with their peering, bird-like stance and their swept back pinions, and they have a phenomenally long season of flowering. They range from the delightful, 8in. 'Beryl' to the 15in. of 'Bartley' (distastefully named 'Peeping Tom' in most catalogues) and they include the celebrated 'February Gold', 'Charity May', 'March Sunshine' and 'Larkelly', as well as others still rather expensive.

There remains, in addition to *cyclamineus*, a great many endearing miniatures, both wild species and hybrids, far too numerous to consider here. Many of them are not at all easy and are quite unsuitable for the hurly-burly of garden borders, requiring either the sharp drainage of the rock garden or to be grown in pots in a greenhouse or porch, where their pygmy charms may be the better scrutinized.

Tiniest of all is *asturiensis*, often mis-called *minimus*, a true little "trumpeter in gold" of 3in. stature, which you must certainly grow in a pot or pan. A trifle taller is *minor* (or *nanus* of catalogues) and at

FIG. 57*b*. Some dwarf daffodils: the "angel's tears" daffodil, *N. triandrus.*

6in. we come to *minor conspicuus*, quite growable outdoors, but never a real success with me; whenever you find a lot of foliage and too few flowers, it usually means too rich a soil.

This is highly probable also of the other delightful dwarf species, *bulbocodium,* the hoop-petticoat daffodil, which blows a little bugle rather than a trumpet, with only wispy perianth segments and grassy foliage. Its chances, I am sure, would be better in a gritty, fast-draining soil. However, two toy trumpeters that I have found most successful are the 4in. 'Little Beauty' and the 6in. 'Little Gem'. Like so many hybrids, they are better garden plants than some of the true species – a statement for which I am certain to be rebuked.

From these you may graduate in time to the elfin charms of

rupicola and *watieri* and to many spritely little hybrids that will entice you at the shows until you discover their prices.

Daffodils have few natural enemies, but there are three insidious ones – the microscopic eelworm, the bulb-scale mite and the narcissus flies. Look out above ground for any stunted, distorted, lop-sided growth, any with discoloured foliage and any that stop growing and

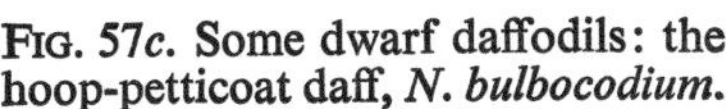

FIG. 57*c*. Some dwarf daffodils: the hoop-petticoat daff, *N. bulbocodium*.

wither at the tip. Dig up and burn all such bulbs, or you may have big trouble. Eelworm, if it comes, sweeps through daffodil colonies like a plague and the average amateur has no remedy.

Dahlias

There are quite a lot of dahliaphobes, but the dahlia has many virtues, for, although not hardy, it is very easy to grow, is virtually free of disease, prolific with its blooms if spent ones are picked off and is a good cut flower. As in the modern chrysanthemum, you would never imagine, from the density of petals in the more popular sorts, that they belong to the same family as the daisy, for in most of them the central disc or eye (an essential part of the beauty of all daisyform flowers) is totally obscured.

The dahlia is another example of a plant which, largely for the benefit of the exhibitor, has been segregated into various clans and cliques. It is all very formalized but anyone who is fired with ambition to specialize can get all the information he wants from the National

Dahlia Society, a very well-run show. They will also profit no end from James Rooke's *Dahlias for Small Gardens*, the best non-boring little book on the subject that I know.[1]

In the meantime, all we need know about this classification are the names that are given to the very diverse floral styles that the modern hybrid dahlia has evolved. These floral styles are:

DECORATIVE. A mass of broad, overlapping, blunt-ended petals, forming a dense rosette. Sometimes of soup-plate size.

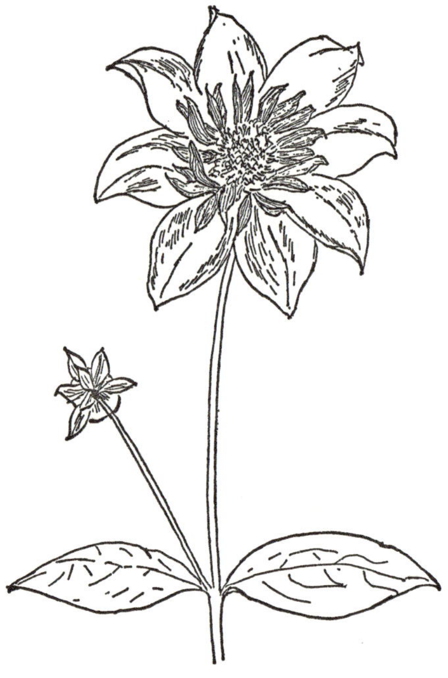

FIG. 58. A collerette dahlia.

CACTUS. The petals roll elegantly into pointed quills. There are also semi-cactus varieties, with the petals less tightly rolled.

COLLERETTES (note odd spelling). These have an outer circle of large petals and an inner one of smaller petals, usually in a contrasting colour, with the central disc elegantly displayed and emphasized.

POMPONS. Perfectly spherical orbs, highly stylized and formal, not more than 2in. in diameter.

BALL. A larger form of pompon, maybe 6in. or more in diameter, but not always completely spherical.

[1] Published by Pan Books, at 5s.

ANEMONE-FLOWERED. A circlet of flat outer petals and a dense cluster of inner ones, obscuring the disc and having a pincushion effect.

SINGLES. A wide range, including the well-known Coltness varieties and other pretty miniatures, all of which are child's play to raise from seed.

PEONY-FLOWERED. A straightforward double flower, with two or more whorls of petals, showing the disc.

When received from the nursery, dahlias are "ex-pots". Except in the mildest, frost-free districts, they should not be planted out before the first week of June. If the plants come too soon (see later) pot them up, water well and give them some form of frost protection at night until planting-out time. For their flowering positions give them as much sun as you can, though they will be quite happy in oblique shade for part of the day. They respond to your hopes in all sorts of soils, but are all the better for good feeding.

Space the large and medium at 3ft apart, the others at lesser spaces down to 12in. for the dwarf bedders. Put a small cane close up to the stem of each plant and tie loosely with raffia. Water well. Pinch out the tips when about, say, 10in. high. As the plants develop, put in three or four 4ft canes round the circumference of each and encage them with strong string. Except perhaps for the monsters, the traditional stout "dahlia stake" is not necessary. Water copiously in dry weather. If large blooms are your ambition, remove the two side buds growing on either side of and below the central one at the end of each branch. If any plants manifest stunted and deformed growth, dig them up and burn them; they have a virus disease.

When frost blackens the foliage in autumn, lift the tubers with care, driving the fork deep, cut the stalks down to a few inches of the base, drain any water out of the hollow stems, dry, clean and store the tubers and label them. Dry peat, sand or sawdust are good storage materials.

Such at least is what orthodoxy ordains. There are, however, plenty of people who, in defiance of the pundits, leave their tubers in the ground all winter in the milder counties, but they take a risk if they go on doing so every year.

Next spring there are three courses open for the treatment of the lifted tubers. The simplest is to replant them outdoors in early May, covered by at least 3in. of soil, and protect the young shoots against night frost. Allow only one or two shoots to develop.

The second method is to divide the tubers, a good and easy method when there is an unheated greenhouse or frame. Dahlias make their new growth from the crown of the plant – that portion which lies between the stem and the lobes of the tubers. In the earliest stage these growth points are discernible as little buds or "eyes", but it is usually advisable to divide the tubers when the new growths are seen to have sprouted.

Division therefore means cutting up the plant so that each portion includes at least one lobe of the tuber together with a portion of the crown bearing a bud or new shoot. This you do by pushing a stout knife hard into the tuber between two lobes and giving the knife a twist. This will usually split the whole tuber in two and it can be further cut up if you wish, provided each portion includes a bud or shoot.

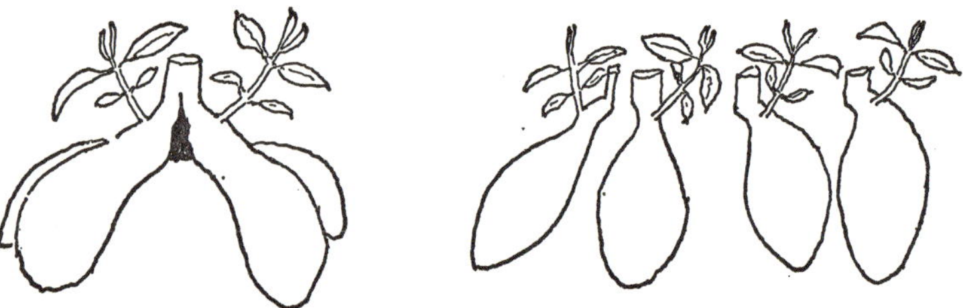

FIG. 59. Dividing a dahlia tuber. *Left:* The black patch shows the initial split made by the knife. *Right:* the stool divided. Diagrammatic only.

This operation you can perform on tubers that have been stored during the winter or on those that have been left in the ground all winter. The divided tubers can be planted straight out in late April, but many people prefer to start the tubers into growth under glass, packing them with fine soil or with peat and sand and lightly watering.

The third method is the orthodox one of growing new plants each year from cuttings, for which a heated greenhouse, frame or propagating case is needed. Start the tubers into growth in February–March, as in the last paragraph, taking care not to bury the crown. When the new growths are 3–4in. high, sever them, just above the crown, with a keen knife, trim the cutting below the bottom node and proceed as for any other cuttings, as outlined in Chapter 6.

When ordering, tell your nurseryman whether or not you have glass, so that he can send the plants at the right time. When I order new ones I get them in April and pot them on by stages into 7in. pots, so that, by planting-out time, they would already be in flower if I allowed them.

I shall not attempt to suggest varieties, for the champion of today is dispossessed tomorrow. The small cactus and small decorative are the best for beginners.

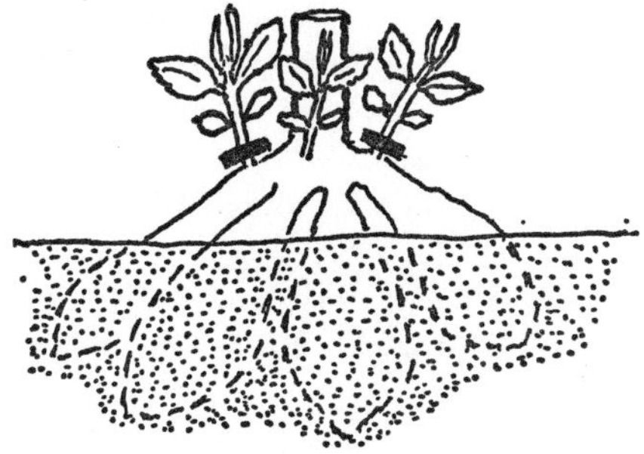

FIG. 60. A dahlia stool started in a box of soil with young growths from the crown for cuttings (diagrammatic only). Sever at the black lines.

Dahlias are worried by few enemies. Aphids are fully inhibited by spraying with a systemic insecticide, as for roses. Earwigs, which nibble the flowers and foliage, can be deterred by dusting the plants and the soil with DDT or they may be trapped, taking a mean advantage of their liking for a warm hiding-place. Mr Rooke annihilates his by simply pouring a few drops of paraffin into the hollow top of one of the supporting canes, when the creatures scamper out and expire in a few seconds.

Lilies

(*Lilium*)

With a very few exceptions, lilies have until quite recently been looked upon by average gardeners with a certain amount of hushed reverence as divinities to be enshrined in the gardens of the wealthy or the experts only. Today, thanks mainly to the hybridists, this is no longer so. There is virtually no garden in which one or other sort of lily will not flourish. Wherever daffodils will grow, there also will many lilies.

An astonishing diversity is at our command today, ranging from the hot, tawny trumpets of 'African Queen', through the gay and colourful hybrids of the Mid-century, Harlequin and Fiesta strains, to the ethereal beauty of 'Limelight' and the true species which still command the highest reverence of the connoisseur. There are lilies of pure colour, others broadly banded in crimson or gold or speckled like a bird's egg or flushed within or without in some contrasting colour, and all are enlivened by bold, thrusting anthers in gold, orange, chestnut or chocolate, dancing in the breeze on slender filaments. Most of them, moreover, exhale a honeyed breath, so that, when the lily season is at its height in July, just as the HT roses finish their first flush, the whole garden is filled with scent.

For many of us the price barrier remains, yet you can still get *L. regale* for half a crown a bulb and a great many others for a crown or less.

Among the hybrids, particularly the newer ones from Oregon, are to be found several that are termed "strains". These are seedling sisters and brothers resulting from a particular mating, all having similar family traits but each liable to be a little different in some point of detail. Out of such a family the raiser may select one of particular merit, give it an individual name and propagate it from its own offsets or scales. This is a "clone" and is usually more expensive than a strain, as it takes longer to work up a stock of bulbs. Thus the now celebrated 'Enchantment' is a clone of the Mid-century Hybrids, though in this particular case there is little difference in the price. These strains are therefore always a good buy unless one's heart is set on a particular clone.

Fundamentals. The lily is a difficult topic to write about in general terms in small compass, for one man's experience is not the same as another's and the needs of the various species and hybrids differ widely. The doctors of lilies disagree just as much as the doctors of philosophy. However, we may at the offset note certain fundamentals.

(*a*) Drainage. All lilies insist on good drainage. This is the very first commandment and one which, the reader will certainly have noticed, I have repeatedly ordained in these pages. In nature, most lily species grow on sloping ground or on mounds, where rain and melting snow thoroughly moisten the soil but run away freely, leaving no underground pools. Thus in our gardens we must make sure that there is no permanently saturated soil within reach of the lily roots. Heavy clay soils are accordingly always unpromising unless they are built up well, with plenty of good drainage material.

(*b*) Feeding. Here the lily doctors are apt to disagree sharply.

Virtually all, however, agree that lilies are damaged by direct contact with fresh manure, but, for the greater part, very much enjoy rotted leaf-soil. It seems best, therefore, to be stingy with all fertilizers, giving only a little as the shoots appear through the ground. In nature some lilies live in pretty poor ground.

(*c*) Shade. Except for the Madonna lily and her offspring the Nankeen lily (*L. candidum* and *testaceum*), all want to have their feet in shade.

(*d*) Lime. Some lilies like or tolerate lime (including chalk), but to others it is poison.

(*e*) Rooting habits. Many lilies, such as the Madonna and the martagon, send down roots from the bases of their bulbs only, but others, such as *regale* and the princely *auratum*, sprout roots from their stems also. This critically affects the depth of planting.

(*f*) Warning. Never buy lilies as a "cheap lot" and never buy them in a shop unless you see that they are stored in damp peat. Buy from reputable growers. Lilies are dormant, if at all, for only a very short period, should be out of the ground the minimum possible time and must not be allowed to dry up. Also, never accept any bulbs lacking their basal roots.

Preparation. Most lilies, the Madonna being an exception, are well suited by any good medium loam in good heart and of a reasonably porous texture; beds that have been manured the previous year are very appropriate. Gardeners who aim above the modest average, however, will go a bit farther. They will prepare the sites in early autumn, cultivating 18in. deep, incorporating plenty of leaf-soil, Cornish or other sharp sand, and a trifle of ancient cow manure if available or other organic food, such as bonemeal or hoof-and-horn.

For the more positive lime-lovers add some form of lime, preferably old lime-mortar rubble if you can get it.

This preparation means taking the soil right out and mixing in a wheelbarrow or, for a larger planting, somewhere on the ground. Better a bold grouping of all one sort (if the purse allows) than dotting about at random. Except for Madonna and *testaceum*, choose a site that is or will be shaded by low shrubs or herbaceous perennials, such as dwarf azaleas, helianthemums, true geraniums, lavenders and so on.

Planting. When the bulbs arrive (which should not be later than November in most instances), plant them immediately, or, if this is impossible, store them in damp peat.

Opinions differ considerably on the right planting depth and the nature of the soil is a qualifying factor, but on the whole I have found that the following is a good rule of thumb (counting from the top of the bulb):

Madonna: barely covered in heavy soil and not more than 2in. deep in light, sandy ones.

Other base-rooters: 4in. deep in light soils, 3in. in heavier ones.

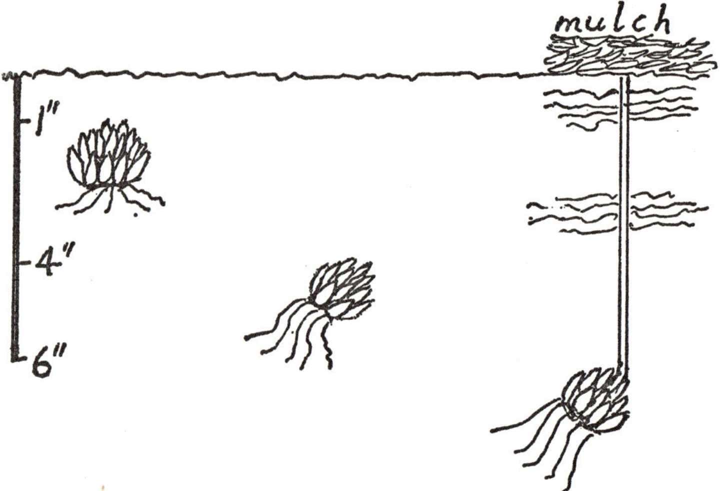

FIG. 61. Planting depth for lilies. *Left:* Madonna. *Centre:* Base-rooter. *Right:* Stem-rooter.

Stem-rooters: 7in. deep in light soils, 4in. in heavier ones, *plus* a deep mulch of rotted leaves or of peat, with a pinch or two of fertilizer, as soon as the tips of the shoots emerge above ground.

The following is the planting drill I practice myself. It may sound a bit fussy, but it is all very quickly done. I dare say that in natural lily soils one may follow a much simpler course.

Dust the bulbs liberally with Botrilex as a protection against fungus disease, by shaking the bulb in a paper bag containing a little of the powder. Plant each bulb on a little mound or saddle built up at the bottom of the hole, as for asparagus and bearded irises (Fig. 29), with the roots well spread out. To keep off the pirate slugs, encase the whole bulb in Cornish or other sharp sand. In heavy soils, plant the bulb on its side, to prevent water from lodging between the scales. Before filling up the hole, plant a cane close to each bulb; this cane may be needed for tying up the stem, though a great many lilies are quite self-supporting. The new stems do not always appear vertically above the bulb, which may be damaged if the cane is put in later. A 4ft cane is usually long enough. Beware of careless hoemanship in spring.

Care. Lilies often sulk in the first year after a move. So don't get shirty if they make a poor show or even no show at all; give them a second chance.

When they finish flowering behead the seed-pods. When the stems have completely withered, cut them down to the ground. When, after a few years, the clump becomes overcrowded, lift the bulbs after the foliage has died down, using a fork driven down very deeply. Then carefully divide the bulbs (sometimes a tough job), damaging the basal roots as little as possible, and replant immediately. In the Savill Gardens at Windsor this is done just after the lilies have finished blooming, but ordinary mortals do it in September, except for Madonna, which is divided in July or August.

The enemies of the lily are few but may be fatal. I have mentioned slugs. A yellow mottling, a curling and twisting of the leaves and a degeneration of growth betray a virus disease, which is spread by greenfly. The tiger-lily, which is a carrier rather than itself a sufferer, is a notorious source of infection. As a preventative against the fly, spray with a systemic insecticide or with gamma-BHC, but plants that are badly diseased must be dug up and burnt.

Two fungus diseases may also occur. One is basal rot of the bulb itself, arising, it seems, from bad drainage. The other is botrytis, which is first manifested by small brownish watery markings on the leaves, which then turn brown and drop. The control is one of the copper fungicides as used for roses, etc., applied at the first sign or as a preventative. The tiger-lily and *hollandicum* (*umbellatum*) are very prone.

Some lilies to choose. I propose to select only a short list, confined to the easier, less expensive and readily obtainable sorts. As the aspirant progresses he may extend his exercises and tackle such difficult ones as *brownii, sulphureum* and *rubescens.*

We ought to note at the outset that lilies have various floral styles which, quite apart from their colour, may strongly influence our choices. Thus we have:

Trumpet-form lilies, such as *regale*, a form for which I have a strong personal predilection.

Turk's-caps, so called because their acutely reflexed "petals" (perianth segments) resemble the Turkish turban of more colourful days; some of these turn their faces to their feet, as in the martagon, others look frankly outwards as in *henryi*.

FIG. 62. The Madonna lily.

Goblet-shaped, a very approximate term for such lilies as *bulbiferum croceum*, which holds up a cup with reflexed lips.

Others of an intermediate nature, some only partially reflexed and having a star shape, others very widely expanded and almost flat.

Here then is my short list. Unless otherwise stated, the flowering season is July.

MADONNA LILY (*L. candidum*). In a class by itself. A familiar, chaste and lovely lily of great antiquity in cultivation, with pure white, sharply reflexed petals in June. Notorious for often shunning the lord's demesne but prospering in the cottage plot. Madonna's requirements are very special but very simple: full sun from head to foot, a plain, stony diet, a fondness for lime and an insistence on being planted close to the surface of the soil, as we have already

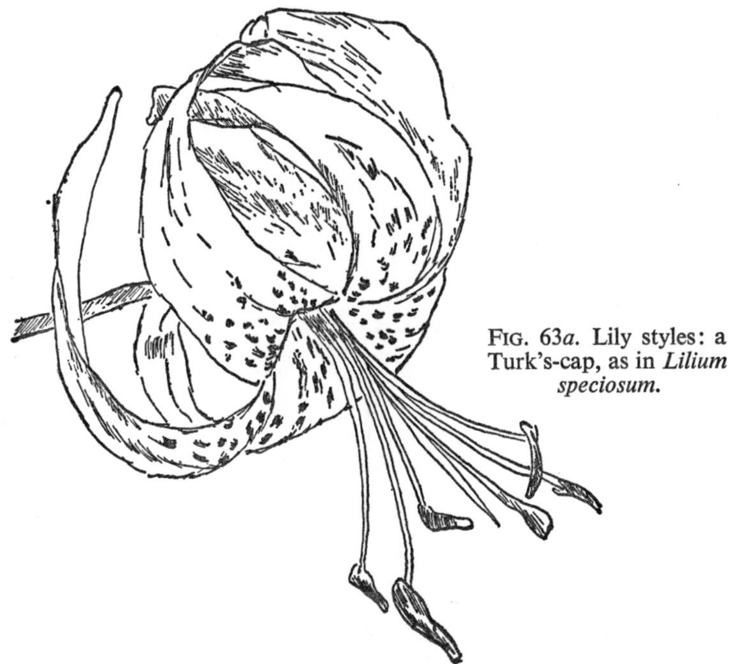

FIG. 63*a*. Lily styles: a Turk's-cap, as in *Lilium speciosum*.

noted. Said to dislike heavy clay, yet flowers magnificently in the sticky stuff of Suffolk cottage gardens. Plant in July or as soon as possible thereafter. The new foliage appears soon afterwards and over-winters.

REGALE. One of the easiest yet certainly one of the most beautiful of lilies. Large clusters of scented, white, golden-throated trumpets with a vinous flush on the exterior and deep gold anthers. Stem-rooting. Content in lime, including chalk. 4ft. Easy from seed.

ROYAL GOLD. A wonderful, warm, deep yellow and melodious version of the regal lily. Very beautiful indeed but a trifle shorter.

HENRYI. Another very easy one, bearing outward-looking orange Turk's-caps, speckled brown, in tremendous quantity on arching stems that occasionally reach 8ft. August–September. Stem-rooting. A lime-lover. Increases rapidly. Very tough and hardy.

HOLLANDICUM (*umbellatum*). Very easy. Erect, wide-open, upward-facing cups, 2½ft. Stem-rooting. June. Lime-tolerant. Several good named clones in catalogues in chestnut, orange and yellow.

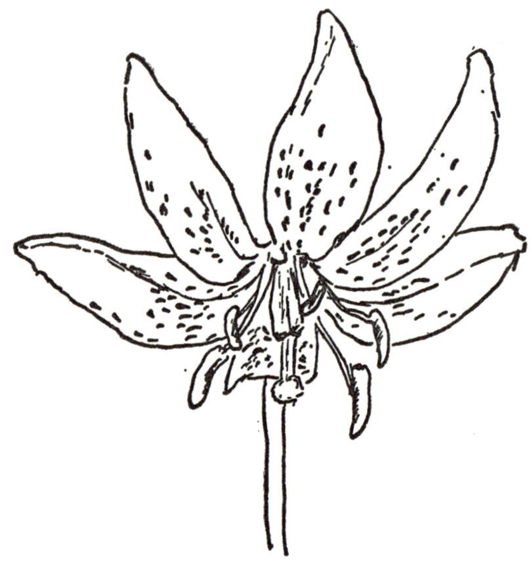

FIG. 63*b*. Lily styles: reflexed, as in the Golden Sunburst strain.

MARTAGON. Typical Turk's-caps, looking down to earth on long foot-stalks, displayed pyramidally. Base-rooting. Lime-tolerant. Variable colours, some disagreeable. The best is the white *album*, beautiful against a dark background.

LIMELIGHT. An enchanting and unique trumpet lily, in clear, cool shining lemon, with the exterior flushed chartreuse and with orange anthers. Give it a dark background, against which it will gleam like a lamp. 3½ft. I don't know about lime.

THUNDERBOLT. A sturdy, 5ft plant, crowned with large and superlative clusters of wide-open trumpets in deep apricot. Stem-rooting. July–August. Lime-tolerant.

GREEN DRAGON. Large trumpets of a thick, waxy substance, glistening white within, deeply flushed with chartreuse without and enlivened with copper-hued anthers. Very impressive. 4ft.

BLACK DRAGON. External flushing of very deep maroon. 6ft.

AFRICAN QUEEN strain. Strapping trumpeters of a hot, tawny orange or a warm apricot, on long, strong foot-stalks. 5½ft.

AURATUM. Perhaps the most sumptuous of all lily species, the huge white flowers opening nearly flat, distinguished by broad gold bands running through each segment, liberally speckled with crimson and extruding bold chestnut anthers. Stem-rooting. Intolerant of lime. 5ft or more in August–September. Seems to do best in a light soil with plenty of old leaf-soil and grit. Sensitive to virus. Quite cheap, apart from a few special varieties. See also the next two entries.

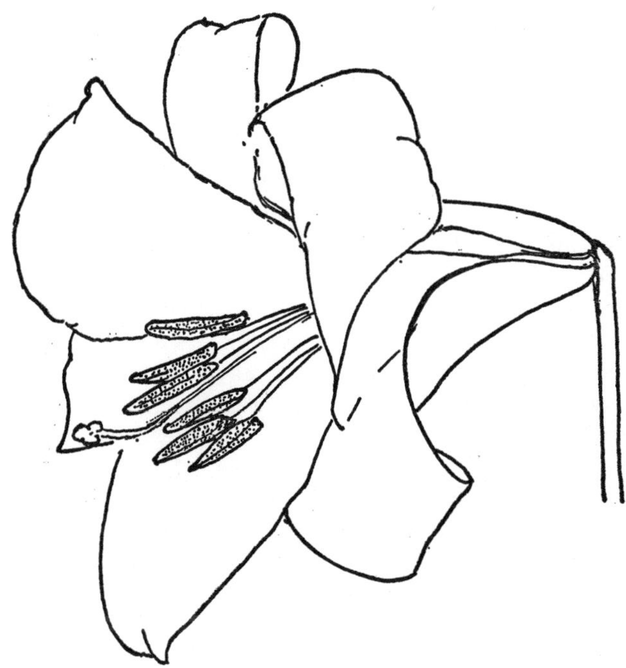

FIG. 63*c*. Lily styles: trumpet.

SPECIOSUM. A gorgeously coloured Turk's-cap, requiring much the same conditions as *auratum* and similarly sensitive to virus. There are a few particularly good varieties, including 'Melpomene' and

'Rubrum', all brilliantly banded and freckled in crimson or ruby, and all 4–5ft in September. *Speciosum* has been joined in marriage with *auratum* to produce three magnificent hybrid strains, to wit:

The IMPERIAL strains – Imperial Crimson, Imperial Gold and Imperial Silver; all 4–5ft and all, of course, stem-rooting, intolerant of lime, more expensive than their parents, but probably easier to grow.

MID-CENTURY hybrids. One of the most successful hybrid strains raised so far. As easy as daffodils, in brilliant colours and self-supporting on strong stems. Widely splayed petals, looking upwards or outwards. Stem-rooting. Average height about 3ft. There are several fine clones, of which the most famous is 'Enchantment', usually described as nasturtium-red and of the easiest culture. All very gay and jolly. All apparently lime-tolerant.

OLYMPIC Hybrids. Very handsome trumpets in white or yellow, often flushed with pink or green and streaked outside in maroon or vinous shades. As easy as potatoes. Fairly lime-tolerant. 4ft.

GOLDEN CLARION strain. Deep gold to pale lemon, widely expanded trumpets. Lime-tolerant. An instant favourite but has died away with me and apparently with others also.

GOLDEN SPLENDOUR strain. Selected from the best colour forms of the Golden Clarions, glowing in dusky, ochreous gold, externally marked maroon. Very handsome. 5ft.

HARLEQUIN strain. Outward-looking Turk's-cap in all sorts of lively colours, with heavy freckling. Stem-rooting. 2½–4ft. June–July.

FIESTA strain. Another coloured galaxy of Turk's-caps, but looking reflectively at their feet. Stem-rooting. Lime-tolerant. Sun-loving. 3½ft.

Some other easy, reliable but not particularly glamorous lilies, of which catalogues should tell you all you need know are: *L. hansonii, davidii* var. *willmottiae*, *pyrenaicum* and *bulbiferum croceum*. The tiger lily (*tigrinum*) is kind to some people, not to others. The beautiful yellow Nankeen lily, which you treat in the same way as Madonna, seems to have lost its vigour.

L. monadelphum and the similar *szovitsianum* are useful for heavy clay soils, lime-tolerant and stem-rooting, but expensive. *L. bulbiferum croceum* is also good in heavy soils.

Propagation. Lilies can be multiplied by division of multiple bulbs, as explained before, and also by the following methods.

STEM BULBILS. Several lilies, such as *tigrinum*, form tiny bulbs in the axils of the leaves up the whole length of the stem. Detach these in autumn and sow them in a John Innes seed compost in an ordinary seed-box or pan. Press them into the soil and scatter more soil on top, so that they are just covered. Top-dress with a little more soil when they begin to grow.

GROUND BULBLETS. These are produced from the base of the stem just below ground by some lilies, such as *auratum* and *speciosum.* The larger ones can be grown on normally and the smaller ones sown in the same manner as stem bulbils or planted 2in. deep in a nursery bed.

SCALES. In late summer, or in May, or when lifting an old bulb for division, detach one or more of the fleshy scales of the bulb and plant them in a seed-box or pan in a mixture of peat and sand. Press the base of the scale in only a quarter-inch or so and then cover completely with sphagnum moss. Small bulbs will form at the bases of the scales in six to eight weeks and these are planted out an inch or so deep in pots, deep boxes or a frame. To obtain scales from a growing plant, it is not necessary to dig up the bulb; burrow down to it and detach a couple of scales without disturbing the bulb.

SEED. Unfortunately lily bulbs may already be infected with disease when bought, unless from firms of the highest repute. Disease is not transmitted by seed, which is therefore the best means of building up a disease-free stock, as well as by far the cheapest. On the other hand seed-raising is not always easy and is often very slow, as in *auratum* and *speciosum*, which take up to two years to germinate, but the beginner will have little risk with *regale* and *henryi.* Indeed, the beautiful *formosanum* will flower within a year from seed, but unfortunately it is the very devil for subsequently attracting whatever disease there may be about.

Tulips

(*Tulipa*)

The tulipomania that swept Europe in the seventeenth century still lingers with us, but in a different form and scale. The dedicated tuliparian nowadays devotes himself mainly to the wild species and the more rare and difficult they are the greater his enthusiasm. We may well salute these *dilettanti* and in time perhaps aspire to their status, but in these pages must confine ourselves to those tulips that are within the compass of the average gardener and that are readily obtainable. Fortunately these do include a few of the species and some exciting developments from them.

Most of the tulips grown today by the million are hybrids and of the easiest culture in any reasonable soil, provided they are given full sun and good, free drainage. They are planted 4in. deep on or about 1st November. Like the hybrid hyacinths, they are very well suited to being martially regimented in phalanxes, battalions and squadrons, unlike the wild species, which prefer to serve as small guerrilla bands. Frankly, I simply line the hybrids out in the kitchen garden for my wife to cut as she wills. In formal gardens, however, they admirably adorn the scene in their coloured regiments, leaving one only with the problem of replacing their empty ranks when their parade is over.

Snap off the seed-pods, let the foliage wither (not quite completely), then lift and store the bulbs. If their ground is needed for some other bedding display, lift the complete plant and treat as in the opening section of this chapter.

Tulips are liable to be attacked by a fungus known as the fire disease, shown by withered, greyish or pinkish patches, on which a grey fur may sprout. Immediate death by fire – bulb, foliage and flower alike – is the only treatment for avoiding a widespread epidemic; nor must any tulips be grown in the same ground thereafter for four years.

Accordingly, whatever this man or that may say from his private experience, you will do well to dig up *all* tulips just before the foliage dies right down and suffer no withered foliage to lie on the ground.

In order, Reader, that you may understand what few catalogues tell you, I must now discharge the tedious duty of explaining what is meant by the terms that nurserymen use for various types of tulip hybrids.

Popular Hybrids

EARLY SINGLES. Bloom with the daffodils in April on short stems, usually about 1ft. Good for bowls and pots.

EARLY DOUBLES. Solid, peony-like blooms in lovely colours on short stems. Very long-lasting. Very good value (if you are not a purist). Good for bowls and pots.

LATE DOUBLES or "Peony-flowered". April–May. Much taller

than the earlies – 18–20in. Shelter from strong winds, which may snap off their heavy top-knots.

MENDELS. Singles in Darwin style, April, 14–18in., often picked out in a second colour.

TRIUMPHS. Follow the Mendels in late April. Single, tall (18–26in.) Darwin style. Are crosses between the Darwin and the Early Singles.

DARWINS. Very familiar, very formal, very tall (up to 30in.). Rather square-based, but having blunt, rounded "petals" (perianth segments). May.

COTTAGE. Very like Darwins but less formal. May.

"HYBRID DARWINS" or "New Darwins". The result of bringing the blood of the brilliant red *T. fosteriana* into the Darwins. Very large flowers in gleaming colours on 24–28in. stems. Good value. May.

LILY-FLOWERED. Of beautiful, urn-like form. The petals are pointed and reflex outwards in the lily manner. 20–24in. May.

MULTI-FLOWERED. Several flowers to a stem. About 2ft. May.

PARROTS. Fantastic in design, with fretted edges often feathered, flared and veined in green to contrast with a brilliant body colour. 18–28in. May.

FRINGED. The edges of the petals are twisted.

"BROKEN". The body colour is striped, flaked or feathered with a second colour. As I understand it, these are the results of a beneficent virus, which has been perpetuated for 400 years. They include the classes called Bizarre, Bybloem and Rembrandt. 16–26in. May.

More Elegant Moderns

The stiffly formed and traditional tulips, popular though they are, are far surpassed in elegance and brilliance by a few groups of modern hybrids or varieties of the wild species. Being rather nearer in lineage to the wild, they have a stronger need for a gritty soil in full sun.

FOSTER'S TULIP. Nothing is more vivid and dashing than the wild *T. fosteriana* from Samarkand. Centuries of hybridization has failed to produce anything to rival its enormous, blazing scarlet goblets. It still outshines its many offspring, which include the Darwins. One need go no further than the old selected forms called 'Mme Lefeber' (or 'Red Emperor'), 16in., and the shorter 'Princeps', but other colours are at one's disposal from hybridizing, as in the yellow 'Easter Parade'.

WATER-LILY TULIPS. Another of the world's most beautiful wildings is the 6in. *T. kaufmanniana*, arrayed in many tones that melt from rusty red to cream, ivory and primrose, with long, pointed petals that reflex and give it its apt sobriquet of "water-lily tulip". Cunning hands have developed these basic colours in the most subtle or the most brilliant combinations or sometimes in self colours. Only rarely do they reach more than 8in., yet the bloom is often longer than the stem. Many are named after famous musicians and some have striped or mottled leaves derived from a marriage with Greig's tulip. The Kaufmanns are perhaps the most elegant of all tulips. They flower with the daffodils at the end of March.

GREIG'S TULIP. *T. greigii* is another scarlet dazzler, distinguished by the mahogany stripes that ornament its leaves. The same stripes have fortunately been transmitted in many, but not all its matings, which have resulted also in some exciting colours and a variety of floral forms, as in 'Plaisir' and 'Red Riding Hood'. 7–10in. April.

GREEN TULIPS. Hybrids resulting from the "greenery-yallery" *T. viridiflora* have given many alluring tulips in which red or white or yellow is flushed or banded with green, while others are a greenish-yellow. The most popular and enticing is 'Artist', a wonderful compounding of chestnut, green, pink and apricot. A warm-hearted and unique tulip of 10in. Others vary a lot in height. Mid-May.

Wild Tulips. Here is an emphatic need for a gritty, fast-draining soil and all the sun possible. They are often grown on the upper slopes of rock gardens or on the edge of embanked borders. They must by no means be planted in regimented fashion. Some gardeners lift the bulbs every year, others do not; the danger of fire disease remains. They are good in pots.

We have met a few of the species already. Most of those that follow are quite small, with a charm all their own, and are fairly easy; start with them first and then become more adventurous.

T. batalinii. Charming primrose. 6in. Late April.

eichleri. Polished scarlet, with black and yellow within. Petals sharply pointed. Grey foliage. 12in. April.

praestans. Several scarlet flowers on one stem. There are several varieties, of which the best known is 'Fusilier'. 10in. April.

tarda (or *dasystemon*). Tinier still. Greenish in the bud, opening widely to sharp, pointed stars of soft gold at the centre, white at the tips. 3in. April.

Tulips in pots. Few tulips succeed in bowls of fibre, the early singles

PLATE 9. *Top*: Dwarf pinks and thymes skirt one of the rose beds.
Below: 'Albertine' on a broad arch linking two rose beds.

PLATE 10.

Left: *Cotoneaster* 'Hibridus Pendulus'.

Below: *Cotoneaster* 'Rothschildeanus' crowns one of the rose-azaleas beds.

and early doubles being the most reliable and the latter making a brave show in a sitting-room. Such old-established varieties as 'Murillo', 'Peach Blossom' and 'Scarlet Cardinal' were among the first that I began with.

Almost any tulip, however, can be grown in a pot, provided that the compost has plenty of grit and the pot is well crocked. Whether in pots or bowls, don't hurry them and observe the following commands:

Plant in September or early October.

Don't take them out of their outdoor plunge bed (or indoor cupboard) until the shoots are 4in. long.

After they have been gradually accustomed to full light, keep them in a temperature of not more than 60° until they are about to flower.

Other Prime Choices

In the following list I have chosen those on which most people would like some guidance, together with a few of the less hackneyed things that are specially recommended. A few that I specially suggest as "something different" are: the ornamental onions (alliums), the "plumed hyacinth", species crocuses instead of the usual hybrids, belladonna-lily, crinum, the easy tigridia and especially the lovely rock and woodland types of anemone.

The general advice that has been given for soil preparation, planting, lifting, etc., will not be repeated save in special instances.

Allium. Though these are garlics, many varieties are virtually odourless unless the leaves are crushed. They are of striking beauty, their rigid stems crowned with splendid orbs in many colours during May and June, with an air of poise and elegance. Very suitable to the herbaceous border or to occasional beds, to which they lend a note of distinction. Quite easy and inexpensive. Plant 3in. deep in autumn and leave undisturbed till overcrowded, then lift and divide. A very few good ones for a start are:

azureum (or *caeruleum*), sky-blue, 2ft.

ostrowskianum, a delightful pink dwarf, 6in.

karataviense, 7in., rose-pink, with broad, diapered leaves in varied colours.

rosenbachianum, 3½ft, pale purple, for the larger scene.

albo-pilosum (correctly *christophii*), huge mauve orbs with a metallic sheen, 2ft.

Anemone. In this sumptuous race there are many breeds. We have seen the herbaceous ones in Chapter 10.

The most widely grown, sold in shops by the million, are the flaunting hybrids of *A. coronaria* called St Brigid and De Caen anemones. Growable in most parts of the country, but best in the warmer ones. Need full sun, a well-dug soil, well drained but moisture-holding, and liberally supplied with leaf-mould or peat, with bone-meal; add sand if the soil is heavy. Not sound perennials and, being very cheap, best grown from fresh corms annually, but can be left in the ground in light, warm soils if the flower stems are persistently cut right down. Can be planted any time of year for a succession, but March and October are best. Plant 2in. deep and 4in. apart, ensuring that the little scar left by the old leaf-stalks is uppermost; if in doubt, plant on edge. Water freely in dry spells. Not difficult from seed sown very thinly in May in a cool greenhouse.

Very like them, but better still, are the hybrids of the peacock-anemone called St Bavo. They have a crisp and brilliant beauty, and are just as easy, but a warm, sunny place is specially important. Grow these rather than the coronarias.

The lesser-known wilding anemones and their varieties however, have a chaste and porcelain beauty much more desirable than the holiday riotousness of the St Brigids and their kind. They are exquisite, having daisy-like petals, and pretty, lacy foliage. Only a few inches high, they flower in spring, *blanda* being first off the mark at the end of February. Their needs vary somewhat. Plant in September or October 2in. deep. Some are apt to be difficult, but specially commended for ease and beauty are:

blanda 'Atrocoerulea' with daisyform rays of fragile and virginal blue – for sun or half-shade in rich, gritty soil, preferably with mortar rubble, where water drains away well. Other pretty varieties of *blanda* are 'Charmer' and 'Radar'.

nemorosa, especially its variety 'Robinsoniana', whose silver-blue rays are adorned with golden anthers; a haunter of moist and shady woodland. The frail blossoms nod over elegantly cut leaves and the plant dies down after flowering but perennates by underground runners.

apennina, lavender, for similar places.

fulgens, delicate in form but vivid scarlet in hue, with handsome black anthers (May); needs the hottest, driest spot possible, with gritty, briskly drained soil in which the water runs away as through a sieve.

All these little, bulbous anemones, especially *blanda*, are very happy in chalk.

Begonia. These natives of moist, tropical countries, many of them tuberous, are remarkable for their exuberance, but they vary tremendously and we should be clear at the outset about what we can or cannot attempt. The main groups are:

Large-flowered hybrids, often grown for exhibition.

Smaller-flowered hybrids called in the horticultural trade "multiflora" or "multiflora maxima".

The small *B. semperflorens* varieties, which are non-tuberous.

The 'Gloire de Lorraine' group; expensive winter splendours raised largely at ratepayers' expense in Corporation hothouses.

The 'Rex' section grown in warm houses for their handsome foliage, demanding the warm, humid shade of the forest.

The hybrids known in the trade as B. pendula, for hanging baskets and the like.

There are, of course, plenty more, some rather *recherchés* and others not at all difficult, such as *evansiana* and *sutherlandii*, which are hardy in the mildest counties. We shall be concerned here, however, with the first three only.

The large hybrids are among the most opulent of summer flowers, set off by very handsome foliage. Exhibitors grow them in greenhouses, as I did once, but you can also weave the most spectacular floral carpets with them in the open ground.

Start the tubers in a warm greenhouse or frame about February in shallow boxes filled with a compost of loam, sand and rotted leaves or peat. Put them in hollow side uppermost, covered by a thin spread of the compost. Keep them moist. When well rooted promote them to 4in. pots and later into 6in. ones before they become pot-bound. Keep the atmosphere of the greenhouse moist by regularly damping the floor and staging. Withhold heat as the sun warms up. Harden-off in May and bed-out in the first week of June.

Give them a soil richly manured and add all the leaf-mould you can. Water copiously and mulch with manure or leaf-soil; begonias prosper in a wet summer.

Lacking any garden glassworks, you can easily raise a small number in the kitchen. If that proposal evokes howls of rage, plant the tubers straight out into the open ground in late April, 3in. deep.

When autumn frost calls off their parade, dig them up complete with roots and a good ball of soil and park them in boxes in a place cool but frost-proof. Leave the foliage and stems to wither and fall off (don't cut them off) and put the tubers to bed in sand or clean soil that is nearly dry.

For real enthusiasts Blackmore and Langdon have a good little pamphlet in great detail.

The "Multiflora maxima" begonias are not classy enough for the greenhouse, but they are easy, gay and flowerful in the garden and in window-boxes. The tubers are started and grown on in the same way as their upper-class brethren. The pendulous begonias are also started the same way, but can then be planted straight into their baskets without being potted.

Skilful gardeners can propagate prized varieties of the tuberous begonias by cuttings. Less skilled ones can do so by cutting up the tubers with a keen and sterile knife, as you do potatoes. Do this about the end of April when the young shoots are growing strongly, with at least one shoot per chunk of tuber. Dust the cuts with flowers of sulphur against fungus diseases and replant.

The *semperflorens* begonias, which are fibrous-rooted, are the most extraordinary mass-production flower factories imaginable. The busy little plants, only a few inches high, are crowded with red, pink or white blossoms among leathery little leaves which are often themselves brightly hued. You use them *en masse* as bedding-out plants. They flower madly all summer and will go on flowering all winter too, if you push them into pots and take them indoors.

Belladonna-lily (*Amaryllis belladonna*). An enchanting but temperamental South African, which all who live in the warmer counties and have the right conditions should ardently woo. It opens its scented, pink, lily-form trumpets in September–October, in clusters at the head of a strong, 2ft scape shooting up from the bare earth without any foliage, which comes into growth in mid-winter and dies down by next midsummer. The belladonna must have the warmest place possible, a light, sandy soil mixed with plenty of leaf-soil and copious watering when in leaf. It tantalizes us madly by not flowering every year, a failing due to its foliage being damaged in a nippy winter and to shortage of sun in its dormancy. At Exbury, Wisley and elsewhere it flowers best just alongside the walls of heated greenhouses.

Plant in June–July, with ample bonemeal, 2–3in. deep in the warm western counties, 5in. deep elsewhere.

BLUEBELL, see Scilla.

Chionodoxa. One of the minor jewels of the bulb world. In earliest spring it throws up blue, starry flowers, 4in. high, looking their best in drifts. Plant 2in. deep in autumn and leave undisturbed. The usual one is *C. luciliae*, with a sparkling white eye, but *gigantea* is larger and *sardensis* is gentian blue. Also successful in pots.

Crinum. Very beautiful; pink-and-white trumpets like swan-necked lilies. 3ft high on thick, strong scapes in summer, much recommended despite their dense, spreading, harum-scarum foliage. Give them about the same soil and situation as the belladonna lilies, though they are far more reliable and hardy. Plant in March, with the shoulder of the long-necked bulb at least 7in. below ground. *C. powellii* is the one.

CROCOSMIA. See in Montbretia.

Crocus. Here we have on the one hand the big, bold, Dutch hybrids, which flower in spring, and on the other hand the smaller, more refined, wild species and their varieties, which come in autumn, winter and spring. Both have their uses. They may be ruined by sparrows unless frustrated by the black cotton dodge, and by voles and squirrels, which eat the corms.

Plant the easy and popular Dutchmen 2–3in. deep in early autumn in drifts and clusters, not as miserable edgings. They naturalize beautifully in grass. Take your pick from the catalogues, with strong leanings towards 'Remembrance', 'Kathleen Parlow' and 'Yellow Giant'.

The little wildings and their varieties delight the heart with their dainty air, especially in the chillier months. Many are enterprising colonists, multiplying freely. You must give them, however, sunny positions and good drainage in a privileged bed, not in grass. The autumn and winter ones you plant in July–August, the spring ones in September. The following is a small posy, many of which have their named varieties also:

AUTUMN. The lilac *zonatus* (or *kotschyanus*), quickly off the mark in September; *speciosus*, forming drifts like pools of deep blue water; and the cooler-coloured *pulchellus*.

EARLY WINTER. The lilac *laevigatus fontenayi*, with feathered petals.

MIDWINTER. The purple *imperati*, from December to March; the little yellow *ancyrensis*, flowering in succession over many weeks; the showy, tangerine *flavus* (or *aureus*).

LATE WINTER. Dominant at this season are the enchanting varieties of *chrysanthus*, particularly 'Blue Pearl', 'Snowbunting', the yellow 'E. P. Bowles' and the bronze 'Zwanenberg Bronze'; challenging it is the resplendent "Cloth of Gold" crocus, *angustifolius* (or *susianus*).

FIG. 64. *Cyclamen neapolitanum* and *C. coum*, with leaf specimens.

SPRING. Now the easy *tomasinianus* takes over, colonizing eagerly; of the several varieties of "Tommy", choose 'Whitewell Purple'.

For the so-called "autumn crocus" see meadow saffron. See also the crocus-like Sternbergia.

Cyclamen. The big, showy hybrids that one gives or receives as Christmas presents are Persian cyclamens and objects of the greenhouse. The hardy, outdoor pygmies, no taller than your finger, are altogether more lovely, have an elfin beauty all their own and induce you to believe in pixies. The few with which we are concerned are all haunters of the shady groves and glades and can, indeed, find contentment in the root crannies at the foot of some fatherly tree or even in the sombre shade of conifers. All are happy in chalk. Several have beautiful foliage.

Start the corms off in a soft bed of leaf-soil, mixed with bonemeal, covering them by only half an inch, and feed them with more leaf-soil and bonemeal annually.

They will outlive you and me and spread into ever-widening colonies through the helpful agency of the ant, which relishes the tiny spot of honey on each seed – unless the mouse, which also enjoys the seed, beats the ant to it. Our chosen few, most of which have colour variations, are:

The deep-rose *europaeum*. Starts off the cyclamen ball in July and goes on sporadically till November. Complete shade.

Next comes *neapolitanum*, by popular choice the queen of all. Its tender pink and its charming stance, like the laid-back ears of a toyland leveret, capture all hearts. The flowers come before the leaves, in masses, throughout September–October. Partial shade.

Third is *cilicium* in early October, likewise putting out its pink shuttlecocks before the foliage. Doubtfully reported not to be quite hardy in the north. Partial shade.

Finally, the several varieties of *coum*, often catalogued as *orbiculatum*, *atkinsii*, etc. September to November or later, the leaves first. Colours vary from crimson to white. Small, four-square little flowers. Partial shade, but not wet soil.

All these wilding cyclamens can be grown in pots in a shady, unheated greenhouse.

Erythronium. Charming and refined little plants putting forth widely expanded, lilyform flowers, 5–9in. high, above diapered foliage in March and April. Nicknamed dog's-tooth-violet: "dog's-tooth" because of the shape of the little bulb, though why "violet" I have no idea; a silly name. Their beauty is not fully appreciated unless they are planted on elevated ground, as on a bank or on the shady side of a rock garden. They must have partial shade and a cool, leafy or peaty, lime-free soil, moist but porous, and, like cyclamen, do well among the roots of trees. The cheapest and easiest are the *denscanis* varieties in several colours. *E. revolutum* 'White Beauty' and the yellow *tuolumnense* will delight all hearts still more and the golden, 15in. 'Pagoda' will challenge one's skill. Plant 3in. deep in August.

Fritillary. (*Fritillaria*). All garden fritillaries nod and some weep poetically, "like Niobe, all tears". Florally, they develop two totally dissimilar styles. One is the curious crown-imperial (*F. imperialis*), which stands regally erect to 3ft, crowned, in the manner of a pineapple, with a topknot of leaves, beneath the protection of which

FIG. 65. The snake's-head fritillary.

clusters a group of several yellow or orange bells. Seen at its best in old cottage gardens. Takes kindly to a wide range of soils and to sun or part-shade.

Plant the bulb on its side 6in. deep in sharp sand in autumn. Usually very shy after moving.

The other group is characterized by the daintier snake's-head fritillary, so called because of the chequered markings that many bear on their drooping, deep-mouthed bells. For the non-specialist the one to have is our charming native *F. meleagris*, which throws up a threadlike stem to some 10in., from which dangle one or two speckled or white bells looking demurely down at the sparse foliage at their feet in April and May. In contrast to the crown-imperial, they are native to water meadows, so do not expect good drainage and must have a damp soil, as heavy as you like, and partial shade. Happy in damp woodland and in grass. Plant 3in. deep in September.

Other fritillaries are captious creatures, but you might try the little yellow *citrina*.

Galtonia. Popularly known as the Cape-hyacinth, *G. candicans* is

FIG. 66. *Galtonia candicans.*

an easy, hardy and most useful summer bulb. It sends up several thick, rigid stems to 4ft or more, from which, in a loose, hyacinthine manner, droop quantities of flowers rather like giant snowdrops. Useful for filling gaps in the herbaceous border, especially among delphiniums and lupins, or elsewhere. Any soil, if reasonably sunny. Plant 4in. deep in March–April.

Not nearly so well known is a little galtonia bearing prettily cut bells in green to 18in. Nice for arrangers. This is *G. princeps* (Christopher Lloyd).

Gladiolus. The big, hybrid gauds of late summer, which are most people's idea of a gladiolus, are child's play to grow in any decent soil in full sun, with copious watering, but for fine bold spikes of large blooms you must apportion them a rich soil manured the previous year.

These gladioli are wretched things in any part of the pleasure garden, for when their blooms are finished the "sword-flowers" look like a shattered army. They are essentially flowers to cut for the house, so grow them in straight lines in the kitchen garden. Plant the corms 4in. deep and 6in. apart any time from March till May. Thus grown, lines of string or wire stretched between occasional stakes will be sufficient support, whereas in the pleasure garden each spike must have a separate cane. When cutting, take the flower stem only, no leaves.

In autumn the corms must be lifted. Specialists tell you to do this as soon as the foliage begins to turn brown, about six weeks after flowering. Amputate the stem half an inch above the corm, dry and clean the corms, then break off the old shrunken corm at the base of the new one and store the new stock in a cool but frost-proof place, dusting them with a mixture of flowers of sulphur and DDT.

The mass of baby cormlets that cluster around the big one, like chickens round a hen, are best thrown away, unless you would like to find yourself, in three years' time, with enough to stock a large nursery.

In addition to these outsize splendours, there are smaller strains, known as "butterfly" and "primulinus" glads. The former have prettily ruffled petals and usually vivid colours in the throat, while in the latter the upper petal is not open, but hooded.

I shall not attempt to suggest varieties for any of them, for the usual reason.

Gladioli are often attacked by thrips – minute, sucking insects. The evidence is a silver or brown streaking and patching. Spray early and often with gamma-BHC. The same treatment does for aphis. Fungus diseases also occur. Destroy all rotten or soft corms and all that are shrivelled, hard and corky. Before planting, examine and discard any corms showing dry, dark, shrunken, scabby patches on the flesh of the corm beneath the papery envelope.

Much more elegant than all these big, conventional glads, but not nearly so easy, are the miniatures known as *G. colvillei* or sometimes as "nanus". These are eminently suited to the borders of the pleasure garden, provided that (in my experience) the soil is rich but gritty and well drained and the position is in full sun; a warm border against a south wall is excellent. They throw up wiry, 18in. stems, bearing up to a dozen charming florets in June. Plant these in the autumn, 3in. deep, with plentiful bonemeal. Do not lift them in autumn but give them a warm, thick blanket of leaves, bracken or other litter. Varieties that I have grown are 'The Bride', 'Spitfire' and 'Peach Blossom'.

Together with these, you could grow the true species *G. byzantinus*, which is of rose-purple and quite easy. There are still more beautiful gladioli that, alas, few of us can attempt.

Some hybrids between *colvillei* and the primulinus glads have been raised by Mr Frank Unwin, but it is too early to pass judgement on them.

GRAPE HYACINTH. See Muscari.

Hyacinth (*Hyacinthus*). Besides being the finest of bowl plants, the hyacinth is very beautiful indeed outdoors, but nowadays its price discourages its use in large numbers. Plant 5in. deep and 6in. apart in a rich but porous soil in October, preferably in sun. Formal regimental planting suits them well. Likely to need staking. Remove spent flower-heads but leave the bulbs in the ground. Very good in window-boxes and tubs.

Choose what colours you like from catalogues but the yellow and oranges are the least satisfactory.

Far cheaper and less trouble outdoors than these top-heavy hybrids are two wild hyacinths of great charm, provided you can give them a gritty, well-drained soil in full sun. They are:

amethystinus, loose racemes of amethyst bells, 7in; May.

azureus, a lovely sky-blue toy of 4in. in February–March, worth planting by the hundred.

Both have white forms. Plant in September, 3in. deep.

INDOOR HYACINTHS. The treatment is as for indoor bulbs generally. The big hybrids are very good in bowls of fibre. If you want them very early, you must get the specially doctored "prepared Christmas hyacinth" or the loose Roman hyacinth, which blooms even before Christmas. "Cynthella" hyacinths are shorter variations on the same theme in several colours; they can be grown outdoors also, planted close together. "Fairy hyacinths", for indoors only, throw up several little spikes from each bulb, flowering indoors in January.

IRIS. See Chapter 9.

Ixia. Pretty stars in various colours borne on erect spikes in gladiolus fashion in June, 15in. high. Suitable only for warm, sunny spots and light gritty soils. Plant 3in. deep in October and fairly close together, enveloping the bulb in sharp sand. No need to lift in autumn if well blanketed with leaves or other litter. Good for cutting and excellent in pots in the unheated greenhouse.

Meadow Saffron (*Colchicum*). Misleadingly called "autumn crocus". There is nothing wrong with the old English name. Its rustic name of "naked lady" is also appropriate for it sends up its large, false-crocus flowers on naked, 6in. stems in autumn without leaves, which do not come until spring and are then very large, coarse and poisonous to cattle. Our native *C. autumnale* is lilac-pink, and *speciosum* is large and late; there are also several showy ones in the catalogues, of which the finest is the pure white 'Album'.

All are for the rather larger gardens and best in open wood or similar settings. Plant 3in. deep in August–September in any reasonable soil.

Montbretia. We are now expected to call most of these gladiolus-style flowers *Crocosmia*, but the old name will stick. The fashionable species is *C. masonorum*, which produces long, bending sprays of blazing orange in summer. Seems quite hardy. Very suitable for the herbaceous border if sited where its hot colour can be tolerated. Over-rated.

The old hybrids still have their place in light soils in the milder counties and among them I have a fondness for the scarlet-and-gold 'His Majesty'.

Plant the corms 3in. deep in March.

Muscari. The lovely little toy grape-hyacinth is one of the earliest and deservedly most popular of spring bulbs. It grows in hyacinthine style, 6–8in. high, with tight clusters of small, closed bells in various tones of blue and in white. Any decent soil suits it, in sun or part-shade. Multiplies rapidly. Never looks better than at the feet of an early-flowering shrub, particularly forsythia. Plant 3in. deep in September. The foliage grows rather long and unkempt after flowering, so site them carefully.

The sovereign choice is the rich and subtle 'Heavenly Blue', but 'Early Giant' is virtually identical and 'Cantab' rivals them nearly. Less familiar are:

'Pearls of Spain' (*M. botryoides* 'Album'). White, small, charming, preferring sun and a gritty soil.

The Oxford and Cambridge grape-hyacinth. Sterile, pale-blue bells at the top of the spike, fertile dark ones at the base. This is *M. tubergenianum.*

The "plumed hyacinth". Grows 10in. tall, massed, as might seem, with amethystine feathers. Unique and decorative. Is *M. comosum plumosum* (or *monstrosum*).

Nerine. Early autumn has few more radiant flowers. Borne on a thick, strong scape or stem, the numerous flowers are displayed in a loose orb and formed of narrow petals that reflex to give a starry-eyed look, with boldly out-thrust stamens. They commemorate the Greek water-nymph Nerine, though they come from South Africa. Thus it is no surprise that they shrink from the colder counties and that even in the south they must be sun-bathed at the foot of a south-facing wall. The nymphs are naked at flowering time, their strap-like leaves not coming till later.

The only species that is safe to grow outdoors here is the pink *bowdenii,* of which there are a few selected forms. Plant with the neck of the bulb only just below ground in November or early March. Even more beautiful ones can be grown in a cool greenhouse.

The nymph's name is pronounced Ne-ry-ne.

Oxalis. This genus includes the English wood-sorrel, one of those plants sometimes called shamrock, which must on no account be allowed in the garden. Those most worth growing are usually planted in the rock garden and very pretty too, if given part sun and a gritty soil. They grow but 3in. high. *O. adenophylla* has silvery, crimped, clover leaves and charming, lilac-pink, upright bells, opening from coiled buds, in June while *enneaphylla* has slightly larger leaves and wide-open glistening white flowers in May. Plant 2in. deep in autumn.

Puschkinia. Wan blue stars are thickly clustered in a 6in. spire in April. Easy and good in sun and light soils and successful in bowls. Is *P. scilloides.* Plant 3in. deep in September.

Ranunculus. The tuberous, oriental buttercups, densely petalled, about 9in. high and flowering May–June, are not very effective garden plants but are fine for cutting and best grown in the kitchen garden. They want heaps of sun, good drainage and leaf-mould or peat. Dampness and cold finish them off. Plant the tiny, dahlia-like tubers, claw downwards, 2in. deep, the "turban" type in November, the French and Persians in March. Lift and store in July. There are also non-bulbous ranunculi, such as the "Fair maids of Kent" (or "of France"!) (*R. aconitifolius* F.P.).

Scilla, or squill in the old vernacular. Until driven out by the botanist this beautiful race included the English bluebell, one of the loveliest of earth's flowers, which was *Scilla nutans* for goodness knows how long but is now *Endymion nonscriptus.* The Spanish edition, which is now *E. hispanicus* (or still *Scilla campanulata* in many catalogues) dresses itself in various shades of pink, blue or white. Plant all a good 4in. deep in a woodland situation.

The smaller squills are enchanting midgets 4 to 6in. high. The sovereign choice is 'Spring Beauty', whose tiny ballerina skirts of gentian blue dance on earth's stage in March–April. *S. bifolia* dares the frosts of February and very soon afterwards the silvery-blue of *tubergeniana* peers out. Plant all 2in. deep in autumn. All make good pot plants.

Snowdrop (Galanthus). The world provides many lovely snowdrops but none, in my eye, rivals the common British one, *G. nivalis,* Wordsworth's "pensive monitor of fleeting years", which enlivens the bare earth in the chill of January and February "for the pale sun's sake". I have a liking for the double one, 'Flore Pleno' because of its prolonged display. There are several other species or named varieties or selected forms, some of which seem to me to lack the true spirit and essence of the tiny commoner. Of such are the "giant" snowdrops 'Arnott's Seedling' (or 'S. Arnott'), which is far too tall at 9in., the early 'Atkinsii' at 8in. and the broad-leaved *elwesii,* 7in. high. These and the donkey-eared 'Scharlokii' and others yet more rare are the darlings of many ardent worshippers at the shrine of the snowdrop, but for my part I am content with the little wilding, "so holy and yet so lowly". Of course, you are not obliged to share my views.

Something rather special, however, is the Greek autumn snowdrop usually called *reginae-olgae,* which flowers in October, the flowers coming up before the leaves, but which otherwise resembles our native, its close blood-brother. For this woodlander you must provide a gritty, fast-draining, leafy soil and a warm, sunny spot.

Snowdrops hate being moved and have the peculiarity that they object least when in full flower or immediately afterwards. If bought as dry bulbs, try to get them in July or August and plant them 3in. deep in shade, even deep shade (except for the Greek), provided it is well drained.

Snowflake (*Leucojum*). Close cousins of the snowdrop and visually almost undistinguishable, except that all its petals are of identical form, whereas some of the snowdrop's petals form a tiny trumpet. *L. vernum*, the spring snowflake, is a 4in. charmer for March. The summer snowflake or Loddon-lily, *L. aestivum*, blooming in May, is too tall at 2ft, the best form being 'Gravetye'. The autumn snowflake, *autumnale*, 6in., flowers from early September onwards. Treat as snowdrops.

FIG. 67. The summer snowflake.

Sternbergia. Considered the most likely contender for the title of the Biblical "lily of the field", *S. lutea* has all the appearance of a yellow crocus, but a leafless, gleaming, buttercup-yellow, as vivid as Solomon in all his glory. It flowers from August–October, but only if given conditions approximating to a Palestinian hillside – hot, gritty and fast-draining. Plant 5in. deep in August and leave it be. The foliage does not appear until the flowers finish and dies down in spring, leaving the bulbs at rest all summer.

The sternbergia flourishes in chalk.

Tigridia. A splash of tropical splendour comes from these cunningly wrought flowers, in which the large outer petals, usually orange, enclose an inner circlet of brilliantly speckled ones. The flowers open after breakfast and shut up at tea-time. They are fleeting but replaced in a rapid and long succession throughout July. Easy in any soil that is not too heavy, but not fully hardy. Plant in April 3in. deep in full sun, fairly close together. Lift and store in September.

Winter-aconite (*Eranthis*). Jolly little elf with a bright buttercup face nestling in a green ruff. Grows anywhere (including gravel paths) but prettiest among deciduous shrubs, whose naked feet it will enliven in the chill of January and February. Plant 2in. deep in August–September. Shy at first. The traditional one is *E. hyemalis*, 3in. high and very cheap, but the hybrid *tubergenii* has much larger, brightly glistening flowers, which, being sterile, give a long display, though not until March.

Second String

Acidanthera. Elegant, amorously scented, white flowers with crimson markings borne gladiolus-wise in September with too much foliage. Erratic and unreliable when planted outdoors. Start them in the greenhouse at the end of March (no heat needed), three bulbs to a 5in. pot, planted 3in. deep, and transplant the whole potful outdoors in full sun at the end of May. Expect two months of dull foliage before the flowers bloom in August. This is *A. murielae*.

Camassia. Tall spikes of small, starry flowers in various colours, for woodland. Plant 4in. deep and 9in. apart in September–October. The best are the blue forms of the 3ft *leichtlinii* and the 2ft lavender *cusickii*. Quite hardy and cheap.

Ipheion. A pretty little flower, *I. uniflorum* has had its name changed four times in recent years. Six-pointed stars, an inch wide, in wan mauve, one flower per 6in. stem in spring, the stems abundant. Plant 3in. deep in September or, if obtainable, when starting into growth in March. Still often catalogued under its older names *Triteleia*, *Milla* and *Brodiaea*. What next?

Ornithogalum. Not a very exciting lot. Possibly the best of the hardy sorts is *O. nutans*, with nodding, silvery green stars on 1ft stems in June. The star-of-Bethlehem, our native *O. umbellatum*, much written up, should be admitted only to hedge bottoms and in the wilder parts of large gardens, for it is a mad colonizer, though a very pretty one with its thronged white stars. Plant both in autumn 4in. deep.

The chincherinchee, *O. thyrsoides*, is a poor garden plant but useful to flower arrangers. Hardy with me in the south, but not apparently elsewhere. Easy in pots in the greenhouse.

Zephyranthes. Beautiful white flower closely resembling a crocus, 8in. high, from August till late October. Flowers well only after a hot summer in full sun and a gritty, sharply drained soil. Is *Z. candida.* Plant 4in. deep in March.

CHAPTER 16

TREES

The "Tall and the Broad" – Planting – Shaping and Pruning – The Larger Conifers – Dwarf Conifers – Magnolias – Cherries and their Kind – Other Trees

TREES are dominant elements in the garden, and their shapes, textures and manners immensely influence its general atmosphere and character. There are tall slim trees, plump round ones, light and airy ones, those with dark-green leaves, others with silvery or purple leaves, and so on. Outline and skyline and architectural effect are critical factors, and variety and contrast must therefore be sought in making one's selections, whether they are to be used as backgrounds or screens, or planted as conspicuous specimens.

I would particularly draw attention to the immense usefulness, especially in the small garden, of that form of tree known as "fastigiate" (see "Gardener's Jargon"). Others, though not strictly fastigiate, have a similar silhouette – slender and narrowly columnar. They both take the minimum ground space and do not overhang and overshadow the soil. One can often get a fastigiate form of a genus normally known only as a standard or as a bush, such as the fastigiate forms of hawthorn, koelreuteria, cherry, mountain ash, and, for rather larger places, the splendid Dawyck beech. Many more are at our command among the conifers, so valuable for creating a tranquil and pensive atmosphere.

Another very desirable form of small tree for providing variety of form and outline is the "weeping" shape, with pendulous branches sweeping the ground like crinolines. Here again there are several, including weeping cherries, looking like great umbrellas of State, mantled in pink or white, the beautiful, silver-leaved weeping pear (*Pyrus salicifolia* 'Pendula'), the dwarf weeping elm beloved of children and, of course, the great weeping willows. Here, in contrast to the columnar trees, we have to allow for a very wide spread.

Another matter of form to consider is the manner in which the tree may have been tailored at the nursery. Except for conifers, many trees, especially the popular flowering cherries and crabs, are available as standards (having a clean stem for about 6ft), half-standards (about 4ft), as well as "bushes", forking a little above ground level. The last is the cheapest, the first the priciest. The advantages of the standard are that it gives immediately some height, that you can plant other things at its feet and that you can walk beneath it.

Be careful to plan according to the ultimate height and spread of each tree. Only a few catalogues give us both these dimensions, a conspicuous example being the *Planter's Handbook* of Jackman's, but we must bear in mind that the soil, local climate and our own care or neglect in cultivation have a considerable effect on the ultimate result. If the catalogue gives no hint of the breadth, we may, for general purposes, assume it to be about three-quarters of the height, except, of course, for columnar and weeping trees.

A problem felt by many people who live in houses close together is that of forming some screening-off of neighbours' windows or masking some hideous prospect. If speed is the prime object, the best tree is Leyland's cypress (*Cupressocyparis leylandii*), but 'Green Hedger' or a good strain of the western arbor-vitae (*Thuja plicata*) are almost equally effective. Or one may use lime trees, pollarded and pleached, at 10ft intervals. See also the chapter on hedges.

Planting

I shall assume that the ground has been thoroughly well prepared in accordance with previous ordinances.

The best time for planting deciduous trees from a nursery is the autumn, the earlier the better, but, except in the colder counties, any time up to the end of March will suit, as long as the ground is not frost-bound or sodden. For hardy evergreen trees (which means chiefly conifers) the ideal season, particularly in the south and west, is October and early November, while the ground is still warm and when plenty of rain is reasonably certain; alternatively, April will suit very well and is the safest time for evergreens of doubtful hardiness especially at the seaside and anywhere else exposed to vicious winter gales. May (though often advised in some writings) is in general too late for evergreens from a nursery. The same seasons apply to shrubs.

Follow the drill laid down in the section on planting in Chapter 5. Use a stake that, after having been driven in, will reach to the lowest branch and tie stake and stem together, preferably with one of the rubber or plastic tree-ties on the market.

After planting follow faithfully the drill for watering, mulching and syringing throughout the first year.

When planting a specimen tree in a lawn, people often make a hole far too small. As we have seen before, the hole should be not less than 4ft × 4ft. This does not mean that the hole need be square; in fact, an oblong one of an equivalent area, with the corners rounded off, makes for a much smoother passage of the mower. Round holes are a curse when mowing. Before planting, prick over the inside walls of the hole with a fork, without breaking them down. In these specimen beds there is a great temptation to mound the earth up above the soil mark on the tree; avoid committing this crime.

Shaping and Pruning

Ornamental trees from a good nursery normally need no pruning at first, except for the amputation of any branches that may have been damaged and except as in the next paragraph. Afterwards, keep an eye open for any overcrowding, any lop-sided growth and any branches that are crossing each other and remove these completely at the point of origin.

Fastigiate trees, other than conifers, profit by some simple pruning in their first year in the garden, to thicken-up the branch structure and correct a tendency to splay outwards. The popular cherry 'Amanogawa' is a typical example. You cut back all the branches, *except the leader*, by about one-third, to an *outward* pointing bud. Do the same thing on any branch that subsequently goes astray, as long as the tree is of manageable size. You can also help the tree by corseting it inconspicuously with string while the sap is running in summer. Big, old fastigiate trees that go haywire are a difficult problem. See Fig. 74.

Trees that grow in a bush or shrub form, forking low above the ground, such as the magnolia, often spread out very broadly in the manner of a bowl. If their growth becomes embarrassing, as it often does in smaller gardens, the outer branches can be severed at or near the base, as in Fig. 72. As the branches next to them develop, these also may be cut out if necessary. Dress the cuts with Arbrex or Medo.

When it is necessary to lop off a complete branch of a heavy tree, start with a saw-cut on the underside, to prevent splitting, and, of course, flush with the trunk or parent bough; then complete the severance from the upper side.

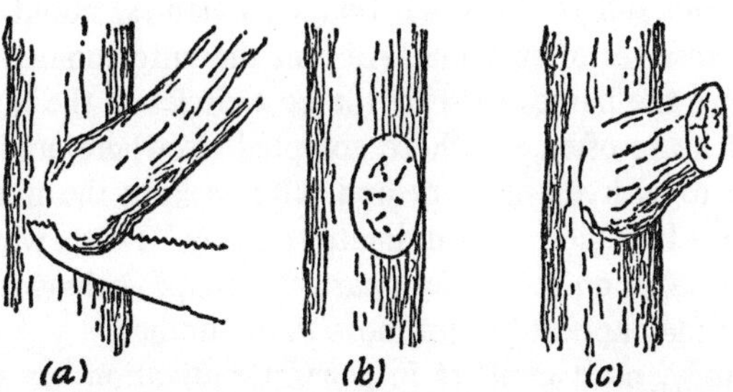

FIG. 68. Lopping a heavy branch. (*a*) Make a small initial undercut flush with trunk or parent bough; (*b*) Complete the cut from above, still flush with the junction; (*c*) Leave no snag.

Sometimes we may want to convert to standard or half-standard form a tree that has arrived as a bush or a "feathered" tree – one having a central stem and several lateral branches. Candidates for this treatment are the liquidambar, maples (particularly those with handsome barks), the Judas-tree, holly, bay, hawthorn, arbutus and silver birch. This you may do by removing the lower branches flush with the stem, but on choicer trees and certainly on evergreens it is best done gradually, over a period of two or three years. Cut clean and remember to paint the wounds with Arbrex or Medo.

Another important thing in the treatment of many trees of erect carriage is to be sure that they have a good "leader" and only one. If a rival to the leader develops, cut it out and tie in the selected leader to a long cane tied firmly to the main stem (Fig. 21).

These and all other pruning operations on trees and on shrubs you must be careful to do at the right seasons, which are:

All prunus species, about the end of May.

Other deciduous trees, soon after the autumn leaf fall.

Evergreens, just before growth begins in early spring (which depends on your latitude and altitude).

Certain trees, notably the liquidambar, the silver birch, and the walnut, will "bleed" and possibly bleed to death if the knife is put to them while in leaf before the middle of July. Winter is safest.

We can now proceed to consider our choices.

The Larger Conifers

This is a fearfully difficult topic, definitely to be ranked among the "ologies" and full of fearsome botanical names, about which the experts themselves often argue. All that the unfortunate author can do is to give the names used by the best circles in the horticultural trade, which are often not those accepted elsewhere, and to exhort his reader to visit the nursery and, after asking the nurseryman's advice about behaviour and ultimate size, say "That's what I want" and put his label on it. Names apart, the shape, behaviour and size of one tree may appeal to him more than another.

Fortunately, most conifers in general cultivation are very much easier to grow than their names are to recite. Judiciously employed, they are tremendously valuable in the garden, giving it dignity and a sense of serene maturity. Handsome all the year round, they need virtually no attention at all once they are established. They exhibit an immense variety of form and feature, from tall, statuesque specimens and broadly spreading ones to absolutely prostrate carpeters, and are clothed in diverse hues of green, blue-green, grey-green, silvery-green and greeny-gold. Some make fine hedges.

The needs of conifers are much the same as those of any other evergreen tree. Above all, after having been properly planted in well prepared soil, give them a thorough soaking of water and follow the drill laid down in Chapter 5 the whole of the first year, which is critical for them. Syringing of the foliage in the first spring and summer in any dry spell is a most positive commandment. The erect species and varieties need care in planting, to be sure that they are absolutely vertical from all viewpoints. Except for small specimens, a firm stake is necessary and a finicky job it can be.

In general, conifers should be in full sun and should not be closely jostled by other plants. They are seldom happy in the atmosphere of large towns unless frequently washed down with the hose. Nor do they care for being moved after the years of infancy, and the eager gardener has to be particularly on his guard against elegant specimens of the columnar types. Some of these may be acquired with reasonable safety up to 5ft high, such as the varieties of Lawson's cypress, but in general wisdom decrees you should be satisfied with trees of no more than 2ft, preferably less. I learnt this lesson many years ago when I planted a "specimen size" Arizona cypress, winning the battle against the wind only after sore trial, and watching specimens of 'Pottenii' and 'Ellwoodii' die in spite of all care.

FIG. 69. Snow damage to a columnar conifer unless tied up.

In general, conifers are best left unpruned, but sometimes they need a helping hand to maintain an elegant deportment. The columnar types should be kept to a single leader, if possible, and any rival cut out. If a tree comes from the nursery with more than one leader, cutting down the rival right to its point of origin may leave a large blank; if so, merely shorten the rival. If a rival appears after planting out, remove it entirely at its source.

Columnar conifers, until they get too large, look much smarter if valeted by running a fairly large, very sharp knife from bottom to top, just skimming the outer surface, so as to snick off the tips of the leaves. This thickens up the foliage attractively. Do it in June. If lacking skill with the knife, use the points of the Greensleeves or Wilkinson's one-handed shears.

Some other conifers that may be of rather loose habit can be thickened up by more careful pruning back of the branchlets to a point where a young lateral is growing (Fig. 70). Do this about

April. Good examples are 'Crippsii', some *pisifera* varieties, the dwarf 'Boulevard' and the thuja 'Rheingold'. The soft tips of 'Boulevard' and of 'Rheingold' are easily plucked off by finger and thumb.

Many low-branching conifers of columnar deportment, especially when young, are liable to severe damage by heavy snow, which may cause the branches to be splayed out and possibly broken. Tie these round circumferentially before the snow arrives; on all conifers knock off the snow with a long pole.

Name hunters may find it useful to note the following equivalents:

Cypress (true) – *Cupressus*
False cypress – *Chamaecyparis*
Lawson's cypress – *Chamaecyparis lawsoniana*
Leyland's cypress – *Cupressocyparis leylandii*
Fir – *Abies*
Douglas fir – *Pseudotsuga*
Redwood – *Sequoia sempervirens*
Spruce (including the Christmas-tree) – *Picea*
Hemlock spruce – *Tsuga*
Yew – *Taxus*

A FEW CHOICES

Cedrus. The blue Atlantic cedar, the cedar of Lebanon and the deodar are all magnificent trees suited to large gardens only (though I have an Atlantic cedar in mine); and the small variations of them are disappointing. If you have anything like an acre or more, you must certainly have *Cedrus atlantica* 'Glauca'.

Chamaecyparis. This popular "false cypress" is distinguished by having flattened branchlets and small cones, instead of the rounded branchlets and larger cones of the true cypress. The trees themselves are also usually smaller overall. Good in chalk. Don't allow cones to form in the first three years; they strip off easily by an upward motion when the branch is clasped in the hand.

There is a whole regiment of these most decorative conifers to choose from, especially in the varieties of Lawson's cypress, of which there are some fifty. The following must satisfy us.

C. lawsoniana vars:

'Columnaris' (or 'Columnaris Glauca'). This I look upon as the best of all, which is saying a lot. It forms a perfect steeple of very dense foliage, richly suffused with blue. A superb specimen tree, but even more impressive when three are planted together. Ultimately about 30ft high by 9ft.

'Ellwoodii'. Slim, elegant, with blue-green foliage, growing slowly to rarely more than 10ft. A tree for any garden.

'Fletcheri'. Another great favourite. A trifle plumper, more feathery, taller, not so blue as Ellwood's variety. Rarely more than 18ft by 5ft, but has been known to exceed 30ft.

'Lanei' (or 'Lanei Aurea') is my own choice from among the many golden forms of Lawson's cypress (Jackman or Notcutt); of softer hue and more compact than the usual 'Stewartii'. Other guilded excellencies are 'Lutea', rather slow, with drooping branchlets, and 'Smith's Variety' (Four Winds Nursery). All can ultimately grow very tall.

Of the other species of chamaecyparis, not slenderly columnar, we may note:

Obtusa 'Crippsii'. An unique tree with foliage of brightest lemon, displayed on horizontal, outspread branches, loosely spaced, so that the whole tree makes a wonderful pattern of light and shade, with the lemon foliage contrasting with the black of the deep shadows. Say 20ft × 12ft. Prune as advised in the introduction of this section and Fig. 70.

Pisifera. This is a species that includes several delightful varieties with soft, feathery foliage and attractive outlines, including some choice dwarfs. Two to choose here are the milky-green 'Squarrosa' or its pale sulphur form and 'Plumosa Aurea' in soft gold (Hillier or Jackman). Clothed to the ground and of plump outline, they may perhaps reach 20ft × 15ft. The latter grows quickly, but can be cut down at 8ft, is quite amenable to clipping with shears and can make a good, close hedge.

Cupressocyparis. This is the now celebrated hybrid Leyland's cypress, already mentioned. About the fastest of all conifers, it will grow a good 3ft a year when established, assuming an erect, broadly columnar deportment. An excellent sea-side tree but liable to get bowled over in extreme exposures. Tolerant of chalk. A fine tree for a quick screen. Get plants not more than 2ft high. It will certainly reach 50ft or more, but remains reasonably slender. Is the child of a marriage between a true and a false cypress.

Cupressus. The true cypress gives us many trees of great beauty,

FIG. 70. Pruning the tip of a lateral branch of the golden *Chamaecyparis obtusa* 'Crippsii' to thicken up the foliage. Certain other conifers can be similarly treated.

but not all are fully hardy in Britain except in the warm, western, Gulf Stream counties. Here are a few outstanding ones:

arizonica 'Conica', the Arizona cypress. A beautifully symmetrical steeple, like the Italian cypresses, but with blue-green foliage, soaring elegantly to 35ft. Now re-named *C. glabra* 'Conica'. More reliably hardy than the classic *sempervirens.*

macrocarpa. The Monterey cypress. Popular, fast, undistinguished, not fully hardy away from the milder seaboards and apt to give up the ghost suddenly. Leyland's cypress is far better.

sempervirens. The elegant and romantic Italian cypress, straight as

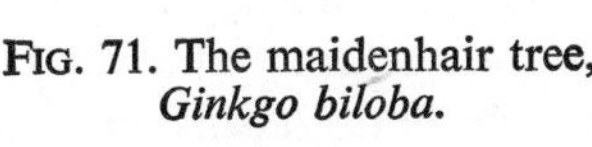

FIG. 71. The maidenhair tree, *Ginkgo biloba.*

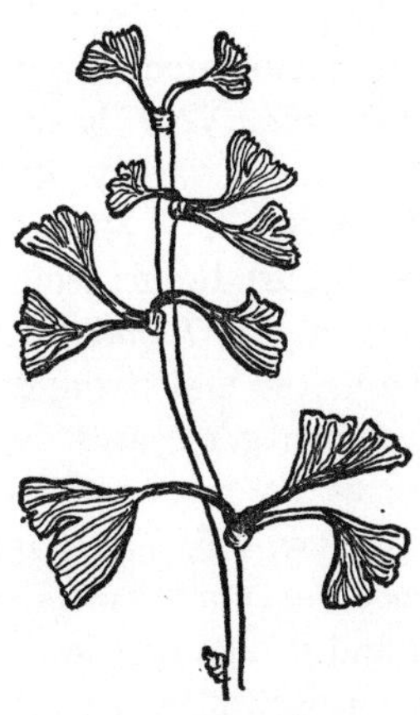

a dart, slender as a wand in the variety 'Stricta', not hardy outside the warmer counties. See *arizonica.*

Ginkgo. *G. biloba* is the maidenhair-tree, most interesting and distinctive, having leaves like pretty little fans, which explains its popular name. The fastigiate form is usually preferred. May become too tall and broad in time for small gardens, but (I am told) a good conifer for towns.

Juniper (*Juniperus*). Though its forms are many and various, it is convenient to group all these among the dwarf conifers in the next chapter.

Libocedrus. The incense cedar, *L. decurrens* is a majestic columnar tree for larger gardens, growing to 60ft in time, yet scarcely 10ft wide. The dark-green foliage is displayed in fan-like formations. A splendid landscape tree and quite hardy in most parts of Britain. Must be got pot-grown. The coarse roots dislike disturbance. Then they strike deep, so that other plants can be grown quite close to it.

Pinus. We can note only three pines, both for the larger scene only: the superb Scotch pine (*P. sylvestris*), with its warm, rufous bole towering high and topped with a mushroom hat, a tree to plant in "tall woods with high romances blent"; the Austrian pine (*P. nigra austriaca*), a very fine, big, rugged shelter tree against rude sea winds and excellent in chalk; and *P. radiata* also used as a sea-side windbreak.

Thuja. The 'arbor-vitae'. Those for our money are:

plicata, especially its variety 'Fastigiata', which makes a very fine, dense, fast screening tree, shooting up 3ft a year. Its variety 'Zebrina' is lightly illuminated with gold, but rather slower.

occidentalis. Very handsome, broadly columnar; particularly attractive in its variety 'Lutescens', in which the foliage is a soft yellow. Only 12ft × 8ft.

Yew (*Taxus*). In this genus pride of place is taken by the handsome old English yew, *T. baccata*, the "Old yew that graspest at the stones that name the underlying dead"; though by no means confined to Tennysonian graveyards. Nowadays, out of its numerous varieties and forms, the most popular for planting as a tree is, paradoxically, the Irish yew, *T.b.* 'Fastigiata', found growing wild by a farmer near Florence Court in Ireland about 1780. It grows in a broadly columnar shape and is seen best in the form 'Aurea', in which the somewhat sombre aspect of the parent is relieved by a golden glitter; it grows slowly to an ultimate 15ft. A pair of Irish yews make handsome sentinel trees (especially for the next generation). More elegantly slim and of an even brighter gold is 'Standishii', but it is a fearful slowcoach. See also in "Hedges".

Dwarf Conifers

Here the thicket of names and synonyms becomes denser still and we are in the realms of the extra-specialist. So we must tread carefully. More than ever is it necessary to visit the nursery to see what you are buying rather than trust to a catalogue, apart from a few well established sorts. I have some pretty toys of my own, but, as no one seems to agree on their names, I must regretfully leave them out.

Commonly, dwarf conifers are plants that you do not come to until rather late in your gardening life. Only then do you find how charming they are in their subtle and often brilliant colours, their diversity of form and their air of peace. You must, however, be careful with their associates and not mix them promiscuously in any sort of company. Their choicest friends are undoubtedly heathers, which are particularly valuable for covering the ground before the prostrate junipers, for example, have made their full growth. To me, the golden dwarfs, sparkling with life in winter as in summer, have a particular appeal. These, even more than the green ones, need maximum sun. A few are susceptible to damage by searing winds.

Most of the true dwarfs have no objection at all to being moved about from one place to another, provided one is sensible about the weather and soaks them thoroughly before and after the move.

Chamaecyparis. Once again it is the false cypress that gives us the largest choice, and here are a few:

lawsoniana 'Minima Aurea' (also called 'M. A. Rogersii'). A beautiful, lustrous, greeny-gold pyramid, with flat, upright branches, one of the very best. May reach 4ft in forty years (I am told!).

lawsoniana 'Minima Glauca'. More rotund in outline, with fanned branches suffused bluish-grey.

obtusa 'Nana Aurea'. A most picturesque shrublet of irregular outline, with golden fan-shaped sprays. 'Nana Gracilis' is a lustrous dark-green, reaching 6ft in time.

pisifera 'Boulevard'. An unique and colourful shrub in which the overall effect is silvery blue or blue-grey according to the light. Attracts everyone. Pyramidal in outline and said to reach 6ft in time. It colours best in shade (but not overhung) and perhaps in an acid soil. Prune as in the introduction to this section.

pisifera 'Plumosa Rogersii'. Beautiful, feathery, golden plumage on a broadly conical little tree, reaching 3ft or so. Said to need some shelter from the keenest winds, but mine stand fully exposed. 'Plumosa Pygmaea' is a greener equivalent.

Juniper (*Juniperus*). For convenience, I am grouping all the junipers here, although some are by no means dwarfs in the same sense as the others in this list. They vary widely in form and size, some being slender steeples, some absolutely prostrate and others shooting out bristly fingers at rakish angles. All have a strong influence on the character of the garden and the prostrate ones are first-class ground-covers, dense, wide-spreading and weed-proof. Many grow in chalk in nature.

chinensis. The most celebrated is 'Pfitzeriana', commonly known as the Pfitzer, a bold, lusty, dark-green shrub throwing out bristly fingers eagerly at angles of 45°, tremendously effective in the garden scene. The strong limbs will reach to 12ft or more laterally with their tips some 5ft above ground. It may also be listed as *J. media* 'Pfitzeriana'. There is a yellow-tinted form.

The Pfitzer now has a handsome young brother named 'Hetzii', which grows much more nearly erect and not so wide, with the upper surfaces of its foliage of a lightly silvered, olive green; mine is a little over 7ft high and wide – much taller and narrower than the Pfitzer.

Another very attractive form of *J. chinensis* (or *media*) and occupying far less space is 'Blaauw's Variety', which is blue-green and grows in the shape of a vase, the stems starting vertically and then arching over. 7ft × 4ft.

communis. Our native juniper, of which we shall have four varieties:

'Compressa', the wee Noah's ark juniper in the shape of a slim little spire, which takes many years to reach 1ft; for rock and sink gardens.

'Hibernica', the Irish juniper, one of the most popular of all; an enlarged edition of 'Compressa', splendid with heathers or as a specimen. 10ft or possibly more with the years, but scarcely more than 1ft wide.

'Hornibrookii'. A dense, prostrate, dark-green carpeter.

'Bonin Island'. A beautiful, absolutely prostrate ground-hugger, following the contours of the soil; its fresh apple-green is delightful at all seasons. Unique and rare.

conferta. Absolutely prostrate, forming a dense and bristly rug of apple-green about 7in. deep, very decorative, quite weed-proof and spreading 10ft wide.

sabina. This is the well-known savin, which bursts out into various forms. The favourite is 'Tamariscifolia', which builds up tier upon tier of close-knit horizontal branches in handsome architectural "tabulations". Say 2ft × 8ft.

Picea. The most popular dwarf spruce is *P. albertiana* 'Conica', a very fine, dense, rotundly conical bush of soft green, growing very slowly to some 5ft × 3ft. Treat it with a systemic insecticide in early June to ward off red spider.

Thuja. Of the several smaller arbor-vitaes, I propose 'Rheingold', a variety of *T. occidentalis.* A gingery-gold, broadly pyramidal shrub, excellent as a specimen among heathers. To 6ft slowly.

Magnolias

These hover on the borderline between shrubs and trees, but, as certain of them are most emphatically trees, I include them all here.

The magnolia ranks among the *élite* of trees and is the pride of many of the largest and most opulent gardens in this country, especially in Cornwall, where magnificent trees of *campbellii* tower

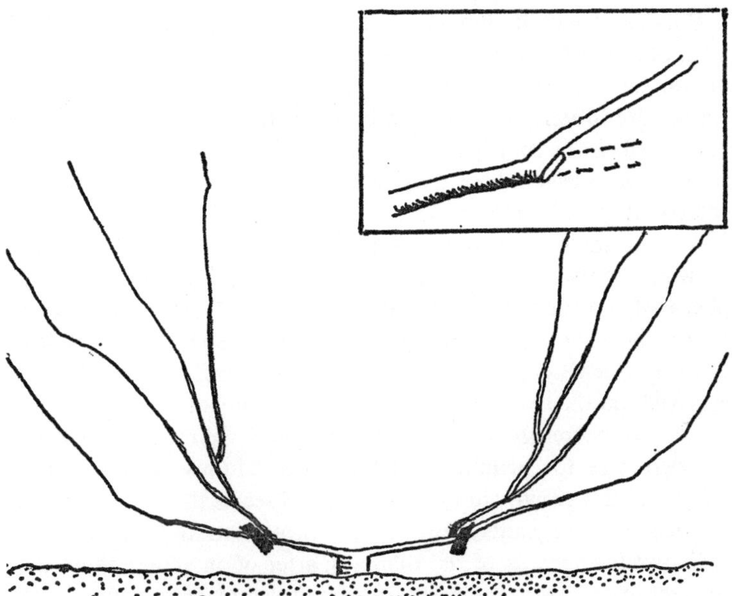

FIG. 72. Pruning a ground-forking tree or shrub that is growing too wide, e.g., magnolia. *Inset:* The actual cut.

as high as a house, laden with the most breath-taking blossoms. Such splendour, however, demands not only the largest scene but also a cheerful faith in the future, for *campbellii* may keep you waiting for twenty-five years or more before it allows you to see its wonderful, pink, tulip-form blossoms. Others, such as *mollicomata* and *kobus*, may hold back for at least half as long. However, those of us who have command over smaller territories and those who are impatient have yet some glories of our own.

Most magnolias are deciduous but all have handsome foliage.

Naturally they fork low above the ground and are of broadly branching habit, often to the embarrassment of people who plant them in small suburban front gardens, but this embarrassment can be avoided by pruning as advised at the foot of p. 272 and in Fig. 72. Their flowers are commonly in the forms of goblets or saucers, often spectacularly embellished by gleaming, crimson tufts of stamens round a central boss of green carpels. The blossoms of some species stand erect but others turn down to gaze at their mother, the earth, and are best beheld by walking underneath them.

Outside the Gulf Stream counties and sheltered nooks inland magnolias must be considered of suspect hardiness in their first year or two and protected accordingly. The buds of all the early flowering species are in danger of rupture by frost, though the plant may be unharmed, as in camellias and early rhododendrons. The majority require, or at least prefer, an acid soil, though fortunately there are some that grow happily in lime and even in chalk.

A good start means everything to magnolias. Prepare a large hole – 5ft wide and two spits deep – enriched with organic material and with plenty of peat in order to hasten the penetration of the soil by the roots. These roots are thick, fleshy and hungry, so do *not* tread them down too fiercely. Apart from a few small bulbs, allow nothing to encroach on the root area, but mulch it very liberally. For the same reason, never fret the soil with fork or spade. Opinions differ about the best time for planting, but for the deciduous ones, especially those that flower early in the year, autumn seems the most desirable, provided that the plants are given some protection for the first winter.

Except for gardens of less than a quarter of an acre, I think that the first prize goes to the evergreen, lime-tolerant *M. grandiflora*, one of the handsomest trees in all our gardens, its branches, forking low above the ground, thickly draped with large, bold, gleaming, dark-green leaves of superb quality among which, before too long, the big, creamy-white goblets, gorgeously scented, shine throughout the summer like lamps in a green shade.

Commonly, *grandiflora* is grown against a warm south wall, a wise precaution in the cooler counties, but not necessary in the warmer ones, provided it gets a fair share of the sun. The wall needs to be an expansive one, with a good 25ft of headroom ultimately and no windows in the magnolia's wide upward path. Plant for preference in the spring and give it some protection for its first winter. The best variety of *grandiflora* is 'Goliath', but 'Exmouth' and 'Ferruginea'

PLATE 11.
Left: The Madonna Lily.
Below: *Ramonda myconii* growing in the peat wall.

PLATE 12. *Top*: Author's un-named seedling lily, near to 'Golden Clarion'.
Below: Lily 'Thunderbolt'.

are also first-class, and, if bought from a nursery of high standing, all will flower when quite young.

Of the deciduous magnolias, the sovereign choice for average gardens is *soulangiana*, so often seen giving lustre to a suburban garden in May. Easy, very beautiful and quite hardy in the north as well as the south. There are several varieties, of which the finest is undoubtedly 'Lennei', opulently laden with waxen, tulip-form flowers in a regal, rosy purple, followed by purplish seed-pods enclosing brilliant red seeds. Flowers when 3ft high and reaches 15ft × 15ft in thirty years.

A smaller, more compact tree, apposite for very small gardens, is *liliflora* 'Nigra', which bears large goblets of very dark purple for a long period, beginning before the leaves, the petals recurving in the form of a lily-flowered tulip to show a paler hue within. Some people think it sombre. Flowers when very young.

The commonest magnolia is one that I don't care for. This is the so-called star-magnolia, *stellata*. The petals are narrow white ribbons which unfurl very raggedly, before the leaves, not at all star-like. But it is easy, lime-tolerant, successful in towns, compact, seldom as much as 10ft × 10ft after many years and flowers (when 1ft high) in March–April if the frost hasn't ruptured the buds. In parts of Wales and Scotland it may grow far larger. The pink form 'Rosea' is much more attractive.

For acid, woodsy soils, rich in humus, and hardy enough for Yorkshire at any rate, there is a sumptuous little magnolia in *sieboldii* (or *parviflora*), carrying, in May and June and often later, the most elegant white cups of porcelain texture accentuated by a crown of crimson stamens and enriched with a heady scent. About 15ft.

Another lovely white magnolia, also hardy in Yorkshire, is the celebrated yulan, *M. denudata.* It flowers when young on leafless boughs in April, its snowy, waxen goblets opening wide, with the scent of lemons. Not often more than 15ft except in the west.

For gardeners in the chalky lands who have room to spare for a loosely spreading tree, the one to have is *highdownensis*, which was born in Sussex chalk and is profusely embellished with opulent, pendulous, scented, white bowls with purple carpels, in early summer.

Another safe choice on chalk is *sinensis*, which much resembles *sieboldii*. May–June. Say to 15ft.

FIG. 73. *Magnolia soulangiana.*

Cherries and their Kind

(*Prunus*)

This very large and captivating genus includes, so far as flowering trees are concerned, the cherries, almonds, plums, peaches, apricots and a few of indeterminate allegiance. The majority are low-forking trees but are obtainable from nurseries as standards or half-standards, priced in guineas. There are also one or two of narrow, columnar carriage, very useful in confined spaces, and some beautiful weeping ones for ampler spaces. Several make good hedges.

All that we shall discuss are thoroughly hardy and easy to grow in reasonable soils and their glory is enhanced when they stand with their feet among daffodils. But I implore you to plant them where they will have room for their full development, for it is heart-rending (as well as possibly dangerous to the tree) to see a fine cherry mutilated because its ultimate spread has not been foreseen.

Indeed, except for those used for hedging, all kinds of prunus dislike cold steel, which may cause gumming, and the right time to prune, if at all, is at the end of May. You are warned also that bullfinches plunder the buds of prunus trees without mercy in winter. If you live in an area plagued by these deceptively handsome vermin you must either give up the idea of growing any prunus or you must drape the trees completely with small-mesh nets down to the ground. Other birds may also attack the buds, but none is so utterly destructive as the bullfinch.

There is such an enormous field to choose from that I can give no more than a few pointers. A few small prunus are usually classed as shrubs, but we will embrace them all here.

ALMONDS AND PEACHES

The almond is *P. amygdalus* and the peach *P. persica.* Their charms lie not only in their ethereal beauty but also in the cheerfulness with which their brave buds challenge the frosts of March and even February. A memory of one of my previous gardens that lives with me is that of an almond tree in full bloom in February, each pink blossom encased in ice as though it were the work of a confectioner to the gods. Yet they have their cross to bear, for, like the fruiting almonds and peaches, they are prey to the disfiguring and debilitating disease of peach-leaf curl. The preventive measure is to spray the branches with Orthocide just as leaf-fall begins in autumn and again just before the buds open in February. The die-back disease may also occur, when all dead twigs should be cut back to live wood.

Of almonds, I suggest that there is nothing more satisfying than the pink, double, late-flowering 'Roseo-plena', small and compact. There is, however, the charming dwarf Russian almond, *P. tenella* 'Firehill', growing to only 4ft and draped in pink blossom from top to toe in April. It spreads gradually by suckers, when some of the older shoots should be cut right out as the buds begin to open and presented to the distaff side with which to make a pretty "arrangement".

Of peaches, which flower in April–May, the most popular variety is 'Clara Meyer', with charming, double-flowered rosettes of true peach-pink, reaching in time to 15ft × 18ft, with edible fruit. Somewhat larger is the splendid 'Aurora', while 'Prince Charming' is of more upright growth in deep rose-pink.

Here also we have a dwarf in *P. triloba* 'Flore Pleno', truly a "perfect peach", when it is not overcome by an uncontrollable forest of suckers, as it often is when bought as a standard (it is always grafted). About 4ft high, it is wreathed in the most enchanting pink rosettes often sold in florists' shops. Spare a few when in bud for the family flower arranger and amputate all other shoots 2in. above ground after flowering. It is sometimes called 'Multiplex'.

CHERRIES

One of the great glories of the spring, the "loveliest of trees" do better in heavy soils than in light, sandy ones. The beauty of the multitudinous blossoms is often accentuated by the coppery or bronzy hues of the young foliage, but, alas, the glory of the cherry is short-lived, seldom lasting more than ten days and strong winds quickly bring down the blossoms, to form a carpet of pink or white on the ground.

The cherries are encumbered with a tiresome complexity of names – English, Japanese and botanical. Botanically, the valid ones are the Japanese. The list at our command is so long and so tantalizing that one just does not know where to stop, but we can begin by segregating a few.

First, the fastigiate varieties that are so valuable in limited spaces. These are the celebrated 'Amanogawa' in pale pink about 20ft × 6ft, and the hybrid 'Spire', a little taller and broader and maybe a better tree. There seem to be slightly different forms of both of these about the country, some of not so good behaviour as others. Prune as in the introductory sections of this chapter.

Next, the weepers, which make magnificent spectacles, like enormous floral ballet skirts. They must necessarily be got as standards and an ultimate spread of a good 20ft allowed for, with possibly 15ft of height. We have the following primary choices.

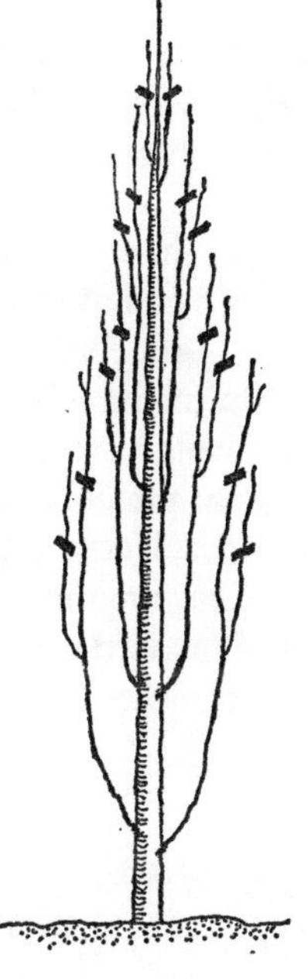

FIG. 74. Pruning a young fastigiate tree, e.g., the cherry 'Amanogawa', to outward-pointing buds, but the leader left alone.

Cheal's Weeping Cherry. A vivid pink fountain.

subhirtella 'Pendula Rubra'. Rose-pink; large.

'Accolade'. A fine modern hybrid.

Coming now to trees of normal shape, there is a huge field, of which I pick the following as the best. Augment my scrappy notes from good catalogues.

'Kanzan'. The sovereign choice of most small gardeners and of local authorities. Also called 'Sekiyama' and (wrongly) 'Hisakura', which is a different, single-flowered cherry. The newer, large-flowered 'Pink Perfection', raised by Waterer, Sons and Crisp, is somewhat preferred.

'Okame'. Prime choice for small gardens. A shapely tree of elegant carriage. Perhaps 18ft × 18ft.

sargentii. One of the glories of the race. Beautiful foliage spring and autumn. Pink flowers. Fairly upright. 25ft × 20ft.

'Longipes' is the easiest name for the superb and graceful small tree that ought to be called 'Shogetsu', but is more often 'Shimidsu-Sakura', or even 'Oku-miyako'. Perhaps a tribute to its popularity. Dense clusters of pendant, blush ballet-skirts. Say 15ft × 20ft.

'Hosokawa'. Very distinctive. Flat topped, the branches spreading horizontally. 15ft × 25ft or more. Usually miscalled 'Shirotae'.

subhirtella 'Autumnalis'. Famous as the winter-flowering cherry, in white or pink forms. Wonderful with a witch hazel at its feet. 20ft × 25ft.

'Tai Haku', the magnificent "great white cherry". Most sumptuous of all, but one of the largest, 30ft × 30ft.

'Tsubame'. An elegant new introduction in which the branches undulate in the horizontal plane, suggesting a bird's wings (the name means a swallow). Very picturesque. From Jackman's.

Look also at the unique yellow 'Ukon' and the robust 'Shirofugen'.

Our two splendid native wild cherries deserve places in larger gardens. They are the gean or mazzard (*P. avium*), best in its double form, and the bird-cherry (*P. padus*), which brandishes very distinctive little truncheons and is choicest in Waterer's variety. Both are white.

OTHER PRUNUS

The Japanese apricot, *P. mume*, is a delightful small tree, often starting to flower in February. There are white, pink and double forms.

The hybrid flowering plum, *P. blireiana.* A beautiful little tree with masses of double pink rosettes esconsed among copper leaves. 15ft × 18ft.

P. cerasifera 'Nigra'. Leaves damson-purple, almost black, with a profusion of pink flowers. 20ft × 20ft.

Other Trees

All are deciduous unless declared otherwise.

Arbutus. The strawberry-tree. One of the few evergreen trees that succeeds in Britain. Glossy, small, dark-green leaves densely clothe a broad-spreading and handsome plant. Choose *A. unedo* 'Rubra'. The flowers resemble pink lilies-of-the-valley in November, developing into small, strawberry-like, tasteless fruit. Flowers and fruit are often borne at the same time. Comes as a low-forking tree, but can be pruned to make a trunk, the warm rufous bark being very handsome. Not reliably hardy in the coldest shires unless in shelter. Usually below 20ft.

More handsome still is the Californian madrona (*menziesii*), a large, noble tree, with a beautiful, smooth, pale trunk and pyramids of flowers in spring, followed by orange fruit. Generally pretty hardy, as seen in the Midlands.

The hybrid *andrachnoides* has gorgeous cinnamon-red trunk and branches. Fairly hardy, I gather.

Bay (*Laurus nobilis*). This is the true laurel, used of old to crown emperors, heroes and poets. For those falsely so called, see under "Laurels" in the next chapter.

The bay is one of our handsomest evergreen trees, besides being useful to the cook. A doubtful choice in cold counties; even in the south it may be cut severely by extra hard frost, but shoots up again. You can trim it to all sorts of formal shapes, but it is best as a free-growing shrub, when its small, warm, dense, holly-green foliage comforts the winter scene. To 20ft, usually less.

Beech (*Fagus*). In general, far too big for most of us, but the handsome, columnar Dawyck beech is quite suitable for many gardens, growing with great dignity to some 35ft by only 10ft wide and clothed to the ground. It is *F. sylvatica* 'Fastigiata'. A pair of Dawyck beeches at an entrance make the most impressive of sentries.

Birch (*Betula*). The beautiful silver birches are acceptable in quite small gardens, where their white trunks and graceful foliage are a great delight, though their roots are greedy. Our very fast-growing native "lady-of-the-woods" is *B. pendula.* Young's Weeping Birch makes a delightful umbrella where a spread of 25ft can be spared. They prosper in almost any soil – sand, chalk, clay or bog.

Catalpa. The Indian bean tree, *C. bignonioides,* is one of the most delightful and umbrageous of trees from the shade of which to watch others work. A beautiful lawn specimen and one of the best trees for large towns (as seen outside the Houses of Parliament). Its wide-spreading branches and large, heart-shaped leaves are companioned in late summer by splendid trusses of bell-flowers, in the manner of the horse-chestnut, the individual flowers, which are white, diapered with pale-gold and mauve, being of great beauty. Slow off the mark, then fast. Say 30ft × 30ft.

Its golden-leaved variety, 'Aurea', is a good deal smaller and a delightful little tree.

Chestnut. The Indian horse-chestnut, *Aesculus indica*, is a distinguished tree of moderate size, dressed over-all with tall, slim, elegant, blush-pink candles at midsummer. For the half-acre garden (Notcutt, Hillier).

COTONEASTER. Several can be bought as standard trees, see Chapter 18.

Crab-apple (*Malus* but still sometimes listed as *Pyrus*). The crabs tend to get overshadowed by the flowering cherries and their kind, for, although beautiful in spring, often having coloured foliage as well as flowers, many look rather commonplace in summer.

Particularly beautiful, however is the small Japanese crab, *M. floribunda*, which erupts in a great froth of soft pink – a superb picture in a full-grown 20ft tree. From the dozens of others, the fairly new 'Profusion', with wine-red flowers in great masses, looks like becoming the best all-rounder.

For floral beauty there is little need to look farther than these two, but if we hanker after fine fruit as well we can have 'John Downie', 'Golden Hornet' and 'Dartmouth Crab', which produce big, handsome, heart-shaped crab-apples, excellent for crab-apple jelly.

Some crabs are liable to the same scab disease as other apples and need the same spraying with Orthocide or lime-sulphur before and after flowering.

Eucalyptus. There is a growing cult for the Australasian gum-trees, some of which have been found pretty hardy in the Gulf Stream counties of the West and elsewhere if sensibly placed. Their evergreen, blue-washed foliage is very attractive. Not suitable for chalk soils, except *E. parvifolia*, which is also one of the hardiest. Get pot-grown plants in *spring*. They grow very fast and young trees are apt to blow over; the recommended treatment is to cut the plant down to 9in. from the ground after its first year and to make a trunk by subsequently removing all shoots except the one that proves strongest and straightest. The best proven species are *gunnii* and *parvifolia* (Treseder).

FIG. 75. The pinnate leaf of *Koelreuteria paniculata.*

Hawthorn or **May** (*Crataegus*). "Our gnarled and writhen thorn" is picturesque, easy to grow and indomitable in all climates. In gardens it is best as a standard. The most striking is Paul's Double Scarlet Thorn, which explains itself. Another valuable one is *C. lavallei*, a sturdy tree with large, orange haws that are usually ignored by birds and hang on till the end of January; also called *C. carrierei.* Almost thornless. Both reach about 20ft × 18ft.

Very rarely seen, but extremely good value in small gardens, is the fastigiate hawthorn, *C. monogyna* 'Stricta', a nice sentinel tree. I have had it in two gardens and have great fun by using it as a host for clematis, sweet-peas and *Eccremocarpus scaber*; people pause and ask: "Whatever's that?"

FIG. 76. Leaf of the liquidambar.

Judas-tree (*Cercis siliquastrum*). A charming small tree, remarkable for the masses of rosy purple pea-flowers that burst forth direct from the naked branches in May, before the nasturtium-shaped leaves. A low-forking tree. Good in towns. Flowers best in a warm corner.

Koelreuteria. A tree that is undeservedly much neglected, no doubt because of its awkward name. *K. paniculata* grows to about 25ft, spreading rather broadly, with long, fluttering, pinnate foliage and trusses of bright yellow flowers in July–August. Easy, hardy and not shy of chalk. Very rare indeed is its fastigiate form, exceedingly slim and admirable for small gardens, which I have grown for several years. (Hilliers.)

K. apiculata closely resembles his brother but is a little smaller and flowers earlier.

Laburnum. Tennyson's "dropping wells of fire" have a few superlative varieties, excellent for gardens of any size. Perhaps the best is the hybrid *L.* 'Vossii', which has very long racemes and does not

FIG. 77.
Acer negundo 'Variegatum'.

set seed. The Scotch laburnum, *alpinum,* is a prettier tree but its seed-pods hang on and, at least while the tree is young, you must patiently remove them all; a boring job on a step-ladder. They are poisonous.

A curiosity is the hybrid between a laburnum and a broom, in which the flower racemes are yellow or purple or both; *L. adamii* is a sufficient name for most nurserymen, though the generic is in fact *Laburnocytisus.*

Liquidambar. The sweet-gum is a most desirable tree, with foliage resembling that of maples. It can grow very large, but, outside the Gulf Stream counties, is not often seen above 30ft or so and much less in width. In the most favourable situations the foliage colours impressively in autumn. To make a trunk, remove the lower branches flush with the stem soon after leaf-fall, not in the growing season, for the liquidambar bleeds badly then. Order *L. styraciflua.*

Maple (*Acer*). Leaving aside the big trees such as the sycamore and the Norway maples, we are left with a varied group of very decorative small trees and with the dwarf, shrubby Japanese maples, which I include here for convenience. Though having no visible flowers, all have a gracious carriage, beautiful leaves, which may be painted in green, purple or silver, and often coloured bark as well.

Pictorially, there are few more decorative trees than *A. negundo* 'Variegatum'. The blanched green-and-white leaves are most effective in the garden scene if not clumsily sited, but for heaven's sake do allow for an ultimate spread of a good 25ft, for a negundo amputated is a negundo ruined. The only time to use the knife is when a young shoot appears without the white variegation. Otherwise it is a very easy tree, tolerant of the most unpromising conditions and prospers in lime.

A. griseum is a jewel, growing slenderly and slowly to a graceful 20ft, and with a trunk of rufous bark that peels annually to disclose the gleaming orange skin beneath. A beautiful creation suitable even for gardens of quarter of an acre. Succeeds in lime.

Akin to *griseum* are the snake-bark maples, in which the trunks are handsomely streaked or marbled, particularly *grosseri hersii, davidii* and *pennsylvanicum* (the moosewood). These are all trees of distinction, with brilliant autumn colours in acid soils.

The dwarf Japanese maples are delightful little trees or shrubs with the most elegant foliage and graceful deportment. Most are varieties of *A. palmatum.* Try to give them protection from cutting winds and late frost, which sere the beautiful foliage. They are doubtfully lime-tolerant. If the stems die back, amputate to healthy wood, even to the base if need be; they don't fear the knife and will sprout afresh. Mulch them liberally. In defiance of Authority, I grow all mine in full sun. For distinguished carriage and brilliant autumn colour, the sovereign choice is 'Osakasuki', which, if it likes you, may grow to 15ft, arching widely.

Probably more popular, however, are the cut-leaf forms of the variety 'Dissectum', in which the delicately sculptured leaves have the appearance of having been finely shredded. Each tree has its own individuality and they grow into low, gnarled, spreading bushes. If you want the form with crimson-bronze leaves, ask for *A. palmatum*

'Dissectum Atropurpureum', which will grow very slowly to 6ft × 9ft, but the less usual green form is equally beautiful and fresher-looking.

Confusingly, there is also *A. palmatum* 'Atropurpureum', in which the leaves are divided into five fingers ("palmate"), but not finely dissected.

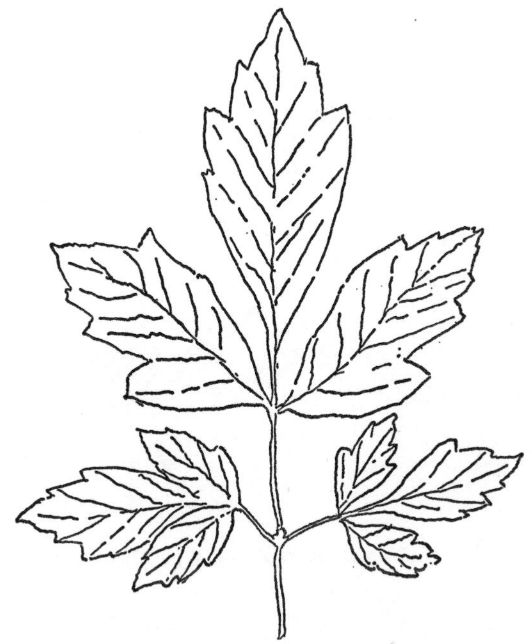

FIG. 78. *Acer griseum.*

Besides *palmatum*, Japan gives us *A. japonicum*, somewhat over-shadowed in popular favour, yet still handsome, especially in the variety 'Aureum', with leaves of pale gold that contrast charmingly with others and branches arranged in tiers. The leaves are relatively broad, with many short-pointed lobes. Remains dwarf for several years. There is a cut-leaf variety of *japonicum* also, known as 'Aconitifolium' or 'Laciniatum'; and for a really fast mover there is 'Vitifolium', whose vine-like leaves become charged with splendid autumn colours and which grows into a handsome tree.

Unless grown in cool and partly shaded places, all these small oriental maples should be well mulched in spring and liberally watered in dry spells and barred from gardens swept by fierce winds.

MOUNTAIN ASH. See Sorbus.

Pyrus. The weeping pear, *P. salicifolia* is one of the most distinguished of small trees, with dense, silvered, willow-like foliage, a beautiful carriage and cream flowers in April. Possibly the finest weeping foliage tree for small gardens. About 20ft × 20ft. Try to give it a dark background and aim to make it, when big enough, one of the main focal points of the garden, companioned with shrubs of contrasting foliage in dark green or in copper. Later in the season the foliage becomes grey. Not cheap.

FIG. 79. *Acer palmatum* and *A. p.* 'Dissectum'.

Robinia. Often erroneously called an acacia, *R. pseudo-acacia* is a big 50ft tree with a furrowed trunk, pinnate leaves and clusters of white flowers in June. The columnar form 'Pyramidalis' is very good value. What is of more interest is the new variety 'Frisia', with the most beautiful golden foliage, but we don't yet know a great deal about it.

Sorbus. This versatile genus provides two valuable groups – the rowans or mountain-ashes, which have loosely pinnate leaves (like the ash), and the whitebeams, which have simple, oval leaves. All are hardy and easy and are celebrated for their loads of autumn berries.

Taking the rowans first, those of special note are:

S. aucuparia. Our fine native (30ft × 25ft), of which there are many forms – a weeper ('Pendula'), a narrowly columnar ('Fastigiata') and a yellow-berried ('Xanthocarpa').

vilmorinii. A beautiful little tree, less than 20ft high, and my favourite. Light, small-leaved, feather-like foliage, delightful berries that turn pale rose.

hupehensis. Another beauty, but much larger, with feathery, sea-green foliage and persistent, pale rose berries.

cashmeriana. A little charmer with fern-like foliage, red in autumn, and white, marble-size berries (Waterer or Sunningdale).

Of the whitebeams, the one of most interest is the 30ft *S. aria* 'Lutescens', with glistening white leaves that sparkle like diamonds when fluttered by the wind. A delightful sight. There are several others, including a charming miniature weeper (Hilliers); all good on chalk and in towns.

Willow (*Salix*). In the smaller gardens much travail can ensue from planting the glorious golden weeping willow. It looks so innocently charming as a juvenile, but its rate of growth and its ultimate size – it reaches 50ft × 50ft – appear rarely to be foreseen. Nor is the tedium of sweeping up the leaves and twigs that it sheds for many months of the year. However, in any garden of half-an-acre or more the golden weeping willow gives a marvellous backdrop to the garden scene and it is quite fallacious to suppose that it needs to be near water, though, to be sure, dry, shallow soils are unfriendly.

Unfortunately this desirable willow has, through the machinations of botanists and others, acquired a list of aliases as long as a burglar's record at Scotland Yard. The current one is *S. alba* 'Tristis' (too sad a name) and others are: *S.a.* 'Vitellina Pendula', *S. chrysocoma* and even *S. babylonica* 'Ramulis Aureis'. Quite a lesson in botanical latin.

There are, of course, any number of willows, large and small, erect and otherwise, but where a weeper is wanted in a small garden a much safer bet is the purple osier, *S. purpurea* 'Pendula', a charming small tree with purple bark, grafted on a standard stem, forming a graceful crinoline. Not cheap (Waterer or Jackman).

Other nice willows are:

The corkscrew willow, *S. matsudana* 'Tortuosa', a smallish tree with curiously twisted branches; quaint rather than beautiful and liable to be plundered by the "arranger".

The "palm" or goat-willow or common sallow, a great favourite for its pretty male catkins; this is *S. caprea* (15ft), of which there is a very small weeping form (7ft × 5ft).

CHAPTER 17

RHODODENDRONS AND AZALEAS

Soil and Climate – Planting and Tending – Ailments – Some Rhododendron Choices – Deciduous Azaleas – Evergreen Azaleas

I ENTITLE this chapter as I do merely as a result of popular usage, but in point of fact all azaleas are rhododendrons, being merely one of the many "series" into which all rhododendrons are grouped.

Given an appropriate soil and climate, the culture of rhodos presents no difficulty whatever. Once planted, they normally need no attention at all beyond removing the dead flowers and an occasional renewal of the soil's fertility. Until recently they were regarded as adornments of baronial acres, but today, so diverse are their forms, features and measurements, there are species or varieties quite suited to the cottage plot and plenty that conform to the scale of suburban gardens.

Soil and Climate

Rhododendrons do not need a particularly rich soil. Overfeeding may result in excessive growth at the expense of flower. Any soil in good heart will do, but it must be an acid one. The notion that it must be a peaty one is fallacious.

As we have seen earlier, the value of peat lies in providing an easy rooting medium, in improving the structure of the soil and in conserving moisture. Some of the finest rhododendrons in the country are grown in stiff clay. Sandy soils present the problem of moisture conservation, so important to rhodos, but this may be in part overcome by the measures we have noted before, particularly by deep annual mulches of oak or beech leaves. Chalk is hopeless.

The most desirable climates are those in which there is ample rainfall, especially summer rainfall, and in which the air is somewhat moisture-laden. Thus the most favourable climates are those of the Gulf Stream counties and the least favourable are those on the dry east coast. However, rhododendrons vary greatly in their insistence on a moist climate and the "hardy hybrids" will prosper with a rainfall as low as 23in. (the mean for London). Of course, what heaven

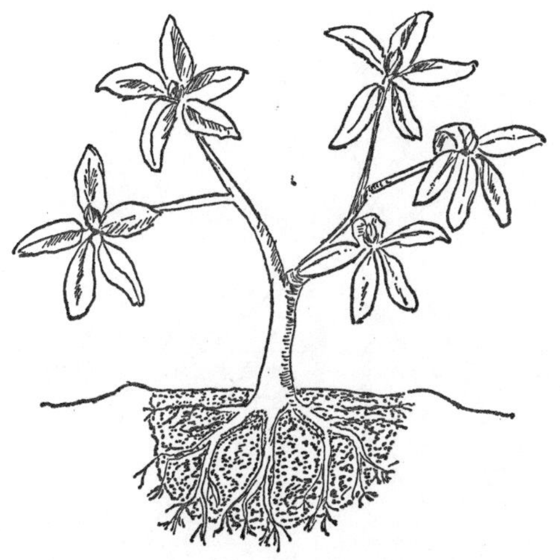

FIG. 80. Planting a rhododendron.

fails to do the gardener can supply through the hose and we need not be seriously frightened by the oft-repeated adjuration that the water must be lime-free; I myself, and of course many others, use water from the pure chalk of the North Downs in Surrey which frequently leaves a trickle of chalk when the sprinkler is taken off the hose.

Climate has further to be considered in relation to frost and to shade. A good many of our most sumptuous rhodos will not stand very low temperatures and there are others that, contrariwise, are spoilt or possibly killed altogether by excessive roasting in the sun. Thus, to sum up, the most promising conditions for rhodos generally are an acid soil, plenty of moisture and preferably dappled shade.

Planting and Tending

This is a simple enough matter, but there are a few points to watch.

Prepare a hole no deeper than the plant's root-ball, but a few inches wider all round. Line the hole, especially the sides, with wet peat and mix up the peat with the soil, adding a trifle of organic fertilizer (e.g. manure, Eclipse, Maxicrop or hoof-and-horn).

FIG. 81. Dead-heading rhododendrons: snap off at the arrow.

Tease out the fine root tips from their ball of soil so that half an inch or more is visible. Plant the rhodo so that the root-ball is *not lower* than the level of the surrounding earth. Fill in round the perimeter. Give a *light* firming all round. Water thoroughly. Some hours later tread in a trifle more firmly and water again. Avoid compacting the soil and damaging the roots by excessive treading.

Planting distances present a problem. You must first discover from the nurseryman how much space each variety takes up and you must then face an awkward question: will you plant the rhododendrons at their ultimate distances apart, filling in with other plants the while, or will you plant at half-distances and move every other rhodo later? Fortunately, rhodos move very willingly, provided a good ball of soil accompanies them. Given the manpower, you can shift them around at any age or size.

Subsequent treatment consists only of the annual mulch of leaves, with manure every now and then, ample watering in spring and summer and dead-heading. This last job you do by clasping the whole truss of dead flowers between thumb and middle finger at a point immediately above the small buds showing in the axils of the topmost leaves and snapping off the whole truss by bending it sharply to one side. Do this as soon as the flowers fade.

FIG. 82. After dead-heading; the three new buds are preserved.

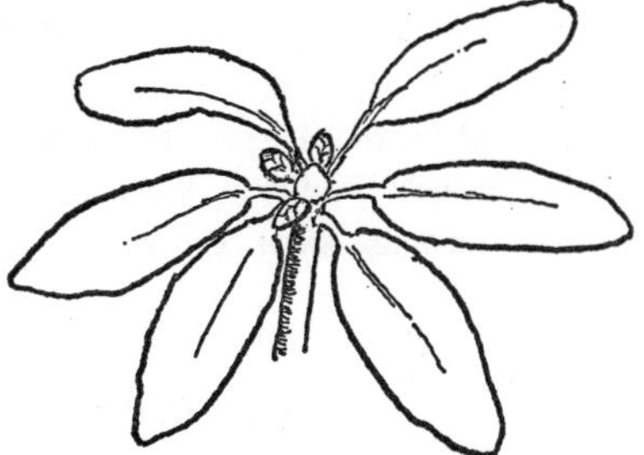

Be particularly careful not to damage the young buds in the leaf axils, which are usually very obvious but sometimes not yet emergent.

One can't, however, be expected to dead-head the dwarf, small-flowered rhodos or the evergreen azaleas; you would need the patience of Job and the temper of a saint. On the larger, deciduous azaleas the whole truss does not always come off easily in one snap.

Pruning has very rarely to be done on rhododendrons. The need will arise only if a branch gets damaged or if the plant grows lop-sidedly or too big. You simply amputate the branch just above any leaf joint. If the branch is very lean and leggy, with no leaves except the top cluster, cut anywhere you like and trim back when new leaf buds appear.

Ailments

Mercifully rhododendrons are bothered by few ailments. The commonest is bud-blast, in which the flower buds become "browned off" and withered in winter and early spring. Pluck off all these and burn them. Bud-blast is due to a fungus carried by the insects known as hoppers, therefore the thing to do is to attack the predator by spraying with DDT every three weeks from July to September.

Two other insects molest the leaf on its under-surface, though not to a serious extent. One is the rhododendron bug, a tiny creature with diaphanous wings that betrays itself by a cream-coloured speckling on the upper surface.

The other is the rhododendron white-fly, a frail, pallid thing that causes a yellow mottling of the leaf and often a curling of the margins. Its "honeydew" drops on to the leaves below, resulting in a "sooty mould" that impairs the leaf function.

In either case spray the underside of the leaf with any of the usual insecticides.

As in other plants, soil deficiencies may be revealed by various discolourations of the leaf. These are analogous to anaemia in man and technical advice is called for.

Some Rhododendron Choices

Now we come to the very awkward stage of considering which rhododendrons are to be recommended, for the range is enormous. For lordly estates there are the huge splendours of *sinogrande* and 'Polar Bear' and for little old ladies in cottage plots there are charming miniatures such as *campylogynum* and 'Little Ben', besides absolutely prostrate ones, such as *radicans*. Except in the milder counties, it is usually advisable to avoid those that flower very early in the year, of which 'Cilpinense', 'Bric-à-brac' and *leucaspis* are examples, for although the plants are hardy enough, their fattening buds will not resist the grip of a sharp frost at the end of February.

In the following short selections I have used a few hieroglyphics, which are based on the official ratings of the RHS. In fact, two systems are current (apart from the system of the American Rhododendron Association), but I am following the older one, which, though less exact, is easier as a quick guide. The ratings are given for hardiness and for floral merit. The first is for hardiness, in which:

- A means hardy anywhere in the British Isles.
- B means likewise hardy, but needing some shade for the best results.
- C means hardy when sheltered and in warm gardens inland.

The further hardiness ratings do not concern us.

The merit rating (in the old system) is represented by a number of stars, from one to four. I omit these stars here, as they are sometimes arguable and as all that I quote are highly meritorious. Neither the hardiness nor the merit rating is by any means sacred, for one man's experience is not the same as another's, and many a class B rhodo is grown well in full exposure.

For very small gardens some ideal rhododendrons are:

'Elizabeth', B. Scarlet. Large flowers.
yakusimanum, A. White. The absolute tops.
'Carmen', B. Dark red, low, spreading, superlative.
'Blue Tit', B. Dense and bushy. The most popular.
'Bluebird', B. Broader than high.
impeditum, A. Near violet in best forms.
keleticum, A. Rosy-purple. A low mound.
scintillans, A. Deep blue-purple in best forms.
russatum, A. Rich, regal violet.
'Songbird', A. Deep violet.

None of these normally exceeds 4ft. In the slightly larger garden we can add:

'Bow Bells', B. Large rosy bells. A charmer.
'Blue Diamond', B. Good colour; highly rated.
'Doncaster', B. Rich red. Good old favourite.

In time these may reach 6ft and a bit more in favoured conditions.

THE HARDY HYBRIDS

Gardens of up to half an acre can easily accommodate varieties up to 7 or 8ft and one or two larger sorts. The gardener here has to choose between the "hardy hybrids" with tightly packed trusses and mostly of old standing, and the more refined or woodland sorts in which the elegance and poise of the lovely Asiatic species are dominant. He will choose the latter if he lives in the Gulf Stream counties and favoured places inland with a little dappled shade, but the former if he is climatically less fortunate. Here is a First XI of easy hardy hybrids.

'Britannia', B. Scarlet. Tops all nursery sales lists.
'Purple Splendour', A. A prince among rhodos.
'Blue Peter', A. Pale lilac with purple eye.
'Betty Wormald', B. Deep pink.
'Pink Pearl', B. Large, soft, voluptuous pink.
'Souvenir de Dr S. Endtz', B. Deeper hued 'Pink Pearl'.

'Scandinavia', B. Dark scarlet. Clothed to the ground.
'Sappho', A. White, with black patch in throat.
'Kluis Sensation', B. Scarlet.
'Goldsworth Yellow', B.
'Lord Roberts', A. Dark red. Trusty old warrior.

THE WOODLANDERS

And here, for the same sized garden, is an XI of the choicer and more elegant sorts, all perfectly easy. In this class of rhododendron we often find what is called a "grex" or group, with several different colour forms (or other variants), known as clones. Thus in the grex Jalisco there are eight clones, all in slightly different tones of yellow.

'May Day', C. Scarlet. Clothed to the ground. 5ft.
'Fabia', B. Orange. Clothed to the ground. 6ft.
'Grosclaude', B. Gleaming scarlet. Compact. Modest size.
'Temple Belle', C. Pale rose. Compact, neat.
'Dairymaid', B. Cream and pink. Early.
'David', B. Blood-red. Large. Fine.
'Day Dream', C. Primrose and pink.
'Idealist', B. Lovely soft yellow. Rather large.
'Jalisco', B. Yellow. Beautiful form.
'Unique', B. Cream and pink.
Naomi, B. A famous grex with many clones, of which 'Exbury Naomi' and 'Naomi Stella Maris' have four-star ratings, in shades of biscuit and lilac. Give them room.

Where one or two plants of about 12ft can be fitted in, one thinks at once of such superlative varieties as the deep yellow 'Crest', the ethereal 'Carita' in various heart-melting colours, the elegant, tubular trumpets of 'Lady Chamberlain' and 'Lady Rosebery', the creamy trusses of 'Letty Edwards' and so on.

Beyond half an acre everything is at our command – the glories of the Loderi grex, the immaculate splendour of 'Avalanche' and its pink clones, the scarlet uniform of the great 'Grenadier'; or, where only the hardier ones must be grown, the almost blue 'Susan', 'Fastuosum Flore Pleno' and 'A. Bedford', or the rosy salmon of 'Mrs R. S. Holford'. Not to speak of the great species, such as *sinogrande* and *falconeri*, for those who have the conditions that suit them.

Deciduous Azaleas

Azaleas present rather less embarrassment of choice, though catalogues seldom explain what the various groupings mean. Initially, we segregate them into two flocks – the evergreens or semi-evergreens, which are low, dense, broadly spreading, and the deciduous, which are taller and of more open growth. We will take the latter first.

Nearly all the deciduous azaleas commonly grown in our gardens are hybrids of complicated ancestry. In catalogues they are found arranged in several groups, all of which have a strong family resemblance. Pictorially, all look most alluring in light woodland shade, but, subject to the usual measures for preserving moisture, they do well enough in the sun, though their flowering period may be shorter.

Mollis azaleas flower in early May on leafless stems. 4–5ft. Often erroneously called "mollis x sinensis".

Ghent azaleas. End of May at the same time as the leaves emerge. Flowers of honeysuckle form and a delightful scent. To 10ft. Very hardy.

Occidentale azaleas. End of May. Soft, pastel tints and sweet scent. About 7ft.

Rustica Flore Pleno. Double flowered, June, to 9ft.

Knap Hill azaleas were an inspired development from other groups, resulting in flowers of a scintillating brilliance and a lively and dancing poise, clustered in large trusses throughout May. They were further and intensively developed by the acumen of the late Lionel de Rothschild and became famous as the "Exbury azaleas", although, in fact, they are only the Exbury strain of the Knap Hills.

These are the ones for the average gardener to go for. Broad-petalled, of great size and substance, of a gay and sprightly carriage, the flowers have a radiant quality and their colours range from fiery reds to tender, silvery pinks and whites. They average 5½ft in height. The strength of the strain through in-breeding is so emphatic that seedlings now come remarkably true to their parents, so that today the gardener may confidently buy "Exbury azaleas" simply by colour, at much less cost than the named varieties. They are extremely good value.

However, he would be a man of strong purpose who could resist these gorgeous named varieties and the following handful will surely open the door to temptation:

'George Reynolds'	'Scarlet Pimpernel'
'Strawberry Ice'	'Basilisk'
'Corringe'	'Clarice'
'Silver Slipper'	'Sun Chariot'

Besides these hybrid splendours, there are also some very nice azalea species, of which the best known is the yellow *Rhododendron luteum* (Azalea pontica), stocky, sturdy, very hardy, colouring gloriously in autumn and spectacular as a hedge.

Evergreen Azaleas

The field here is smaller but no less rich in treasure. The leaves are small and the flowers of the majority are small also, but are borne in such profligate abandon that they often completely obscure the foliage. Their low stature makes them very welcome in small gardens, but many of them spread laterally more than vertically.

In my experience the best evergreen azaleas are not the most pubcized ones, but are the Dutch strain known as the Vuykiana azaleas. These remain dwarf, have relatively large flowers in fine colours and excellent, dark-green foliage. They include the incomparable 'Palestrina', finest of all white azaleas, 'Vuyk's Rosyred', 'Vuyk's Scarlet', 'Purple Triumph' the finest of purple azaleas, together with several named after famous musicians (Slocock).

The best known evergreens, however, are the Japanese Kurumes, small-leaved, very dense, smothered with multitudes of small flowers in brilliant or tender hues in April–May. Not wholly evergreen outside the softer counties and not fully hardy in the coldest ones.

From this great band one could make a dashing start with the scintillating pink 'Hinomayo' (best of the lot), the blazing crimson 'Hinodegiri', the gorgeously barbaric 'Hatsugiri' in magenta, and 'Rashomon' in soldier's scarlet. Among those of softer tones there are 'Kirin' in silvery rose, rather tender when young, 'Apple Blossom' and 'Takasago' in pale lilac.

There is a medley of other evergreen azaleas, all very beautiful and all of very mixed parentage. They are usually to be found in catalogues as "Malvatica-kaempferi" hybrids. Some of these form themselves in tabulations or layers 4ft or more high, usually in May. Partial shade is always best. We will pick just a very few; all are completely hardy as far as I know, but not all are fully evergreen.

'Addy Wery'. Deep scarlet, tough.

'John Cairns'. Orange-scarlet. Deciduous in my garden.

'Kathleen'. Sparkling rose-pink.

'Orange Beauty'. Vivid and arresting.

'Pippa'. Beautiful, soft amethyst. Very hardy. Stands sun.

'Eddy'. A blending of reds. Superb. To 5ft.

'Naomi'. Salmon. Outstanding. To 6ft or more. June.

'Leo'. Orange-pink. Low and leafy. June.

The last four, which were raised at Exbury by Lionel de Rothschild, are often erroneously listed as *oldhamii* hybrids; there is no sap of that species in them.

CHAPTER 18

A DIVERSITY OF EVERGREENS

Something for All – Camellias – The Heather Family – Other Desirable Shrubs

We have much rich treasure to explore here in addition to the rhododendrons. There is something for everyone, for all conditions and all seasons. The list will include a few deciduous shrubs also, for, when a genus has both evergreen and deciduous species, I have, for convenience, brought both sorts together in this chapter. The viburnum is an exception, for, having very few evergreen forms, I have reversed the method.

Grey-leaved shrubs, which have a powerful effect on garden atmosphere, are assembled in the chapter "Silver and Grey".

In this chapter we have to keep a wary eye open on hardiness, for, as a rough generalization, evergreens not native to our shores are less hardy than deciduous shrubs. For this reason some are best grown in the shelter of a warm wall, where they look extremely elegant and become one with the architecture.

For the same reason one is often advised to plant out evergreens in May rather than in the autumn or winter. This may possibly be the right advice in the iciest of all regions, where "milk comes frozen home in pail", but elsewhere it is too late. Normally the best time is early autumn (September–October), when the ground is still warm and when ample rain will succour the plants until they get a foothold. The exceptions to this norm are two: wherever violent winter gales vex the land and when the plants themselves are of sorts that funk their first winter outdoors, e.g. ceanothus and escallonia. In such instances the best planting time is April, especially at the seaside.

Whenever they may be planted, all evergreens need copious watering for their first year of life. Accordingly, after planting, obey strictly the ordinances laid down earlier to water, mulch and thereafter spray the foliage liberally in all dry spells, especially in spring and summer.

Camellias

One of the great glories of the garden, their sumptuous flowers set off by the most handsome, dark-green, highly polished leaves, which densely robe the whole plant, so that it is beautiful at all seasons of the year. I own to a partiality for camellias above all other flowering shrubs, except roses. It is a perennial cause of wonder to me how such tender-looking flowers can outface the bitter breath of February and March or even, as some do, burst out at intervals throughout the winter.

If they were a little cheaper and a little quicker off the mark, camellias would surely be one of our most popular shrubs, for, given a few basic provisions, they are so easy to grow. They are far hardier than was supposed at one time, when, except in the west country, they were grown only in the ample greenhouses of rich uncles. Today, however, we know that the most popular camellias, which are *C. japonica* and its many beautiful varieties, are completely hardy in most parts of the country and so also is the fine, new, Cornish-bred hybrid *williamsii.*

Before and after planting. The basic provisions for growing camellias are:

lime-free soil, fairly rich in plant food,
plenty of water,
free-running drainage,
partial shade (for most species).

In other words, pretty much the same conditions as for rhododendrons, but with a trifle more care in positioning. Avoid situations facing either south or east.

Plant if possible in early autumn, in soil that has been fairly well enriched with manure or other organic matter, mixed with plenty of peat in the top spit. After planting obey the following few cultural precepts.

Give copious and *regular* watering when rain is not vouchsafed, especially in the period from April to September and extra-specially in July, when next year's buds are forming.

Feed fairly liberally, though not to excess, the important period being June–July. Mulch thickly with leaves every autumn, adding a lump or two of manure or a little nitrogenous fertilizer to prevent de-nitrification of the soil. Camellias seem very fond of tea-leaves, which are their own natural top-dressing, the tea plant being itself a camellia.

Carefully pick off the small, round seed-pods, at least while the plant is young.

Take whatever precaution you can to prevent the branches from being broken off by heavy falls of snow.

Much heartache and wringing of hands is suffered when, just as the big, fat buds are about to burst open to enrich the world, they suddenly drop lifeless to the ground. This is a physiological ailment, due to one of the following causes:

waterlogging of the roots,
sudden heavy rain after drought (so water regularly),
sudden frost after a mild spell,
sudden thaw, when plants are in an east exposure.

Selections: the Williams varieties. If I were starting a new garden, I would put my best dress shirt on the exquisite varieties of *williamsii.* They flower when very small, are less sun-shy than the japonicas, grow fairly fast and usually shed their flowers neatly as soon as they fade, which most other camellias do not. They flower in a long succession from February to May and, indeed, one or two begin in November and go on for five months. The pick of this stunning new race are:

'J. C. Williams'. The first of these hybrids to face the world. Large, single, pure pink petals ornamented with a handsome boss of golden stamens. A bush of open habit, growing to some 8 ft. 'St Ewe' is a tone deeper.

'Elizabeth Rothschild'. Near J. C. W. in flower, but, with me, the shrub is much more compact and dense.

'Donation'. One of the world's most beautiful flowers. Very large, double, soft, heart-melting pink blossoms, deepening slightly as they age. Begins to flower when a few inches high. A bush of erect habit, about 8 ft × 5 ft.

On these *williamsii* camellias do not hesitate to cut back fairly hard, in April, the long, spindly stems that several of them throw out.

Selections: japonica varieties. Close upon their heels in estimation come the many varieties of *C. japonica*, which, apart from their initial slowness (and their price), are almost all that a man could wish for. There is a far bigger range of colour and of form than among the *williamsii*, but the one that I would go "nap" on for a first choice is the superbly generous 'Adolph Audusson', with splendid, blood-red flowers and gleaming brushes of golden stamens; an easy plant and most eager to please the considerate gardener.

Otherwise, the choice of japonica varieties depends mainly on one's ideas about colour, though there is some diversity in floral style also. Some of the most reliable and popular are:

'Jupiter', dusky scarlet, single.

'Elegans' (or 'Chandleri Elegans'), light rose, spreading habit.

'Gloire de Nantes', rose, semi-double, begins at Christmas.

'Contessa Lavinia Maggi', blush, variably streaked carmine, double.

'Lady Vansittart'. White, faintly flushed and often flecked pink, semi-double; narrow and acutely pointed leaf, dense habit.

'Latifolia', rose-crimson, broad-leaf, spreading, very hardy.

The pink 'Lady Clare' is beautiful in blossom, but the shrub has a floppy habit. For a white, the single 'Alba Simplex' or the double 'Nobilissima', which starts in December.

The reticulatas. Even more gorgeous florally, because larger, are the varieties of *C. reticulata*. These, however, are not hardy in the open outside the Gulf Stream counties, but in favoured areas elsewhere they can be grown against a wall facing west or north-west, for which they make the most sumptuous adornment. In the warm counties they are highly successful on north walls as well as out in the open, in some shade.

Of the dozen or more varieties of *reticulata* one has only to pick one's preference for colour, but most people go straight for 'Captain Rawes' (also known as 'Semi-plena'), which breaks out into superlative, semi-double flowers of rose-red, often nearly 6 in. wide, and borne on quite small plants. Another great success is 'Noble Pearl' in oriental red (Hillier).

Other very desirable camellias for the milder places are:

C. saluenensis. Beautiful soft pink, decidedly tender.

'Salutation' and 'Inspiration'. Opulent flowers of silvery pink and dark red respectively, the former fairly hardy.

C. sasanqua varieties. Delicate and charming, flowering in the depth of winter, but doing well in the most genial localities only. Sun-hardy.

The Heather Family

Here we encounter three very similar types:

the calluna, which is the ling or Scotch heather;
the daboecia, the Connemara or St Dabeoc's heath;
the erica, of many and diverse affiliations.

Although some of the beautiful South African heaths prosper in Cornwall, we shall have no dealings here with any that are not hardy or nearly so in the British Isles generally.

To certain purists the only one of the three that we ought to call "heather" is the calluna, the others being "heaths". Like other sensible people however, we shall pay no attention to this triviality and call them all either heathers or heaths as we please.

The flowers of the heath make delightful and trouble-free gardens, once established. They bloom for astonishingly long periods and need no attention beyond a light clipping over once a year when the flowers are spent. There are species for virtually every month of the year, those that sparkle bravely in winter being particularly warming to the heart. And from the "tree heaths" we can make excellent hedges.

If blended with likeable consorts, heathers create in the garden an air of serenity and evoke a whiff of the moorland and the hillside. There are no better consorts for this purpose than dwarf conifers, especially the golden ones, but others with which they mix happily are the richly jewelled pernettyas (if not allowed to encroach), the dwarfer rhododendrons and kalmias, halimiums, *Pieris floribunda*, dwarf lavenders and brooms. Nothing rampageous. Certainly no bulbs at all. In designing, the great thing is mass effect. If you can afford only six heathers, have all of the same variety and plant them all together. When space and means allow, plant in squads of twelve to twenty-four of each variety. Except for the tree heaths, never dot them about.

The setting also is important. Within the wooden palings of a small suburban villa or against a brick wall heathers would, I think, look incongruous and not all of them settle down well in average small-garden conditions, except in rural atmospheres. The easiest are the winter and spring heaths (*E. carnea, mediterranea* and *darleyensis*) and the Cornish heath (*E. vagans*); unhappiest of the lot in confined spaces is the June bell-heather, *E. cinerea.*

Heathers need an open, sunny position. Only a very few will prosper in shade and I would plant none beneath the boughs of any deciduous tree. Full, all-day sun is absolutely essential for what are called the foliage varieties – those grown more for the beauty of their foliage than for the flower – particularly the golden-leaved ones.

Planting and caring. The great majority of heathers expect an acid soil, the exceptions being the winter and spring heaths, the tall Corsican heath (*E. terminalis*) and, to some extent, the Cornish heath. Very dry soils are not propitious. Peat is not always vital but extremely valuable, especially when planting. The soil is best dug two spits, but should not be enriched with manure or fertilizers unless in poor shape. The things to dig in are peat or rotted leaf-soil and, according to my usual recipe, some broken-up turf, well down. In heavy clay be very liberal with the peat.

Plant in autumn those that bloom in winter or spring and the others any time from October to March. Work some peat liberally into each pocket and plant rather deeply, so that the lower branches are in contact with the soil or even buried. Tread or press in firmly. Stake the taller "tree" heaths. Then top-dress the whole with peat.

Planting distances depend upon the ultimate spread. Thus a variety that the catalogue tells you has a spread of 15in. (which is a good average for all but the tree heaths) should be planted not farther apart than that distance. I do not agree with the advice sometimes given for wide spacing. For the tree heaths, 3 ft is enough.

Thereafter watering is very important indeed, especially during the first year. So also is weeding. Weed rigorously in the first few years, after which you will find that the enemy has to a large extent been suppressed.

Pruning. As soon as flowering is over (except on the Cornish heath), cut the flower spikes back to a point just below the lowest flower or thereabouts. On young plants do this patiently and meticulously with secateurs; after that, when the plants have filled out well, the best tools I know are the Wilkinson or Greensleeves one-handed clippers, before the advent of which I used the old-fashioned sheep shears.

Don't prune too hard, but pay attention to preserving a comely outline. The winter and spring sorts will be satisfied with a pruning every two or three years only, but it is then important to do it the moment that the main flowering is over, as they begin to make their new growth very quickly.

Propagation. If planted deeply, as I have suggested, the lower branches of heathers will take root and provide you with ready-made new plants. Alternatively, take half-ripe cuttings in July or August and set them in a compost of peat and silver sand. Keep your eye open for self-sown seedlings also.

Horses for courses. To a large extent, one's choice of heathers is conditioned by one's soil. I have mentioned the lime factor and the disadvantages of other extremes. Otherwise there is a pretty wide tolerance, but if your soil is one of the following sorts I would give these priorities.

Clay soils (or any other not too dry or too wet): *E. carnea, darleyensis, mediterranea* and *terminalis.*

Medium loams: *E. arborea* and the Cornish and Connemara heaths;

Light loams: the lings and the hybrid 'Dawn'.

Warm, sandy soils: the June bell-heather.

Damp spots: the cross-leaved heath (*E. tetralix*), the Dorset heath (*E. ciliaris*) and the Connemara heath.

Partly shady places: *E. carnea* and *arborea* and the Dorset and Connemara heaths.

Bearing this soil factor in mind, we may now select our teams according to their seasons.

WINTER AND SPRING HEATHERS

Here the ericas have the field to themselves. The first three are the easiest of all heathers and growable in any reasonable soil. Nor frost nor snow deters the exuberance of their flowering.

Erica carnea (now threatened with a new name), the mountain heath, has some forty children, so fruitful is its seed. They make low, shapely domes, usually about 8in. by 15–18in. Six of the best are:

'King George', rose-pink, December–February. Everyman's choice.

'Queen Mary', pale pink, November–February, wants lime positively.

'Vivellii', red, February–March.

'Springwood White', and 'Springwood Pink', February–April.

'Winter Beauty', soft lilac-pink, November–February.

'Praecox Rubra', deep rose-red, December–March.

'Aurea' is a particularly beautiful golden-leaved variety, lovely the whole year round, but it must be in full, all-day, direct sun. Avoid 'Eileen Porter', a sensitive lass.

E. mediterranea, (questionably known as "hibernica"). Three fine varieties for early spring:

'Brightness', pink, 3ft in roughly pyramidal form, March–May, space at 2ft.;

'W. T. Ratcliff', February–April, white, 2ft;

'Superba', pink, 5ft, March–May, space at 3ft.

E. darleyensis, a splendid hybrid erica of 18in., hard as nails, determined to win in any soil. Pink flowers all the way from November till April. Two superlative varieties are the robust 'George Rendall', deeper pink, and the white 'Silberschmelze' ('Silver Beads'). Space at 2ft.

E. arborea alpina. A tree heath growing 10ft or more, with very long, erect and elegant spikes sheathed in white. March–May. From its roots are "briar" pipes made.[1] Not totally hardy everywhere. Apt to get broken by heavy snow, but sprouts again if pruned back. Space at 3½ft.

SUMMER AND AUTUMN

Again the ericas carry on the theme, staying with us right up till October, but the Connemara heath intrudes in June for four months, and in August the lings make their magnificent two-months' display, though their golden-leaved varieties are a joy throughout the whole year. They, the lively domes of the Cornish heath, and the hybrid 'Dawn' are the soundest choices in average soils from among the following rich variety.

E. tetralix, 9in. A long innings from June to October, but not a sparkling one, except by the crimson 'Con Underwood'.

Dawn. A beautiful rose-pink hybrid. July–September, 9in.

E. cinerea. Ardent sun lovers, disliking wet, cold soils. July–September, 1ft high or less. 'Atrorubens' is a glowing deep pink, lasting till October. 'C. D. Eason' is not quite so deep but first-class. 'P. S. Patrick' is a vivid purple. The lavender 'Cevennes' is also of high rating, but tricky.

E. ciliaris. For damp soils in sun or half-shade. July–October, The wood is brittle and needs a little care in handling. The pink 'Mrs C. H. Gill', 1ft, is the best, but the blush 'Wych', 18in., is also charming.

[1] Corruption of the French *bruyère*, heather.

E. terminalis, the rose-pink Corsican heath, another of the "tree" types. About 5ft. July–September. Happy in lime.

E. vagans, the Cornish heath. The best of the summer heathers for average soils, but the shortest in flower – August–September. The spent flower spikes, however, continue to be attractive in the winter in their russet apparel and may be left on till the end of February. The three outstanding varieties, all 18in., are the deep rose 'Mrs D. F. Maxwell', the bright salmon 'St Keverne' and the white 'Lyonesse'.

FIG. 83. The Connemara or St Dabeoc's heath, *Daboecia cantabrica.*

Daboecia cantabrica. Its generic name commemorates an Irish saint and its specific one a region of Spain, where also it is a wilding, as in Connemara. Also known as *Menziesia polifolia.* 2ft. Relatively large, pendulous, egg-shaped florets on long stems, loosely borne and not having the mass effect of ericas and callunas. June–October. Choose the purple 'Atropurpurea', the white 'Alba' or the pink 'Praegerae', which is rather tender.

Calluna vulgaris, the ling, called "heather" in Scotland. A radiant and versatile clan, some with long, tapering, lissom spikes, others of compact, pincushion outline and yet others distinguished not by their flowers but for their gloriously coloured foliage. August–

September, some longer. There is a host to choose from, of which the following will do you well:

For flower: 'Flore Pleno' (as good as any with a fancy name), 'J. H. Hamilton', 'Elsie Purnell', 'H. E. Beale', 'Peter Sparkes', 'County Wicklow' (all pink) and 'Alportii' (red).

For beautiful foliage: 'Gold Haze', 'Golden Feather', 'Sunset', 'Robert Chapman'. All-day sun imperative.

Dwarfs: 'Humpy Dumpty' and 'Foxii Nana' make very tight, solid, green hummocks, the flowers being of no account. 'Sister Anne' is prostrate, tight, spreading, with twisted shoots and pale-lilac flowers, effective in mass.

Other Desirable Shrubs

Here will be found many evergreens familiar to the general reader, but there are other treasures not so familiar which are of great beauty and which will add distinction and grace to gardens of all sizes. Among those that I invite you to study, Reader, are the elaeagnus, splashed with gold and one of the joys of wintertime, the fast-growing piptanthus, once considered tender, the tall, white-and-gold eucryphias, the streamer-hung itea and a rich and lustrous quartet for gardens that have a rhododendron soil: the pieris, sumptuous in leaf and in flower, the little pernettya, heavily encrusted with coloured berries, the kalmia with its big trusses of porcelain cups and the glorious scarlet embothrium.

None of these is a Sixth Form plant; all will reward you if you have apt conditions, and treat them aright. If you have not the right conditions, pass them by. Not all in this section are fully hardy in the open, but if you garden in the milder shires or in a sheltered nook elsewhere, take a close look at the clianthus, the coronilla and the myrtle – all shrubs of great beauty.

Nor will everything here satisfy the impatient gardener. Others, however, are so easy-going as to flourish in the poorest and stoniest soil if such be yours, as we see in the helianthemum, the halimium and the cistus. Yet others will handsomely adorn the shadiest places, such as the mahonia and the hypericum, and a special few will hug your walls and fences in a close embrace or form themselves into dense hedges, especially the pyracantha and the cotoneaster. Several, of which the ceanothus, the escallonia, the rosemary and the hebe are examples, are lovers of the seaside, though not of the seaside only.

Besides all these, there are a few superlative shrubs that need special conditions of warmth, moisture and shade which are in the category of Sixth Form plants and which I have had to rule out here. They include the crinodendron, hung with crimson lanterns, the scarlet-and-gold, holly-leaved desfontainea, the starry leptospermum, the golden-bowled fremontia, the elegant, ferny-leaved sophoras, hung with golden bells and several others that, if you are interested, you will find discussed at some length in my *Climbing Plants for Walls and Gardens*.

Where I do not say otherwise, it may be assumed that all will succeed in limy soils as in acid ones.

Certain shrubs, particularly the cotoneaster, can be bought from a nursery in the form of standard trees and others can be tailored to that form by the gardener himself.

Abelia. Small shrubs of quiet charm and gracefulness. Not fully evergreen outside the warmer shires. The most reliably hardy is *A. grandiflora*, densely beset with small, pointed, gleaming leaves and sprays of small, blush-pink bells from July till autumn on a 5ft shrub of lax and gently arching habit.

More handsome is *schumannii*, with flowers of deeper pink and growing gracefully to 5ft, but not fully hardy, though safe in most places against a south wall.

Barberry (*Berberis*). Evergreen and deciduous. A very large, prickly and often handsome family that gives us flower in spring and berry in autumn. Several need no pruning. They thrive in any reasonable soil and don't mind shade.

As a whole, the evergreens are the most handsome, but they loathe being moved, and having to be obtained as small plants, usually look awful in their first year and grow much too slowly for impatient gardeners. The best all round is *B. stenophylla*, which throws out gracefully arching cascades of deep gold that make a glittering display in May – a thing of strong, masculine beauty, maybe 9ft high, succeeding equally in clay, sand or chalk. Stenophylla also has some fine semi-dwarf children ideal for small gardens, including 'Brilliant', the golden 'Gracilis', the ruddy 'Coccinea' and the very dwarf 'Corallina Compacta', excellent consorts for heathers.

There is no need to give a long list of other sorts, but two to be picked out are:

darwinii. A noble bush of 8ft in time, a-glow with orange flowers in April, followed by blue berries.

verruculosa. Exceptionally good for small gardens. Very dense and compact, the branches bending in sickle-wise, the leaves glossy, white beneath, with yellow flowers in May–June. 5ft × 6ft. Good also for hedging. If the plants have been grafted on a common rootstock, look out for suckers.

FIG. 84. *Abelia schumannii.*

Two other evergreen barberries much written up are florally splendid, but become straggly; these are *linearifolia* and *lologensis.*

Of the deciduous barberries, the ones to be taken most notice of are:

temolaica. Rare and remarkable for its beautiful young foliage, which is conspicuously blue-green, matched with pale yellow flowers, followed by red berries with a plum-like bloom. Vigorously upright and spreading (Hillier). I have not seen it full-grown.

thunbergii 'Atropurpurea'. One of the best purple-foliaged shrubs.

7ft. There is a remarkably fine dwarf form, 'Nana', only 2ft high and little wider; good with heathers.

Three fine new hybrids with dazzling red or orange berries and gorgeous autumn colours: 'Barbarossa', 'Buccaneer' and 'Pirate King' (Hillier's, Notcutts).

CANDYTUFT (*Iberis*). These dwarf shrublets are in Chapter 21.

Ceanothus. Both evergreen and deciduous. Valuable as being one of our few blue-flowered shrubs. When, upon the background of its small, dense foliage, it becomes animated with a haze of little blue tuffets, it provides an element well suited to the British scene. The colours range from rich, dark blue to pallid wood-smoke ones and there are a few in pink or white.

All ceanothuses grown in Britain hover on the borderline of hardiness. In general terms, those that flower in the spring are evergreen and of varying degrees of tenderness, while those that flower in summer or autumn are deciduous and pretty hardy.

The evergreens grow in the open in the more temperate counties only; in other parts of the country they are better thought of as wall plants, a role in which they excel. All seem to do best on poor, stony or sandy soils rather than fat loams and they make good seaside plants. To plant in spring is an absolute command. Once settled, they grow very fast indeed, becoming tougher, but they very often give up the ghost after about nine years.

When grown on a wall the ceanothus needs a little training and pruning. Fan the stronger branches out well, tying them in close to the wall. Pruning is governed by the fact that, with a few exceptions, the evergreen ceanothus, like other spring shrubs, flowers on the "old wood" grown the previous summer. This means shearing the flowered shoots hard back to a couple of buds from the parent branches as soon as flowering is over. The few that break the rules and flower in late summer or autumn are best pruned in April, discouraging any attempt at spring flowering.

The hardiest of the evergreens is *thyrsiflorus*, but it is rarely a good garden plant. I must be content with the following few selections.

'Autumnal Blue'. A hardy, light-blue hybrid that breaks the rules and flowers from July onwards; prune in April.

'Cascade'. Magnificent fountain of soft blue, but on a wall grows to 20ft and arches outwards, so needs room. Not 100 per cent hardy away from the south.

'Delight'. One of the hardiest and finest. Soft-blue, 20ft on a wall. My No. 1 choice.

C. dentatus floribundus. Dense clusters of powder-blue. Fine.

'Dignity'. Large spikes of clear-blue in autumn. Prune in April. 15ft on a wall.

C. rigidus. Bright indigo-mauve. March. Very reliable.

The deciduous ceanothuses, flowering from June to September in large trusses, are less vigorous but hardy enough to grow in the open in most places. Prune very hard in early spring, nearly back to

FIG. 85. *Choisya ternata.*

the base of last year's shoots. The best known is 'Gloire de Versailles', in powder blue up to 10ft, but 'Topaz' is a rich indigo. 'Henri Desfosse' is almost violet, but of lower growth. The pink varieties are not much catch.

Choisya. Often called "Mexican orange-blossom" in magazines, but never in real life, *Choisya ternata* is a handsome evergreen, with glossy, three-foliated leaves and white, richly scented blossoms in May and sometimes later. Almost fully hardy in the west and south, but likes protection from east winds and, oddly, from the full glare of the sun also, which discolours its foliage. Cut back to sound wood any shoots withered by cold wind. Best plant in spring. 6ft × 8ft (more in the west). Very easy from summer cuttings.

Cistus. Beautiful shrubs with poppy-form flowers of tissue-paper substance, breaking out in succession in June from crisp, aromatic foliage. Good substitute for the late deciduous azaleas when the soil is not acid. Alas, they are not hardy enough to survive a hard winter, though I find that they stand a better chance (and flower better) in a lean, stony soil rather than a rich one. Don't call them by the equivocal name of "rock-roses" or you may get something different. Plant in spring, in full sun, and pinch out the tips of the shoots. Expect to

FIG. 86. *Cistus ladaniferus*, typical of the genus, having crimson splashes on the white petals, beautiful in flower but not hardy.

have to replace them every seven years, for they do not grow old gracefully, but replacement is not difficult from 3in. cuttings in July.

For all-round excellence the one to go for is *C. lusitanicus decumbens*, a low, dense, dark-green, scented shrub, 2ft high by 4ft wide, with large, white flowers splashed with maroon, from June to September. Where something taller is wanted, I should choose *C. cyprius*, a luxuriant, pretty hardy shrub growing to 7ft × 6ft with gummy stems and handsome, white flowers splashed with red, or alternatively the white-flowered *laurifolius*, 7 ft × 4 ft.

Probably the hardiest of the cistuses, however, is *corbariensis*, another dense, low shrub of 4ft × 6ft, with crenulate leaves and small white and yellow flowers in June. 'Silver Pink', 3ft × 4ft, has delightful pink flowers but the foliage is leaden.

Clianthus. Quite hardy in the favoured west and often seen decorating houses in Cornwall, the gorgeous "lobster-claw" can be grown elsewhere in warm, south-facing ingle nooks only. Its bizarre flowers hang in opulent clusters of the most vivid red, suggesting to the imagination the claws of a lobster (cooked), accompanied by frond-like foliage. This is *C. puniceus*. June onwards. To 15ft on a wall. An open, sandy loam is best (Hillier or Notcutt).

Coronilla. Beautiful shrubs bearing yellow pea-flowers over an exceptionally long span of the year, starting in April, but needing warmth and shelter in most areas. The best bet is *C. glauca*, a choice creation with small, pinnate, sea-green leaves and sweetly scented flowers of rich yellow in large clusters. Charming on the walls of either cottage or mansion. Full sun. To 8ft, but can be kept pruned back. Its offshoot 'Variegata' has luscious cream foliage.

C. valentina is a smaller edition, may be more tender.

Cotoneaster. Chiefly evergreen, or semi-evergreen. A large and versatile genus, from tall shrubs to creepy-crawlers. Extremely hardy, of very fast growth, flourishing in any soils, in sun or in shade, bursting out into fuzzy white or cream flowers in spring and a crop of red or yellow berries (for the birds) in autumn. There is such an enormous choice that I can pick out only a few of the more significant ones.

LARGE, RATHER OPEN SHRUBS

C. frigidus (usually deciduous), vigorous, fast and of spreading habit.

The three fine, nearly evergreen Exbury hybrids, 'Cornubia', 'Exburyensis' and 'Rothschildeanus', of willowy elegance, the last two having yellow berries. All grow very fast to 15ft high and wide, or more. In harsh climates a safer bet is *salicifolius*, of very similar habit and a parent of the last two.

C. lacteus. A lusty shrub with widely flung arms. Evergreen olive foliage and persistent red berries. 12ft × 12ft. A noble shrub for larger gardens only.

Except for *lacteus*, all these make fine standards, excellent for small gardens.

MINI-WEEPER

C. 'Hybridus Pendulus', grafted on a standard stem. The arching branches cascade to the ground, jewelled with red berries, like oriental bead or bamboo curtains. Plant it in a prominent and solus position, preferably in a bed raised a foot or more above ground level. Rarely evergreen.

FOR TRAINING ON A WALL

C. wardii is the usual one, but the one sent out by most nurseries is really *franchetii sternianus*, which is in fact a better shrub.

Much more unusual, and first-class for a wall up to 10ft, is *microphyllus* and its varieties, dealt with in the ground cover chapter, a valuable all-round species.

FOR HIDING AN EYESORE

C. horizontalis, the ever-popular, deciduous "herring-bone" cotoneaster. In nature it fans itself out in a more or less horizontal plane, and so is useful for hiding a manhole or other hideosity. Planted against a wall, however, it will fan out gracefully in the vertical plane, leaning flat against the wall, to 8ft or more, where, especially after leaf-fall, its branch structure shows clearly its resemblance to the skeleton of a fish.

There is a delightful variegated form, with tiny, silvered leaves, which are prettily suffused with red in autumn; slow (Hillier).

FOR DENSE GROUND CARPETS

C. dammeri and the invaluable 'Autumn Fire'; see chapter on ground cover.

FOR HEDGING

C. simonsii (rarely evergreen) and *lacteus*.

WARNING!

Cotoneasters, pyracanthas, hawthorns, apples and other plants of the rose family are subject to attack by the fire-blight disease. This is evidenced by blackened blossoms, withered leaves and discoloured stems, often with seemingly healthy sections between clearly diseased ones. The disease is carried by bees. Some local authorities require you to destroy the whole plant, others allow you merely to cut back to healthy wood. In the interests of oneself and one's neighbours, complete destruction is the best course, unless the infection is trivial.

Daphne. Evergreen and deciduous. Ardently to be desired for both their beauty and their heavenly scent, the daphnes, not inappropriately, are among the most capricious of creatures, sharing with the madonna lily and the gentianella the perverse habit of bestowing their charms freely upon your neighbours but denying them to you. Yet even next door, after a few years of enchantment, they may suddenly fall into a decline and die for no obvious reason.

There is, Mr Eliot Hodgkin told us[1], no golden rule for wooing them successfully, but, in general, the conditions to aim at are: a sunny position, plenty of humus (especially leaf-mould) and, thirdly, that condition so often described in this book – a soil that holds sufficient moisture yet is well drained. Lime, say the most experienced fanciers, seems to make no difference one way or the other.

Of evergreen species, I think that the most wooable are *tangutica* and the very similar *retusa*, which have lustrous, dark-green foliage and grow slowly to 3ft, with rose-purple, scented flowers, the first in April and the second in May.

Brief notes on some other amenable ones:

cneorum 'Eximia'. Prostrate. Terminal clusters of rich rose-pink, exquisitely scented, in May. Mainly for rock gardens. Have none but the form 'Eximia', unless it be the very slow white variety.

collina neapolitana. Scented, soft purple flowers for two months from April onwards. A beautiful shrub, 4ft × 5ft. No fear of its dying back like some others.

odora. Rapturously scented flowers of rose-purple while the frosty breath of winter still lingers. To 3ft. Have none but the variety 'Aureo-Marginata', which is the hardiest form. Full sun. Plant on a south wall beneath a sitting-room window.

Of the deciduous daphnes the outstanding one is our old cottage garden friend, *D. mezereum*, known of old as the mezereon, a 4ft shrub with sprays of soft purple, scented florets that "startle the sloth of February", blooming before the leaves. Hates moving and cold steel. Easily raised from seed. There are various white forms.

[1] *RHS Journal*, November 1961.

D. burkwoodii is a partially evergreen 3ft hybrid, with clusters of pale pink florets in May. 'Somerset' is a more vigorous form of it with a slightly different floral arrangement.

Elaeagnus. The golden-leaved elaeagnus with foliage heavily splashed with daffodil and margined with olive, is one of the handsomest of all our variegated shrubs, especially in winter, when it glows and glitters like the massed candles of an olden-time Christmas. This is *E. pungens* 'Maculata' (or 'Aureo-variegata'). It should certainly be very high on everyone's gardening lists and should be sited where you can see it from the house. Expect it to grow a good 10ft in time. Watch for any shoot lacking the yellow pigment and cut it clean out at its point of origin. Quite happy in part shade and prospers in chalk. Not to be confused with *pungens* 'Variegata', which has just a cream edge to the leaf; less attractive.

There are also some elaeagnuses with brightly silvered leaves. One is deciduous, smaller and increasing by stolons; this is *commutata* (or *argentea*). Another is the very big, tree-like oleaster (*E. angustifolia*), also deciduous, its willow-like leaves looking as though dipped in aluminium paint; apt to become ungainly. All happy in chalk.

Embothrium. The chosen varieties of this exotic genus are highly dramatic shrubs, robed in May in dense clusters of small, tubular flowers of fiery scarlet. Anyone in the not-too-cold counties who can provide it with a cool, acid soil and a station protected from north and east winds should be able to delight in its splendours, but must be prepared for it to grow pretty large in time. In short order, all you need ask for is *E.* 'Norquinco Valley', which is the finest form of *E. coccineum*. Plant in spring.

Escallonia. Handsome, fast-growing shrubs with small, glossy leaves and strung with little red, pink or waxen bells from June onwards. Some are rather loose, gracefully cascading shrubs, others more compact and yet others of erect carriage. Excellent for the seaside as elsewhere, especially for hedging, formal or informal according to their habit.

They vary also in hardiness and in the north some may become deciduous and others may need wall protection. Plant in spring. Expect their breadth to equal their height. Prune back the flowered shoots when spent.

Opinions differ widely on the best varieties and species, but the following is a very good basketful.

'Donard Seedling'. Cascades of blush-pink, 9ft. Pretty hardy.

'Langleyensis'. Cascades of rosy-red, 7ft. Very hardy.

'C. F. Ball'. Tall and strong. Red. Great favourite. 10ft.

'Donard Brilliance'. Pendulous. Rose-red. Fine small garden sort. 5ft. Repeat flowering.

'Donard Radiance'. Compact. Large-flowered, deep pink. Very fine. 8ft.

FIG. 87. Pruning an escallonia; the old, flowered wood is cut back to its junction with a new one.

'Edinensis'. Lax pink cascades. 7ft. Very hardy. Long-flowering.

I would avoid 'Apple Blossom', which is not always of good habit. Propagate all by half-ripe cuttings in July–August.

For hedges, see especially Chapter 24.

ERICA. See "The Heather Family"

Eucryphia. Evergreen and deciduous. These are what you might call rather classy shrubs, often of tree-like proportions, not very tough and, with rare exceptions, having a distaste for lime. They grow slowly and take years to flower but, when they at last do, they break out into a splendid display of white saucers enlivened by a bold brush of stamens, like a white rose-of-Sharon.

The hardiest and safest evergreen is the hybrid *nymansensis*, but you must make sure of getting the clone called 'Nymansay', other forms being indifferent. This is a mat shrub of slenderly columnar silhouette to 16ft or more, dressed in dark, evergreen foliage, handsome in summer, but distinctly sad when wind-bitten in the sharpness of winter. August flowering. Tolerates lime, even chalk, and well suited to small gardens.

On some counts, however, the two parents of the Nymans eucryphia are to be preferred. One is the beautiful *glutinosa*, quite as hardy, wonderfully coloured in autumn, but lime-hating, usually deciduous and more broadly spreading. The other is *cordifolia*, evergreen, possibly lime-tolerant, but certainly for the Gulf Stream counties only.

Euonymus. Evergreen and deciduous, very diverse. *E. japonicus* is a sombre and thoroughly plebeian evergreen, whose only use is as a seaside hedge.

On the other hand, its little sister, *fortunei*, in one of its variegated forms, is one of the gardener's most willing handmaids.

One should regard this as though it were an ivy, whether to creep over the earth as a ground-cover, or to be trained, as our grandfathers did, as a little low skirting to a bed or – the prettiest of its tricks – to climb a wall, to which it clings by little holdfast pads and where its small, parti-coloured leaves make a delightful pattern. It will do the same sort of useful trick over an old tree-stump. On reaching maturity after several years it begins, again like ivy, to lose its holdfast pads and to become stiffly shrub-like and it should then be prevented from growing up by a sharp clipping, when it will continue to behave in an attractively juvenile manner.

Long familiar to us as *E. radicans*, this useful helpmeet is now *E. fortunei*, and it has several variegated forms, such as 'Gracilis' and 'Silver Queen'.

The deciduous species of euonymus are not very exciting. 'Red Cascade', however, is a showy variety of our native spindle tree, *E. europaeus*, laden with quantities of cute little rose-red fruits in autumn, but it needs a spouse to fertilize it – either our wilding or else *E. hamiltonianus* (Jackman).

Garrya. A much publicized plant, *G. elliptica* is in truth a very ordinary evergreen bush which can look pretty shabby in winter, except for its pretty, 6in. bunch of dangling, pale-green catkins. Needs the shelter of a wall in most areas. Specify male plants. About 8ft.

GAULTHERIA. See Chapter 23.

Halimium. One of the very best of our low-level, summer-flowering shrubs, especially where azaleas cannot be grown, flowering from late May to late July, with some sprinkling till the end of summer. It grows about 2ft high by 4ft or more wide, beset with small, grey-green leaves and jewelled with flowers rather like large buttercups. An excellent ground-cover plant, but not fully hardy. In the record freeze of 1963, six out of my eight were severely damaged above ground though not all were killed and were easily replaced from a reserve of cuttings. Well suited to dry, stony, warm soils.

The choice lies between three sorts:

H. lasianthum, in which the yellow flowers have a maroon patch at the base of the petal,

its variety *concolor*, which lacks the patch and looks like a buttercup, and

H. ocymoides, having flowers like those of *lasianthum*, but smaller and a bit more brilliant.

A marriage between an halimium and a cistus brought forth the hybrid *Halimiocistus*, of which the best known is *H. sahucii*, with small, white flowers inferior to those of either parent, but profusely borne on a ground-hugging plant that spreads to 6ft; extremely hardy.

Plant all these in spring. O.K. in lime.

Hebe. This is the name by which the shrubby species of the veronica race should now be known, but they are still to be found under *Veronica* in many catalogues.

The hebes are small, evergreen shrubs, usually no more than 4ft high, with small, close-packed foliage and terminal tufts of little florets, which you must behead when flowering is over. They have an uncommonly long flowering season, usually in late summer and autumn, and are particularly good sea-side plants, but their degrees of hardiness vary a lot, as does the quality of the numerous varieties, many being very commonplace.

Quite in a class by itself is *H. hulkeana*, a superlative, 3ft shrub, with large, foaming trusses of lavender in the utmost profusion in May and June, but you must give it the protective warmth of a south wall. Tie it up to the wall and behead its sumptuous panicles after flowering. Other tender and beautiful hebes for warm places, are 'La Séduisante', 'Simon Deleaux' and 'Alicia Amherst'. Plant all these in spring.

Moderately hardy are the elegant 'Great Orme' and the tall, lavender 'Midsummer Beauty'; and hardier still are 'Autumn Glory', 'Marjorie' and 'Margery Fish'.

Where the need is for a low, dense, weed-conquering evergreen of distinctive character, *subalpina* is agreeable to the eye, especially in winter, with its fresh, apple-green foliage; fully hardy and a nice labour-saver as a low, informal hedge, 2ft × 4ft (Waterer or Sunningdale).

For the useful *pinguifolia* 'Pagei', see the ground-cover chapter.

Increase hebes by 4in. half-ripe cuttings in August.

Helianthemum. These splendid little shrubs, often ambiguously called "sun-roses", prove themselves again and again to be the answer to the gardener's prayer. Hardy, flowerful, compact, expecting no luxuries, they will serve him well in a dozen ways, provided he gives them a fair ration of sun. Will flourish on the stoniest diet (including a gravel path) as on rich soil. A packet of seeds will quickly provide you with platoons of good plants in many colours, from which you can as easily multiply your favourite ones by cuttings. Of course, there are plenty of named varieties also. The singles are florally the prettiest, but the doubles (particularly 'Jubilee' and 'Cerise Queen'), give the longest show. Among the singles go rather for those of dense, compact foliage, such as 'Croceum' (from Jackman's, particularly good) and the extra-vigorous 'Wisley Primrose' and 'Wisley Pink'.

Be sure to trim back all the single varieties, a trifle sharpish, as soon as they have finished flowering; the double ones, if still flowering in November, may be left till early spring. Don't let them get straggly.

Holly (*Ilex*). One of the handsomest of our evergreen shrubs when properly grown, but a slow starter. There are quantities in the lists, but none better than the many varieties of our common English holly (*Ilex aquifolium*), whether prickly or smooth, green or variegated, red-berried or yellow. They succeed in any reasonable soil, in sun or shade, but, with a few exceptions, are uni-sexual, the berries being borne only on the females and then only if pollinated by a near-by male.

One of the most successful of holly marriages for producing berries is that between two very handsome parents: the prickle-free, green-and-gold 'Golden King', which, paradoxically, is a female, and the prickly, green-and-cream 'Silver Queen', which, equally surprisingly, is a male.

However, there are some varieties that are bi-sexual, one of the finest for a specimen tree being 'Polycarpa' (or 'J. C. van Tol'), which has few spines, berries profusely, has leaves of dark olive and makes a bold, spreading bush, but can freely be clipped to formal shapes. Another, likewise self-berrying and virtually spineless, is the hybrid 'Camelliaefolia', whose name explains the form of its foliage.

FIG. 88. *Hypericum patulum* 'Hidcote'.

It has a very distinctive outline, like that of a pagoda. If you are prompted to buy any other varieties, ask the nurseryman's advice.

Hypericum. One of the easiest and most useful of small, all-purposes shrubs, most familiar to us all in its dwarf shape known as the rose-of-Sharon or St-John's-wort, with gleaming, golden salvers and a bold brush of gold stamens. This is *H. calycinum*, so valuable for flourishing under trees, though it grows even more proudly in full sun, and marvellous on an awkward bank and for brightening town gardens. Shear it down almost to the ground early in March, or, as too often happens, it becomes a ragamuffin.

By implication the popular names also get applied to the taller hypericums, the most valuable of which is *H. patulum* 'Hidcote', which bears larger salvers in a great, golden, continuous profusion. Like its little brother, it will flourish in deep shade, right up to the boles of trees, as well as in sun. An Everyman's shrub. Trim it back by about one-third every March to keep it a tidy, compact 4ft. 'Hidcote' has largely displaced *henryi*, which is also good.

The most handsome of the hypericums, however, is 'Rowallane', with large, opulent, slightly drooping, golden bowls on long, arching stems. Unhappily not fully hardy, but is the one to have in the softer counties, where it will top 6ft.

Besides these, all other hypericums seem to me to be outclassed, but flower arrangers like *androsaemum* and 'Elstead' for their berries. In the bleakest northern regions and in grimy towns 'Elstead' vividly enlivens the austere scene with its bright red fruits; cut it to the ground each March. There are also several delightful dwarfs to be found in Chapter 21.

All very easily increased by summer cuttings.

Itea. An elegant and unusual shrub with holly-like foliage festooned with long, pendulous streamers of minute, sweetly-scented, green-and-white florets. Very decorative. This is *I. ilicifolia.* August onwards. Give it a snug and sunny position on a soil that does not dry out. If it gets too big for its boots, cut some of the old wood right out (Treseder or Hillier).

Kalmia. A handsome, rhododendron-like shrub, *K. latifolia* breaks out in June into trusses composed of many, small, bright-pink cups with crimped margins, the plant ultimately reaching 6 to 8ft. It wants the same acid, well-watered soil as rhododendrons, but, contrary to much that is written, prefers the sun to the shade, where (like those I first grew) it may never flower. Remove the flower trusses when spent. I gather that northern gardeners should give its foliage some protection against icy winter blasts.

For smaller gardens there are two charming dwarfs: *polifolia,* a wiry 2-footer with purple flowers in terminal clusters in April, and the extra-hardy *angustifolia* 'Rubra', with many, very small cups of deep rose from June onwards. A favourite in my garden, but slow.

LAVENDER. Included in the chapter "Silver and Grey".

LUPINUS. For tree lupins, see under Lupin in Chapter 10.

Laurels. For the true laurel, *Laurus nobilis,* see "Bay" in the chapter on "Trees". There are also several phoney "laurels".

The Japanese laurel, with large leaves, often spotted, and white flowers followed by large red berries if males and females are consorted together, planted in whole regiments by our great-grandfathers, is *Aucuba japonica,* now out of favour except as a hedge, for which it is splendid. It prospers in full shade and in sooty cities.

The Portuguese laurel is *Prunus lusitanica,* densely beset with oval, dark-green leaves and bearing tassels of scented, white flowers in June followed by grape-like berries – a fine background shrub or hedge.

The cherry-laurel or "common laurel" is *Prunus laurocerasus,* a large shrub also used for hedging and windbreaks, of which Hillier lists a dozen varieties.

Mahonia. A small group of shrubs (once included among the barberries) with bold foliage and yellow flowers that enliven the land when the year is cold, valuable for flourishing in deep shade.

Finest of all as a young plant is *M. lomariifolia,* with very long, sea-green, compound leaves divided into some seventeen leaflets, topped with cockades of erect spikes of deep yellow florets in winter. Alas, this is a Gulf Stream plant and becomes leggy. Some hybrids have been raised from *lomariifolia,* of which the best known are 'Charity', and 'Hope', but these also have a leggy tendency.

Almost as good however, and entirely hardy is *M. japonica* with leaves of similar design, but shorter, and crowned in winter with luxuriant clusters of long, outspread, semi-pendulous, primrose tassels, scented of lilies-of-the-valley. Grows 6ft high and wide. One of our finest winter shrubs. There is a confusion of names with the less favoured *M. bealei,* which has stiffly erect flower spikes, but your safeguard is to go to the best nurseries.

The other mahonia to be noticed is the common *aquifolium,* a low-growing shrub with small, polished, holly-like leaves, tinted purple in winter and much used as a ground-cover beneath trees, for which purpose it is excellent, spreading by suckers; prune back after flowering. Its variety *undulata* is an 8-footer with wavy leaves of many-tinted colours.

Myrtle. Beloved of the old poets and renowned for its aromatic leaves, the common myrtle (*Myrtus communis*) prospers in the open in Cornwall and may be enjoyed in all but the coldest counties also against a snug south wall. If cut back by extra hard frost, it comes on

FIG. 88*a*. A truss of *Mahonia japonica. Inset:* Two florets.

again. The one to have is the variety 'Tarentina' (also known as 'Jenny Reitenbach'), a compact little charmer, with a beautiful pattern of small, lustrous, dark-green, wind-hardy leaves and frothing in July–August with a profusion of little, sweet-scented, white flowers that have a dense, fluffy brush of protruding stamens. A delightful plant beside a door or window on a sunny wall.

Several other myrtles are at the call of those who live in the pampered shires, such as *luma*, the tree myrtle, *ugni*, the small Chilean guava, etc. (Treseder or Hillier).

Olearia. The "Australian daisy-bushes". See section on "Seaside" in Chapter 25.

Osmanthus. Handsome, densely foliaged shrubs succeeding in any reasonable soil, in sun or half-shade. The best is *O. delavayi*, a shrub of rotund outline, growing slowly to 6ft, with small, densely packed, dark-green leaves, among which, in April, sparkles a profusion of white, tubular, jasmine-like florets that embalm the air with the richest of scents. Plant in spring or, if in autumn, give it some protection for the first winter; in the very coldest counties plant it against a wall. If in age it gets leggy, trim it back all over after flowering.

Another good species of osmanthus is the holly-like *ilicifolius*, flowering in September–October, of which there are several varieties, including the handsome, olive-green 'Gulf Tide' (Jackman).

Osmarea. *O. burkwoodii* is a first-class hybrid, having Delavay's osmanthus as one parent. Though not having quite the same air of distinction as its parent, it inherits its other good qualities, is entirely hardy and grows rather larger.

PERIWINKLE (*Vinca*). See Chapter 23.

Pernettya. If your garden has an acid, rhododendron-type soil, you are mad not to plant *P. mucronata*, in dozens, hundreds or thousands. They are possibly the finest berrying shrub we have, bursting out in early autumn into a profusion of large, white, lilac, pink or red berries that look as though they were made of porcelain. Growing normally some 4–5ft high, the shrubs are densely beset with small, neat, glossy, slightly prickly leaves and they spread freely by suckers, so that a few plants soon develop into a weed-defying thicket, which you may easily extend by transplanting the suckers. In spring they are smothered in a fuzz of white, heather-like flowers, and they are, in fact, genial companions for the heathers if not allowed to encroach.

Pernettyas do best in sun or part-sun and the important thing when ordering is to stipulate one male plant to about every five females, for they are self-sterile. There are several good variations or strains, including the red Bell's Seedling and Davies's Hybrids, in various colours.

PHLOMIS, the Jerusalem sage. See "Silver and Grey".

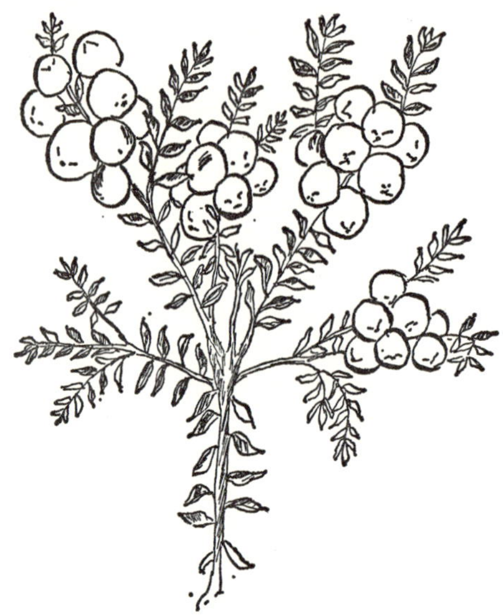

FIG 89. A sprig of pernettya in berry.

Pieris. Numbered among the world's most sumptuous shrubs, but needing rhododendron conditions – an acid, well-watered soil and, in some instances, a shady situation. Distinguished by their handsome foliage, they develop (slowly) into dense, close-packed shrubs of comely, rounded outline, from which, in favourable conditions, they throw out bountiful tassels of exciting, scented, lily-of-the-valley flowers in late winter or spring.

The monarch of them all is *P. formosa forrestii* (usually contracted to *forrestii*). Its glory is chiefly in the brilliant flames of its young foliage, seen best in the forms known as 'Wakehurst' and 'Forest Flame'. If the winter be mild, these splendid heraldic cockades are accompanied in spring by the beautiful fountains of small, white bells. Take note, however, that this gorgeous young foliage will be ruined if the beams of the sun are allowed to strike directly on it and that sharp frost may shrivel up the flowers. Normally 8ft × 10ft, more in Gulf Stream climates.

Other very fine pieris are:

japonica 'Variegata'. A delightful shrub of moderate size with dark, glossy leaves margined with cream. One of the most beautiful of variegated shrubs, but slow. Drooping sprays of waxy, white flowers that may be caught by frost.

floribunda 'Grandiflora'. The easiest and hardiest, growable in full sun, bearing its flower trusses erect above the leaves in April; usually about 4ft only (Hillier).

taiwanensis. Pretty hardy, reaching 7ft or so. A great mound of dark green smothered with large, boldly displayed flower trusses in April and young leaves unfurling in copper cockades. Sun-hardy.

FIG. 90. *Pieris japonica.*

Piptanthus. Once considered tender, the excellent *P. laburnifolius*, has now proved itself to be perfectly hardy, at any rate in the south and certainly in my garden. This is fortunate, for it is a most welcome and decorative plant in any but the smallest of gardens, growing, and growing very fast, to about 8ft and resembling the laburnum both in its trifoliate leaves and in its yellow pea-flowers, though the flowers are much larger. Blooms for six weeks from April onwards. Admittedly a bit raggle-taggle in a sharp winter. Any reasonable soil, but full sun if possible. Easy from seed or plants from Christopher Lloyd.

Pyracantha. Small-leaved, slightly thorny, hard as nails, the pyracanthas are most familiar as wall shrubs, but they also make very fine open-ground shrubs and dense, solid hedges. All burst into a fuzz of white or cream flowers in June, followed by crowded clusters of red or yellow berries in autumn. The birds soon loot the red ones, but often leave the yellow till winter. Beware the fire-blight disease, mentioned in the cotoneaster entry, above.

The best all-rounder is *watereri*, with white flowers and red berries. Dense and twiggy, it makes an imposing specimen of 8ft × 9ft and a very fine low hedge and can be beautifully tailored to hug a low wall.

Broader and virtually as good is the yellow-berried variety usually catalogued as *P. rogersiana* 'Flava'. Makes a splendid 6ft hedge, as seen at Wisley, and a handsome specimen bush, arching gracefully and clothed in bright green.

Much more vigorous than either is *atalantioides*, with long, oval, glossy leaves, growing 16ft high and splendid for a large wall. Not so good a tall hedge as *rogersiana*.

A variety much written up is *coccinea* 'Lalandii', but its foliage is dull, compared with that of the others.

The usual method of training a pyracantha as a wall-hugging shrub is to treat it as an informal espalier. Run up a main shoot and allow lateral branches to grow out from it every foot or so, training them horizontally. Tie all in fairly closely and flat to the wall. Rub out all excess buds or incipient young shoots, particularly the "breastwood" shoots growing outwards and those growing inwards into the walls. From the main framework branches can be led up between windows, athwart porches and round corners.

In April prune back all the sub-laterals that have finished fruiting to within about 3in. of their parent branches. The result should be a tightly packed display of fruit on very short spurs.

Rosemary (*Rosmarinus*). Though a very old favourite, is much abused. As on lavender, in order to get compact, well-clothed bushes the vital thing is to prune the shoots moderately hard after flowering is over. Do not cut back into the *old* wood; shoots do not break from wood more than a year old. Choose one of the several varieties of *R. officinalis* or the more showy *angustifolius* 'Corsican Blue'. The former is a good sea-side plant and hardy enough in all but the colder northern areas, but the latter is not safe outside the warmer ones, so plant in spring. Full sun and, preferably, light soils for both.

Increase by summer cuttings.

RHODODENDRON. See previous chapter.

Salvia. We have met some sages among the annuals and others in the herbaceous border. There are also several shrubs of great beauty, many of them tender, particularly *S. grahamii*, which bears quantities of brilliant scarlet flowers from July right through till autumn, but is definitely a Gulf Stream plant for a hot wall. Also called *S. microphylla.*

Our common sage, however, *S. officinalis*, offers us some splendid variations on its culinary theme wherever low, wide-spreading shrubs with coloured foliage are the gardener's requirement. One is 'Purpurascens', the purple-leaved sage, a most handsome foliage plant growing only 2ft or less, high but spreading easily to a neat, dense circle of at least 6ft diameter; a valued old friend, with soft, velvety leaves, a wonderful foil to other plants and a good companion for heathers. Others are 'Icterina', whose grey-green leaves are flaked with yellow, and 'Tricolor', where cream and pink tints creep in.

None of these coloured sages, however, seems to be reliably hardy in the colder shires, the purple one being safest. However, I believe that the smaller Spanish sage is quite hardy. This has grey-green leaves that charmingly set off the lavender-blue flower, arranged in a compact bush reaching 2ft × 4ft. This is *S. o. hispanica* (Sunningdale and Jackman).

The leaves of all are good for the pot. If the plants show signs of getting bare-wooded, pinch them back here and there. Very easily raised from summer cuttings.

SANTOLINA. Cotton-lavender. See "Silver and Grey".

Skimmia. People who know more about skimmias, particularly *S. japonica*, than I do contradict each other so much about both their habits and their very names that I shall not attempt to lay down the law. Suffice it that skimmias have dense, attractive foliage, grow from 3 to 6ft high, succeed in both sun and full shade, make excellent ground-cover, are satisfied (with exceptions) with any good soil, become massed with small, scented off-white flowers in spring and are thickly clustered with large, red berries from autumn right through till next May.

Most if not all of the japonica skimmias, however, are uni-sexual and there will be no berries on the females unless they are given a male. Opinions differ about which is which. People of undoubted authority assert that the variety 'Formanii' is hermaphrodite, others say not, so I suggest that you simply ask your nurseryman to send you both 'Formanii' and the best male of *S. japonica* 'Fragrans', an undoubted male (but deliciously scented!). One gentleman to five ladies.

VIBURNUM. As all but a few viburnums are deciduous, I deal with them all together in the next chapter.

VINCA. Periwinkle. See Chapter 23.

Yucca. I have never been able to get accustomed to these in the British scene, especially when stuck in the middle of a lawn. If you yearn for one, the usual is *Y. filamentosa*, whose bell-hung spires may go to 6ft in August, but the dwarfer *flaccida* may suit you better. Better avoid the dangerously spiked *gloriosa*. Once established these species should flower nearly every year. Cut the flower stems to the base when spent. They are robustly tolerant of seaside wind and salt.

CHAPTER 19

THE BEST DECIDUOUS SHRUBS

Their Versatility – Brooms – Fuchsias – Hydrangeas – Lilacs – Other Excellences

Their Versatility

MORE treasure here. The dross has been omitted, except where it needs to be mentioned; no "moth-ball bushes", no "Elisha's-tears".[1] Most are amenable to lime and none is exacting, though there are a few that need things rather dry and stony, others that want them wet, and a sprinkling that want them warm and sheltered. Some grow too big for small gardens and there is much more pruning to be done than on the evergreens.

In the list that follows are several first-class shrubs with which the gardener of limited experience will be unfamiliar and unfortunately many of them are labelled in multi-syllabic botanese, which probably explains why so many owners of smaller gardens fight shy of them. Of such are the following in particular:

Perovskia	Caryopteris
Abeliophyllum	Ceratostigma
Indigofera	Kolkwitzia

Look these up and consider them carefully in preference to such commonplace things as the flowering currant, the kerria, the tree-mallow and even the lilac, which is often so dowdy when its show is over.

Brooms

Three very similar genera go by this name: the cytisus, the genista and the spartium. They have blossoms like those of peas, usually in

[1] *Symphoricarpos* species (note spelling) and *Leycesteria formosa.*

some shade of yellow. All are attuned to warm, sunny places, to poor, dry, sandy or stony soils and to long spells without rain, though a few are quite happy in clay. They grow fast and flower lavishly, but most of them have a life of only eight years or so. After planting out, never attempt to move them.

Most brooms have got to be hard pruned, cutting back the spent flowering twigs to a couple of inches of their starting point, or else they get very bare-legged and scruffy. This is done, of course, immediately after flowering, except for the few that bloom after midsummer.

Propagation of the true species is usually pretty easy from seed and that of the hybrids by heel cuttings in August.

The **cytisus** gives us several fine species and whole platoons of hybrids. Particularly valuable are the low, wide-spreading ones, especially the pallid *kewensis*, the bright yellow *beanii*, the miniature *ardoinii* and the mauve *purpureus*. All bloom in May with great dash.

The Warminster broom, *C. praecox*, is one of the splendours of

FIG. 91. The golden truncheons of the Morocco broom, *Cytisus battandieri*.

late April, throwing out great sheaves of gently arching stems, festooned with flowers of pale primrose, maybe 5ft high by 6ft. But the tall white Portuguese broom does not grow old gracefully and *nigricans* may also fall short of expectations.

Among the hybrid cytisuses, there is a tempting gallery in the catalogues in all sorts of colours. Take 'Johnson's Crimson' or the pretty dwarf 'Peter Pan' as your first pick. Remember to prune immediately after flowering. They need firm staking or will flop drunkenly.

Quite different from all these is the unique Moroccan broom, *battandieri*. In late June this brandishes remarkable truncheons of tightly packed florets, richly scented of pineapple, on upright branches that may reach 12ft, with copious laburnum-like, blue-washed leaves. Hardy but wants warmth and, outside the softer counties is best against a south wall. Unlike other brooms, it produces new basal shoots, so that you cut out old, spent shoots as the new ones appear. Easy from its own seed.

Of the hardy **genistas**, badge of the Plantagenets, easily the first pick for most gardeners is the delightful *G. lydia*, which forms itself into a low, widespread mound of wiry, many-branched shoots that curve like bows or scimitars, encrusted in May and June with golden flowers. Fit for the very smallest garden, but not keen on heavy clay. Its full beauty is shown when planted at the top of a terrace or bank, where it will shoot down like a miniature golden rain rocket.

For the larger garden the Mount Etna broom, *G. aethnensis*, is a magnificent spectacle at midsummer, growing in tree-like fashion to 15ft or more and, with its semi-pendulous branches, perfectly representing a glittering, golden fountain. But you must do all you can to prevent it from becoming top-heavy and leggy. Stake it securely and shorten the stems after flowering. Long-lived.

Two other genistas that make large and graceful shrubs of about 9ft are the silky-leaved *cinerea* and the very similar Madeira broom, *virgata*, blooming in June–July in elegant profusion. The short, spiny "Spanish Gorse", *hispanica*, is an awkward customer, but its dwarf form, 'Nana', is most effective where a low, densely packed evergreen mound, glittering with golden sequins, is the need; mixes jolly well with conifers. Very hardy.

There are also several very nice creepy-crawlers, especially *pilosa*, which is hard as nails and featly spreads a yellow mat over an area of 5ft, moulding itself to the contours of the ground; excellent for dry banks and satisfied with clay if really well drained.

The broom of the Plantagenet Kings, by the way, was the petty whin, *G. anglica*, dwarf and spiny.

Our third genus is the Spanish broom, *Spartium junceum*, a tough shrub that thrives in chalk, at the sea-side and almost anywhere else in sun. The flowers are large and borne for three months from June onwards. Grows very fast to 9ft or more. Inelegant carriage. The way to grow it, if you have room, is to plant several 4ft apart and annually to cut every other one almost down to the ground; the result will be an all-over blaze. Propagate by seed in March.

Fuchsias

Our great-grandparents would have been delighted to see here another revival of Victoriana, for the fuchsia, out of fashion when I began gardening, has come back into the limelight, bringing with it a breath of gay Caribbean air. It has many virtues that appeal to gardeners of today; it grows fast, is disease-free and flowers with prodigality from July right through till the frosts with its constant succession of ballet-skirted columbines or long, pendant earrings.

The varieties of *F. magellanica* and a nice trugful of hybrids are quite hardy in most parts of the country (certainly in Yorkshire and Lancashire), especially if we regard them as herbaceous perennials liable to be cut to the ground by frost. Indeed, regardless of frost, we may profit by deliberately cutting them down in late March (early April in the north), for new, strong shoots then spring up eagerly from below ground level. They prosper in sun or shade and their chief needs are for a rich soil, retentive of moisture, and plenty of water. They much enjoy a wet, warm summer.

Prepare the soil a little extra well, with plenty of manure if you have it. Do not plant until the end of May (early June in the north). Plant very deeply, with the crown buried some 4in. or more. Water copiously in dry spells. Pinch out the growing tip when four or five pairs of leaves have developed and, for good measure, pinch out the tips of the subsequent side-shoots also, for the more tips there are the more flowers there will be.

In the mild west, which is the fuchsia's happiest hunting ground, little seems to be needed for winter protection, but elsewhere the usual practice nowadays is to hibernate the plants by building a little mound over each to a height of 6 or 8in. at the end of October in the north and mid-November in the south. The mound may be of ashes, provided they have been thoroughly well weathered, otherwise of gravel or a very gritty soil.

At the end of March remove the hillocks and cut what shoots there are down to ground level. There are other dodges also for hibernation, which require potting them up.

As for selections, there is a large array, from the charming little 'Tom Thumb', of 15in., to the big 'Riccartonii', a variety of *F. magellanica* and the largest and hardiest of all, growing to 6ft or more and making a marvellous floral hedge, as any visitor to Cornwall will have seen, and not needing, as a rule, to be cut back to more than 3ft.

A more graceful variety is the slender, erect, crimson 'Thompsonii', excellent for very small gardens but not, I am told, hardy everywhere.

Even more beautiful than the Magellan fuchsias, and sometimes included among them, are 'Gracilis Tricolor' and 'Gracilis Variegata', in which, on 3ft bushes, the scarlet-and-purple flowers are marvellously displayed against foliage that is suffused with rose-pink and other tints in the first and margined with cream and pale pink in the second.

Other safe and well tried choices are:

> Mrs Popple (fails in some northern gardens), Mrs W. P. Wood, Mme Cornelissen, Uncle Charlie, Princess Dollar (fat, low, gorgeously barbaric), Chillerton Beauty, Enfant Prodige, and Susan Travis.

There is particular charm in the fuchsias of weeping habit, but to enjoy them fully you must hoist them up on a bank or terrace or plant them in tubs. Here 'Marinka' and 'Lena' are good choices. For hanging baskets (to be taken indoors in autumn) there are 'Cascade', 'Marinka' and a few more.

In very favoured regions, such as the Channel Isles, *F. excorticata* makes a stunning small tree, with flowers of violet, yellow and green accompanied by bright blue pollen, upon which birds become tipsy and which the Maoris used as a face powder.

If you are tempted to buy other species or varieties, ask the nurseryman's advice about their suitability for growing outdoors. In a greenhouse you can, with minimum difficulty, grow many an opulent, Caribbean splendour, and, with more difficulty, train them as standards, fans or what you will. If you are moved that way, join the British Fuchsia Society.

Propagation of fuchsias from cuttings is very easy any time from spring to autumn, June being the best. Give them the normal "close" conditions; a flowerpot-ful in a plastic bag will do.

Hydrangeas

Influenced by the pot-grown splendours of hotel lounges and at mayoral receptions, many people suppose that hydrangeas ought to be blue. This is quite fallacious, for the red, pink or white varieties and species are equally splendid and often inevitable. The behaviour of hydrangeas outdoors is to a large extent unpredictable. There are many that can never be anything else than pink or white. Nor can you have any blue hydrangeas (if you want them) unless you have an acid soil *and* choose the right varieties. They may then go blue quite naturally, but may, on the other hand, have to be induced by large dressings of aluminium sulphate; old horseshoes and rusty nails are no-go for blue, though a useful tonic to health.

All this, of course, concerns mainly the popular varieties of *H. macrophylla* and more particularly the mop-headed ones, known as the Hortensias, in which all the visible florets are sterile, thus in part accounting for the fact that, when they are taken indoors in early autumn, they become dry and papery but they still live on as very beautiful flowers, flushed and tinted with half a paintbox-full of subtle colours, more lovely than when alive.

A second limb of *macrophylla* is provided by the "lace-caps", less suited to the mayor's parlour and much more refined, being nearly flat and composed of a central bevy of very small, demure, densely crowded fertile florets, imprisoned within an outer ring of bold, showy, infertile ones. Both sorts are subject to the same blueing factors.

Cultivation. The conditions required by hydrangeas in general are:

- rich feeding with plenty of manure and top-dressings of the same from time to time,
- deep mulches of leaves every autumn accompanied by some fertilizer,
- copious watering,
- avoidance of frost pockets,
- partial shade for the majority.

The macrophylla hydrangeas need no normal pruning. They flower mainly from the tips of the shoots grown the previous year and if you behead them you may have no flowers next year. Nor should you rob the plants of flowers for the house until the plants are large enough

PLATE 13. Roses interplanted with azaleas at the skirts of the weeping willow.

PLATE 14. *Top*: A section of the old peat-wall garden.
Below: The ever-blooming *Potentilla fruticosa*.

to spare a few, and these only with very short stalks; for the new, soft shoots that result may not harden up before winter. Always leave the old flower heads on right through the winter until early April. On the other hand, when the plant ages, you do prune away, completely and to the ground where necessary, all decadent old stems, so as to rejuvenate the plant with strong, young ones.

Blueing. First choose varieties that have a natural inclination that way. If your soil is very acid they will probably display their Oxford or Cambridge allegiances without artificial prompting, those of a Cambridge persuasion especially needing a very acid soil. If, on the other hand, the soil is only mildly acid, any of them may come quite a nice mauve or perhaps a shade that you don't care for. Then is the time to give them chemical encouragement. Either use a proprietary article or else water them, every week from April onwards, with quarter of an ounce of aluminium sulphate in a gallon of water. Do this liberally, particularly at the root-tips, which correspond more or less to the circumference of the foliage. White varieties cannot be induced to colour and should always be planted in shade, for hot sun burns the sepals.

Choices: the mop-heads. Many catalogues (Sunningdale's and Jackman's being notable exceptions) are curiously unhelpful in the matter of colouring, but the following is a good "short list" of the mop-heads:

Altona. Very deep pink or deep blue, 5ft.
Ami Pasquier. Fine crimson, 5ft.
Goliath. Pink or deep blue, large, good at seaside.
Mme E. Moullière. Always white, 6–7ft.
Maréchal Foch. Rose or deep blue, very fine, 5ft.
Mouselline. Pale pink, blue in very acid soil, 6–7ft.
Parsival. Deep rose or very deep blue, 5ft.
Générale Vicomtesse de Vibraye. Soft pink or vivid sky-blue in very acid soils. Very fine indeed, 5ft.
Westfalen. Fine crimson or violet, 3½ft.

The lace-caps. Of the lace-cap macrophyllas, there is a limited choice. The favourites are: the robust 'Blue Wave', which is blue only in acid soils and grows 5ft high by 8ft wide;[1] the sun-loving 'Lanarth White', 6ft in the west, much less elsewhere; and 'Veitchii', 6ft, not for full sun.

[1] Sometimes wrongly labelled 'Mariesii', its parent, which has a bun-shaped truss.

In addition to the macrophylla varieties, there are several other very fine lace-caps, of which the following is a selection.

H. serrata varieties, most of which (but not the first) prefer light woodland conditions:

'Lilacina'. Tough and hardy, beautiful colourings in any soil, the outer florets prettily fringed, 5ft. Preferred to 'Blue Wave'.

'Blue Bird'. Blues readily, a pretty plant, 3½ft.

'Grayswood'. Erect habit to 5ft × 3ft. Domed trusses in many changing tints of pink or blue and white. Often leggy in youth.

Lastly, there is the species *villosa*, with very long, furry leaves and wide lace-caps in tones of lilac and rose-lilac, flowering late. Dreary as a juvenile, it becomes a handsome and strapping 8-footer. Thrives on lime, but needs a cool and partly shaded spot, as on a north wall or in open shrubland.

In exposed seaside places the very old 'Joseph Banks' puts up a brave show, as may be seen in the Isle of Wight, but it is useless inland.

Plumed hydrangeas. Of a style entirely different from these mop-heads and lace-caps is a very fine, utterly hardy hydrangea that throws out long, broadly conical plumes, anything up to 1ft long, that start green, develop white and slowly turn to a russet pink, on show throughout August and often beyond. This is *H. paniculata* 'Grandiflora'. Quite sun-hardy and excellent in herbaceous borders as elsewhere. Feed it richly. May top 8ft, splaying out with slightly pendulous arms to 6ft. In the open ground, you should cut it back half-way every March.

Alternatively, 'Grandiflora' makes a spectacular little standard tree, in the fashion of a rose, very formal and prim, very pretty as a little avenue or in pairs on a terrace, etc. (from Hillier). In this form prune harder still.

Hydrangeas multiply with the greatest of ease from heel or nodal cuttings any time from May to September.

For the climbing hydrangeas see Chapter 22.

Finally, may I persuade everyone to pronounce the name so that the second syllable is not "drain", in the manner of the multitude, but "dran", which is not only U but also Oxford Dictionary and good etymology.

Lilacs

(*Syringa*)

You should already have noted that the botanical name *Syringa* applies to the lilac (or layloc in the vernacular of some counties) and not, according to popular fallacy, to the philadelphus. Those of the most popular appeal are varieties of *S. vulgaris*, the common lilac, but we have also to look at the fine Canadian hybrids and a few species and dwarfs that are beautiful, very hardy and splendid for small gardens.

Lilacs are greedy and you should feed them richly and give them full sun. They relish lime in any form and do well in smoky towns, but hate bad drainage. Except as we shall see in a moment, they call for little effort from the gardener and normally need no pruning beyond the prompt removal of the spent flower trusses.

The vulgaris lilacs. It is in these, which are the ones most commonly grown, that may cause the gardener a little bother, for, if they have been grafted on a common rootstock, he may find himself plagued with a forest of suckers. Opinions differ on whether these give better or worse results than plants "on their own roots" raised from cuttings or layers. Thus, Notcutts, the lilac specialists, supply only grafted plants of *vulgaris* sorts, but Sunningdale, a nursery of equal repute, have them on their own roots. Find out which yours are and, if any suckers of a wild rootstock appear, immediately *wrench* (not cut) them out below ground level.

After planting, cut back the young shrubs to make them bush out and remove all flower buds in the first year. Do not expect them always to be true to colour for the first two or three years.

Having dull foliage, these lilacs are boring plants after flowering, but can play a second innings if partnered by one of the less vigorous clematis (see chapter on climbers). They also call for some sort of ground-cover at their feet and suitable ones are given in the appropriate chapters. Old, neglected lilacs can be rejuvenated by cutting out whole branches or even by cutting the bush down to 4ft or so.

Of the *vulgaris* lilacs, the best whites are 'Maud Notcutt' for a single and the old 'Mme Lemoine' for a double. In the former the buds are cream, opening to very large, white florets in a huge cluster. Of other colours, I suggest that you look particularly at:

Masséna, deep purple-red. Very large and splendid.
Souvenir de Louis Spath. Deep wine-purple.
Katherine Havemeyer. Deep lavender, double.
Clarke's Giant. Immense trusses of lavender and mauve.

The extra-hardy **Canadian hybrids** (*S. prestonae*) grow very quickly indeed, very large (perhaps too large for some gardens) and carry huge, multiple trusses of long, tubular florets, several in shades of real pink, after the *vulgaris* varieties have finished. I have grown all the following satisfactorily: 'Bellicent', 'Elinor', 'Isabella' and 'Virgilia'. I should have had the pink 'Fountain' also. These Canadians are usually, or should be, on their own roots, as they do not have the spreading habit of the *vulgaris* lilacs.

Other lilacs. A charming dwarf lilac that gave me great delight for many years is *S. microphylla* 'Superba'. Small-leaved, dense, compact, it grows to about 5ft × 4ft in a broadly pyramidal form, with quantities of small trusses of scented, rose-pink florets, first in May and again in September, with occasional trusses throughout summer. Very hardy. Has an alias in some catalogues as *palibiniana*, which is something different, but also good.

Another delightful dwarf is the Persian lilac, *persica*, of about the same size. The slender branches incline gracefully at the tips. The pearly white form, 'Alba', is charming.

The Roman lilac, perversely named *chinensis*, grows to about 10ft with quantities of small, scented, drooping trusses of warm lavender and small leaves. There are a few colour variations, as in 'Rubra'. Early-flowering.

A genuine Chinaman, *sweginzowii* 'Superba' is the most sweetly scented of all lilacs and makes an elegant bush of 9ft with trusses of flesh-pink florets loosely arranged. Good in cold northern counties.

Other Excellences

Abeliophyllum. An unusual and charming little shrub. Imagine a small forsythia of 4ft wreathed in very small, blush-pink florets, waning to ivory, enlivened by the bright little golden eyes of its stamens, and almond-scented to boot, and you have *A. distichum*. The plant is quite hardy, but the buds dare the frosts of February and in some seasons pay the penalty; so give it the protection of a warm south or west wall.

Prune the spent twigs back by two-thirds immediately after flowering (Waterer or Notcutt).

Abutilon. Slender, graceful shrubs, occasionally very large, with vine-like leaves and flowers that often resemble those of the hollyhock. None is fully hardy in the open outside the Gulf Stream counties but there are a few that handsomely decorate a south wall in many other parts.

FIG. 92.
Abutilon megapotamicum.

The best known is *A. vitifolium*, a beautiful plant, happy at the sea-side, liable to grow to 12ft, with abundant flowers of soft lilac in June–July.

A more exotic but less hardy creature is *megapotamicum*, which needs the protection of a warm wall outside the more cosseted counties. A slender and graceful shrub of 4ft or less, it dangles long, pendulous flowers theatrically dressed in red, yellow and purple, like tiny dolls. 'Ashfold Red' and 'Golden Fleece' are handsome varieties (Hillier or Notcutt).

ARTEMISIA. See "Silver and Grey".

BARBERRY (*Berberis*). See previous chapter.

Buddleia. The common one with purple plumes in July–August is *davidii*, a plebeian thing that would be more acceptable if cut back hard to 2ft from the ground every spring, or even lower. The variety 'Royal Red', which is not red but a crimson-purple, is the showiest variety, but better still is a graceful, grey-leaved species with the same habit as Father David's buddleia, but rarely growing more than 6ft and having plumes of rich blue; this is the hybrid 'Loch Inch'.

The "orange-ball tree", *globosa*, is a 12ft shrub which tosses up tightly packed orange orbs in June. Apt to become gaunt and ill-clad. Prune to new growth after flowering.

The most beautiful of all hardy buddleias is the species *alternifolia*, which flings out long and elegant parabolas wreathed all the way along with tight little clusters of soft lilac in June, delicately scented. Prune spent shoots immediately after flowering, removing about one-third of the plant annually. At 12ft × 15ft it is too large for many small gardens, but reaches the height of elegance in gardens of any size when tailored as a standard tree. I raised mine by growing from seed (very easy) and training the strongest seedlings up a tall stake on single stems, plucking off all shoots except the topmost tufts. Some reached 6ft in the first year and in the second year built up their gracefully arching topknots. You can do the same thing from nursery plants by choosing strong basal shoots when the plant is two years old, pinching out the tip at 6ft and removing the remaining growth completely. Alternifolias transplant only when very young.

FIG. 93.
Caryopteris clandonensis.

Caryopteris. Delightful 4ft shrubs with grey, scented foliage and clusters of blue florets in the leaf axils in August–September. Would be seen in thousands if 100 per cent hardy. The name is *C. clandonensis* and perhaps the best forms are 'Heavenly Blue' (Hillier) and 'Kew Blue'. Cut hard in early April nearly to the base of last year's flowering shoots. Full sun. O.K. in the south and sheltered places elsewhere.

CEANOTHUS. See previous chapter.

Ceratostigma. Charming and easy shrubs with pretty bright-blue flowers in clusters like those of the phlox or the plumbago. Excellent for mingling with herbaceous plants. August–October, 30in. Prune to the ground each April (not before) if the frost has not done so for you. Fearsome full name: *C. willmottianum*, the best of the ceratostigmas. Easily increased by division or by summer cuttings.

CHAENOMELES. See Quince, below.

CHIMONANTHUS. See Winter-sweet, below.

Clerodendrum. Loose, 12ft shrubs grown mainly for their autumn display of small but jewel-like fruits, in which turquoise berries are brilliantly set in crimson, star-shaped calyces; but it needs a warm autumn for them to materialize. Small, scented flowers. Otherwise dull. This is *C. trichotomum*.

Cornus. The cornels or dogwoods are a large race, broadly divisible for our purposes into two groups – large, open, tree-like shrubs, some reaching 20ft, and those that make dense, widely spreading thickets of brilliantly coloured stems in winter, 6–8ft high.

Of the tree types, the best in the long run is the gorgeous *C. kousa chinensis*, subject to these provisos: that your garden is not too small, not in a cold county and that you are patient. After many Junes it becomes lavishly plastered with large white flowers, which are in fact bracts, and which age picturesquely to rosy pink. When at last it blooms it is a stunner. Quite hardy but flowers poorly in cold climates. Of the same nature and indeed more beautiful still, but able to do themselves justice in the hottest spots only, are *florida rubra* and *nuttallii.*

A cornel that is iron-hardy anywhere is *C. mas* 'Variegata', which bursts out gallantly into a froth of minute yellow blossoms clustered in short spurs on leafless boughs at the end of February. Lovely against the winter sky. The foliage, when it comes, is margined in white. Much nicer than the plain *C. mas*, which is a humdrum thing after flowering is over.

The dogwoods grown for their brilliant stems look marvellous in a pallid winter sun and they prosper in boggy ground, but may spread too much for some gardens.

Those that find most favour are the brilliant red Westonbirt dogwood (*C. alba* 'Sibirica'), and more particularly still its form with leaves beautifully margined and splashed with white. This is *C. a.* 'Variegata', one of the loveliest of shrubs (in some catalogues it is *atrosanguinea* 'Elegantissima').

Its counterpart with golden leaves instead of silver is 'Spaethii' and, for a dogwood in which the stems are yellow instead of red, you can have *stolonifera* 'Flaviramea'.

Amputate these thickets right down to a stump at the end of March each year.

For the little *C. canadensis*, see Chapter 23.

COTONEASTER. See previous chapter.

COTINUS. See under Sumach, below.

Currant, Flowering (*Ribes*). Easy suburbanites that have their brief reign in April and for the rest of the year are boring. For rich colouring get 'King Edward VII' (6ft), or 'Pulborough Scarlet' (9ft). Prune fairly hard after flowering.

Much more interesting is the prickly "flowering gooseberry", with glossy, semi-evergreen leaves and strung all along the branches with hanging, rich-red, fuchsia-like flowers, beginning in February (7ft). This is *R. speciosum*.

CYTISUS. Included in Brooms.

DAPHNE. See previous chapter.

Deutzia. Only too familiar as a slovenly, scraggy, unpruned shrub of 10ft, with clusters of small, white flowers; this is *D. scabra*. Even if pruned after flowering, as you should do, it is not nearly so desirable as the smaller and more compact sorts. High marks go to *rosea* 'Carminea', whose slender limbs swing elegantly outwards, laden with small flowers of soft rose at the end of May; 4ft × 5ft. Just as good and a trifle taller, are the erect, scented *elegantissima*, a wonderful sight in June, *kalmiiflora* and 'Mont Rose', all in slightly different shades of pink.

Prune away the old flowered wood at once, if necessary down to the ground.

DIERVILLA. See Weigela, below.

Forsythia. Few shrubs are better known to us all, yet still counted among the world's finest garden plants, than the varieties of *F. intermedia*, whose thickly clustered sprigs of golden bells break out in March. They prosper almost anywhere and are lovely underplanted with blue scillas. The variety most written-up is 'Lynwood', but the older 'Spectabilis' is just as fine. Sometimes available as standards (Waterer). I should avoid the cock-eyed 'Beatrix Farrand'.

Diverse opinions are voiced on pruning, but probably the best system is simply to cut the old wood back very hard every three or four years. Cutting long sprays for the house is a good way of annual pruning.

For growing on walls, the species usually employed is *suspensa*, the most attractive of which is the black-stemmed 'Atrocaulis'. Of course, these forsythias are not really climbers but floppers and, like the winter jasmine, must be patiently tied in and the flowered shoots cut back regularly, or they become a fearful mess. The best use of *suspensa* and its varieties ('Sieboldii' is extra floppy) is tumbling down a terrace or bank.

Forsythias are very easy from summer cuttings.

Hibiscus. I did not think that the Syrian hibiscus was much catch until, many years ago, I saw a perfectly splendid short hedge of it in a small suburban garden near Hampton Court. Expect no South Seas splendour, but imagine hollyhock flowers on a bold, branching shrub 8ft high and wide in August–September and you have *H. syriacus*. Fully hardy but often dormant the first year and not at its best in a cool summer. There are several varieties, of which you could start with the very fine 'Blue Bird', the red 'Woodbridge' or the pink 'Hamabo'. Full sun essential.

Indigofera. Beautiful and very easy shrubs draped in elegant, airy, pinnate foliage, from the leaf axils of which comes a constant succession of pea-flowers all summer. The popular one is *I. gerardiana*, rose-purple, 3½ft. Very decorative and now known to be quite hardy in most parts of Britain. Cut hard back nearly to the ground in April; new shoots spring up readily. Full sun.

"JAPONICA". See Quince, below.

Kerria. Kindergarten cottage favourite with green, nearly upright stems spangled liberally with bright yellow flowers; usually seen in the double, rosette form. Connoisseurs prefer the single form, with yellow saucers. Best not in full sun. Cut all the flowered stems right down to the ground every May, or it will degenerate miserably. Propagates easily by division or offsets. Shun the variegated forms.

Kolkwitzia. One of the most beautiful and gracious of moderate-sized shrubs for May–June. The slender stems form themselves into graceful arches, 7ft high and wide, producing masses of pink, orange-throated pouches in clusters at the tips of the short, lateral twigs. Any good soil. Prune the flowered shoots back to a point where a good new shoot is starting; when aged, cut old, gnarled stems to the ground The name is *K. amabilis,* of which there is a beautiful variety 'Pink Cloud' (L. R. Russell). Increase by summer cuttings.

Mallow. The "tree mallow", *Lavatera olbia,* partially evergreen, is no aristocrat, but useful as a temporary fill-in. The best is 'Rosea', giving a good scattering of pink hollyhock-flowers all summer. 6ft. Cut back hard in March.

Perovskia. Not quite sure whether it was going to be a sage or a lavender, a shrub or an herbaceous plant, the delightful hybrid 'Blue Spire' sends up very slim, erect, pointed wands of proud bearing to 4ft or so, sheathed in silvery grey and green and decorated with quantities of small florets in deep lavender. A lovely colour association, displayed throughout August and September. Wants hot sun and is probably sad in wet soils. Looks best slightly elevated on a bank or terrace but also consorts harmoniously with the flowers of the border. Splendid with heather. In April, cut hard back to the base of last year's shoots.

Its parent with the atrocious name *P. atriplicifolia* is just as good but has paler flowers.

Philadelphus. You should know by now that this genus has no right to the name *Syringa,* as the uninstructed call it. Even the fancy name "mock orange" is ambiguous, for it is sometimes applied to *Choisya ternata,* the "Mexican orange blossom".

Philadelphuses are known for their showers of white blossoms, usually scented, at midsummer. Of no interest after flowering. Usually allowed to degenerate into gangling skeletons through lack of pruning. Do this immediately after the flowers are spent, cutting the stems back to a point where a strong new shoot appears. The result will be an enormous outpouring of blossom the next year.

There are some beautiful dwarfs, particularly 'Manteau d'Hermine' of 3ft, which develops into a thicket in a few years, and the smaller flowered, denser, more richly scented *microphyllus*. Of the larger sorts, nothing beats the old *P. coronarius* for pure scent (which Gerarde found "troubling and molesting in the head in a strange manner"), but it is a very plain Jane. Its offspring 'Aureus' has beautiful young foliage of bright gold, but is slow. There is no point in examining the long list of named varieties, but, ignoring all that lack a sweet breath, you might look kindly on the purple-throated 'Belle Etoile', the double 'Virginal', the like 'Bouquet Blanc' and the delightful, small 'Sybille' of 5ft.

Potentilla. We have seen some herbaceous and rock garden potentillas. The shrubby ones, if of no romantic glamour, are one of the most useful of shrubs, especially in small gardens, for they never stop blooming all summer and half the autumn and give absolutely no trouble at all.

Their flowers, when yellow, are rather like flattened buttercups or, when white, like those of the strawberry. The bushes are very compact, usually 3–4ft high; those that grow taller, such as 'Katherine Dykes' and 'Vilmoriniana', are too tall. In winter all turn russet, like dead bracken; the wood is brown right through, and thus may seem to be dead when you make the usual test of scratching the bark.

All those normally grown are varieties of *P. fruticosa* and there are now a lot of them. I have grown a good many and find some difficult to distinguish from others, while the bees have provided me with varied seedlings. Three that stand out are the dwarf 'Beesii' (alias 'Nana Argentea'), 12in., with small flowers and small leaves agreeably "silvered o'er", the more typical 'Elizabeth', a fine lass of 3ft with large flowers of medium yellow, and 'Primrose Beauty', 3ft, dense and compact and particularly good for a little hedge. Good dwarfs or near-dwarfs are 'Woodbridge Gold', 'Klondyke', 'Minstead Dwarf' and 'Tangerine' (low and spreading).

Quince (*Chaenomeles*, formerly *Cydonia* and *Pyrus*). The beautiful and lively flowering quinces, which adorn walls and beds with so much festive splendour in winter and spring for three long months, have been cruelly treated by those people whose business is to lay down the law about the names of things. The result is a hopeless confusion in catalogues. As Mr Christopher Lloyd says: "Well may the multitude groan."[1] Usually the safest name is the varietal one, ignoring the specific one; and we really ought now to discard for ever the pointless old fancy name "japonica".

The flowering quinces are very hardy, prosper in any reasonable soil, in sun or in part shade, though better and earlier in sun. Their normal season is from February to the end of May. Of the many offered to us, look first at the following.

'Simonii'. Vivid, velvety blood-red. One of our very finest low shrubs, 2ft high, spreading horizontally to 4ft. Often wrongly shown under *japonica* (which used to be famous as *Cydonia maulei*). Really a *speciosa*, but what boots it?

'Knap Hill Scarlet'. A variety of *superba*, but usually catalogued under *speciosa*. Badly named, as the flowers are not scarlet, but salmon and terracotta; 5ft, spreading densely.

alpina. A true variety of the aforesaid *C. japonica* of today. Another good dwarf in brick-red, suckering freely and spreading to 8ft or so.

Then we come to several named cultivars of what is now called *C. speciosa*. This is the species out of which the botanists have weaved the most tangled of all webs. In my lifetime it has been known successively as *Pyrus japonica, Cydonia japonica* and *Chaenomeles lagenaria* before it got to its present one – a list of aliases that look like a burglar's record. Any of these may be found in catalogues. This is the species that gave rise to the popular name of "japonica" for all flowering quinces, *not* the species mentioned above that is now called *Chaenomeles japonica!*

Well now, the speciosas make quite large shrubs, sometimes up to 10ft in the open, but are particularly celebrated for growing against a wall, where they may spread very widely. They prosper on any walls, including a north one, but do better still on a south or south-west one, which brings out their heart-warming flowers as early as Christmas in some places.

The craft in growing them on a wall is to train and prune them in the same manner as cordon or espalier apples. First build up a basic framework, by running up a leader and training out lateral branches, the while removing any outward thrusting breastwood and any

[1] In *Shrubs and Trees for Small Gardens* (Pan Books).

growing inwards to the wall. As soon as sub-laterals form, pinch out their tips in June, cut them back to five leaves in August and in winter cut them hard back to two buds. They flower, like many apples, on short spurs on shoots one or more years old, not on "young wood".

Good speciosa varieties for growing this way are:

'Rosea Flore Pleno', rose-pink, double.

'Falconnet Charlet', salmon, double.

'Moerloosei', pale-pink and white.

'Boule de Feu' red, possibly a *japonica* variety.

'Nivalis', white.

The above are the correct spellings; many catalogues err.

The blood-red, widely spreading 'Rowallane Seedling', 'Pink Lady', and 'Knap Hill Scarlet' may also be grown on lowish walls but I think it spoils the beauty of their form and I prefer them as open-ground shrubs.

RHUS. See Sumach, below.

RIBES. See Currant, Flowering, above.

Rubus. These are the brambles, of which there are some beautiful forms for the flower garden, provided there is ample room. The best is the hybrid 'Tridel', which, all along its long, arching shoots, is starred with large, single, beautiful, white flowers adorned with a brush of golden stamens in May. A plant of distinction. 6ft × 10ft or more.

I have also found the Tibetan bramble very enjoyable for its beautiful, wraith-like white stems, most attractive in the winter scene and not so large as 'Tridel'. This is *thibetanus.* Very good and picturesque in shade. Of the same white-stemmed elegance is *cockburnianus*, but more ground-consuming, spreading by suckers; good for woodland spots.

Cut the old canes of all brambles right down to the ground after flowering.

Spiraea. All the old herbaceous spiraeas (Chapter 10) have been rechristened, so that strictly the name now applies only to the shrubs. There are a great many, very variable, very easily grown in any decent soil, comely in habit, very flowerful and nearly always white. Unless pretty regularly pruned, however, they become shabby. Follow the normal rules for those that flower before or after midsummer respectively, as ordained in Chapter 7. Taking them in seasonal order:

thunbergii. March–April. Twiggy bush of 4–5ft. Virginal sprays of small white stars. Fresh, slender, apple-green foliage, which breaks out surprisingly in January. Makes one of the loveliest low hedges.

arguta, known as the bridal-wreath. Most beautiful of the spring spiraeas. April–May. 6–7ft. Festooned with bunches of little white flowers all along the upper sides of its twigs.

vanhouttei. May. 8ft. Arching shrub with flowers grouped in little domes all along the branches.

menziesii 'Triumphans'. July–August. 8ft. For woodland, spreading by suckers. Accords more to popular image of spiraeas. Tall plumes of rose-purple. Not for poor or very dry soils. Prune hard in February.

'Anthony Waterer'. 4ft. July–September. Over-praised shrub with flat trusses in dull carmine. Dead-head the early blooms when spent. Prune half-way in March.

Sumach (*Rhus*). The sumachs include two or three old friends of the easiest cultivation, prospering in poor soils and noted for their stunning autumn colours. They often stay dormant in their first year.

The stag's horn sumach, so called because of the shape of its branch formation, reaching 12ft, with very long pinnate leaves that colour to a brilliant orange-crimson, is *R. typhina.* I go, however, for its variety 'Laciniata', which has deeply cut, shredded leaves that turn orange and lemon.

The Venetian sumach or smoke-plant, known by its billowing masses of silken hairs and fawn-pink flowers that turn to a smoke-grey haze, is *R. cotinus,* though we are now expected to call it *Cotinus coggygria.* Go for the gorgeous 'Foliis Purpureis', which unfolds crimson, turns vinous purple and dies a light red.

Even more fiery autumn tints are produced by *R. cotinoides,* but it should be grown only in the stoniest soils.

Tamarisk (*Tamarix*). Light, airy, feathery foliage and multitudes of little pink florets. They "do like to be beside the sea-side" and will grow in almost pure sand, as in any other soil that is not too heavy. Growing very fast, they become sprawling, 12ft shrubs, unless sharply pruned. The best is the species *pentandra* or its varieties 'Pink Cascade' (Waterer or Jackman) and 'Rubra'. August. Cut back as hard as you like every April. Longer-flowering but less choice is the common French tamarisk, *gallica*; same treatment. For earlier bloom (May–June) there is *tetrandra*; cut out old, exhausted stems and shorten others just after flowering. See also page 436.

Syringa. See Lilac for the true syringa. For the plant fallaciously so called, see Philadelphus.

Viburnum. A tremendously versatile troupe, a few evergreen, some flowering in winter, others varying in their floral forms and yet others grown for their foliage and berries. In the popular image the best known are those with "snowball" trusses. All easy in any reasonable soil and most very suitable for small gardens. Our native wayfaring-tree, *V. lantana* is one of the troupe. The following are usually the most esteemed; all flourish in chalk.

WINTER FLOWERING. On the whole the best today are *V. bodnantense* 'Dawn' and 'Charles Lamont', both slight improvements on dear old *fragrans.* Domes of pink buds opening white, voluptuously scented of almonds. 10ft.

The old laurustinus (*V. tinus*) is a fine, dense evergreen of the easiest culture, valuable as a screen, with pink-tinted snowballs for many months and an excellent host for clematis. There are several forms, not all hardy.

SPRING FLOWERING (April–May):

carlesii. 4ft. Pink buds opening to white snowballs, carnation-scented, beautiful in flower, dull afterwards.

juddii. 5ft. Similar in flower but a much finer shrub.

burkwoodii. 9ft. Also similar in flower; a fine big shrub, partly evergreen.

Nurseries often graft these spring viburnums on the wild *lantana*, which may throw up wretched suckers, not easy to identify.

LATE SPRING (May–June). Now arrive the more spectacular viburnums:

opulus 'Compactum' is a dwarfish form of our native guelder-rose. Flat trusses of scented, white flowers, followed by a profusion of sparkling berries, like red currants. Handsome leaves, like a maple's, colouring well in autumn. 5ft.

opulus 'Sterile' is a big "snowball tree". 12ft × 12ft.

tomentosum 'Sterile' (or 'Plicatum') is the Japanese snowball, a superlative shrub with its snowballs borne in opposite ranks all along the tiered and gently arching branches. 7ft. In the top class of shrubs and champion for small gardens.

tomentosum 'Lanarth' or the almost identical 'Mariesii'. Of equal merit to 'Sterile', but needing more elbow room. A noble shrub, characterized not by snowballs but by large floral plates, in the manner of a lacecap hydrangea, lying flat, facing upwards and laid out the whole length of the horizontal tiers of which the shrub is so handsomely and architecturally composed. Maybe 12ft × 15ft in time. A very handsome specimen shrub in isolation.

All these are propagated with little difficulty from cuttings.

I have used the names given in the best catalogues, which are not botanically correct. Thus the Japanese snowball should be *V. plicatum* var. *plicatum* and the next one *V. plicatum* var. *tomentosum* 'Lanarth'.

FOLIAGE SPECIES. *V. davidii* is a low-growing, wide-spreading evergreen with handsome, dark green, leathery, deeply veined leaves and small trusses of turquoise berries on female plants if consorted with a male. 3ft × 5ft. Often recommended as a "ground-cover" in shade, but far better in sun.

No pruning for viburnums. For large gardens other species are available, such as *betulifolium*, bearing glistening red berries. A big one much written up is *rhytidophyllum*, a coarse-leaved evergreen which is the picture of misery in winter.

Weigela (or *Diervilla*). Easy and useful shrubs, excellent for towns, with strong stems that usually grow about 7ft high and arch out in all directions to the same extent. The flowers are pink or red funnels, borne in profusion in May, but partly hidden by the foliage, which is rather commonplace for the rest of the summer; except in the outstanding *W. florida* 'Variegata', which has cream-margined leaves and pale-pink scented flowers that bloom while the leaves are still very small.

Among the numerous garden hybrids the ones that stand out are 'Styriaca', rose-pink, and the sparkling 'Bristol Ruby', both flowering in terrific form. 'Eva Rathke', dark red, has some merit in small places, growing only 4–5ft and flowering all summer.

You must give weigelas a good, rich, loamy soil, with occasional mulches of manure. Prune the majority as you do other early shrubs, cutting the flowered shoots back to a strong new growth. Use your discretion on 'Eva Rathke' and go easy on *florida* 'Variegata', which is rather twiggy. Aged weigelas need to have some of the tough old stems cut right out.

Increase by summer cuttings.

Winter-sweet. A rather boring shrub, but one which, if you can wait several years, produces clusters of little yellow and tawny florets with a marvellous scent all winter. Of value only for cutting. This is

Chimonanthus praecox (or *fragrans*). 9ft × 10ft. The variety 'Luteus' is showier but my nose detects no scent.

Witch-hazel (*Hamamelis*). Loveliest of all winter shrubs, *H. mollis* has a piquant and captivating charm. From Christmas till late February it bears on its straight, naked stems quantities of ingenious little twisted ribbons as of spun gold, scented of cowslips – a merry bush that ought to be the haunt of elves. In summer it has leaves like the hazel's. Lovely for cutting when the bush is big enough to stand it. A stunning picture where partnered by *Iris histrioides* 'Major' or the mauve Rhododendron *mucronulatum* (in the milder counties) or by winter heathers. Full sun and a fairly meaty soil. Allow 10ft × 10ft. No pruning. There are several other witch-hazels, such as the variety 'Pallida' and the Japanese species, but plain *mollis* beats the lot.

CHAPTER 20

SILVER AND GREY

High, Dry and Sunny – The White Company

THE priestesses of flower "arrangement", and their occasional male equivalents, have been largely responsible for popularizing all manner of plants that have foliage wholly or partly "silver'd o'er" with a metallic sheen or coated with a soft down that may be almost pure white or dove-grey or pewter. Our gardens have benefited from this cult, which has influenced our ideas of design and colour groupings. We may use them as foils or contrasts or as consorts for other soft colours. Attempts at all-white gardens or parts of a garden, however, have always made me feel chilled and a bit shivery.

In nature most of the silvers and greys come from open, sunny, arid places and their leaves are actually green but, in order to counteract the aridity, they restrict transpiration by putting on a coat of very fine hairs or a sheath of white or pearl-grey bloom. It is this protective clothing that give the leaves their steely or downy appearance and we begin our understanding of the plants when we appreciate this fact.

We have two main classes of plants to consider: shrubs (together with a few small trees) and herbaceous plants. Their cultivation differs a little in some points but, by and large, all have three basic needs:

a dry, stony soil with extra fast drainage,
all-day sun,
lime.

The last is perhaps the least important; many grey-leaved shrubs will prosper in mildly acid soils but lime seems particularly important for the herbaceous plants and in all cases it seems to intensify the silvery or pearly bloom. Many revel in chalk.

The other two conditions are compulsory, with such few exceptions as we shall note. Shade takes all the life out of them and the slightest risk of a wet collar or wet feet, especially in winter, will send them into a mortal decline. So will manure. Sandy, stony, gritty, impoverished soils are excellent. Clay is most unpromising for the majority unless on a steepish slope or a mound, well worked and lavishly sprinkled with grit or gravel (I use Cornish sand) and preferably charged with lime. These conditions are not difficult to create artificially and, in the rock garden chapter, we shall see how many plants prosper in a dry wall or a scree. Thus "high, dry and sunny" is the prescription we must stipulate for all but a few of the plants on our panel.

The silvers and greys are, of course, grown chiefly for the beauty of their foliage, particularly when the leaves are so deeply incised, slotted or shredded as to look like filigree, lace, ferns or what you will. The flowers of many are of no account and should be strangled at birth. Others need an occasional, or even frequent plucking of their foliage, to keep them compact and to induce fresh, young shoots. There is quite a lot of annual pruning to be done also and this you do rather late in spring.

On the whole, the herbaceous plants are the hardiest and these you plant in early autumn in the ordinary way, while the soil is warm. The shrubs, unless of the tougher sorts, must be held back till spring. Some of these are sensitive not only to winter wet but also to frost, so that in those counties that get it both cold and wet in winter you may have to put on cloches or lift, pot and park the plants in the greenhouse, or propagate afresh each year. The ever-grey shrubs are not very happy in big towns, their hairy coats getting clogged with grime. Conversely, nearly all, whether shrubs or perennials, very much enjoy life at the sea-side, because of their protective coatings.

Propagation of the silver and grey shrubs by cuttings is usually even easier than that of green ones. They want lots more grit in the compost and must not have the usual "close" conditions of a glass-covered propagation box. Make your compost of loam, peat and grit in the proportions of 1:2:3 and put your boxes or pots in a shady place but uncovered – a cold greenhouse, an uncovered frame or the shady north side of a big shrub. If any of the cuttings have woolly stems, scrape off the wool on the lower parts. Go slow with the watering.

Of course, several of the greys and silvers are only varieties of green-leaved plants. These have been included with their own kin in other chapters, so here I give them mere references. Nor do I include here those many shrubs in which the silver or white is no more than a variegation of the leaf, as in hollies, maples, ivies, euonymus and so on. Other classes omitted here are the many silvers of rock gardens and the silver or white-dusted primulas. And before going on with this list of shrubs and perennials let me remind you of that beautiful silver-leaved tree, the willow-leaved pear, *Pyrus salicifolia* 'Pendula'.

The White Company

(HP = herbaceous perennial)

Achillea, HP. See Chapter 10 for the silvery-leaved yarrows *clypeolata,* 'Moonshine' and *taygetea.* All tough and easy in any reasonable soil.

Anthemis, HP. See Chapter 10 for *A. cupaniana.*

Artemisia, shrubs and HPs. Known of old as wormwood, the artemisia supplies us with one of our largest trugfuls of greys and silvers, though some of them are appreciated more by arrangers than by gardeners. Among them are some pernicious infiltrators, such as *A. stelleriana,* fit only for semi-wastes of wet clay. Avoid *palmeri* also.

Out of this big trugful let us pick the following:

absinthium, HP. Famous, or infamous, for providing those "hot and rebellious liquors" in which old gentlemen in France drown their sorrows. The best one now is 'Lambrook Silver', raised by Mrs Marjorie Fish, having mimosa-like flowers and tussocks of cascading, silvered leaves as delicately shredded as those of the carrot. 3ft.

abrotanum, shrub. This is the southernwood, lad's-love, old-man, so delightful to pinch and sniff as you pass the cottage gate. Densely bushy and feathery, with grey-green foliage. May need to be cut hard back in spring occasionally. 3½ft × 18in.

arborescens, shrub. Billows of silvery, silky filigree foliage. Not fully hardy, but magnificent in very dry soil on a warm wall. Plant in spring. 30in.

ludoviciana, HP. The "white sage". One of the most popular for borders. Slender, willow-like, almost white leaves on erect stems and plumes of tiny, off-white flowers in July–August. Has running roots and becomes a thicket. Untidy after heavy rain unless staked. 3ft. 'Silver Queen' is denser, shorter and flowers less.

pedemontana (or *lanata*), HP. An aromatic, 6in. dwarf, with ever-

silver leaves, delightful all winter and spreading out to make a silver carpet.

schmidtii 'Nana', HP. Another sparkling dwarf making a gleaming mound of finely spun silver, turning russet in winter. Keep this old foliage as a protection for the young shoots in spring. Take precautions against the piratical sparrows.

Centaurea, shrub. One of the arranger's pets is the silver cornflower or knapweed, *C. gymnocarpa.* Curving, skeletonized leaves

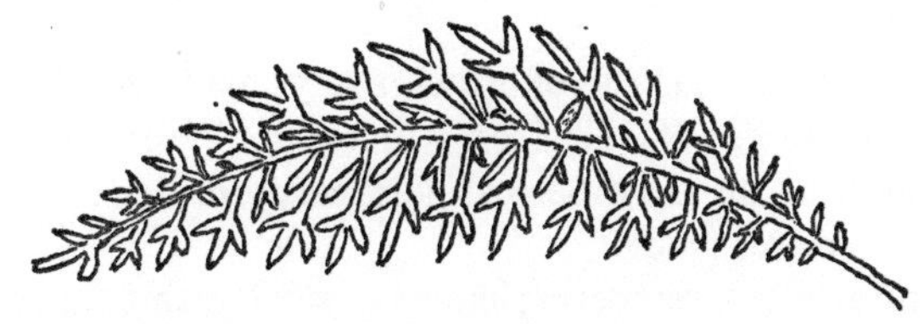

FIG. 94. The silver filigree leaf of *Centaurea gymnocarpa.*

often 15in. long, like fish bones dipped in silver. Very elegant, but only half-hardy and best raised every year from cuttings or from seed in heat in March. Amputate the stalks of the cheap little mauve flowers as soon as apparent.

C. candidissima, much used in bedding schemes, has leaves like silver dandelions (my wife says) and is still less hardy (Christopher Lloyd).

Chrysanthemum, silver. See Tanacetum, below.

Convolvulus, shrub. Not conforming at all to the multitude's image of a convolvulus, *C. cneorum* is a lovely little plant, low and open of habit, clothed all the year with simple, silken leaves, gleaming like pewter, and crowded at its finger-tips in May and in September with florets flushed with pink and freckled with gold at the base. Full sun, gritty, fast-draining, scree-like soil. A Sixth Form plant on the danger-list of hardiness. No pruning apart from dead-heading.

Much rarer is the pretty *C. mauritanicus,* a trailing plant covered with soft, white hairs and giving a long succession of lilac flowers. Tolerably hardy and very nice for hanging baskets (Christopher Lloyd).

Elaeagnus. For the brilliantly silvered species, see Chapter 18.

Eryngium. For the metallic-tinted sea-hollies, see Chapter 10.

Euryops, shrub. A recent immigrant from South Africa, enthusiastically acclaimed. Brilliantly aluminium all the year round, growing about 9in × 12in. or a bit more, it gleams in the garden like a little mound of treasure from the Spanish Main and is prettily garnished for a brief spell in summer with yellow marguerites. Surprisingly hardy, but it is one of those that you must plant "high and dry" in full sun. Its name is *E. acraeus* (formerly *evansii*).

Helichrysum. Mainly shrubs. A race known for their small, papery, daisyform, "everlasting" flowers. Not my cup of tea but may be yours. Few if any are hardy unless in ideal conditions. They include (but I shall exclude) the hot-smelling curry plants. The most reliable seem to be:

splendidum. Round shrub of 3ft with very small, grey-felted leaves and small yellow flowers. Gets leggy unless you give it an occasional cutting back in late May. Seems quite hardy in dry soils. Aliases: *alveolatum* and *trilineatum.*

petiolatum. Pliant, wandering shoots of small, heart-shaped, white-felted leaves. A pretty carpet-bedder for other plants and good in towns, but far from hardy and best raised afresh from cuttings every year.

The above and others from Christopher Lloyd or Mrs Underwood.

Lavender. (*Lavandula*), shrub. Lavenders qualify for enlistment in the Greys by their pewter foliage, so excellently matched by nature with their scented mauve flowers. Look their smartest when paraded as little hedges. Have a wide tolerance of soils, provided you don't post them anywhere damp or shady. Their useful life is not a long one and you should raise new plants from cuttings about every five years – a very simple business.

Lavenders get terribly shabby unless pruned every year. Give them a light trim after flowering and a slightly harder one in spring, bearing in mind the essential fact that new shoots do not sprout from old wood; so cut down to some promising whorl of new, young leaves.

If pallor of foliage is the main consideration, one would have the dwarf, white-felted, purple-flowered *L. lanata*, provided one could give it a thoroughly dry, gritty soil in a hot spot. Otherwise, for all-round excellences, one would choose from the many varieties of the old English or Mitcham lavender or the Dutchman, which is superior as a grey foliage plant but inferior in flower. Catalogues usually call them respectively *spica* and *vera.* Both reach 3ft × 4ft. The best of the many children of the Englishman are:

'Hidcote', dwarf, 15in. × 15in., dense, pewter foliage and very deep purple flowers; a modern classic for a dwarf hedge. There is also a 'Hidcote Giant', 2ft × 2ft, with big flower-heads (Sunningdale).

'Twickle Purple'. This is big brother, broad and bushy, 2½ft × 3ft with spikes of rich purple fanning out to right and left.

'Folgate'. About the same size as 'Hidcote', but flowers of softer hue.

You may have pink lavenders if you wish, but I find them insipid. The old 'Munstead Dwarf' is now outclassed and 'Grappenhall' is too big for most people

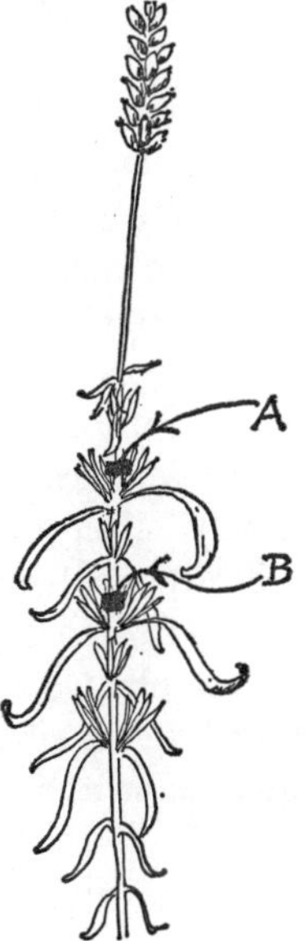

FIG. 95. Pruning a lavender: A, in autumn: B, in spring.

Lychnis, HP. For the old, grey-felted cottage flower *L. coronaria*, and the charming *L. flos-jovis*, see Chapter 10.

Onopordon. Gardeners who fancy having their borders haunted by a gibbering skeleton may invite one or other of the giant thistles into their grounds. *O. arabicum* is an 8ft ghost sheeted in silver and green with purple thistles, and *O. acanthium* is the common cotton-thistle, draped in white wool to about 5ft. They are biennials only and vanish, in disarray, after flowering, but you can get a whole Macbeth-full of more ghosts from their seeds.

Phlomis, shrub. The handsome Jerusalem sage, *P. fruticosa*, only just qualifies for election to White's Club. The wrinkled leaves are more or less grey-green with a white reverse and the whole plant has yellow undertones and a soft texture, with whorls of hooded flowers of dusky yellow in June. Very nice indeed, but of dubious hardiness in colder counties. After flowering cut back below the flower stalks. 3ft × 4ft.

For warmer places a phlomis that is felted all over in a delightful soft old-gold is *P. chrysophylla* (Jackman).

Phlox. See Chapter 10 for the pallid 'Norah Leigh'.

Salvia. The grey-leaved shrubs, very desirable, are in Chapter 18 and the herbaceous sorts in Chapter 10.

Santolina, shrub. The cotton-lavender or, of old, lady-flax, is a great friend to the gardener – easy in any reasonable soil, tidy and well-mannered, not afraid of cold steel and making delightful miniature hedges. There are four very nice ones.

Cut them back hard each April almost to the base of the shoots that grew out in the previous summer and suffer none of the flowers to show their plebeian little noses.

Our first was for long known by the agreeable name *S. incana*, but we must now take a deep breath and say *S. chamaecyparissus*. It has dense, feathery, silver-grey aromatic leaves, but its most delightful form is its dwarf one, 'Nana', which send up spikes of small, densely packed, heavily frosted leaves, and makes the prettiest pygmy hedge a foot high, when planted a foot apart.

Even more brightly silver than the old *incana* is *neapolitana*, but it has a looser habit and texture and longer, more finely shredded leaves.

Not in the least silver, but brilliantly green is *virens*, an absolute aristocrat among dwarf hedges; nothing else quite like it (Hillier or Christopher Lloyd).

Senecio, shrub. The "old man" of ancient Greece and his several children (some herbaceous and annual) are among the big shots of the White Company. Indeed, in a First Eleven of the best all-round shrubs for any soil, one that always finds a place is *S. laxifolius*, though it is often badly treated by neglectful gardeners.

Growing about 3ft high and spreading rapidly to a circle of 6ft or more in diameter, *laxifolius* makes a dense and compact dome, its olive-green leaves coated in a dove-grey felt and its stems thickly dusted with frost-white talc. Late in June it throws out bouqucts of quite jolly brassy daisies.

To get a dense effect, however, you must prune constantly, cutting back by about one-third in April and frequently pinching out the tips of the shoots in summer. If you let it bloom (I don't), cut the flowering stems right down afterwards. Old neglected plants that have degenerated into a core of woody midribs are quickly rejuvenated by amputation right back to the bare bones at ground level. It propagates with extreme ease from cuttings and always layers itself freely. Laxifolius is very hardy and is an absolutely first-class shrub, in almost any kind of soil, not necessarily gritty, but in the colder districts spring planting seems advisable.

FIG. 96. *Senecio cineraria* 'White Diamond': a mature leaf and a tuft of young ones.

Other senecios, especially those that are the high kick of fashion among arrangers, are more *recherchés* and tender. High among them is *S. cineraria*, previously known as *Cineraria maritima*. There are two outstanding varieties of it, of which the hardiest is 'White Diamond', which is thickly plastered with a whiter-than-white talc, its leaves being decoratively indented. Looks miserable after hard frost, but survives. This *must* have a high-and-dry position in lean, stony soil in full sun and you must cut it back sharp about 1st May to about 6in. from the ground, when the new leaves that result will start green. Strangle at birth its ragged little flowers. Usually about 15in. ×

20in. To ensure continuity, take summer cuttings and over-winter them in a frame.

The other outstanding variety of *S. cineraria* is 'Ramparts', with beautifully dissected leaves, but less hardy.

Of again quite a different character is *leucostachys*, a white-robed wanderer, with fine, comb-like foliage that likes to meander among other plants. Its prettiest trick is to climb up into the branches of a plant growing on a south wall, where it may reach 12ft or more. Again the law is high, dry and hot; not hardy (Mrs Underwood).

Stachys, HP. Known as lamb's-ears, donkey's-ears, etc., *S. olympica* (better known as *lanata*) is a tough, kindergarten plant, growable more or less anywhere, including chalk, in sun or part-shade. Large, soft leaves covered with pearl-grey down, which appear to have been cut out of felt. 1ft. Eliminate all flower stalks. Becomes a thick, rampaging mat before long and needs occasional renewal. Easy from seed. The variety 'Silver Carpet' does not flower and is dwarfer but is not so white.

Another nice stachys, but with dark-green, wrinkled, hairy leaves, is the old betony of cottage gardens, decorated with tiers of rich mauve, hooded, nettle-flowers in May–June. This is *S. macrantha*, 18in.

Tanacetum, HP. A very welcome recent introduction, for the leanest, stoniest soil in all-day sun, is a plant that you may call a tansy for simplicity if you wish, for it is blood-brother of our old herb. Botanically it is now *T. densum amani.* Silvered, fern-like leaves, incredibly finely shredded, forming a dense mat eventually 9in. × 18 in. The flowers are worthless. Also known as *Chrysanthemum haradjanii.* From Hillier.

Verbascum. See Chapter 10 for the ghostly mullein, *V. bombyciferum.*

CHAPTER 21

ROCK, STONE AND PEAT

The Lure and the Hazard – The Rock Garden Proper – Dry Walls and Banks – Moraine and Scree – Cultivation – Peat Walls – What to Plant – Pavement Plants – Floral Walls – Moist, Peaty Beds – Sink Gardens

The Lure and the Hazard

I HAVE already warned you about rock gardening. If you allow this particular siren to ensnare you, you are likely to be her slave for life, your soul committed to the worship of the pygmy darlings that dwell in her miniature grottos.

Few branches of gardening reach a higher degree of specialization. Your Sixth Form rock gardener deals with cool familiarity with the most forbidding botanical names, which trip off his tongue like the periods of an Horatian ode, and he adores most ardently those elves and sprites that are euphemistically described as "specialist's treasures". If his purse allows, he will not think his cult complete until he has provided himself with an "alpine house", within the glass shelter of which he can cultivate the "high alpine" plants that, though they withstand the deep mountain snows, will perish in the alternating cold and warm spells of our mild winter.

These higher realms are not within the scope of this catholic book. Indeed, they are somewhat beyond the author's knowledge. Most of us can aim no higher than the Fifth Form and welcome any dwarf plant of good quality, whether from mountains, stony places, heaths, seashore or woodland. For those who are eager to climb high and discover these specialist's treasures, there are some excellent specialist books and a good little beginner's book, valuable for quick reference, is *The Small Rock Garden*, by E. B. Anderson, a top rock gardener, in the Pan Series. There is very good value also in membership of the Alpine Garden Society and the Scottish Rock Garden Club.

The beginner must naturally start on simple lines, but they should be the right ones. A rock garden which is well conceived, well built, and well stocked with carefully chosen plants will be a joy for many years; wrongly done, it will be an eyesore and a source of constant trouble. You are warned that to do the job thus is not cheap, though the first cost is the last, except for occasional replacement of plants. Good stone is heavy and expensive, and a ton does not go far. You can, of course, start with a wee garden of a few square yards and add to it yearly, but my advice, however large or small your intentions, is that if you are not prepared to do the job properly, don't do it at all.

Fortunately, however, there are several ways of employing rocks, and growing flowers among them, which do not constitute true rock gardens, and we can enjoy many of the lovely creations of mountain-side and cliff in settings which do not profess to simulate natural scenery and are frankly the artificial work of man. For these artifices we can economize by using old, mature bricks or one of the fabricated stones, such as Thakeham or Marshalite.

In particular there is the so-called "dry wall", which can be employed in many forms. It can be a retaining wall supporting a terrace or the edge of a raised flower-bed; or it may be a stone facing to an awkward bank, or it may be just a free-standing wall expressly designed for saxatile plants. There is also the more restricted medium of the pavement, into the crannies of which we may insinuate prostrate plants that suffer being trodden on. Similarly, there are steps and sunken paths on the flanks of which other prostrate ones may tumble down in profusion. And, over and above all these stony places, one can employ a great many rock plants almost anywhere one likes in the garden.

The Rock Garden Proper

In your true rock garden the objective must be to simulate a natural outcrop or other formation of rock, seemingly unmolested by the hand of man. It is difficult to define in print just what this implies except in general terms. The environment may be a dictating factor, although a little art may contrive a convincing rock garden even within the unpromising wooden palings of a surburban villa. Taste and judgement must be our guide. Obviously the middle of a lawn is an unnatural place in which to suffer rocks to erupt, and on any flat site there is always a danger of incongruity. But the end of a lawn – yes, with the grass gradually merging into a low and scattered outcrop.

The shape and the design of the rock formation must be informal, irregular, and loose, but not an unplanned jumble. The outline may be compounded of bays or jutting promontories. Advantage should

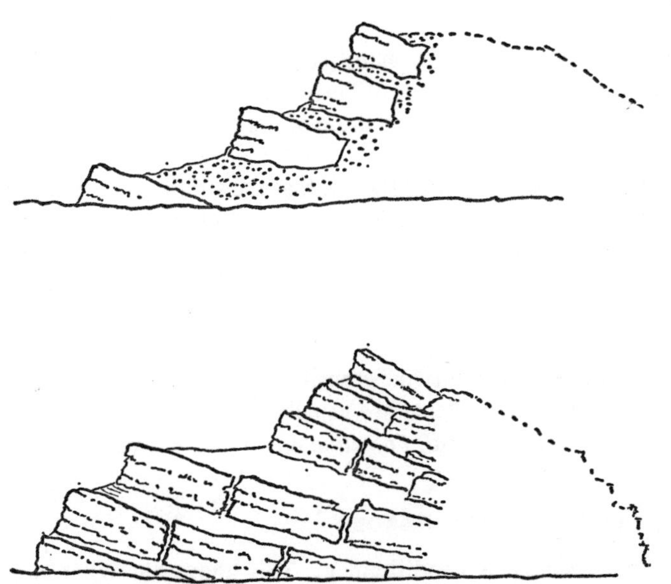

FIG. 97. *Top:* Sectional sketch of naturalistic rock garden; drainage not shown. *Bottom:* Profile of a simple scheme, showing striations running stratum by stratum.

be taken of any unevenness of ground there may be, and a naturally sloping bank or depression is a great opportunity for a naturalistic design. Unless something specialized is intended, the rock garden should be in full sun for the greater part of the day and not under trees, but if part of it can have a north aspect, with a little shade from its own rocks, a greater variety of plants can be introduced.

At the start it is wise to make only one or two small rock beds, but having their extension in mind, and to add to them after some experience. By this means one may have beds for different purposes, as, for example, one made up of lime-free soil for dwarf rhododendrons, autumn gentians and the like. But it is an absolute law that the rock must be the same throughout and, if lime-hating plants are to be grown, limestone is forbidden, unless it be Westmorland stone, which is very hard and almost insoluble.

In laying out these beds, a convenient width for cultivation is six feet, with as much length as one likes.

TYPES OF ROCK

Excellent stone comes from many parts of this country, but there is a good case for using the stone of the locality if there is any. The stones should be of varying sizes, and those of roughly rectangular shape are easiest to manage.

What is particularly important is that the striations or graining of the stone should all run one way, as they do in nature, and, in like manner, when the stones are built into the new garden they should all lie more or less in the same plane, stratum by stratum. Lumpy rocks are not amenable to quite the same law, but should still be arranged to simulate a natural outcrop.

Certain specialist plants like growing in tufa, which is a soft, porous limestone; but these plants are usually the "specialist's treasures", such as *Campanula zoysii, Potentilla nitida* and *Phyteuma comosum.*

BUILDING THE ROCK GARDEN

The first essential is good drainage. This above all. What is most wanted is protection from damp, not frost. If natural drainage does not exist, dig out about 18in. of soil (preserving the top spit), lay in a bed of broken bricks or clinkers, and dig a channel to a soakaway or to some other outlet if there is one. On top of this drainage lay a mat of close-set turves upside-down. The excavated soil serves for building up the mounds.

In any case, remove the top spit from the selected site and keep it on one side. Using this top spit as a base, prepare a soil mixture that will include plenty of grit and leaf-mould or peat. The grit may be of coarse sand, stone chips, gravel or road grit. A loamy soil will need up to a quarter of its bulk of grit; sandy ones need more peat or leaf-mould. Such a mixture will be fast-draining but will retain enough moisture through the agency of the peat or mould.

The soil for rock gardens should not be rich and for most plants it should be neutral or somewhat limy, except where rhododendrons, heathers and the like are to be grown. The gritty matter that is incorporated should be of limestone chips or ¼in. gravel or lime-mortar rubble if obtainable, but of sandstone for the lime-haters.

Assuming the rock garden to be a raised one, work from the bottom upwards over the whole expanse, placing the rocks layer by layer. The function of the rocks is to provide the plants with a

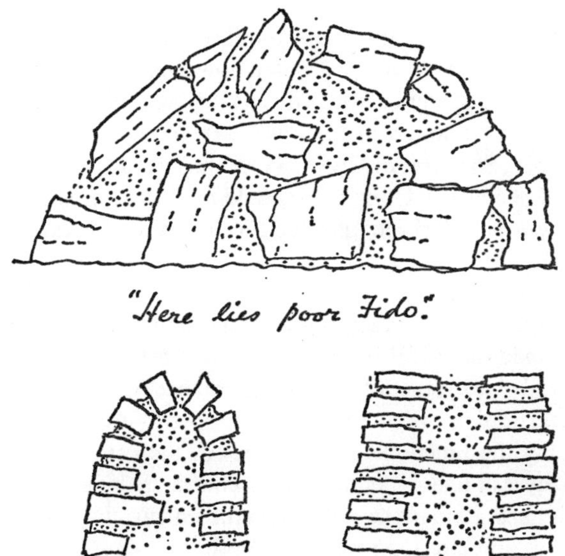

FIG. 98. *Top:* Calamity – the "dog's grave" rockery. *Bottom:* Two methods of finishing the top of a dry wall.

cool root-run. In general, about one-third or so of each rock should be buried. The rock should *emerge* from the soil, not appear to have been dumped on top of it, and there should be an impression that a mass of solid rock lies hidden below the surface. Tilt all the pieces slightly backwards and their noses just a little upwards, but always preserve the graining parallel, for one rock standing erect, or otherwise out of plane, will spoil the whole picture. Don't put a big rock on top of a small one.

Bed each rock in firmly, ramming the earth well down with a pick helve or something of that sort. Make each stone or boulder so firm that it does not rock when you stand on it. Fill every cranny and crevice, and make sure that there are some vertical crevices for plants that like that sort of home. If you are clever enough to plan things scientifically, have ready the plants intended for crevices and slip them in as you build. The areas of soil between rocks should vary in size from a few square inches to broad, 3ft, sloping expanses.

Dry Walls and Banks

A dry wall is one which is made without cement or mortar. It may be a wall supporting a terrace or a raised flower-bed or it may be a free-standing wall specially designed for displaying rock plants.

One orders "walling stone", of which there are several good sorts, such as York, Somerset or Cotswold walling, as the purse may allow. All should be fairly flat, and they should not be too dissimilar in size. Bricks, especially dark, mature ones, can be used instead or can be mixed with stone; alternatively, one can use one of the artificial stones at less cost.

If the wall is to be much more than about 18in. high, give it a strong foundation of fairly large stones just below ground level. As you proceed give the face of the wall a slight backward tilt or "batter", as architects call it. "Bond" the stones properly – those of one course overlapping the junction of two stones in the course below – and spread a layer of fine soil between each course, making sure that there are no air gaps. Ram in the soil behind the wall firmly. Every here and there put in an extra long stone, in depth, as a tie-stone, to give the wall stability.

Walls of less height than about 18in. are not likely to need buried foundation stones, unless the ground is soft and sandy, nor tie-stones, and a batter is not needed for those of a foot or less.

Ideally, you should put in the plants as you build the wall, but one seldom attains such perfection of planning. What one can do is to push in a small plug of turf in each selected spot, to be pulled out when the plants arrive. These positions should be at the bottom of a junction between two stones, with a solid stone in the course below (Fig. 99).

Free-standing dry walls can be great fun and very beautiful, but they should have a positive purpose *qua* wall. Stuck out in isolation, they are incongruous. Employ them as you would any other wall, fence or hedge – to divide one part of the garden from another, or, in surroundings not too towny, as the front wall of the property.

PLATE 15. Delphinium 'Melora', an old variety now little used by the exhibitors, but still beautiful in the garden. (*By courtesy of The Delphinium Society*)

PLATE 16. The value of a "frame". Rose 'Zephirine Drouhin' gives on to the old herbaceous borders.

The free wall, of course, has two faces. Each must be on the batter, so that the base is broader than the parapet, and the tie-stones, where necessary, should go right through both faces. Fill the space between the two faces with the same gritty soil mix as for the rock garden and ram the soil well in.

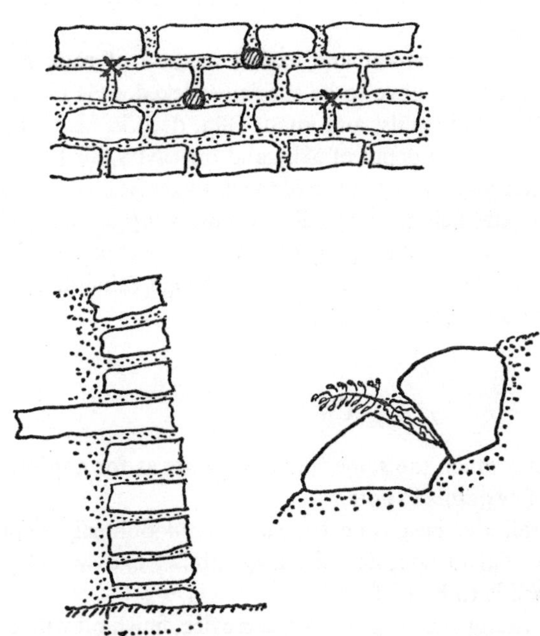

FIG. 99. *Top:* Front view of a dry wall; the circles show the right place to stow plants and the crosses the wrong ones. *Below, left:* Sectional view of a dry wall, showing "batter" and tie-stone. *Below, right:* Cruel planting, the roots trapped in a stone prison.

Both sides, as well as the parapet, can be studded with plants, all of which should be such as will stand a good deal of dryness, especially those near the top. If the wall runs more or less east and west, choose shade-tolerant plants for the northern side.

Watering a dry wall in periods of drought is a problem, but a dodge I learnt from Mr Ingwersen is to insert, as you build, a few polythene tubes punctured with small holes every few inches. Long live progress!

Moraine and Scree

These are specially stony conditions prepared to simulate the detritus of falls or erosions of mountain rock and grit that have become mingled with a little soil. A moraine has a controlled water supply underground (usually a pipe drilled with a few small holes) and a scree has not.

A scree is the cheapest and easiest method of rock gardening, but the plants for it have to be specially picked. It is usually about 12in. deep in sandy soils, and about 18in. deep in heavy ones. The soil is excavated to a depth of 18in. and the cavity filled with broken brick or other hard core. On top of the drainage hole the scree is built up with an extremely porous soil-mix, consisting of one-half gravel, stone chippings or road grit, one-quarter loam and one-quarter moss-peat. Increase the gravel, etc., in areas of high rainfall. One or two fair-sized rocks improve the picture.

Cultivation

This is pretty much the same for rock plants as for any others, but there are a few points to note.

In general, the best time to plant is undoubtedly September–October, except in counties of heavy rainfall and wet clay, where March–April is to be preferred.

When planting otherwise than in a crevice, finish off with a surface dressing of stone chips or gravel, close up to the collar of the plant. In the face of a wall, remove the plug of turf you had put in, squirt plenty of water into the hole, shake some of the soil off the roots, insinuate them delicately into the hole, then fill in with some moist soil, using a small wooden wedge to push the soil well back to the extremity of the roots.

On a scree, moisten the hole, put in the plant, fill up with the scree mixture and water again, but avoid firming in the usual way.

Every winter give the sunny parts of the rock garden a top-dressing made up of 14oz. bonemeal and 2oz. sulphate of potash, sufficient to give the appearance that the beds have been dusted with flour. In the shady parts use instead a mix of 5 parts of leaf-mould or moss-peat, one part Maxicrop powder and half a part of dried blood. These are Mr Anderson's prescriptions.

Rock garden soil often sinks, leaving the crowns of some plants standing up in the air and tufted plants sinking in the middle. When this occurs top-dress with the same sort of gritty soil mixture as before, using it in a dry state and working it in with the fingers.

In your plan arrange the compact and tufted plants for the greater part in the upper strata and the wide-spreading ones in the lower, though little floral waterfalls from an upper stratum will look very engaging if you ensure that they do not submerge others in their tumbling course.

Many plants will flower for long periods or give a second blooming if the spent flowers are removed; those that make close and dense growth should be trimmed back with shears (the "Greensleeve" shears are particularly good) after flowering, notably aubrietas, dwarf phloxes, candytuft, geraniums, soapwort, helianthemums, violas and thymes.

Some of the Sixth Form plants, such as androsace and soldanella, cannot stand winter wet and need a roof over their heads in the shape of a pane of glass held up on wire or wooden struts fashioned to prevent the glass from being blown away by wind.

Peat Walls

Peat wall gardening is a fairly new dodge of which I was a very early practitioner. It is the cheapest, quickest and easiest method of building little walls and terraces and is heartily enjoyed by a large range of plants. It implies nothing more than the substitution of featherweight peat blocks for heavyweight stone.

Two types of block can be used – large ones cut to order from peat firms or the small, roughly flat ones sold for fuel and often called "peat turves". The latter are laid just like bricks, properly bonded. Like dry walls, they are best built with a slight batter, but 15in. is about the maximum height that should be attempted. The turves are seldom perfectly flat and the gaps caused by undulation should be thoroughly plugged and rammed with soil. Here and there, especially at corners, a 6in. nail should be driven right down through the blocks.

The difficulty with these turves is that they are excessively dry and one is told that they need a long soaking before building. This is quite a problem unless one builds only a small portion of the wall at a time or unless one has a pond into which sackfuls of the turves can be thrown and weighted down. My own experience, however, is that, if the walls are built in autumn, they will get thoroughly well soaked by winter rains and snow and planting can be done in spring.

I once terraced a bank 5ft high, 9ft wide, and about 120ft long in this way with the most satisfactory results, the gentians seeding freely in the turves themselves and the roots of dwarf rhododendrons, roses, ferns and many other plants penetrating them with obvious satisfaction. The walls were quite firm enough to walk on. This was in Surrey, with an average rainfall of only about 24in. a year.

You are warned that many weeds will seed themselves in the turves as readily as other plants and it is a good plan to encourage very small creeping plants, such as *Arenaria balearica*, and *Raoulia australis*, to grow over them.

What to Plant

I am keeping this list rather short, and restricted mainly to the simpler things. However, I have made bold to include just a few Sixth Form plants, such as lewisias and shortias, for the benefit of gardeners who have the right conditions and for those not afraid to be adventurous.

If expense is at first an obstacle, one can in the first year or two fill up with small annuals easily grown from seed. The gentian-like *Phacelia campanularia* is perfectly compatible with the rocky scenery. The pretty little leptosiphon, the pimpernel (*Anagallis*), annual candytuft, kochia (which looks just like a dwarf cypress), the tiny violet-cress (*Ionopsidium acaule*), alyssum in various colours, and that pleasing little nuisance *Limnanthes douglasii* are all acceptable, easy and cheap. In hot, dry places the Livingstone-daisy and the portulaca will clothe the sunny slopes with the gayest colours; while the amaranth, though unsuited to the rock garden proper, will droop with wistful elegance down the retaining wall of a raised border.

Apart from these temporary tenants there are, broadly speaking, three groups of plants for the rock garden – dwarf shrubs (especially rhododendrons and conifers), bulbs of miniature size, and the general run of soft-wooded plants, some evergreen and some deciduous.

Many of the little bulbs will gaily enamel the rock beds from January to May. The wild anemones will claim a high place in one's choices: the dashing, scarlet *fulgens* where it is hot, dry and fast-draining and the woodlanders *nemorosa* and *apennina* where it is shady and cool. *Iris histrioides* 'Major' will make brilliant sapphire clusters in January and February and later there will be the dwarf daffodils, the dog's-tooth violet, the starry little chionodoxa, the small, wild tulips and the better behaved species of wood sorrels or oxalis. Then in early autumn, in the hot, gritty places we can enjoy those two beautiful crocus-like bulbs so difficult to grow elsewhere – the white zephyranthes and perhaps even the sternbergia.

DWARF CONIFERS

These are marvellously effective in rock gardens, giving them an air of maturity and serenity. I have included them in Chapter 16. Even the smallest rock garden is safe with the toy sentinel juniper, *J. communis* 'Compressa', aptly called by some the Noah's Ark tree. Plant it half-way up the rock garden, not at the top. If space allows, one should also include the obtuse shapes, the spiky ones and the prostrate.

The following is a small picking from those that I describe in Chapter 17.

C. lawsoniana 'Minima Aurea'. A prime choice.
C. pisifera 'Plumosa Rogersii'.
C. pisifera 'Boulevard', for shady places.
C. obtusa 'Nana Aurea'.

Then of other conifers:

Picea albertiana 'Conica', for the not-too-small garden.
Pinus sylvestris 'Beauvronensis', the dwarf Scotch pine.

OTHER DWARF SHRUBS

Brooms. Both the cytisus and the genista of Chapter 19 offer themselves to tumble down rocks, banks and terraces in golden rain. Our choices are:

Cytisus ardoinii, beanii and *purpureus* for small places and *kewensis* for larger ones.

Genista delphinensis and *pilosa minor*.

Cotoneaster. See Chapter 18. There are several low or prostrate species, but most of them are much too overpowering for the average rock garden. The following will suit us very nicely:

C. adpressus, congestus (which creeps along and then bunches itself up in series of little mounds) and *microphyllus thymifolius.*

Daphne. See Chapter 18. The one for us is *D. cneorum* 'Eximia'. Plant it on top of a rock wall.

Euryops acraeus (or *evansii*). A heartily welcome silver newcomer for dry, sunny, rather gritty spots in any setting. See Chapter 20.

Heathers. Somehow they don't appeal to me in rock gardens, but you can use any but the tree heaths if you like. Most need an acid soil. See Chapter 18.

Helianthemum, or sun-rose if you like. See Chapter 18. All are admissible to the simple rock garden, the pavements and other stony places. Two that are better seen among the rocks than elsewhere are the little yellow *H. lunulatum* and the prostrate *alpestre.*

Rhododendrons. The finest of all rock shrubs, I think, provided the soil is acid. There are a great many at our command, from the tiny *campylogynum* upwards, according to the size of the garden. My first choices would be 'Carmen', *radicans, keleticum* and *impeditum,* but see Chapter 17.

Roses. The tiny *Rosa* 'Roulettii' (or *chinensis* 'Minima') is a perfect miniature of elfin charm, 6in. high (if on its own roots), pink, and in bloom on and off all summer. 'Pompon de Paris' is nearly identical, but 12in. high.

Spiraea. The variety of *S. bumalda* called 'Nyewoods' is an excellent little shrub, 1ft high by 2ft broad, flowering exuberantly in flat trusses of rose-pink in July–August; but you must have 'Nyewoods'.

SOFTWOOD ROCK PLANTS

This must, I fear, be a short selection of the rather easier sorts only.

ACHILLEA. See Chapter 10.

Aethionema. Toy shrubs like celestial candytufts with roseate crowns. Only for warm, sunny, gritty, limy soils. Not for cold counties. Excel in dry walls. The sweetest is the 5in. 'Warley Rose', a gem of a plant, but rather easier is *grandiflorum,* a loose and lovely 10in. bush, cascading in bright pink.

For scree conditions there are the grey-leaved *iberideum* and *opposititifolium* in white and lavender respectively.

Alyssum. Everyone knows the familiar bright yellow alyssum,

A. saxatile. Better than this are its double form 'Flore Pleno', the dwarfer 'Compactum' and the paler 'Citrinum'. Cut these back after flowering. Sun. Any soil. April–May.

Androsace. Most of the enchanting little "rock jasmines" have to be given the protection of an alpine house and even those growable outdoors usually need to be roofed over with a sheet of glass in the winter. The easiest is *sarmentosa,* composed of woolly rosettes and trusses of pink flowers 3in. high in May, increasing by strawberry-like runners. There are several named varieties. Give these a glass roof, unless planted in a dry wall or on a sharp slope.

Others growable outdoors are the trailing, lilac-pink *lanuginosa,* with silver-furred leaves, needing no protection if on a steep slope or in a crevice, and *sempervivoides,* like a tiny house-leek, with green-leaved, glossy rosettes and rose-pink flowers, not at all difficult and very charming. Full sun for all. Other species present their challenge to the experienced gardeners.

Anemone. See Chapter 15. The brilliant *fulgens* suits the top of hot, sunny, gritty places, *magellanica* 'Major' a moister place in the sun and the little woodlanders the shady side.

In addition there are the perfectly lovely little hepaticas, which are virtually identical with anemones to anyone but the botanist and often catalogued as such. They want a moist, cool, shady place, with or without lime, and gladden the heart in the chill days of February–March, but take time to settle down, after which they will be yours for ever. The easiest one is *H. triloba* (or *nobilis*), in various colours, of which the blues are surely the loveliest; but it is surpassed by the beautiful hybrid *media* 'Ballardii', with large and heart-melting lavender flowers (Broadwell Nurseries).

Antennaria. Little, grey-leaved carpeters. Not good enough for the best rock gardens, but useful in pavements and other stony places. The flowers are not much catch except in the pink 'Nyewoods' variety of *A. dioica.* 3–4in. Spring.

Arabis. Proletarian but pretty, the common white, rampant arabis (*A. albida*) is excellent for covering some unsightly spot. Much better are the double form 'Flore Pleno' and the red 'Coccinea'. Sun and lime preferred.

Arenaria, the sandwort, gives us two very different but easy plants. *A. montana* is a beauty, with gleaming flowers like white buttercups, over dense, fine, 4in. high foliage, which spreads widely, in May–June. By contrast, *balearica* has leaves so tiny that the plant is a mere film of green over the soil, except when it is studded with a thousand minute white stars on ½in. stems. It creeps freely over damp stones and peat blocks. Both easy from seed.

ARTEMISIA. See Chapter 20 for the dwarf sorts.

Aubrieta (note spelling). Familiar and easy. Get a packet of seed from a leading seedsman and you will soon have dozens of plants of various colours. Alternatively, there are plenty of named varieties in the catalogues. Cut back hard after flowering.

Campanula. The beautiful dwarf bellflowers are as imperative in the rocks as their tall brethren are in the border. They will clothe formal rock gardens, tumble down terrace walls, cover the occasional stonework or can be used almost anywhere else in the garden. Some thrive in the shade, even dense shade, though they flower better in the sun, and have attractive leaves, often deckle-edged or shell-like. The following must serve as an introduction.

carpatica. Easy. Widening mounds capped with large floral saucers on 6in. stems more or less all summer in blue, lavender, white or violet – 'Blue Moonlight', 'White Star', 'Isobel', etc.

turbinata. Really a variety of *carpatica,* but smaller and neater, as in 'Pallida', milky blue, and 'Jewel', deep blue.

cochlearifolia (better known as the old *pusilla*). Roams about gregariously, making a low, dense mat, with multitudinous little nodding bells on 3in. stems. Best kept clear of anything specially precious. Good varieties are 'Miranda', 'Miss Willmott' and the pretty white 'Alba'.

'Covadonga'. Very like our native harebell, but in rich purple, 4in., flowering almost continuously from June onwards, but demanding a warm, sunny place (Broadwell Gardens). Delightful.

garganica. Radiating stems and blue, starry flowers over kidney-shaped leaves in June–August. Full sun, except for 'W. H. Paine', which seems best in half-shade.

portenschlagiana. More agreeably known as *muralis.* Purple. Vigorous spreader to be kept out of choice rock gardens, but effective in walls or terraces. Flowers the whole season.

poscharskyana, the Serbian harebell. A terribly rampageous invader and colonizer. Use it only in the wilder places or as a carpet among shrubs, for which its close foliage and large, lavender bells are quite useful. Grows in deep shade and the poorest soils. If planted at the foot of a wall, it will ramp up it like a climber. Its progeny 'Birch Hybrid' is less aggressive.

Plenty more campanulas are in the best catalogues or specialists' books, some very tricky indeed. I would start with the carpaticas, turbinatas and pusillas. For a scree you might open your innings with:

arvatica. Large violet stars on 2in. stems, or white in the lovely variety 'Alba'.

rotarvatica. An offspring of the above, upright, with purple bells; a fine, vigorous little plant.

Candytuft. (*Iberis sempervirens*). This familiar little cottager is an evergreen shrublet, handy for all sorts of uses about the garden. Spreads into a wide mat over the years or can be clipped as a toy hedge. Use the named varieties, 'Snowflake', 12in., 'Little Gem', 6in., or *saxatilis,* 4in. Cut all back after flowering – very important. The annual candytufts may also be used.

CHRYSANTHEMUM. See "Silver and Grey" for the plant usually called *C. haradjanii.*

DIANTHUS. See Chapter 11 for many pretty little pinks.

Dryas. Our mountain-avens, *D. octopetala*, forms a close, ground-level mat of miniature oak leaves, with flowers like white wild roses in May. In some soils the flowers are sparsely borne and *D. sundermannii* is perhaps better (Hillier).

Erinus. Very easy and gay miniatures, forming compact tufts and seeding themselves readily. Best suited to walls, including brick walls. The usual ones are the pink 'Mrs Charles Boyle' and the crimson 'Dr Haenaele' (variously spelt), both about 3in.

Gentian (*Gentiana*). To most of us the gentian is the assured queen of the rock garden. She wears her many crowns in diverse territories – in acid and in limy ones, in sun or in shade, in woodland and among border plants as well as among rocks. We have therefore to consider her particularities with some care.

In general, one may say that all gentians expect a rather richer soil than most rock plants, so let them have a little cow manure or fortified leaf-soil if you can. They also in general hate being dry.

Instead of following the usual system, I shall group them according to the diverse environments that each expects.

(*a*) Chiefly for woodland or other shady, moist places:

asclepiadea, the willow-gentian. Arching wands up to 2ft long, with leaves in pairs and blue or white trumpets in August. Also effective in moist or shady clefts in the larger rock garden.

(*b*) Easy ones for the border or anywhere in sun in any decent soil that does not get dry:

septemfida. Bright-blue trumpets in dense clusters at the ends of lax stems which start upright and then lie down on the ground. I grow them at the feet of pink floribunda roses. July–August. There is a good hybrid called *hascombensis*; and *gracilipes* is very similar in deep blue.

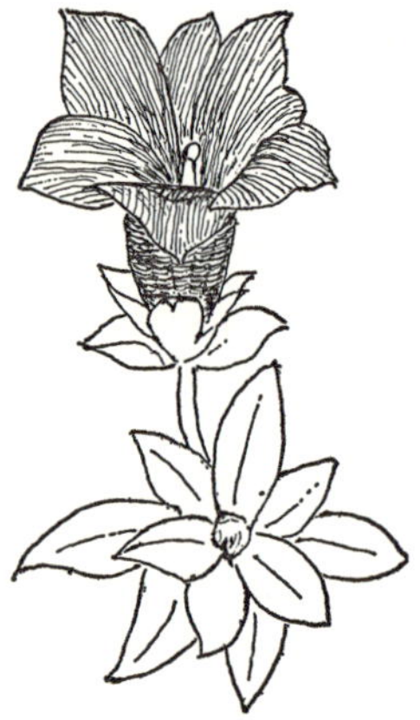

FIG. 100. *Gentiana acaulis.*

(*c*) Choice ones for gritty soil, with or without lime, in full sun and flowering in spring:

acaulis. This is the celebrated gentianella of deep, unfathomable blue, most rapturous and most notoriously wayward of all. As you gaze, like D. H. Lawrence, into those cavernous trumpets, "where blue is darkened on blueness", you wonder what its secret is, but no man can answer you with certainty. My own prescription is a raised bed of gritty soil, with or without lime, but heartened with some old cow manure, facing full south, with plenty of water in spring. Plant firmly.

verna. This is the beautiful little star-gentian, with small flowers of the most vivid blue imaginable. It grows wild in upper Teesdale and in County Clare but turns shy when brought down into cultivated gardens. Its life is short. It appears to want a moist, sandy, peaty or leaf-mouldy soil, in full sun, with frequent watering. The very similar *G. angulosa* is better.

(*d*) For moist, lime-free, leafy or peaty soils in half-shade, flowering in autumn:

There are a good many of these, all on the highest plane of beauty. Their happiest hunting ground seems to be Scotland, but I have grown some of them quite satisfactorily in lime-free loam in Surrey, especially in my old peat-wall terrace (now buried beneath a block of flats). Choose from these:

FIG. 101. *Gentiana sino-ornata.*

sino-ornata. Perhaps the most beautiful, with trumpets of a fine China blue with bold, blackish pencillings and paler zones. Quite easy in a lime-free loam in part-shade. September–October.

farreri. Light blue with white throat and olive pencillings, giving an overall effect of an ethereal greeny-blue. The only autumn one (except the New Zealanders) to tolerate lime. Begins in August.

macaulayi. The lovely child of a marriage between the two above, with large, turquoise trumpets and dark pencillings; 'Kingfisher' is a very fine clone in brilliant violet.

'Inverleith'. A sumptuous hybrid with huge trumpets of a uniform, brilliant, deep blue in August–September.

Geranium. See Chapter 10. Delightful ones for any rock or stone situation are 'Ballerina', *subcaulescens, farreri* and, where there is room, *dalmaticum.*

GYPSOPHILA. See Chapter 10 for some pretty dwarfs.

HEPATICA. Dealt with under Anemone, above.

FIG. 102. *Left: Campanula arvatica. Right: Geranium subcaulescens*

House-leeks (*Sempervivum*). Old cottage favourites of odd charm and special usefulness for bare rock ledges, crevices of dry walls and roofs of outhouses. Tight rosettes of thick, fleshy leaves, with curious flower stems crowned by flat or domed clusters of small, starry florets. Need virtually no depth of soil, but best started on a 1in. spread of good quality. Content with the driest possible conditions, but must have sun and not get waterlogged. Readily increased by removal of baby offsets once they have rooted.

There are quantities to choose from, the most attractive being the varieties of the cobweb house-leek, *S. arachnoideum*, the rosettes of which are covered all over with white, cobwebby filaments. The grey-green *ciliosum*, with hairy incurved leaves and yellow flowers, is also delightful. At the other end of the scale are the numerous clones of the plump, common house-leek or St Patrick's cabbage, *S. tectorum*, especially its variety 'Calcareum', with no cobwebs but with hairy flower stems.

Hutchinsia. For moist places or for any shady spot the little *H. alpina* is a pretty tenant, forming deep, mossy, evergreen cushions, sheeted with tufts of small, white flowers from April to July. Quite a little charmer with many uses.

Hypericum. The common rose-of-Sharon or St John's-wort, has several happy little brothers that are immensely gay and flowerful with their big buttercup-form flowers and prominent puffs of stamens. They scatter their golden treasures with abandon for long periods in the summer, in sun or part-shade, heedless of the botanists' disputes about their names. All the following are first-raters:

coris. A 6in. heather-like shrublet, flowering in succession.

fragile. Low, foot-wide mounds smothered in gold. June–August.

olympicum, of nurseries. Up to 10in. with large, rather shaggy flowers; there are pale forms as in 'Sulphureum' and 'Citrinum'. *polyphyllum* is a sub-species of it.

FIG. 103. *Hypericum olympicum*

repens. Heath-like foliage, low-growing, but not a creeper.

reptans. Prostrate, leafy, with large flowers tinted with red. June–September. Delightful when trailing down a bank or wall.

rhodopeum. Also prostrate, with soft dove-grey, hairy foliage and soft-yellow flowers. May–July.

Lewisia. One of the chief splendours of the rock garden, lewisias form a handsome basal rosette of fleshy leaves, from which pointed, rose-pink buds arise and open to daisyform flowers of iridescent apricot, pink or rose-red. They are, however, definitely Sixth Form plants and expect you to provide them with very special conditions: plenty of warm sun, sharp drainage, a soil somewhat richer than for most rock plants and – most difficult to provide outdoors – a place where there will be an absolute minimum of winter rain. If you attempt them outdoors, plant them in a crevice or on a very steep slope with the rosette of leaves lying more or less in a vertical plane. Thus the conditions of a dry wall suit them, with the leaves lying flat to the face of the wall.

Beginners had better start with one of the hybrid strains such as are offered by Ingwersen, Jack Drake and Hillier. The choicer sorts, such as the celebrated *L. tweedyi*, succeed outdoors only in ideal conditions and are safer in pots in a greenhouse (no heat needed).

It now seems well established that lewisias will tolerate some lime but would probably not survive in chalk, Mr Anderson tells me, unless in the presence of plenty of humus.

Lithospermum. At its best *L. diffusum* is one of the most beautiful of all prostrate plants, with dense, evergreen foliage and small, vivid blue flowers that suggest the star gentian. It often grows, however, into a sprawling, untidy mess with few flowers. This I believe to be due to its being grown in a 'fat', rich loam, instead of a spare, gritty rock soil. The outstanding variety is 'Grace Ward'. It *must* have a lime-free soil and full sun. Trim it back sharpish after flowering.

There are, however, lithospermums that like lime, but must still have sun. They include *graminifolium*, with 9in. tufts of grass-like foliage and sprays of clear-blue flowers, and the rather taller *intermedium*, which makes a rounded dome, with clustered, nodding flowers of deep blue. We may ignore for a while that all these are now supposed to be called something else.

Omphalodes. Very like forget-me-nots. *O. cappadocica* is a lovely and easy enough plant in a moist and shady soil, with large flowers of true blue up to a height of 9in., flowering in spring and again later and spreading itself amiably. Less desirable is *verna*, the blue-eyed-Mary, for, although a real charmer as a juvenile, she becomes a confounded nuisance.

Only after experience should one attempt the beautiful *luciliae*, for it is one of the "specialist's treasures".

OXALIS. See bulb chapter p. 265.

Penstemon. Besides those mentioned in Chapter 10, there are a good many more in some catalogues. Nearly all dwarf penstemons are good for really warm, fast-draining places, except *confertus* or *procerus*. Trim back after flowering.

Phlox. The moss-like prostrate brothers of the big, border phloxes, nearly all flowering in May–June, are one of the mainstays of the rock garden, walls and all sorts of stony places, which they completely cover with dense mats, the leaves obscured by their massed blooms in gay or tender hues. They vary somewhat in their tastes. "Some like it hot, some like it cool". The most popular are the named varieties of *P. subulata*, of which 'Betty' and 'G. F. Wilson' will start you off handsomely. These prefer things somewhat dry. So also, but even more, so do the tight cushions and stemless pink flowers of *kelseyi* 'Rosette', a much neglected beauty, and the dainty children of *douglasii*, which will like a place as hot as you can give them for their dense hummocks, and of which 'Boothman's Variety' and 'Eva' will serve you devotedly.

On the other hand, there is a group that likes things cool, shady and lime-free, with leaf-mould or peat for their comfort. These temperamental little charmers include the rose-pink *amoena*, the salmon, white-eyed *adsurgens* and a little beauty named 'Blue Ridge', which displays delightful flowers of tender blue on 9in. stems.

PINKS. See Chapter 11.

POLYGONUM. The chosen one is *P. vaccinifolium*. (Chapter 10.) Use only to cover wide expanses, not among choice plants.

Potentilla. The versatile potentilla offers us several fine little plants for rocky places, in addition to its shrub and herbaceous forms of Chapters 19 and 10 respectively. Their strawberry leaves are usually accompanied by simple, bright-yellow flowers that flourish for a long season. The outstanding one is *P. nitida*, a jewel of a plant, with little, pink, wild-rose flowers above compact, 6in. cushions of silver foliage; but it seldom flowers well unless the summer is very hot. It must get full sun and it seems to do best in the very gritty soil of a scree or else in tufa.

Others are much easier. The little *alba* is quite a sweetie, 4in. high and spreading neatly, with leaves like grey-green fingers and white, orange-eyed flowers in spring and autumn. In bolder fashion *tonguei* builds up a dense mound and throws out streamers of apricot, crimson-eyed flowers most of the summer. I grow it as a carpeting, weed-resisting plant beneath floribunda roses.

Much smaller is the pretty little *verna* 'Nana', only an inch or two high and spreading into neat, circular mats adorned with gold in spring; easy as pie and useful anywhere in the garden. I shrink from quoting the jaw-breaking new name with which it has been branded.

Primula. I deal with primulas generally in Chapter 9. Those most to be desired in rock gardens are not among the easiest, but 'Linda Pope' (a variety of *P. marginata*) will assuredly engage your heart and impel you to woo her. The toothed leaves are dusted as with talc powder and from them spring soft lavender flowers of a wonderful tone and of a rare purity of form. Like other marginatas, however, it gets very leggy and is therefore best planted between a pair of rocks, from which it will hang down. If on the flat, pack the stems round with small stones as they lengthen. A Sixth Form plant.

Other desirable little primulas that are attainable are the varieties of *pubescens* and the smaller auricula varieties and hybrids, such as the beautiful little 'Blairside Yellow' (Jack Drake).

Saxifrage (*Saxifraga*). The saxes are a very large, very diverse, very complicated family, ranging from our dear, easy-going old London-pride to the most finicky of "specialist's treasures". So the eager gardener haunting flower shows and nurseries must be well on his guard whenever his heart seems in danger of being captivated by some enchanting little creature that very often appears to have been fashioned out of pure silver and embellished with rubies or gold. Some want sun, others shade and many are only for stony screes or the controlled environment of the alpine house.

However, we are considerably helped in our choice by having had the saxes neatly bundled into horticultural pigeon-holes, according to their garden needs. These are the Mossy, the Silver or Encrusted, the Kabschia, the Engleria and the inevitable Miscellaneous. All we can do in the small compass of this book is to review the needs of each section, with only a very few specimens from the innumerable lists, which constitute so vast a horde that one does not begin to penetrate their ranks until one becomes a dedicated fanatic. Let us begin, however, from the basis that all saxifrages form a close-set rosette of leaves at ground level and that, as a rule, they increase by gradually spreading colonies of rosettes.

We will dispose first of the:

MISCELLANEOUS

The outstanding one is London-pride, with its airy plumes of little pink florets borne high aloft over the basal green rosette. It colonizes eagerly, forming dense mats and should be barred from the company of choice plants, whether of the rock garden or elsewhere, but is one of the best carpeting plants for use under trees in sun or shade. For generations London-pride has been known as *S. umbrosa*, but some clever fellow has recently discovered that it is really a hybrid and expects us to call it *S. urbium*. There are several pretty miniature varieties, including 'Primuloides', 'Elliott's Variety' and the pygmy 'Ingwersen's Variety'.

MOSSY

Very easy and familiar. The small, loose rosettes form a dense, spreading, moss-like, evergreen mat or hummock with gay little flowers on thread-like stems from April to June. Very useful for clothing shady places, rock or no rock. Trim back after flowering, or else the mat gets "browned-off". New colonies are easily started by pulling up a few tufts and planting them again where wanted. Pick at your pleasure from the many named varieties.

SILVER OR ENCRUSTED

So-called because their rosettes of leaves are a silver-grey and coated with lime on the margins. The rosettes die after flowering, but reinforcements come up quickly to fill and add to the ranks. All need full sun and a typical rock garden soil – gritty and fast-draining, preferably with lime – and their flowering times are late spring and early summer.

Typical of them are the numerous varieties of *S. aizoon* (*paniculata*), with little sprays of flowers in many colours. A favourite association is that of the yellow 'Lutea' with 'Rosea', both 8in. The smallest is the tiny, white 'Baldensis', 2in., a pretty silver carpeter.

More spectacular is a group of Silvers that you should plant in vertical crevices or in dry walls, from which they thrust out handsome arched plumes in white in June–July. They include:

cochlearis, 6in. plumes from heavily silvered domes.

cotyledon 'Southside Seedling', 12in. plumes freckled with red.

lingulata lantoscana, narrow leaves, 9in. plumes.

'Tumbling Waters', a spectacular hybrid that shoots out magnificent plumes nearly 2ft long, but you should decline any plant not showing two or more offsets, or you are likely to be disappointed.

The Silvers also include some other fine hybrids, among which, the beautiful pink, long-flowering 'Kathleen Pinsent' and the white-and-pink 'Dr Ramsay', both about 9in., are outstanding.

KABSCHIA

These form themselves delightfully into tight, slow-growing hummocks of closely packed leaves, in green or grey, which become studded with charming, miniature flowers on 1in. stems. In their case what is wanted is an *extra* gritty and limy soil and a spot where they are shaded from noon onwards. Thus the best prospect is a partially shaded scree, but they are delightful also for a trough or sink garden. Many surprise one by flowering in February. The multiplying rosettes, after flowering, must be dressed with a mixture of grit and loam to prevent the cushions from getting hollow.

Of the hundred varieties and hybrids, the following are generally considered the easiest:

apiculata, 'Elizabethae', 'L. G. Godseff', 'Primrose Bee', *haagii*, and 'Jenkinsae'.

After which a small picking of the more desirable would include:

'Cranbourne', 'Faldonside', any variety of *burseriana* (especially 'Major' and 'Gloria'), 'Christine', 'Queen Mother', *marginata*.

Details of all in catalogues.

ENGLERIA

A smaller group appealing to gardeners who are excited more by quaint forms rather than floral beauty.

The outstanding one is the Wisley variety of *S. grisebachii*, which has silvered leaves and curious, slightly arching, dark-red, velvety stems and calyces of a similar colour in early spring. Give all the same gritty conditions as the Kabschias but a bit more sun. Best in crevices and not beginner's plants.

Sedum. We have met the herbaceous border species in Chapter 10. Here we have the species that justify the vernacular name of stonecrop, for they flourish in any stony setting and are particularly suitable for little walls, the flanks of steps and so on. They abide any dry, poor, stony soil, but expect a reasonable amount of sun. All that we are considering here have small, thick, fleshy leaves, themselves often beautifully coloured, and are prostrate mat-formers or tumblers down walls, flowering densely in little, bright trusses at various seasons.

The most handsome is *S. cauticola*, which has richly blue-green foliage and dense trusses of glowing rose-crimson, which smother the plant in September–October. I grow it along a little wall of a built-up bed of yellow roses. Other desirable ones sufficiently described in catalogues are:

spathulifolium, especially its delightful, dusty variety 'Cappa Blanca';

spurium in its variety 'Schorbusser Blut' ('Dragon's Blood'); and *douglasii*, yellow flowers on a fleshy green mound.

Avoid 'Coral Carpet' in any choice position.

Silene. The old cottage campion or catch-fly, which looks like a sparsely petalled pink with a very long calyx, has a few nice juniors for rocky places in full sun. A very easy-going little fellow is *S. schafta* 'Abbotswood', sprinkled with rose-purple on 4in. stems in August–October, but a bit untidy. In *alpestris* we have a better 6in. plant with tufts of glossy leaves and abundant white, starry flowers from June often into August. For the scree there is *acaulis exscapa*, the moss-campion, which makes tight green cushions with pretty pink spring flowers. (Hillier.)

Soapwort (*Saponaria*). *S. ocymoides* is a kindergarten plant that makes large waterfalls or wide lakes frothing with rosy-pink throughout early summer. Grows anywhere. The Bressingham Hybrid is more compact, but the pernickety 'Rubra Compacta' is best avoided.

Thrift (*Armeria*). See Chapter 10. Very suitable to any kind of rocky place, particularly pavements, are *Armeria caespitosa* and 'Vindictive'.

Thyme (*Thymus*). The thymes give us the most refreshing of scents and often delightful evergreen foliage and miniature flowers also. They are suitable for any stony place in the sun, flourishing in the leanest soils, and are particularly appropriate in pavings. In fact, the prostrate thymes are the first of all choices for pavings, whether crazy or sane. The best of all are the several varieties of *T. serpyllum*, particularly the red 'Coccineus', the pink 'Annie Hall' and 'Pink Chintz' and the woolly, grey-leaved *lanuginosus*.

These spread out their eager little fingers over the stone, with no height at all and are smothered in high summer with sheets of brilliant blossom, adored by the bees. In *herba-barona* we have the scent of caraway, with flowers of deep pink. All these thymes have no objection at all to being trodden on as you walk by.

A companion to these creepy-crawlers is the dwarf, lemon-scented bushlet, *T. citriodorus* 'Silver Queen', a pretty toy of 9in. with variegated foliage. I grow it encircled by the mats of *serpyllum* (which also closely surround clumps of dwarf pinks in the pavement).

Trim all these thymes back somewhat firmly after flowering.

Tunica. A very easy and pretty little plant is *T. saxifraga* 'Rosette'. It has flowers like a pink, double gypsophila on thread-like stems, 6in. high and about 9in. wide for a long time in summer. Full sun. Accept nothing but 'Rosette'.

Veronica. It is in their dwarf forms that the veronicas are most charming and usually very easy. They are either trailing plants or neat little shrubs. The shrubby ones were of late broken off to join the new race of *Hebe* and a few others have become *Parahebe*, but most people and catalogues still call them by the older name. All grow in any decent soil in sun or part-shade.

At the head stands *V. prostrata* (alias *rupestris* and *teucrium dubia*), which forms a mat a yard wide of dark-green foliage and innumerable little blue spikes, 6in. high, throughout most of the summer – a wonderful plant for banks, walls, the flanks of steps and so on. There are several variants, such as the pink 'Rosea' and the gold-leaved 'Trehane'.

Another good spreading veronica is *satureioides*, which makes a beautiful blue mat, completely prostrate, for a short season in April and sometimes again in autumn.

Among the shrubby veronicas, now called hebes, the sovereign choice is the hybrid New Zealander 'Carl Teschner', which has been widely distributed by Mr E. B. Anderson. This forms a trim, evergreen shrublet of 9in., profusely robed in violet in June–July; a wonderful little plant.

Intermediate between these two types is a dense, low, spreading plant of box-like foliage and pretty, small, modest flowers for most of the summer, about 1ft high. This is *catarractae*. It is a semi-woody plant of the genus that we are now expected to call *Parahebe*.

There are a great many other veronicas, but beware of *V. filiformis*, pretty enough in some large, wild place, but an insidious fifth-columnist in any pleasure garden.

Viola. See its own section in Chapter 9.

Pavement Plants

Stone or brick paths or terraces, especially those of crazy paving, though designed to be walked upon, do not limit the embellishment of the garden, but, on the contrary, extend the opportunities; for they invite adornment by many pretty floral toys which look better in a stony floor than anywhere else.

All that has to be done is to see that there is a certain amount of tolerable soil under the stone at those points where the plants are to be set. This is easily done if the path is made by the gardener himself; otherwise, using cold chisel and hammer, he must excavate a little and, if there is hard core beneath the paving, remove some of it.

The creeping thymes are the first of all choices. They spread out the gayest little floral mats, which give out a spicy scent when trodden on. Others that tolerate the foot of man and that will succeed in the poorest soil are:

Mentha requienii, the Corsican mint, a prostrate scented mint with fresh, apple-green leaves that creep about wherever there is the tiniest crevice. Excellent for shady, moist paths. Prevent it from invading flower beds. Avoid the pennyroyal (*M. pulegium*), much written-up in horticultural columns, but of no interest whatever and liable to become a curse.

Cotula squalida. A prostrate plant with leaves like wee ferns, building up into dense little cushions and spreading freely in sun or partial shade. Useful but not glamorous.

Frankenia thymifolia. A pretty plant with minute leaves and quite conspicuous little lilac florets (Christopher Lloyd).

Acaena microphylla. A prostrate New Zealand burr; for hot and dry places. Don't let it invade flower beds.

Dryas octopetala, the mountain avens, will not object to an occasional footfall.

In addition there are a good many plants that look delightful in pavements in those parts less likely to be trodden on, though they will not mind an occasional buffet. Nothing looks more charming than the dwarf pinks (Chapter 11) and on wide terraces the evergreen helianthemums, with their gay little sun-roses, will be in proportion to the scene. Other jolly good ones for pavements are:

The lemon-thyme, *Thymus citriodorus.*

The dwarf thrifts.

Antennaria dioica varieties.

Hypsella longiflora. A pretty creeper, with mauve, lobelia-like flowers all summer. For moist places.

Toadflax (annual or perennial species of *Linaria* with wee snap-dragon flowers) will wander along pavement cracks. Very easy from seed.

Erigeron mucronatus. An endearing little daisy, very effective on steps. Very easy from seed.

Mazus reptans. Quite prostrate, with bronze leaves and little mauve snapdragons; a nice little chap.

Floral Walls

The following selection may be useful as a guide for planting free-standing walls or the retaining walls of flower beds and terraces.

The three kindergarten A's: aubrieta, alyssum and arabis, the best being *Alyssum saxatile* or its varieties, which hang down in yellow waterfalls.

Aethionemas (not in severe climates).

Dwarf brooms; e.g. *Cytisus kewensis, ardoinii* and *beanii*; and *Genista lydia,* superlative for large walls and terraces (Chapter 19).

Campanula garganica and *muralis* (now *portenschlagiana*), preferably in the lower courses.

The silver-leaved *Anthemis cupaniana,* but not in cold counties (Chapter 10).

Pinks of almost any kind, especially the Cheddar pink, the maiden pink and the pretty dwarf hybrids.

The mountain avens, *Dryas octopetala.*

Candytufts, perennial or annual.

Erigeron mucronatus, seeds freely, sometimes too freely.

Erinus 'Mrs Boyle'.

Euphorbia myrsinites (Chapter 10).

Euryops acraeus (*evansii*), the dwarf silver-leaved shrub.

Gypsophilas, the creeping species.

Helianthemums.

House-leeks.

Hypericum, the glittering dwarf species.

Lewisias, superb if conditions right.

Linum 'Gemmell's Hybrid'.

Phlox subulata varieties, making mossy mats.

Polygonum vaccinifolium, but not among choice plants.

Potentilla tonguei, to hang down.

Ramonda myconii, in shade.

The rumbustious soapwort, *Saponaria ocymoides*, to hang down.

Saxifrages; use the Silvers – *aizoon, cochlearis, cotyledon, lingulata,* and *longifolia.*

Stonecrops, especially *Sedum cauticola* and *spathulifolium.*

Thymes; creepers and shrublets, at the tops of walls.

Tunica saxifraga.

Wormwoods, the dwarf silvery species, such as *Artemisia pedemontana* and *schmidtii* 'Nana' (Chapter 20).

Moist Peaty Beds

Most of the plants that we have been considering so far have a taste for lime or tolerate it and the majority do not crave a lot to drink. There is another and beautiful group, however, that have an ardent thirst, or a partiality for an acid soil, or both, and like to recline in the shade for part of the day.

As we have seen, an acid soil is by no means synonymous with a peaty one, but we tend to associate these plants with peat or with leafy, "woodsy" soil and I particularly associate them with the peat wall garden that I used to cherish. What is more difficult to provide is the moist atmosphere of the west coast that many of them need to be really successful. Shade is to some extent a corrective and the requirement for shade is reduced in the northern and the wetter counties and at high elevations.

Limy soils are to be avoided for the following, except where I state otherwise:

Astilbe. See Chapter 10 for several choices. No objection to lime.

Cotyledon. If you imagine a little, pendulous spray of laburnum, 4in. high, this is the pretty plant long known as *C. simplicifolia.* Not a lime-hater. Sun or shade. Plant it where its golden tassels will hang clear of the soil. Now inflicted with a terrible new name – *Chiastophyllum oppositifolium.*

Gentians. See section on First Choices, above. Here come in the lovely autumn gentians, loving shade and moisture and hating lime.

Haberlea. These are charming little plants with a basal rosette of hairy, deckle-edged leaves and 4in. stems clustered with several five-petalled funnels, in which the lower petals protrude, like a lip. They are lavender, with yellow throats. Plant them vertically in the manner of lewisias, or, if on the flat, with the leaves held off the ground by stones. The best species is *rhodopensis*, smaller but more flowerful than the one named after King Ferdinand of Bulgaria.

FIG. 104.
Haberlea ferdinandi-coburgi.

Hepatica. See under Anemone in First Choices. Acid soil not necessary.

Meconopsis. The beautiful Himalayan poppies of Chapter 10 fit happily here, provided that the atmosphere is not too dry.

Omphalodes. See First Choices. *O. cappadocica* fits here. No objection to lime.

Primula. In this superlative genus, reviewed in Chapter 9, are some of the main glories of damp gardens of all sorts. For the smaller and daintier sorts appropriate to the conditions we have in mind here, we go to the charming Farinosae section and we choose any of those enumerated under that heading.

Ramonda. Always associated with haberleas, but rather more charming, I think, with its little, golden eye protruding from the centre of its lilac petals. Has the same sort of crinkly leaves and needs the same treatment. The one to have is *R. myconii* (or *pyrenaica*).

We finish this short list with three of the most bewitching little alpines, all having an affinity with one another, particularly in the little fringed bells which all of them dangle. They want a cool, moist (not wet) soil and partial (not complete) shade and flourish most in areas where there is a moist atmosphere. They are usually regarded as plants for experienced gardeners only, but I had reasonable success with them in my peat wall terrace, due more, no doubt, to the "genius of the place" than that of the gardener. These three S's are:

Schizocodon. Little evergreen plants that produce tufts of enchanting, pink, fringed bells to a height of some 6in. The only species is *soldanelloides*, of which there are a few varieties. Difficult to get started if you buy too small a plant.

Shortia. If possible even more lovely than the schizocodon. The leaves are glossy and evergreen, turning bronze in autumn. The one normally offered by nurseries is *S. uniflora* 'Grandiflora'.

Soldanella. Once again the most touching little fringed bells, but this time in lavender on thread-like stems over small, rounded leaves. Where happy they spread into wide mats. You must protect them against winter rain by a sheet of glass, and against slugs, which devour the buds that are formed in autumn. Probably the easiest species is *villosa*, on 6in. stems, but more endearing are the sweet 3in. *alpina* and *pusilla*. Apparently no objection to lime, unlike the other two S's.

Sink Gardens

The sink or trough is a delightful means of rock gardening in miniature. It can be enjoyed in the smallest possible place and is an excellent means of keeping you out of mischief when you have reached the non-bending age.

Old stone sinks and horse troughs are no longer to be had for the asking and you may have to spend guineas on a modern version made of concrete or sandstone. Be sure that it has one or two drainage holes. Set the sink in an open position, preferably in full sun, and raise it to whatever level you like by obvious methods.

Cover the drainage holes with a fairly large crock and add a layer of smaller crocks or pebbles all over. On this drainage system spread a layer of coarse, fibrous material, such as fragments of turf, upside-down, to prevent the drainage from being clogged by the filtering down of the fine planting mixture above.

Make this planting mixture of: two parts good loam, one part moss-peat, or leaf-mould, one part or more of gritty matter (Cornish sand, sharp silver sand or road grit) and about 8 oz. of bonemeal per barrow-load of the mixture. Mix all together and fill the sink nearly to the brim, firming as you go.

You now have to create a miniature landscape. For the love of Mike cut out all infantile notions of willow-pattern bridges, nasty little gnomes, rabbits and anything else that is sham. Start by inserting a few small rocks to some design that pleases your aesthetic impulses. Have one or two relatively large rocks and a litter of small ones. Leave inch-wide crevices between the larger ones. Bed the rocks in deeply and firmly and fill all crevices. As you build insinuate any plants intended to fill the crevices.

In your planting scheme include the Noah's Ark juniper, *Juniperus communis* 'Compressa'. Other dwarf conifers unfortunately present difficulties. Next, break up the harsh outline of the sink by placing several bushy little plants close to the rim and one or two (not more) trailers to cascade over the edge. Most trailers are too rumbustious for a sink, but suitable ones are *Dryas octopetala* 'Minor' and *Alyssum serpyllifolium*, which has tiny silver leaves and little yellow flowers.

Fill in with anything small, neat and unaggressive; don't overdo it, remembering that there is terrific root competition in the sink. Suggestions:

Aethionema 'Warley Rose'.
Rosa 'Roulettii'.
Miniature thrifts, such as the varieties of *Armeria caespitosa.*
Potentilla verna 'Nana'.
Antennaria dioica 'Minima' or 'Rosea',
Miniature pinks, such as 'Little Jock'.
Morisia monantha (or *hypogaea*), yellow saucers from little ferny rosettes, 1in.
Raoulia australis, which spreads a mere film of silvery green on the surface and will creep over the edge.

For the little rock crevices, use the tight little cushions of various saxifrages, such as 'Jenkinsae', 'L. G. Godseff' and *cochlearis* 'Minor.'

You can, of course, have several of these sink gardens, devoted to special purposes, and wheelchair gardeners, as Mr Leslie Snooks shows in *Gardening for the Elderly and Handicapped*,[1] can have a whole series of them mounted at table height in a little paved garden.

[1] Pan Books.

CHAPTER 22

CLIMBERS AND SCRAMBLERS

Their Many Uses – The Clingers – Clematis – Other Twiners

IN *Climbing Plants for Walls and Gardens* I have written at some length on this subject, so my notes here will have to be brief.

Climbers are of great importance in "painting the garden picture". They add a third dimension to our plots. They can throw a becoming mantle over an outhouse or obscure some distant hideous object. They can be displayed on walls, fences, long screens, tall tripods or can put a shroud around and over an arbour, where the scented ones will be particularly welcome. They can also be set to scramble over other plants, a trick at which several of them are both dextrous and decorative. They are particularly good value on small town houses, where the wall area is often larger than the garden area.

For the purposes of usage, we may divide climbing plants into four categories – the clingers, the twiners, the floppers and the roses, which are in a class apart. The clingers mount their host by means of little hold-fast "roots" and need no help from man. The twiners, however, must be provided by the gardener with an artificial host unless they are intended to climb a tree, shrub or hedge as in nature. The twiners are themselves divisible into two classes – those that climb by little tendrils or leaf-stalks (such as peas or clematis) and those that twist their stems round their host, such as the honeysuckle. The third class, the floppers, are not climbers at all, but are bullied by man into behaving as such; for example, the winter jasmine. Obviously these all need an artificial host.

In addition to these four groups there are also plenty of shrubs that can most impressively be grown on walls of any sort, either to hug the wall in a close embrace, as we use the pyracantha, ceanothus and flowering quince, or just growing freely at the foot of the wall, particularly those shrubs of doubtful hardiness that need the shelter of a warm wall facing south.

The best host that I know for the twiners when grown on walls, fences or arbours is the plastic-covered chain-link fencing that can be bought from builders' merchants or hardware shops. You simply hang it up on a few strong nails, let it fall down to the desired distance and put in an occasional nail at sides and bottom. Use the unobtrusive black instead of a coloured one. The very light square meshes now on the market are O.K. for light, tendril climbers. More orthodox is a system of wires strained through vine-eyes.

Wooden trellis is also excellent, of course, for many climbers, but the ready-made thing bought from ironmongers is poor stuff, with a short life and of fixed dimensions. Much better to build your own with 1in. × 1in. timbers and have it plugged securely into the wall.

A word of warning, however, about climbers and their hosts on the walls of the dwelling house. Unless you are careful, they can be an infernal nuisance when the house has to be painted. If the wall itself has to be painted, better not have any climbers unless, like most roses, they can be unloosed. A warning of another kind is needed for anyone with a tile-hung wall: avoid any climber that is likely to insinuate its eager young shoots underneath the tiles. Wisteria is a bad offender.

One of the most delightful ways of growing climbing plants is to let them behave as they do in nature – climbing on trees and shrubs. The clematis is the genus *par excellence* for this, the strong ones, such as *montana* and *chrysocoma*, on tall trees and the usual smaller ones on shrubs and small trees. However, you must be careful in your choice of the host plant. Avoid choicer shrubs and trees with beautiful foliage. Choose decadent old trees or else shrubs (which must be mature) that are comely but not of delicate leafage; laurustinus and holly are excellent. Use honeysuckles only on old trees, for their twisting stems are stranglers. Another charming custom is to set one climber to climb another, such as clematis on climbing roses or on wisterias.

The cultivation of climbers differs in no way from that of other shrubs. Most of them want hearty feeding, though the Passion-flower is a prominent exception. On house walls the absolutely paramount demand is to post them a good 10in. or more from the wall. The soil at the footings of house walls is very dry and nearly all climbers need plenty of water; they are seldom given it except by heaven.

Roses are left out here having been covered in Chapter 14. On walls of houses avoid the lax ramblers and use the strong, thick-stemmed climbers or the pillar roses.

The Clingers

AMPELOPSIS. See under Virginia creeper.

Campsis. Very handsome plants with big clusters of trumpets, usually orange, and foliage rather like that of the wisteria. Sometimes called "trumpet vine". Better plant in spring except in the warmest

FIG. 105. *Campsis radicans.*

shires. Pretty hardy once they get their toes in. Give them a south or west wall or (very impressive) a pergola in full sun. Begin to flower in late autumn, but drop their buds if subjected to alternating hot days and chilly nights. The soundest variety is *C. radicans.* The deep-salmon-red 'Mme Galen' is more impressive but needs a hot spot.

Some catalogues still show the campsis under the older names Bignonia or Tecoma.

Euonymus. See Chapter 18 for the excellent, *E. fortunei* (*radicans*). Hardy, easy and decorative.

Hydrangea. There are three or four climbing hydrangeas, the best bet being the species *petiolaris.* Deciduous and hardy. Good on a north wall or for climbing into the loftiest trees. Sulks at first and does not bear flowers for the first few years.

Ivy (*Hedera*). To people who have eyes to see the ivy presents many beautiful forms and colours at all seasons of the year. It may adorn the walls of houses, shroud outbuildings, clothe old fences, clamber to the tops of decrepit trees and cover bare ground with golden carpets tinted with silver, gilt, pink or cream. Most flourish in dense shade under trees as also in sun. Our best choices are among the following:

The Canary ivy (*H. canariensis*). Choose the variety 'Gloire de Marengo'. Olive-green leaves, heavily splashed and margined with pewter and cream, with some flecks of pink. Said to be not hardy in the coldest areas unless on a south wall.

The Persian ivy (*H. colchica*). A very fine ivy for every use. Best in the form 'Dentato-variegata', in which the large, ovate, untoothed leaves are heavily splashed butter-yellow. Bone hardy.

The English ivy (*H. helix*). Most famous of all, with numerous varieties and much confusion about names. Go to a nursery and take your pick. Many have tiny leaves. Look for 'Buttercup', 'Tricolor', 'Jubilee Goldheart' and 'Glacier', but distrust 'Aureo-variegata' in this species (also listed as 'Chrysophylla' and 'Angularis Aurea).

When ivies reach the gutterings of a house, cut them back a foot. When they start throwing out branches and producing berries, shear back the bushy parts.

Pileostegia. A little known, evergreen clinger valuable because of its limited growth, not exceeding 20ft. Leaves like the rhododendron's and masses of fluffy cream flowers at summer's end. Quite hardy. Any aspect.

Schizophragma. Similar to the climbing hydrangeas but distinguished by the very large, fluttering sepal of the outer, sterile florets.

Virginia creepers or virgin ivies. Familiar enough for their dazzling crimson draperies in autumn, but cursed by an appalling muddle of names. They include genera formerly called *Vitis* (the vine) and *Ampelopsis* (vine-like), now all assembled under the apt and charming name *Parthenocissus*, which means "virgin ivy", but still called by their out-of-date names in some catalogues.

Whatever their names, the virgin ivies provide brilliant and well-fitting cloaks for any really large wall (no other), but their most dramatic act is to climb into the heights of large trees.

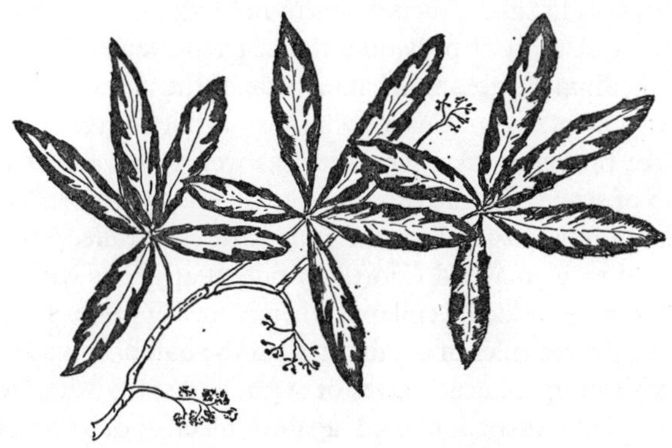

FIG. 106. A charming "virgin-ivy", *Parthenocissus henryana.*

The true Virginia creeper, found in that State by the Pilgrim Fathers, is *P. quinquefolia*, having usually five lobes to the leaf. Another one sold under the same popular name, but less refined, varying greatly in its leaf shapes and a cruder crimson in autumn, is *P. tricuspidata*, but it is frequently catalogued as *Vitis inconstans* and *Ampelopsis veitchii.*

More beautiful than any to my mind is the virgin ivy with very slender leaflets broadly banded along the veins in silver and pink. This is *P. henryana*, but nearly always listed as a Vitis. It colours best in the shade. Needs the help of a few pea-sticks before it starts to cling properly.

Clematis

The most versatile of all climbers, adept at climbing up any reasonably good artificial host of thin section or diameter, at twining up among climbing roses and at scrambling on the backs of big bushes or scaling trees. I implore you not to loop it up in a stranglehold with a few old nails and a bit of string.

Clematis flourish both in limy soils (including chalk) and in mildly acid ones; in very acid ones, add a handful of lime. They have certain cultural essentials:

rich feeding,
copious watering, especially when young,
their roots in shade, their heads in full light.

The usual method of providing the last requirement is to plant a small or medium shrub on the sunny side of the climber. Where this is not convenient, as in a narrow border, a thick layer of fair-sized stones, like broken bricks, serves just as well and is better than the large slab of stone often advised.

Clematis often succumb to the fungus disease called "wilt". The young plant may go ahead vigorously but, at any time within its first three years, may suddenly collapse when in its full pride. This may be overcome by three rules of conduct: plant the ball of roots 2in. below ground, collect up all dead leaves or stems and spray with Orthocide or any similar concoction used against black-spot on roses. The small-flowered clematis species do not seem liable to this malady, only the large hybrids.

Having chosen your site with great care and generously enriched it, plant with equal care. Make a good-sized hole, spread the roots out, uncoiling them gently if they have become pot-bound, and plant with the old ball of soil on a slight slant and 2in. below ground. Return the soil, water copiously and firm the soil next day, not aggressively. Keep the nurseryman's cane in place for a while and protect the frail young stem with wire netting or a cage of twigs against careless hoemanship and ravishment by cats.

Pruning. The thing that worries most people about clematis, when they have got going, is how to prune them. The simplest plan of all is to stick to those species and varieties that bloom after midsummer, all of which you just amputate thigh-high about the end of January. This group, which I call Group 3, includes 'Hagley Hybrid', 'Perle d'Azur', 'Gipsy Queen', 'Ernest Markham', 'Comtesse de Bouchard', *jackmanii* 'Superba', *orientalis* and *tangutica.* The popular 'Ville de Lyon' may also get this treatment.

However, if you become a clematis addict you will not be satisfied with these alone, in which case you will have to deal with two other groups, which are:

GROUP 1. These are the spring-flowering species and their offspring, particularly *montana, chrysocoma, alpina* and *macropetala*, all plants of great beauty. They flower on limbs that have developed in the previous summer. Therefore the basic precept is to cut back the shoots that have borne flowers immediately their display is over. On no account prune them in winter, when all other clematis are pruned. This group is relatively easy if you start by training the shoots out widely and keeping control.

GROUP 2. These flower in May and June, and often a second time in early autumn. They include many spectacular old friends, such as 'Lasurstern', 'Nelly Moser', 'Beauty of Worcester', 'Marie Boisselot' and 'William Kennett'. Unfortunately, they are the most difficult not only to prune but also to explain how to prune. While the first flowers are forming on side-shoots from last year's limbs, other new limbs are growing out also. The practical advice to give to the busy amateur is to be sure to fan the first shoots well out; afterwards, having taken out all dead growth, prune lightly. If subsequently it becomes a horrid tangle, chop it down low, and start again.

Selections. I have already, in passing, mentioned those that I have found to be the best in their groups. Good catalogues will give you other details. My own findings are that 'Lasurstern', clothed in regal plum-purple, is the most beautiful of all, but that the pink 'Hagley Hybrid' has peculiar merits in small places and for growing with roses, as it reaches no more than eight feet.

Try to find room also for one or both of the yellow species – *orientalis*, with sepals like lemon peel, and *tangutica*, like little Chinese lanterns.

Avoid the alluring *florida bicolor*, which looks rather like a Passion-flower, unless you can give it a hot spot, a very rich soil and copious watering.

A species in a special class of its own is *armandii*, which is evergreen, very lusty but not hardy. It has large, leathery leaves and dense clusters of scented white flowers. Good for the Gulf Stream shires and snug corners elsewhere. Group 1.

Other Twiners

Actinidia. An interesting tribe, hardy, ornamental, easy, stem-twining, good for arbours, for strong artificial hosts or for climbing up a decadent tree. The one usually grown is the "Chinese gooseberry", *A. chinensis*, a robust, fast twiner to 20ft, coated in a fuzz of gingery

FIG. 107. *Actinidia chinensis* in blossom; a small fruit is shown separately at foot.

hairs. Large, oval leaves, clusters of buff flowers followed in a hot August, if you are lucky, by fruits which are like plump, 2in. sausages with a mild gooseberry flavour.

Another nice actinidia is *kolomikta*, a slender and elegant beauty, noted for the pink or pearly-white splashes on its leaves. Essentially a shrub for a south or west wall.

Celastrus. Stem-twiner which is dull in summer but later breaks out into a copious and brilliant display of small orange-and-red fruits, rather like those of our native spindle tree, borne in elegant, branching sprays. Excellent tree-climber. The one for our money is *C. orbiculatus*, which carries its big, beaded swags all winter; beautiful for cutting. Fully hardy. Be sure to order a bisexual form.

FORSYTHIA. See in deciduous shrubs.

Honeysuckle (*Lonicera*). Stem-twiner. Also known of old as woodbine, our dearly loved wanderer of the woods and hedgerows is grossly misused by many gardeners. You must give it a very moist soil, liberal waterings, a shady, cool root-run and an annual mulch of leaves. Do not expect it to prosper on a hot wall. To grow it well on any wall, in fact, requires some skill and it shows its graces best when used to cover an arbour, which it will "over-canopy" in the fashion that enchanted Oberon, or when employed in the delightful cottage habit of climbing over arches or gateways or sprawling over sheds. Its stems grasp very tightly, so do not use to climb a tree, except a derelict one.

Honeysuckles are often attacked by greenfly. At the first sign spray with a systemic insecticide, such as Abol X or Murphy's.

For garden usage we put honeysuckles in two pigeon-holes: those that are scented and those that are not. Don't be surpised that the ones with the sweetest breath have the plainest faces.

SCENTED HONEYSUCKLES

See the best catalogues for colours and dates. The following four are hardy:

The "Early Dutch" and the "Late Dutch", respectively *L. periclymenum* 'Belgica' and *L. p.* 'Serotina'.

americana (alias *italica* and *grata*). To 30ft.

japonica 'Halliana'. Evergreen, rampant, not beautiful but with a swooning scent and useful for screening. Some people also care for the variegated form, whose leaves are netted with yellow.

DISPLAY HONEYSUCKLES

brownii. The "scarlet trumpet honeysuckle". Not too rampant and ideal for small gardens.

tellmanniana. Large, opulent clusters of long, copper-gold trumpets. Very impressive and vigorous. Needs almost complete shade.

tragophylla. The most sumptuous of all. Very large clusters of long, golden trumpets. Almost complete shade.

Passion-flower (*Passiflora coerulea*). Many a gardener has suffered heartache from his experience with this exquisitely wrought, exotic and tantalizing flower, whose intricate design symbolizes the incidence of Christ's Passion – the crown of thorns, the nails, the five wounds and the apostles.

The Passion-flower seems to be completely hardy in this country, but numerous complaints come to me of its failure to flower. The reason is that the Passion-flower must not be grown in a rich soil, but in a poor, harsh, stony one. It is quite happy if its roots run under a gravel path. Where the soil is rich, it can be devitalized by mixing in plenty of stones and by constricting the roots, as one does for figs, within a wall of bricks, corrugated iron or the like sunk below ground for 18in.

Despite the exceptional cases, I would always prefer to plant against a warm south wall. There is nothing that it likes more to climb on than the plastic-covered chain-link fencing of which I have spoken. Cut the stronger shoots back moderately in February. 'Constance Elliott' is a connoisseur's piece delicately chiselled in ivory.

Polygonum (*P. baldschuanicum*). Express-speed scrambler foaming in creamy waves in late summer. For throwing floral cloaks over outhouses. Cut back hard if it exceeds bounds.

Schizandra. *S. rubrifolia* is a handsome, showy and curiously neglected climber. It has slender, ruddy, intertwining shoots and pendulous, rather small, crimson flowers in April and May. Dislikes too much direct sun. Train it out on a north wall or over a large arch or summerhouse in partial shade. Said to prefer an acid soil. To 15ft (Christopher Lloyd).

Trachelospermum. A beautiful genus of stem climbers unaccountably neglected by gardeners in general. They have lustrous, evergreen leaves with scented, jasmine-like flowers in July and August and, although admittedly at their best in the warmer counties, some are hardy enough for all but the coldest ones. They display themselves best on walls, and, in all but the mildest localities, prefer a warm south or west one, though they tolerate some shade. The most charming is *T. jasminoides*, which delights us with clusters of little flowers like white jasmine, breathing a swooning scent. Blooms when a few inches high. Hardy for me in Surrey so far, facing south-east.

Hardier and less vigorous but less pleasing to eye and nose is *asiaticum*; *major* is also hardy but will cover a whole house.

Tropaeolum. The so-called "flame nasturtium" of popular garden literature is *T. speciosum* and is one of the most gorgeous of our climbers, but one that you just can't grow well unless you live where the soil is moist and acid and the atmosphere humid. See it on the west coast of Scotland or in Cornwall and it will take your breath away; try it in Kent or Norfolk and you are likely to watch it die.

If you do live in the right sort of place, choose a moist spot in *full shade*, dress the ground liberally with well-rotted leaves and old cow manure and, if the heavens fail you, water it copiously and regularly from the rain-water tank. Set it to scramble over a fair-sized shrub or else to climb up another climber on a north wall. Gorgeous on yew or holly. Mulch liberally with leaves in autumn. Propagate from seed in April or by division.

Vines (*Vitis*). Any of the Bacchanalian vines that are cultivated specially for wine or for dessert can, subject to hardiness, quite well be grown on walls or fences. These are the "fruiting" vines, varieties of *V. vinifera*. Two very good ones are 'Royal Muscadine' and 'Muscatel'.

What we are concerned with here, however, are the "ornamental vines", grown for the beauty of their foliage, which is often of dramatic splendour; some are themselves varieties of *vinifera*. Virtually all climb by means of curling and twisting tendrils. They are just the thing for draping around and above an arbour for shade and seclusion in the heat of the day and, in the old, old way, for creating an "alley cool and green" along a pergola. More prosaically, they do splendid service as screens if given a framework of trellis or rustic poles to climb on and they will quickly cover outhouses of all sorts.

Vines need sun and a richly fortified soil, with or without lime. Plant in autumn. Amputate the cane at about 3ft 6in. before the end of December without fail; if cut after that date they are liable to bleed to death. Train out the resulting side branches at your will. To thicken up the foliage, nip back the laterals very lightly once or twice in summer. Next winter, before January, cut the laterals hard back nearly to their main stem.

Here are some prize selections.

coignetiae. The lord of them all. A magnificent creature of strapping physique, with very big, wrinkled leaves that colour superbly in autumn, accompanied by little branches of grapes. Needs a large host and is unsurpassed as a climber of tall trees. No pruning.

flexuosa parvifolia (alias *wilsonii*). A small and dainty variety, ideal for small places. Slender stems and small leaves enriched by a lustrous metallic sheen.

vinifera varieties. The finest of the lot is 'Purpurea', with lovely claret leaves that turn purple. Very fine with grey-leaved plants. Another splendid vine is 'Brandt', whose leaves do not colour until autumn, when they assume stunning hues of crimson and pink. The grapes make excellent vinegar.

Wisteria. Stem-twiner and noblest of climbing plants. Its prodigious vigour, however, make it unsuitable for growing in too confined a space, where some skill is required to restrain its impetuosity.

FIG. 108. Pruning a wisteria. Summer-prune at the broken line, winter-prune at the thick black one.

Its great strength and speed may also result in some damage unless carefully supervised. Don't let it slip behind the drainpipes of a house and don't grow it at all on a tile-hung wall.

You must be its master from the start, not allowing it to get tortuously wound round itself or anything else. Train out the shoots in the direction that you dictate while it is still young, to create a permanent framework and then concentrate on producing the maximum floral effect by pruning both in summer and in winter. In August cut back to about the fifth compound leaf and in late December cut further back to two buds from the parent stem.

Unlike the majority of natural climbers, the wisteria is quite happy with its roots in full sun. Magnificent when trained along the main beams of a long pergola. Of the several species none is better than *W. sinensis*, unless it be the white 'Alba'.

Annual Climbers

THE SCRAMBLERS

These, if grown on walls, must be featly tied up by man. We have already noted *Forsythia suspensa*. Others are:

Jasmine. The winter favourite, with golden bells on leafless, green stems, is *J. nudiflorum*. Keep it neat by cutting back the flowered shoots as in Fig. 20. The summer jasmine is the white, sweetly scented *officinale*, of great vigour, which is in fact a scrambling twiner. Prune in February. Yet more beautiful, but for warm places only, are two evergreens: *primulunium*, the primrose jasmine, spring-flowering, unscented, a rambling shrub, and *polyanthum*, a richly scented twiner.

Solanum. Rompers, with pretty flowers like those of their brother, the potato, good for sheds, etc. The usual one is *crispum* 'Glasnevin'. More beautiful, but for warm counties only, is *jasminoides*. Prune both hardish in March.

The few to note should be raised from seed in the manner of half-hardy annuals. They look most attractive when set to climb another climber or a slender shrub.

Eccremocarpus scaber is truly a perennial and jolly nearly a hardy one. It rockets up to 10ft, throwing out lateral trusses of small, tubular, orange flowers. Often over-winters safely and seeds itself.

Cobaea scandens is an even faster rocketer, clinging by corkscrw tendrils and breaking out into large, plump bells ornamented with very prominent stamens and pistils.

"Morning-glory" catches all eyes as it opens its beautiful bugles of vivid, luminous blue from slender, coiled buds, but it needs a good summer and the flowers shut up in the afternoon. The plant is a stem-twiner, corkscrewing neatly round its host. Rather poor and stony soil is best. The botanical name is *Ipomoea rubro-caerulea* (or *Pharbitis tricolor*), and there are red and pink varieties also. Sow in peat pots to avoid root disturbance when planting out.

Gourds. The ornamental gourds are great fun. Sow the seed singly straight into pots, pot-on if necessary and plant them out in due course where you can train them over an arch or trellis; they have no climbing mechanism.

CHAPTER 23

CLOTHING THE EARTH

The Objective – Self-sufficient Plants – Groundling Shrubs – Herbaceous Cover – Beware!

"GROUND-COVER" is a gardening vogue of the day and a very good one it is if practised with understanding. A great many typewriters have tapped diligently away on this topic, but the objectives are not always clearly expressed, the drawbacks not set out and the differences between one set of circumstances and another not emphasized. We have at the outset to distinguish between those plants, mainly evergreen shrubs, which are grown as the primary adornments of the garden and which fully provide their own ground-cover (here called primary plants), and those ancillary ones that are grown specifically for covering the ground. It is the latter that we shall be mainly concerned with in this chapter.

The usual purpose of ground-cover is to clothe the soil, particularly beneath trees, with a fairly dense carpet of low-growing vegetation in order to do away with the labour of weeding. It can also be of very good value, however, for throwing a shroud of decency over some raw and naked soil where nothing choice will grow and for putting to profitable use some bank too steep or rough to cultivate.

The most suitable plants for these situations vary a great deal, as also do those for the different circumstances of woodland, shrubland and herbaceous plots and other situations. The cover plant should harmonize with the primary plant and it should be one that has its own beauty of leaf or flower rather than have a mere utility value. Only very few, of which the true geraniums are an example, fit almost every situation. Some of the cover plants often recommended themselves become weeds and others quickly throttle the choicer plants. In many situations we shall need plants that suffer being trodden on or buffeted when one tends the primary plants.

There are certain beds and borders in which covering plants should never be planted at all. Chief of them are beds of hybrid tea-roses, carnations and pinks, irises, dwarf plants generally and most things that require a good baking by the sun. Roses other than hybrid teas are not spoilt by underplantings, but, as I have said in the appropriate chapter, the HT's, for several reasons, are entirely unsuited to any heterodox company, except of the most refined, and their drawing-room elegance is ruined if they are jostled by such rough-and-tumble creatures as "lamb's-ears", Serbian campanulas and pennyroyal, as I have seen recommended.

Ground-cover may also be at odds with the greater requirements of feeding the primary plants by mulches of manure, compost or leaves. One cannot spread a mulch on top of a mat of growing shrublets, though one can do so on dormant herbaceous plants in winter. Mulching is much more important than ground-cover.

Self-sufficient Plants

Thus we must not be deluded into supposing that the new vogue is the complete answer to the gardener's prayer. What is important is that, right from the start of his thinking, the gardener should (subject to his likes and dislikes) choose as his primary plants those that will be sufficient to themselves, when they have become well established, and will never thereafter need any auxillaries around their feet. Virtually all plants that clothe themselves right down to the ground, especially the evergreens, are of this character, but even most of these will have bare spaces around them in their early years. They include:

Many rhododendrons and evergreen azaleas (Chapter 17).

Nearly all heathers.

Pieris.

Pernettyas, develop into dense thickets.

Viburnum davidii, first-class in sun or shade (Chapter 19).

The prostrate junipers, unsurpassed in this test (Chapter 16), sun.

The purple-leaved salvias, extremely good, sun.

The lower-growing cistuses (chiefly *lusitanicus decumbens* and *corbariensis*), in sun.

Senecio laxifolius, extremely good (Chapter 20).
Choisya ternata, extremely good.
Helianthemum and halimiums, in sun.
Barberries, evergreen species.
Mahonias, in half-shade.
Escallonias.
Skimmias.
Osmanthus and osmarea.

The first four are for acid soils. Except where shown otherwise, all are covered in Chapter 18, so are not included in the lists that follow unless there is a reason.

Several deciduous shrubs are also most efficient suppressors of weeds, especially those with branches sweeping close to the ground. Outstanding among them are the handsome "tabulated" varieties of *Viburnum tomentosum* (which, in my garden, have absolutely annihilated all weeds), the mop-head and lace-cap hydrangeas (but not the plumed *H. paniculata*), the shrubby *Potentilla fruticosa*, the flowering quinces and (rather surprisingly) the dwarf Japanese maples.

On the other hand, there is always a crying need in all gardens, large or small, to embroider the naked territories at the feet of all shrubs that have bare legs and an upright or arching carriage, especially lilacs, philadelphus, deutzia, forsythia, weigela, a great many roses other than HTs, deciduous azaleas and sometimes camellias and rhododendrons. Ground that is given over to spring bulbs may also need summer cover.

There are a few preliminaries to bear in mind. First, before expecting any plant to suppress weeds for you, do your own part. Clean the ground of all existing weeds, particularly the deep-rooted ones. Your ground-cover plant will, in time, prevent the germination of annual weeds, but it will not compete with dandelions, thistles, ground-elder and bellbind (also called bindweed and other names in some counties).

Secondly, avoid consorting one vigorous ground-cover plant too closely with another; they will quarrel and one is likely to suppress the other. No use planting a troop of lilies-of-the-valley in some shady corner if squadrons of periwinkle are allowed to gallop over them. Give each its allotted territory to conquer and, where there is a danger of a clash, put between them a barrier of peace-keeping neutrals such as hostas and bergenias, which make first-rate wardens. I tried once a mixture of lady's mantle with the white-splashed dead-nettle, thinking that they would make a good colour harmony, but theory was overcome by fact.

Groundling Shrubs

Among these we have at our choice low shrubs that spread widely from a single crown, others that throw out running stems which take root and expand rapidly, like strawberries or ivy, and those that invade the surrounding territory by means of underground runners, a class to be careful of.

Box (*Buxus*). Both in shade and in sun, in chalk or elsewhere, the dwarf species named in the chapter on hedges, make very good, dense, evergreen shrouds where a 2ft high mini-forest is the thing.

Cotoneaster. Several prostrate species are absolutely first-class. One of the lesser known has evergreen, willow-like leaves and red berries, entirely happy in complete shade beneath trees, and spreading rapidly as its pointed fingers run eagerly along the surface, taking root here and there, so that there is no limit to its extension. This is *C.* 'Herbstfeuer' ('Autumn Fire'). Equally happy of course in full sun, as, for example, tumbling down a rough bank. Does not incommode choice plants. Mine run along beneath cherries and between rhododendrons, camellias, mahonias, etc. Plant 5–6ft apart.

Better known, also evergreen, but less vigorous are:

C. dammeri, with smaller, glossy leaves, moulding itself to the contours of the soil and crawling over rocks. Good for partial shade. Rather dull if the ground is quite flat.

C. microphyllus cochleatus has tiny, densely-packed dark-green leaves, which make a splendid, close cover. Starts growing up a foot or so then fans out. Rather slow at first but perhaps the most handsome. Mainly for sun. Also excellent for climbing a wall or swooping down a bank.

Cornus. The pygmy Canadian dogwood, hardly recognizable as a brother of the big shrubs, is one of the prettiest of ground plants, but it needs an acid soil of loose tilth, such as sandy peat or woodsy leaf-mould. This little charmer is *C. canadensis.* Growing only a few inches high, it forms a trim, flat rosette of pale-green leaves, from the centre of which, in early summer, appear star-like flowers composed of four white bracts, dark-eyed where the minute true petals are, and when these fade there comes a little red berry. Spreads 2ft a year in the right soil. Keep it away from anything likely to swamp it. Best in shade, even full shade beneath trees.

Euonymus. The variegated forms of *E. fortunei* (*radicans*) (Chapter 18) make delightful, dense ground-cover in sun or shade, rooting along the ground like ivy. A good bank climber.

Gaultheria. Here are several of the very choicest ground plants, with splendid evergreen foliage, extremely hardy, but for acid soils only. They have glossy leaves with charming tufts of lily-of-the-valley flowers, followed by white, pink, red or purple berries. The broad-leaved *G. shallon* is for large estates only, making a 6ft high thicket in sheltered woodlands and swamping everything in time; but it is useful for an awkward bank on a cold, northerly aspect, where it grows only half that height. Choicest of the lot is *miqueliana*, a neat, dense, pretty shrublet 9in. high, with oval leaves. I have failed repeatedly with it, for it wants a soil that is moister, more acid and of more open texture than mine. Part-shade is best.

Much easier and growable anywhere in soil not limy is *procumbens*, the partridge berry or wintergreen, a very dwarf, 4in. plant with more pointed, dark-green leaves and red berries, spreading with considerable gusto by underground shoots, which may sometimes penetrate the roots of choicer primary plants. Apart from this, it carpets the ground delightfully and offending shoots can be yanked up and planted somewhere else.

Other desirable gaultherias are the tiny, slow-spreading, pretty *itoana* and the 12in. *cuneata*, which is rather like *miqueliana*. Hillier, Sunningdale and Jackman cover the various species.

Hebe. The low, spreading bushlet long known as *Veronica pageana* becomes a blue-green mat which is as nice in winter as in summer and in May bears quantities of little, pearly-white flowers, which should be guillotined when faded. Easy and tolerant and good in towns. Is now *Hebe pinguifolia* 'Pagei'. See also *Hebe subalpina* in Chapter 18.

Ivies. Nearly all ivies are expert ground scramblers, whether in woodland, where they usually begin to climb any tree they encounter, or creeping up (or down) a steep bank in shade or sun. The most beautiful for all purposes is the primrose tinted Persian ivy, *Hedera colchica* 'Dentato-variegata' (Chapter 22).

Junipers. See Chapter 16. The prostrate junipers when established are complete and ruthless masters of weeds as well as being very decorative. Among the most expert are *J. conferta* and 'Hornibrookii'; the elegant 'Bonin Island' is equally good, but slower. Sun only.

Mahonia. Where a knee-high cover is wanted *M. aquifolium* is excellent and decorative all the year with its glossy foliage, yellow flowers and quickly spreading habit. Shade or sun.

Periwinkle (*Vinca*). Old friends with starry, blue flowers enduring dense shade, but slow off the mark and take time to thicken up. There are two for us: the larger periwinkle (*V. major*) and the lesser (*minor*), both evergreen. The larger leaps about with gusto when established, is suitable for woodland in large gardens and prospers in any kind of soil, including chalk. The lesser, of which there are several varieties, is much prettier and denser. Better avoid those with variegated leaves, pretty though they are, for they are slow. 'Bowles Variety', 'Superba' (Jackman) are the best. Though usually seen in shade, periwinkles prosper also in sun. Cut them down nearly to the ground in late winter.

Roses. The ground-hugging roses mentioned in the appropriate chapter are marvellous at overpowering weeds over a large area, and are primary plants in their own right.

Rose-of-Sharon. Perhaps the best-known of all groundlings, with its big, buttercup flowers, is *Hypericum calycinum* (Chapter 18).

Rubus. Quite out of character with one's idea of a bramble, *R. fockeanus* makes a close, flat, warmly evergreen carpet in shade or sun. It creeps and roots along the ground in the manner of ivy, with small, broadly scalloped leaves like those of some pelargoniums, but with a puckered and glossy surface. The name is a bit phoney.

Herbaceous Cover

Here also are some plants grown as primary choices but which spread thickly to cover the ground, such as lilies-of-the-valley, astilbes and the true geraniums. There are also some little charmers not often grown for their own sakes, but entirely suitable for growing among choice plants, such as vancouveria, maianthemum and the horned violet. The following is a selection for various uses. Where descriptions are not given refer to Chapter 10, unless I say otherwise.

Ajuga reptans. Our common bugle, with many pretty leaf forms. A plant much recommended, but one that I have learnt to discard except in the roughest places. A throttler.

Barrenwort (*Epimedium*). One of the widely recommended cover plants, but one which has never stirred any enthusiasm in my breast. There are several species, averaging about 9in. high, with plentiful small leaves and very small flowers that are often half-hidden unless the leaves are cut away. Their dense root masses are good weed barriers, but the plants are slow to increase. For ground-cover the two best are *E. pinnatum* and *perralderianum*. For half-shade.

Campanula. That pretty weed, *C. poscharskyana*, the Serbian bell-flower, finds its true vocation as a groundling where no choice plants are grown. In my garden it tries to grow everywhere, including gravel and stone paths, in sun or shade.

Dead-nettles. Two sorts are commonly grown, both keen invaders. One is the variegated form of the yellow archangel, known to some hitherto by the forbidding name of *Lamium galeobdolon*. This variegated form (*L. g.* 'Variegatum') has a very attractive, grey-green white-flaked leaf and keeps low to the ground, except for its plumes of small yellow flowers. But beware! This dead-nettle is a furious galloper, leaping and charging pell-mell across the territory that it invades and colonizing at random all over the place. Use it only in large places as an undercover for trees, or in desolate territory that breeds only barbarian stock. Reverting in part to an ancient Roman name, we are now asked to call it *Galeobdolon luteum variegatum*.

The other dead-nettle is a steady, dense, compact spreader rather than a galloper, and fairly easy to keep in check. It lies nearly flat on the ground and has a delightful leaf of dark green boldly diversified with a broad cream patch. This is *Lamium maculatum*. There are forms with mauve, pink or white flowers. Use it under trees or deciduous, bare-legged shrubs or in any patch of poor, rough soil in sun or part-shade. If it were not such a choker when unchecked, we should account this a choice plant.

Geraniums. Among the very best all-purposes cover plants.

Lady's-mantle (*Alchemilla mollis*). Acceptable for their beautiful, round grey-green, velvet leaves and their large plumes of small yellow flowers. They procreate with abandon and have surprisingly tough roots, dangerous to choice plants. For deep shade or sun, poor soils or good.

Lamb's-ears. See Stachys, Chapter 20.

Lily-of-the-valley. Seldom thought of merely as a groundcover plant, but extremely effective when it has colonized well. Shade or half-shade.

London-pride. Our dear old friend is magnificent at overpowering weeds, for it spreads rapidly into a dense mat of thick-leaved rosettes. Sun or shade.

Maianthemum. This charming little plant looks at first glance like a miniature lily-of-the-valley. Spreads widely and neatly by underground runners. For sun or part-sun among shrubs, but put it in a place where it can be seen. Is *M. bifolium* (Jackman's).

Pachysandra. An elegant and evergreen ground-cover, thriving in deep shade as in sun, but for acid soils only. Tufts of glossy leaves about 9in. high and small white flowers in March. Spreads by underground shoots and makes a dense cover. Very widely used in the States for carpeting under trees. Is *P. terminalis.*

Pulmonaria. These easy cottage plants make excellent cover beneath the taller roses and other deciduous shrubs, but are not spreaders.

Polygonum. For a fairly moist soil in sun. 'Donald Lowndes' is a picturesque and rapid colonizer in pink and bronze among such shrubs as lilac and philadelphus.

Potentilla. Any of the lower-growing, shrubby potentillas of Chapter 19 are fine weed conquerors, but one would hardly plant them *en masse*. Among the herbaceous sorts, *alba* and *tonguei* are very nice for small-scale plantings, as at the feet of floribunda roses and other small shrubs.

Rodgersia. Noble plants of masculine character, 3ft to 4ft high, grown particularly for their large and splendid foliage, though their plumes of cream or pink flowers are also impressive in summer. For fairly moist soils in larger gardens only, where they become dense thickets, overpowering all weeds. The species *aesculifolia* has leaves very like those of the chestnut, with cream flower stems unfurling crozier-fashion, *pinnata* 'Superba' has pink flowers. Sun or part-shade (Sunningdale).

Stachys. See Chapter 20.

Tiarella. In *T. cordifolia* we have a 9in. plant sometimes called the "foam flower" for obvious reasons. A good, fast-running and decorative cover for shady places where the soil is not dry, flowering May–June. *T. wherryi* is a prettier plant, but not so good for coverage.

Vancouveria. Another pretty miniature spreader, having foliage like the maidenhair fern, from which rise slender stems hung with tiny, dangling cream flowers in late summer. Increases by rhizomes. For shade among deciduous or other shrubs, but plant it where its charms are not hidden. Is *V. hexandra* (Sunningdale, Jackman, Hillier).

Viola. See Chapter 9 for my favourite little pest, the pretty little Labrador violet. Another good mat-former is the charming horned violet, *V. cornuta*, usable among the choicest plants.

Waldsteinia. My last is one of the best for all sorts of purposes. Lying almost flat on the ground, it has strawberry-like leaves and buttercup flowers in early spring. Quickly forms a dense mat by underground runners. You can tread on it without qualms. Easily pulled up if it breaks bounds. Excellent among any shrubs and a good cover for bulbs.

Beware!

There remains an unholy trio of plants that are often recommended for ground-cover, but which are the most insidious of fifth columnists, all the more so because they are pretty or have a sweet scent. They are:

Winter heliotrope (*Petasites fragrans*).

Snow-in-summer (*Cerastium tomentosum*).

Veronica filiformis.

These have their uses in the roughest, wildest or most desolate places in very large gardens, but elsewhere must be classed as prohibited immigrants and liquidated on sight.

CHAPTER 24

HEDGES HIGH AND LOW

Pryen Wights – Fitness for Purpose – Good Hedgers – Pleaching

IN this chapter we shall consider briefly the various sorts of plant barriers and screens that may be needed in gardens large or small – thick hedges along boundaries, lighter ones between one part of the garden and another and dwarf screens to flank a drive or footpath and low edgings for various purposes.

Unless one specifically wants a decorative, open type of screen, as might be provided by certain sorts of roses, the first essentials of a hedge are that it should be thick, dense, as tall as you want it and clothed right down to the ground with foliage:

> As thick as is a castle wall,
> That who that list without to stand or go,
> Though he would all day pryen to and fro,
> He should not see if there were any wight
> Within or no.

Even in Chaucer's day they thought so. A straggly, moth-eaten hedge with shameless, naked legs is an abomination in the eyes of all wights and a failure in its twin tasks of defeating the pryen ones and keeping out predators on two or more legs. To enable it to do its job properly and to look comely into the bargain, we must bring it up properly from its earliest days, for to cure an adult hedge that has gone wrong is as difficult as to reform an old lag.

The formula for its early training is: sound preparation of the ground (this above all), proper spacing and strict pruning (in most cases) so that young plants will throw out strong side branches and make dense bushes.

Hedge cultivation differs from that of other plantings chiefly in the fact that the plants are set very closely together. It follows that the preparation of the ground must be particularly thorough. Do this in accordance with the precepts of earlier chapters. Make the trench at least 3ft wide for a double hedge, 2ft for a single one and two spits deep.

When digging, give thought to constricting the root growth. Many of the stronger-growing hedges are greedy, with far-ranging roots – none more so than privet – and they gobble up the best of the plant food for 5ft or more on each side. The preventive treatment is to bury sheets of corrugated iron on each side of the trench, to form underground walls. By this means you will be able to grow the choicest plants close to the hedge.

The proper spacing of hedge plants is important. The spacings given in catalogues are often unnecessarily close and you can save a bit by increasing the distances in most cases. Thus instead of 15in. you may read 18in. Usually one row is enough. When a hedge is planted close to a fence, it should be at least 18in. away from it.

If the situation is a windy one, or if the plants are very bushy, stake them firmly until the roots have taken good hold. Water very thoroughly and keep on watering all through the critical first year. Evergreens may lose some foliage after transplanting without any need for alarm, but if the leaves shrivel and *stay* on the plant something is amiss; in such an event cut the plants back fairly sharply, water them often and give shade if possible.

Pruning. Bushy growth must be encouraged from the start, but the methods and degree of pruning will depend on the type of plants. The general rule to remember is that in the first year or two *frequent* pruning is even more important than hard pruning, and that the fast-growing species, such as privet, lonicera and quickthorn, need harder and more frequent cuttings than the slow ones, such as yew and holly. Broad-leaved plants, such as laurel, you should never clip with the shears; prune them with secateurs.

Hedges of flowering plants require slightly different pruning treatment, and here one should follow what has been said in Chapter 7 of flowering shrubs generally – that is to say, according to their season of flowering.

In all cases bear in mind the ultimate shape of the hedge from the beginning; and here there is one governing rule: make all tall hedges narrower at the top than at the bottom, except possibly for strong trees such as yew or holly. Do not cut them square at the top, especially in districts liable to heavy snow; tailor the top instead so that it is either rounded or else in the form of a pointed ridge. This, of course, need not apply to dwarfs or to open screens of roses, etc.

I need hardly say that the best gadget for clipping is a power-driven trimmer. People without a really straight eye haven't a hope of maintaining a long hedge that needs neat tailoring and should employ an experienced professional. In any case, the beginner should use a garden line and a few laths as guides. The standard time for clipping non-flowering evergreens is about 1st August.

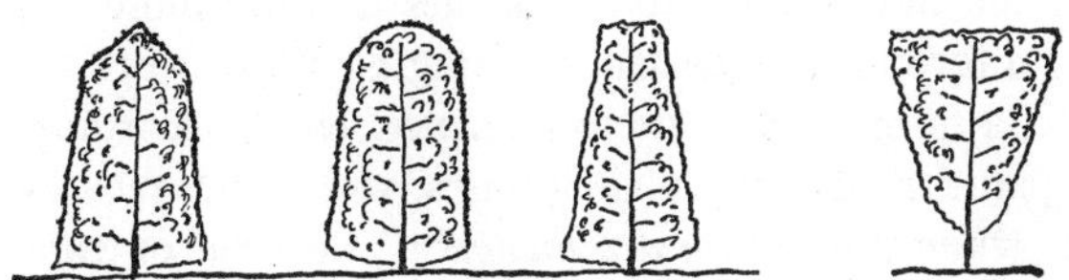

FIG. 109. Three good shapes for hedges – and a bad one.

It is too often forgotten that hedges need food as much as other plants, perhaps more so. Top-dress every two or three years with manure or a good all-round fertilizer in spring and mulch annually where that is acceptable.

Fitness for Purpose

Apart from personal preferences, one's choice for a hedge may be governed by local factors beyond one's control. Chiefly, these are:

the nature of the soil – whether sandy or heavy, acid or limy, etc., and

the nature of the exposure and the locality – whether cold or warm or windy, sea-side exposures having their special problems of salt plus gales.

Accordingly these are the first factors to weigh. For a boundary hedge, most people will want something that will ultimately become fairly tall, proof against pryen wights as well as boy- and dog-proof. This usually means an evergreen, though beech and hornbeam are nearly as good. Boundary hedges abutting on pavements had better not be too scratchy, though this does not eliminate holly.

We should try to use floral hedges much more than we do, for a long hedge in its full beauty of blossom is a picture not to be forgotten. Where there is room and where the climate is not severe, we should make greater use, for example, of the escallonias. Forsythia makes a glorious spring show in any climate and roses of many sorts fill out the summer days.

Internal hedges, dividing one part of the garden from another, allow you to put spurs to your imagination and override conventions. Here mere utility has no merit, even if the purpose is merely to mask the compost heaps and the cabbages. So use the hedges that make flower or beautiful foliage.

Very often one wants internal hedges that are quite low, as surrounding a formal rose garden, flanking a path or steps or forming as it were, a floral balustrade to a terrace. Here, according to scale, we may plant the dwarf philadelphuses, with their spicy breath, the beautiful, white-starred *Spiraea thunbergii*, the large or dwarf lavenders, the ever-flowering potentillas, the silvery cotton-lavenders or their bright-green brother or even, on the smallest possible scale, the little perennial candytufts (*Iberis sempervirens*), which are admirable in this office.

Good Hedgers

In the following brief notes "shear" means use hedging shears, electric or hand, and "prune" means use secateurs. Those not noted as evergreen are deciduous. Refer to the appropriate Chapters 18 and 19 respectively for fuller details in those instances where my entry is very sketchy. Always bear in mind the ultimate breadth as well as the height.

Atriplex. Close to the sea *A. halimus*, a tough, ever-grey shrub, makes a good utility hedge, braving wind and salt.

Barberry. Evergreen and deciduous sorts. Use any of those in Chapter 18. Splendid for both spring flower and autumn berry, but slow. Most beautiful if left alone but, if necessary, prune after flowering. Spacing 18in. to 2ft according to variety. Allow plenty of width. The star performer is *stenophylla*, reaching 8ft high and wide and *verruculosa* is highly favoured as a 4-footer. Space at 2ft and 18in. respectively.

Beech (*Fagus sylvatica*). Famous for keeping its russet foliage well into the winter. Much at home in chalk, but not in heavy, wet soils.

Shear the side shoots hardish in early August (some gardeners prefer February), but leave the leading shoots alone until they reach the height you dictate, which may be anything up to 14ft. Space 21in. The copper beech (*F. s. cuprea*) is champion but expensive. See also Hornbeam.

Box (*Buxus sempervirens*). Evergreen. Dense, handsome and valuable for prospering in shade, but somewhat out of fashion in an impatient age. Very good on chalk. Queen Anne and Gerarde hated its scent, but some noses relish it. For a whopping 12ft hedge I would have 'Handsworthensis' (from Waterer) and for a dwarf "box edging", trimmed 1ft high or a trifle more, the pretty, cream-margined 'Elegantissima', better than the usual 'Suffruticosa' and a beautiful shrub in its own right as a specimen. Space at 18in. and 1ft respectively. Shear in spring and summer.

Cotoneaster. Very good species for hedging are the deciduous *simonsii*, the fine evergreen *lacteus* and the half-evergreen *franchetii* (of nurseries). All to 8ft if required. Space at 18, 21 and 18in. respectively. Prune after flowering or shear lightly if you are impatient (Chapter 18).

Cotton-lavender (*Santolina*). For a miniature hedge see Chapter 20. Space 1ft. Shear in April and inhibit flowering.

Cypress. Evergreen. Possibly the best hedger nowadays is Leyland's cypress, especially for very tall barriers. Jackman's 'Green Hedger', a beautiful colour, rivals it and can be kept to a moderate height and trimly tailored with shears. Good at the sea. Space 3ft. Varieties of chamaecyparis usually grown as specimens, such as 'Fletcheri' and 'Lanei' make handsome but rather expensive screens and are best untouched by steel. Avoid *macrocarpa* except as a stopgap, but it is good near the sea.

Erica. Evergreen. Where heathers are appropriate, *E. arborea alpina* makes 6–7ft. Acid soils only. Space 2ft. For a 5-footer, *terminalis*, space 18in., and for a fine, dense 2-footer, *darleyensis* at 18in.

Escallonia. Nearly all escallonias make superlative evergreen floral hedges, according to their habits of growth, as set out in Chapter 18. Spacing 30in.

They are first-class close to the sea, the gummy coating on their leaves guarding them against salt and wind. The chosen ones for this are the rose-crimson 'Macrantha' and 'Crimson Spire' (Treseder).

In the frostiest inland regions the safest ones are 'Langleyensis' and 'Edinensis'. Shear or prune all after flowering.

Euonymus. The evergreen *E. japonicus* is a sombre and dowdy thing unless well cultivated and tailored, but on the south and east coasts it is valuable for its defiance of sea salt.

FLAMBOYANT. See Myrobalan, below.

Forsythia. The varieties of *F. intermedia* make glorious flowering hedges to about 6ft. Space 3ft. Prune lightly after flowering. *F. ovata* is O.K. for a 4-footer, but flowers for only ten days.

Fuchsia. The one to have is the splendid *magellanica* 'Riccartonii', where the climate is not severe. Fine at the sea. To 5ft. Space 2ft. Prune as in Chapter 18.

Gorse (*Ulex europaeus*). Evergreen. One of the most glorious of our natives, but suitable only for rustic or seaside places, where they excel for resistance to salt and wind, as well as for their golden splendour. Contrary to popular teaching, they should have *good* soil, at least for a start. Get the double-flowered variety (5ft, spacing 2ft). Must be pot-grown. Single gorse can be grown from seed.

Griselinia. Evergreen. Beautiful, fresh, apple-green foliage. A fine windbreak, but only for light or medium soils in the milder sea-side counties. Hardy to wind and salt. 12ft. Space 2ft. Shear early summer. Order *G. littoralis* or its beautiful white variegation.

Holly. Evergreen. One of the finest of all hedges, but slow for the first two years. Stands a lot of shade. If a thornless one is wanted, choose 'Polycarpa' or 'Camelliaefolia'. Spacing 2ft. Shear June and August.

Holm Oak, or Evergreen Oak (*Quercus ilex*). Normally a large tree, but a most effective utility wind-break right on the sea-shore up to 12ft or so. Gets gnarled and wind-bitten. Must be got as small, pot-grown plants. Spacing 4ft. Shear early July.

Hornbeam (*Carpinus betulus*). Resembles the beech and is preferred for heavy soils. Differentiated by its pointed, saw-edged, slightly corrugated leaf.

Laurel. See Chapter 18 for the several sorts so called. Space all at about 4ft. Prune the aucuba with secateurs always, but the others may be sheared when your patience is taxed, in early August.

Lavender. Space 'Twickle Purple' at 2ft and 'Hidcote' at 1ft (Chapter 20).

Lonicera. The evergreen, shrubby honeysuckle, with its very small, close-set leaves, is the smartest of all small hedges when properly tended but a ragged urchin when neglected. Give it a fairly rich soil. Guillotine it at 9in. from the ground when planting. Spacing 15in. Drops its leaves on transplanting. Must be trimly tailored, the top nearly pointed. Shear closely in June and August. The best one is *L. nitida* 'Fertilis'. Degenerate old loniceras are incorrigible.

Myrobalan or cherry-plum (*Prunus cerasifera*). A farmer's hedge, cheap and easy. Cut new plants down to 1ft in March. Space 2ft. Shear June and August. Its purple-leaved variety with blush-pink flowers usually called 'Pissardii' or 'Atropurpurea', is very handsome indeed, but not cheap. Space 2ft. Shear after flowering in late March. "Flamboyant" is a name sometimes given to a mixture of selected strains of both these plums, making a green and purple hedge up to 10ft (Notcutt).

Philadelphus. The dwarf 'Manteau d'Hermine' makes a dense and beautiful flowering and scented hedge of about 3½ft. Space 18in. Prune after flowering.

Pittosporum. Evergreen. Greatly hankered after by florists and flower arrangers for its elegant, undulating leaves on slender shoots. For the milder regions only and particularly sea-side ones. The most reliable is *P. tenuifolium* (alias *nigricans*), of which the variety 'Silver Queen' is madly popular. About 6ft., more in the west. Spacing 18in. or more. Shear early May, after frosts.

Privet (*Ligustrum*). A great improvement on the common *L. ovalifolium* but not so cheap, is *ionandrum* (also called *delavayanum*). This has dark-green, very small, close-set leaves and makes a handsome, solid, springy hedge to 6ft or so. Space 15in. Its roots go deeper than those of the common privet, so do not rob the adjacent soil. Remember not to cut the top square. Shear three times at six-week intervals, starting 1st June.

Prunus 'Cistena'. A brilliant and lively dwarf with purple-crimson leaves but useless on light soil. Space at 21in. and keep it down to a height of 3ft, shearing after flowering.

Pyracantha. Evergreen. Exceptionally fine, easy and tough hedgers. Excellent for exposed north or east aspects. The finest I know is *rogersiana*, but *watereri* and *atalantioides* are also splendid. To 7ft if needed. Space 2ft. Prune after flowering or shear lightly if impatient. Caveat as to the fire blight disease.

Quickthorn, or May. Cheap, fast, impenetrable, somewhat looked down upon (because usually neglected) but altogether excellent if cared for. Feed it! Space 15in. preferably in a double row. Amputate 4in. above ground level in the first April. Shear as for privet. To 7ft or more. Is *Crataegus monogyna.*

ROSES. See appropriate chapter.

Spiraea. One of the very prettiest of all floral hedges is made by *S. thunbergii,* dense and smothered with little stars to about 4ft. Spacing 18in. Shear after flowering. For taller, broader hedges, *vanhouttei* and *arguta* are also most effective.

Tamarisk. (*Tamarix*). Of particular value for salt-resistant seaside screens. The toughest for the seashore are *anglica* and *gallica,* which will grow in the sand. Cut down by two-thirds after flowering in May. See also page 362.

Thuja. Evergreen. Very fast and good. Space 3ft. Prune (if at all necessary) in summer.

Yew. Evergreen. Finest of old hedges, but no go in smoky cities. Also rather slow, but, from 2ft plants, you should get a 6ft hedge in eight years. Soil must be well drained. Space 21–24in. Leave the leading shoots to reach the desired height but shear the sides meantime in May and August.

Pleaching

This is the ancient craft of training trees to form "alleys cool and green" or high-level enclosures for meditative repose or lovers' meetings. Traditionally the trees used are those known by the multitude as limes or lindens (*Tilia*), but hornbeam can also be bent to your will.

Get young standard trees, plant them 9ft apart and leave them to grow until they have reached about 12ft.

Behead them at that height in winter and proceed in much the same manner as when training espalier fruit trees. Using strong, soft cord, firmly tie in thick bamboo canes all along the alley in continuous lines about 3ft apart. Bend the best branches to these and tie them in, after cutting them back by about a quarter to stimulate further growth. Cut out excess branches and thereafter get rid of any shoots growing in the wrong directions.

CHAPTER 25

PROBLEM PLACES

Shade – Chalk and other Limy Soils – Sea-side – Towns

Shade

PEOPLE are often worried what to do about the shady parts of a garden, particularly the north-facing wall. Except for the dense gloom of a beech or pine forest, however, there is almost no situation where one plant or another will not prosper and we must begin by appreciating that there are many degrees of shade, so that it is very often begging the question to say that such-and-such is "a good plant for shade". There is the heavy shade immediately beneath trees, the "dappled shade" through which the sun filters and which is so very much enjoyed by rhododendrons, camellias and many other of our most beautiful plants, and the oblique shade cast by house or tree for part of the day.

Nor is shade a factor to be considered in isolation. Wet shade is usually far more acceptable than dry shade and where the shade is dry, either from the nature of the soil or by reason of the greediness of the trees that create the shade, liberal watering will make life much easier for anything else that you want to grow there.

Among shallow-rooting trees root competition is often a greater hardship than lack of direct sun and is to a large extent counteracted by water. When the roots of the trees plunge deep, however, you can grow almost anything beneath them, even right up to the bole (as I do beneath an Atlantic cedar), especially if you remove one or two of the lower branches.

A great many plants will prosper beneath trees. Nearly all the shade plants listed at the end of Chapter 10 will do. So will the majority of ground-cover plants in Chapter 23, as will several of the larger shrubs in Chapters 17 to 19, priority being given, where the shade is not dense, to rhododendrons and camellias in acid soils and to mahonias in limy ones. In simplified terms, I would say that the first plants to choose for growing in dense shade right under trees are the rose-of-Sharon in its various species, the campanulas tall or dwarf, foxgloves, lilies-of-the-valley and ivy or other of the creepy-crawlers in Chapter 23.

The north side of a house, wall or fence is also no obstacle to suitable adornment, provided it is not unduly overhung. Here you can grow many fine fruits, particularly red currants and Morello cherries, and any of the shade plants. The wall of the house itself can be clad with strong climbers, such as ivy, the climbing hydrangeas, schizandra and honeysuckle, which in turn will serve as splendid hosts for clematis, which illuminate the dark better than any other plant, especially if you choose the bicolour varieties such as 'Nelly Moser', 'Barbara Dibley' and 'Barbara Jackman'.

Several climbing roses also excel on the north wall and enliven it, such as the white 'Mme Alfred Carrière' and the old, buff 'Gloire de Dijon'.

Among the pseudo-climbers, the winter jasmine, *Forsythia suspensa* and pyracanthas will be entirely at home. Several shrubs will also handsomely clothe the lower reaches of the wall, particularly camellias, flowering quinces and the choisya.

Chalk and other Limy Soils

We have to study lime in two ways: first, as an element residing permanently in the soil, whether we like it or not, and, secondly, as a deliberate dressing that we may have to apply for a definite purpose. We need not, however, delve into the profundities of either chemistry or geology (both being sciences in which I am totally unqualified) and all we need to do is to contemplate the subject as practical gardeners.

Limestone is a very variable product of the earth's crust and is found in several forms: chalk, oolite, lias, magnesium limestone, dolomite, the Furness limestone of parts of the Scottish Highlands and so on. While obviously most conspicuous in the limestone hills and chalky downs that traverse many parts of our islands, it may also have been spread far away from them by glacial action. The texture of the soil is no real guide to its presence, for clays, sands and peat may all be either limy or not limy.

The chief chemical element of lime is calcium and some chalk deposits are almost pure calcium carbonate. Now calcium is an element that is necessary to most forms of plant life, but it may be found in excessive concentrations for certain plants.

Testing for lime. The extent to which a soil is impregnated with lime is measured by what is known as the pH scale, in which those apparently mystic letters are followed by an indicative numeral, but which is merely a convenient yardstick based on a logarithmic scale of 0 to 14. Neutrality in a soil is represented by pH 7; numerals below 7 degrees of acidity, those above it the opposite.

Lime is a very important element for vegetables, fruit and a limited range of flowers, but for general garden purposes the best results come from a neutral or slightly acid pH reading – say from 6·5 to 7. Below 5·5 acidity is so pronounced as to create a "sour" soil, as may be found in very old town gardens; in such a condition it smells unpleasant and becomes green, slimy and mossy, and a heavy dressing of lime is at once called for.

The amateur can assess the acidity of his soil quite simply by one of the inexpensive soil testing kits on the market, such as the Sudbury, the British Drug Houses or the Pan Britannica. The methods often recommended of using hydrochloride acid or litmus paper tell you very little. Your County Horticultural Officer will give you a more detailed analysis if you send him a sample of soil from root level. There may, however, be variations in different parts of the garden; in old gardens, for example, the vegetable plots and orchards (and old agricultural land even more so) may show the results of centuries of liming, while the shrublands may be acid.

Calcicoles and Calcifuges. There is, I regret to say, a lamentable snob element in the possession of an acid soil. "Poor chap," you will hear it said, "he gardens on lime." Be not dismayed; if certain desirable plants are denied you, much yet remains of beauty and of usefulness. The question we have to ask ourselves is not, in fact: "What can be grown in a limy garden?" but: "What *cannot* be grown?" For the number of plants ruled out is relatively small, those that need to be particularly noticed being the following:

Camellias.
Virtually all rhododendrons.
Most of the heather family.

Several lilies.

Lupins.

A few choice shrubs, principally pieris, kalmia, pernettya, cassiope, gaultheria, corylopsis, embothrium, liquidambar, tamarisk, *Tropaeolum speciosum* and most of the eucryphias.

A few difficult irises.

The gentians of autumn.

Himalayan poppies.

Nearly all other plants in this book will prosper in lime and those that are conspicuously successful include:

Clematis.

Nearly all carnations.

The grey- and silver-leaved plants.

Most irises, especially the flags.

Junipers.

Many rock plants, as noted in Chapter 21.

Of flowering shrubs: lilac, laburnum, tree peony, buddleia, helianthemum, forsythia, *Spartium junceum* (revels in chalk), lavender, rosemary, hawthorn, most daphnes, nearly all viburnums (revel in chalk), euonymus, sorbus, cherries, crabs, *Acer griseum* and *negundo* and *Elaeagnus pungens.*

Of herbaceous and annual plants: gypsophila, scabious, geum, antirrhinum, wallflowers, mignonette, sweet-peas, agapanthus. All these revel in chalk.

Together with a great many bulbs, especially tulips; all cyclamens and all the little, bulbous anemones of Chapter 15 are happy in chalk.

Of course, all these succeed on soils with a low lime content also and, in brief, it may be said that, with the exceptions of the positive calcifuges in the first list, the great majority of plants of all sorts don't really care a fig whether the soil is acid or alkaline, provided neither condition is extreme.

Chalk, however, is a different kettle of fish. It is the extreme form of lime and, although the geologist may well call it a "soft rock", the gardener may equally well retort: "Come and dig it yourself, then."

For, if the chalk is close to the surface, the cultivation of it is no job for a weakling or a lazy bones. You must delve down 18in. with a pick and mix into the chalk all you can of chopped-up turves, compost, leaf-mould or manure by the methods prescribed in Chapter 6 and you must renew this underground feeding annually with heavy surface mulchings of some sort; for whatever organic matter you apply is rapidly absorbed, its decomposition being accelerated by the chemical action of the calcium. Peat is very useful as a kick-off for young roots when planting and breaks down much more slowly than manure, compost and leaf-mould, which are all quickly lost in chalk.

To the gardener the critical issue is proximity of the chalk to the surface. If it is a good two feet or more down he has little to worry about beyond accepting the limitations of an alkaline soil. If it thrusts up close to the surface, he must delve as I have said. Experience and opinions conflict on the need for watering. In the late Sir Frederick Stern's famous Highdown garden in Sussex many plants grow in almost pure chalk with no watering at all other than what comes from the firmament. But in general terms it may be said that in the top spit and on high ground chalk is porous, dry and hot, like sand, but below that it is nearly always moist and may in some places become waterlogged.

Given a regimen of ample supplies of organic matter below and above ground and plenty of water when the need is apparent, most plants other than those in the first list will regard a chalky soil with equanimity, though there are some that will find it a tricky wicket. Of such are hybrid tea-roses and many of the modern floribundas, the ceanothus and the Japanese and American maples. Several magnolias will also be ill at ease; Japanese and American magnolias cannot face chalk, whereas many Chinese and European ones can.

I doubt very much whether we really yet know why calcifuges fail in limy soils and the old term "lime-hater" is of suspect validity. It may be that, like human addicts, they merely take more than is good for them.

The application of lime. We have seen that, as a rule, the deliberate application of lime is not often needed in the flower garden, though it will be needed for old, sour town gardens and may be important for particular flowers and for vegetables and fruit gardens in acid soil. As a top dressing it has many very valuable qualities. It provides a plant food in the form of calcium. It breaks down obdurate clay into small crumbly particles; though it should not be applied to a clay which is already alkaline. It curbs club root in cabbages and allied plants. It promotes the decomposition of organic matter and has various other useful properties.

To the gardener who needs it, lime is available in various forms.

For carnations, many irises, rock and other plants, it can be supplied in permanent form by limestone chips or dust. Old lime-mortar rubble is also very valuable but the modern building practice of using cement instead of lime-mortar has made it as difficult to get as manure. A good substitute is finely ground (i.e. powdered) chalk or ground limestone as sold for poultry grit. These forms should be applied at root level and renewed as surface dressings (for plants that need it) every few years.

For more widespread dressings, lime is available in several other forms. In my young days we used to get quicklime direct from the quarry, slake it with water and spread while fresh and "hot". Nowadays most people buy hydrated lime from the shop (though carbonate of lime is better on light soils). You simply spread the stuff on the surface in winter and lightly fork it in later. Your County Horticultural officer will advise you on the proper rate if you send him a sample of your soil, but a good rule of thumb is 6oz. per square yard.

Never use lime at the same time as any other soil dressing, especially animal manures. With animal manures and sulphate of ammonia, it causes the loss of nitrogen. Apply it at least a month after manuring and at least fourteen days before chemicals, including soil fumigants and soot.

Sea-side

Those who garden near the sea have certain advantages over inlanders. In particular, they enjoy a warmer soil and atmosphere. Many of our most splendid gardens lie along the west coast and others on or near the south. The east coast faces rather harsher conditions, lacking the warm air of the Gulf Stream and the plentiful rain of the west, yet the east has many sheltered nooks that turn and face to the south.

All sea-side gardens, however, lie at the mercy of one of the roughest of all enemies – wind. Violent gales anywhere can be devastating, but at or near the sea they charge in laden with salt and particles of sand. Salt is actually beneficial to the extent that it tempers the severity of frost, allowing quite tender plants to be grown within a few miles of the sea. On the other hand, it is fearfully destructive to the foliage of a great many plants, especially to evergreen ones in winter. Sand, which is not usually carried very far inland, tears and blasts the foliage and wood of plants with its abrasive action when hurled against them by fierce winds. The greatest danger area, in respect of both salt and sand lies within a quarter of a mile of the sea.

The first need of those who live very close to the shore, therefore, is to provide some form of shelter from the blast. The best is not a solid wall or fence, for the wind leaps over the obstacle and swoops down to ground level again on the inner side, creating an area of swirling wind-turbulence which is even more damaging than the direct blast. The best shelter therefore is one which *filters* the wind and thus reduces its velocity. In larger places one does this by an exterior belt of trees that are resistant to wind and salt and an internal one of lower shrubs. In small gardens where this cannot be done the wind may be filtered by a hedge or by an open-work fence which consists of about 60 per cent solid matter and 40 per cent aperture. Such a barrier will provide reasonable shelter for a distance up to 40 times its own height, so that one of 5ft high will protect up to 200ft. One of the cheapest and most effective is ordinary chestnut paling interlaced liberally with spruce or other branches. It also makes a good shelter for individual plants and is removable at need in summer.

For your external belt, probably the best of all trees, but slow to start, is the holm-oak (*Quercus ilex*), which is a noble evergreen tree, resistant to all the furies of nature, entirely happy in chalk, or which, as we have seen in an early chapter, can be used as a tough hedge right down on the sea-shore. Sycamore, the Cornish elm and the wych elm are also good in large gardens. In the mild counties of the west the first tree to have is the Monterey pine, *Pinus radiata*, in spite of the needles that it sheds all over the place, to the detriment of other plants. The common ash also makes quite a good shelter tree. On the west coast of Scotland the Austrian pine is used a great deal. Where all these are too big, the Swedish whitebeam, *Sorbus intermedia* and the hawthorn are excellent wind-breaks, resistant to exposure and tolerant of most soils.

For hedges, the sea-side gardener is rather well off. We have noted several in the chapter on that subject. In the Gulf Stream counties the griselinia is a first favourite, beautiful, freshly green (or elegantly pallid in its variegated form), and quite salt-hardy. We have also noted the escallonias, the splendid gorse, the pittosporum, the fuchsia, the Japanese euonymus, the silver-leaved *Atriplex halimus* and the tamarisk.

Even tougher still is the sea-buckthorn (*Hippophaë rhamnoides*), which will stand with its toes in sea-washed sand. Fiercely thorned, it is clothed with silver, willow-formed leaves and the female plants bear clusters of orange berries if a male is planted to every eight. It spreads by suckers and forms a thicket.

FIG. 110. The sea-buckthorn, *Hippophaë rhamnoides.*

One good group of hedges that we have hitherto omitted are the olearias, only too familiar to suburban gardeners in the dowdy *O. haastii* or "daisy bush". The most handsome olearias are unfortunately too tender for most of our coasts, but *O. albida* has thoroughly proved itself along the cliffs of Yorkshire, particularly at Scarborough. This is a compact shrub, with leaves that are white-felted beneath and clusters of white daisies in summer. Mr J. H. Clark, the Parks Superintendent of Scarborough writes: "I cannot speak too highly of this shrub both as a hedge and as a nurse to protect less hardy plants." It can be planted close to the sea, but needs pruning by secateurs if you want it to look comely. It roots readily from hardwood cuttings in early April. *O. haastii* can be used similarly.

Of other plants for sea-side gardens, there are legion. Among shrubs the following are outstanding:

> the grey-and-white *Senecio laxifolius*, unperturbed by wind, fuchsias (particularly in the West Country), yuccas (highly resistant), all brooms (especially *Spartium junceum*), pampas-grass (*Cortaderia*), cistuses, rosemary, the ceanothus, which, except in the colder regions, will revel in the sand itself, the hebes (the more tender ones being reserved for the west), hydrangeas and the little cotton-lavender.

As I have remarked elsewhere, all evergreen shrubs, for the seaside, should be planted in the latter part of April, when the winter gales are over, and securely staked.

Among herbaceous plants, those that prosper most conspicuously include: red-hot-pokers (quite outstanding, highly resistant to wind and salt), the sea-hollies (*Eryngium*), the sea-lavender or statice (which we now call *Limonium*), the catanache, many sedums, the old Greek acanthus, the globe thistle (*Echinops*), and the edible globe-artichoke.

More surprisingly, one of the very best plants to filter wind and resist salt is an annual. This is the mallow *Lavateria trimestris*, which I have extolled in Chapter 8.

Towns

I write here not of those pleasant, smaller, county towns, which may have quite sizeable gardens and which enjoy semi-rural conditions as far as gardening is concerned, but of the larger, denser towns in which, as a rule, the gardens are very small indeed and usually much shut in by the houses that crowd in on them on all sides.

Apart from the primary handicap of being very small, such gardens are liable to suffer from excessive shade, from starved or sour soil, from impure atmosphere and from proximity of tall buildings, which causes plants to be drawn up. They are also very often handicapped by having no garden entrance or side-door, so that all the needs of the garden have to be brought through the house, and by having little space to spare for compost heaps and nursery beds.

On the other hand they have a warmer climate than the adjacent countryside, are protected from the fierce winds that sweep the moors, the hill-tops and the sea-shore and the very impurities of the air that are damaging to many plants are a blessing to others, particularly roses, hollyhocks and antirrhinums, protecting them against the diseases of black-spot and rust.

I suggest that the first thing to do in a town garden is to clothe the walls of the house and the walls or fences of the garden with climbers. As I have remarked before, the wall area is usually greater than the garden area. There are plenty to choose from: ivies, virgin ivies, the sweet trachelospermums, the practical pileostegia, the gorgeous *Vitis coignetiae* and so on. Winter jasmine in the darkest, coldest corner will always be a joy. On the walls or fences of the garden, built up to 9ft or so with robust, home-made, square trellis and hung with plastic-covered chain-link fencing, clematis of many sorts will sumptuously display themselves, including the tender, evergreen *C. armandii*. Here also the flowering quinces can be trained espalier fashion.

In those very small, shut-in gardens lawns usually stand a very poor chance. They are very often best replaced with paving stones, relying on plants to provide the greenery, and if the paving is augmented by little built-up walls or terraces of stone or brick the flatness will be relieved and the plant opportunities increased. A further accompaniment to stone and brick which at once raises the little garden above the level of the commonplace is a little pool. This is easily made. It need be only three or four inches deep, which will be safe for children. You have merely to sweep the water out with a broom at need and replace it. Make it with sloping sides and put round the margin one or two plants that can admire their own reflection.

In the gardens of old towns, especially London, the exhaustion of the soil is often a great problem. With much difficulty and some expense one can clear it all out and import new soil, but a great deal can be done, and done easily, by buying some turves and chopping them up, together with one of the new composted manures in polythene bags, plus peat and any other organic stuff you can lay your hands on. Sometimes, when the soil is sour, a dressing of lime suffices.

No garden is better suited than the town one for growing plants in tubs, vases, pots, and any sort of container. There used to be a small house near Eaton Square where virginia creeper and clematis grew splendidly in large tubs in the gloom of the basement, the plants rising high up the walls, while the less hardy jasmines and *Solanum crispum* fell down from the balcony in leafy and floral veils. All sorts of plants can be grown in tubs – small spring bulbs, lilies, pelargoniums (very good summer value), trailing plants and small shrubs, the evergreen ones needing frequent hosing or watering to keep the foliage clean. Of course, there is also the obvious medium of the window-box, in which, if you are clever, you can have a succession of plants nearly all the year by growing in pots which are replaced at need. And it is in towns that the "sink" or trough garden comes into its own, giving a tenure to many little rock plants.

It is difficult to recommend plants to grow in town gardens, as conditions vary so much. In shady places, many of those in Chapter 23 will be entirely suitable. Roses of all sorts do very well. Of trees, the catalpa and the tree-of-heaven (*Ailanthus altissima*) prosper exceedingly where there is room. The Judas-tree presents no problem. The bladder-senna (*Colutea arborescens*) will be more welcome than in the country. Nearly all spring bulbs are happy, too. *Cotoneaster horizontalis* will cover eyesores such as oil-tanks.

A few other preliminary suggestions are, of shrubs:

Forsythia	Prunus of various sorts
Buddleias, very good	Hibiscus
Viburnum davidii, excellent	*Senecio laxifolius*
Hawthorns	The Moroccan broom
Sumachs	Hypericums, very good
Helianthemums	Lilac

No conifers I fear.

Of herbaceous plants:

Hostas	Hellebore
Lily-of-the-valley	Evening primrose
Hollyhocks	Sedums
Ferns (very nice)	*Stachys lanata* (*olympica*)
Euphorbias	Thrift
Helichrysums	*Artemisia arborescens*
Viola	Monardo

APPENDIX

Some Good Nurseries and Suppliers

The following is a relatively short list of nurseries that have national reputations. For reasons of space I have had to confine it to those with which I have had dealings, together with a few others included for special purposes.

GENERAL

Hillier and Sons, Winchester (the most comprehensive lists in nearly all departments, particularly of trees and shrubs of all sorts, herbaceous and rock plants, etc.).

George Jackman & Sons, Woking, Surrey (a very good, select list in most departments, specialists in clematis).

R. C. Notcutt Ltd, Woodbridge, Suffolk (the like, but specialists in lilacs).

John Waterer, Sons and Crisp, Bagshot, Surrey (for trees and shrubs); the Floral Mile, Twyford, Berkshire (for herbaceous plants, roses, etc.).

Sunningdale Nurseries, Windlesham, Surrey. Several specialities, including rhododendrons and old roses.

John Scott and Co., The Royal Nurseries, Merriott, Somerset.

Reginald Kaye, Silverdale, Carnforth, Lancs.

Bakers, Boningale, Albrighton, Wolverhampton (specialists in lupins and delphiniums).

Dobbie & Co., Edinburgh (also seeds, dahlias and bulbs).

Bees Ltd, Sealand Nurseries, Cheshire.

Christopher Lloyd, Great Dixter, Northiam, Sussex (a small but good mixed bag, specialist in clematis).

TREES AND SHRUBS (in addition to several of the above).

Donard Nursery, Newcastle, County Down, Northern Ireland (many "Gulf Stream" plants).

Walter Slocock, Goldsworth Nurseries, Woking, Surrey (chiefly rhododendrons, camellias and tree peonies).

L. R. Russell, London Road, Windlesham, Surrey.
D. Stewart & Son, Ferndown, Dorset.
James Smith, Scotland Nurseries, Tansley, Matlock, Derbyshire (modest prices).
G. Reuthe, Keston, Kent (rhododendrons).
Four Winds Nursery, Holt Pound, Wrecclesham, Farnham, Surrey.
Knap Hill Nursery, Knaphill, Woking (especially for azaleas).
Treseder's Nursery, Truro.

HERBACEOUS PLANTS

Bressingham Gardens, Diss, Norfolk.
Blackmore & Langdon, Bath (specialists in delphiniums, polyanthus, begonias, phloxes and greenhouse cyclamen).
Thomas Carlile (Loddon Nurseries) Ltd, Twyford, Reading.
Robinson's Hardy Plants, Greencourt Nurseries, Crockenhill, Swanley, Kent (also for rock plants).
John Forbes Ltd, Buccleuch Nurseries, Hawick, Scotland (also for rock plants and many old-fashioned flowers).
Gayborder Nurseries, Melbourne, Derbyshire.

ROCK GARDEN SPECIALISTS

Jack Drake, Inshriach Nursery, Aviemore, Inverness-shire.
W. E. Th. Ingwersen Ltd, Birch Farm Nursery, Gravetye, East Grinstead, Surrey.
Joe Elliott, Broadwell Nursery, Moreton-in-Marsh, Gloucestershire.

ROSES

R. Harkness & Co., Hitchin, Hertfordshire.
John Cocker & Sons, Aberdeen.
Edwin Murrell, Portland Nurseries, Shrewsbury.
Dicksons of Hawlmark, Newtownards, near Belfast.
Samuel McCredy & Sons, Portadown, Northern Ireland.
E. B. LeGrice, Rowland Nurseries, North Walsham, Norfolk.
John Sandy Ltd, Almondsbury, Bristol.
John Mattock Ltd, Nuneham Courtenay, Oxford.
Cants of Colchester, Mile End, Colchester.
Harry Wheatcroft & Sons, Edwalton, Nottingham.
C. Gregory & Sons, Ltd, Chilwell, Nottingham.

BULBS

Walter Blom & Sons, Leavesden, Watford.

Wallace & Barr, Marden, Kent (also for irises).
Broadleigh Gardens, Sampford Arundel, Wellington, Somerset (for dwarf daffodils and other small bulbs).

PELARGONIUMS

Anthony Ayton Ltd, Kibble's Lane, Southborough, Tunbridge Wells, Kent.
Gamble and Sons, Highfield Nurseries, Longford, Derbyshire.
Wyck Hill Geraniums, Stow-on-the-Wold, Gloucestershire.

VARIOUS SPECIALISTS

John Crutchfield, Snow Hill, Copthorne, Sussex (dahlias).
Orpington Nurseries, Gatton Park, Reigate, Surrey (irises, etc.).
John Galbally, Fairfield, Upper Dicker, Hailsham, Sussex (auriculas and pinks).
House of Douglas, Edenside, Great Bookham, Surrey (auriculas).
Wansdyke Nurseries, Hillworth, Devizes (dwarf conifers).
W. H. Rogers & Son, Red Lodge Nursery, Chestnut Avenue, Eastleigh, Hants (dwarf conifers).
John Letts, Foxhollow, Westwood Road, Windlesham, Surrey (heathers).
Maxwell & Beale, Ltd, Broadstone, Dorset (heathers).
Mrs Desmond Underwood, Bergholt Road, Colchester (silver plants and pinks).
Allwood Brothers Ltd, Hayward's Heath, Sussex (carnations and pinks).
Lindabruce Nurseries, Lancing, Sussex (carnations and pinks).
E. Riley, Alfreton Nurseries, Woolley Moor, Derbyshire (chrysanthemums).
H. Woolman, Ltd, Shirley, Birmingham (chrysanthemums).

SEEDS

Thompson and Morgan, Ipswich (a very comprehensive list, including many rare sorts, with seeds of trees, shrubs, herbaceous and rock plants, etc.).
Samuel Dobie & Son, Chester.
Thomas Butcher, Shirley, Croydon, Surrey (a long and comprehensive list).
Geo. B. Roberts, Faversham, Kent (some very good specialities).
W. J. Unwin Ltd, Histon, Cambridgeshire (sweet-pea specialists).
R. Bolton & Son, Birdbrook, Halstead, Essex (the like).
Sutton & Sons, Reading.

Alexander & Brown, The Scottish Seed House, Perth.
J. L. Clucas, Ormskirk, Lancs.
Vilmorin-Andrieux, 4 quai de la Megisserie, Paris.

COMPOSTS, etc.

Walter Uwins, Spring Lane, Woodside, South Norwood, London, S.E.25 (J. I. Composts, horticultural sands, peats, etc.).
L. S. Beckett Ltd, Manor House, Whixall, Whitchurch, Shropshire (J. I. Composts and peat from own beds).
"Levington" Soil-less Compost (Fison's) from retail shops.
Croxden Gravel Ltd, Cheadle, Stoke-on-Trent, Staffordshire (soil-less and other composts).
"Shamrock" Irish Moss peat, from retailers.
Alexander Products, Burnham-on-Sea Somserset (peat and peat blocks).
Eclipse Peat Co., Ashcott, Bridgewater, Somerset (the like).
Natural Fertilizer Co. Ltd, Whitelands, Hatfield Peverel, near Chelmsford (for "Stimgro" composted manure).

INDEX

Plants are entered under both their botanical and English vernacular names. When the entry is short, the page numbers are likewise entered under both, but in longer ones they are under the botanical name only, except when it better suits the general reader's convenience to do otherwise, as in Poppy and Daffodil. Cross-references are given fully.

When more than one page reference is given, the main passage dealing with the cultivation or nature of the item referred to is in **bold** figures. Other references may also be material, but casual mentions in the text are not always included; nor are terms already set out alphabetically in "Gardener's Jargon".

F refers to "Figures" (line drawings).

Pronunciation. For the benefit of readers who may like some guidance, a few pointers are given in square brackets [ ] where it seems necessary. In most instances only that syllable which seems in doubt is given, the remaining syllables being represented by short dashes. The separation of syllables is marked by colons. Y means a long i. The single e is short, as in "ante". S is soft. I give usually the generally accepted pronunciations; there are no laws on the subject.

Index

Index